CONSORTING WITH ANGELS

Modern Women Poets

edited by DERYN REES-JONES

Modern Women Poets is the companion anthology to *Consorting with Angels*. While its selections illuminate and illustrate the essays, this wide-ranging and exciting anthology also works in its own right as the best possible introduction to a whole century of poetry by women.

Tracing an arc from Charlotte Mew to Stevie Smith, from Sylvia Plath and Anne Sexton to the writing emerging from the Women's Movement, and to the more recent work of poets such as Medbh McGuckian, Jo Shapcott and Carol Ann Duffy, the anthology draws together the work of women poets from Britain, Ireland and America as one version of a history of women's poetic writing. It draws important connections between the work of women poets and shows how – over the past century – they have developed strategies for engaging with a male-dominated tradition. *Modern Women Poets* allows the reader to trace women's negotiations with one another's work, as well as to reflect more generally on the politics of women's engagement with history, nature, politics, motherhood, science, religion, the body, sexuality, identity, death, love, and poetry itself.

Eliza's Babes

Four centuries of women's poetry in English, *c*.1500-1900
edited by ROBYN BOLAM

This comprehensive anthology celebrates four centuries of women's poetry, covering over 100 poets from a wide range of social backgrounds across the English-speaking world. Familiar names – Anne Bradstreet, Aphra Behn, Elizabeth Barrett Browning, the Brontë sisters, Emily Dickinson, and Christina Rossetti – appear alongside other writers from America, Australia, Canada, India and New Zealand as well as the UK. The poets range from queens and ladies of the court to a religious martyr, a spy, a young slave, a milkmaid, labourers, servants, activists, invalids, émigrées and pioneers, a daring actor, and the daughter of a Native American chief. Whether writing out of injustice, religious or sexual passion, humour, or to celebrate their sex, their different cultures, environments, personal beliefs and relationships, these women have strong, independent spirits and voices we cannot ignore. In 1652, speaking of poems she had published as her 'babes', a woman we know only as 'Eliza' answered 'a Lady that bragged of her children': *'Thine at their birth did pain thee bring,/ When mine are born, I sit and sing.'*

DERYN REES-JONES

Consorting
WITH Angels

ESSAYS ON MODERN WOMEN POETS

BLOODAXE BOOKS

Copyright © 2005 Deryn Rees-Jones

ISBN: 1 85224 393 9

First published 2005 by
Bloodaxe Books Ltd,
Highgreen,
Tarset,
Northumberland NE48 1RP.

www.bloodaxebooks.com
For further information about Bloodaxe titles
please visit our website or write to
the above address for a catalogue.

Bloodaxe Books Ltd acknowledges
the financial assistance of
Arts Council England, North East.

Printed in Great Britain by
Bell & Bain Limited, Glasgow, Scotland.

For Eira and Felix
with love

'Away with it, let it go'
− STEVIE SMITH

CONTENTS

LIST OF ILLUSTRATIONS

ACKNOWLEDGEMENTS

Grateful acknowledgements to the editors of *Women: A Cultural Review*, and *Kicking Daffodils: Twentieth-Century Women's Poetry*, ed. Vicki Bertram, where earlier versions of some of these essays first appeared.

Thanks to Isobel Armstrong who supervised my thesis on which some of this book is built, and more generally to the editors of *Women* and *Poetry Review*, whose support of my writing gave me the encouragement to persevere. Liverpool Hope University helped with their award of the Sheppard-Worlock Fellowship which gave me some time to write, and Sue Zlosnik was a backbone of help in her enthusiasm for my research during my time at Hope. More recent thanks also to Philip Davis and Dinah Birch at the University of Liverpool for their generosity in arranging my maternity leave. Irralie Doel ordered and added to the chronology with care and interest at short notice and was an enthusiastic and invaluable researcher. More general thanks to my students and colleagues at the University of Liverpool for providing such a warm and sustaining context in which to think and write, both critically and creatively.

This book has been a long time in the making. Very special thanks to Alison Mark for her friendship and conversations about women's poetry over ten years; to Maurice Riordan, Gwyneth Lewis, Sally Kilmister, Julia Damassa, Gill Gregory, Matt Simpson, Penny Iremonger, Judith Palmer, John and Pauline Lucas, Hester Jones, Ralph Pite, Andrew Hamer and John Redmond. Jill Rudd gave thoughtful and sharp comments on drafts which, coupled with her cheerful and robust encouragement in the gruesome final stages made a enormous difference. Thanks are due also to Sheila Rowbotham, Caroline Gilfillan and Stef Pixner for offering some personal insight into the role of poetry in the development of the Women's Movement; and to Ric Latham at the Bow Windows Bookshop, Sussex for generously scanning the image of the cover and title-page of the first edition of *Wheels* and not minding that I didn't buy the book. Grateful acknowledgment, too, to Selima Hill, Carol Ann Duffy, Medbh McGuckian, and especially Vicki Feaver and Jo Shapcott, who have, over the years, given interviews and produced material which has fed usefully into this book.

Michael Murphy has been a part of this book in all its reincarnations, and shares my delight, no doubt, in its completion. His ways of thinking and writing about poetry have been an important part of the book as well as my life.

I am grateful to the following people for permission to reproduce poems:

Dorothy Thompson for 'Wheels by Nancy Cunard, from *The Selected Poems of Nancy Cunard*, edited by John Lucas (Trent Editions, 2005).

David Higham Associates and the Estate of Edith Sitwell for lines from 'Elegy on Dead Fashion', 'The Hambone and the Heart', 'Jodelling Song', 'Lullaby', lines from *Gold Coast Customs* and 'Anne Boleyn's Song' from *Collected Poems of Edith Sitwell* (Sinclair-Stevenson, 1993).

Hamish MacGibbon and Penguin Books Ltd for Stevie Smith's 'The Songster', 'Pearl' and extracts from 'Mrs Arbuthnot' and 'Phèdre', and for the drawings listed on page 8, from *The Collected Poems of Stevie Smith* (Penguin, 1985); and to Hamish MacGibbon and Virago Press for 'Miss Snooks, Poetess'.

The Estate of Sylvia Plath and Faber and Faber Ltd for lines from 'Female Author', 'The Disquieting Muses', for 'An Appearance', for lines from 'Daddy', 'The Detective' from *The Collected Poems* (Faber, 1981); and to the Lilly Library and the Estate of Sylvia Plath for permission to quote material from Plath's essay on Sitwell from 1953.

The Estate of Anne Sexton and Houghton Mifflin for lines from 'To John, Who Begs Me Not to Enquire Further' 'The Waiting Head', 'The White Snake', 'Briar Rose (Sleeping Beauty)', 'Talking to Sheep' from *The Complete Poems* (Houghton Mifflin, 1999).

Vicki Feaver and Random House Group Ltd for 'The Handless Maiden' from *The Handless Maiden* (Cape, 1994).

Jo Shapcott and Faber and Faber Ltd for lines from 'Electroplating the Baby' from *Her Book: Poems 1988-1998* (Faber 1999) and 'Rosa nitida' from *Tender Taxes* (Faber, 2001).

Lavinia Greenlaw for 'Electricity' from *Night Photograph* (Faber, 1993).

Alice Oswald for lines from *Dart* (Faber, 2002) and from 'Woods etc' and the poem 'Leaf' from *Woods etc.* (Faber, 2005).

Bloodaxe Books Ltd and these authors for the following work:

Selima Hill: lines from 'Do It Again', 'The Villa' and 'The Island' from *Trembling Hearts in the Bodies of Dogs* (1994).

Gwyneth Lewis: lines from 'Chaotic Angels' from *Chaotic Angels: Poems in English* (2005).

Jackie Kay: lines from 'The Adoption Papers' and 'Dressing Up' from *The Adoption Papers* (1991) and from 'Sign' from *Other Lovers* (1993).

Moniza Alvi: lines from 'The Country at My Shoulder' from *Carrying My Wife* (2000).

Kathleen Jamie and Bloodaxe Books Ltd for lines from 'The Republic of Fife' and 'The Queen of Sheba' from *Mr and Mrs Scotland Are Dead* (2002); and to Macmillan Publishers Ltd for lines from 'Stane-Raw' from *The Tree House* (Picador, 2004).

Introduction

What does it mean to consort with angels? Angels appear in various guises in women's writing of the 20th century. For Virginia Woolf the angel was an image of Victorian femininity embodied in Coventry Patmore's poem 'The Angel in the House'.[1] In her essay 'Professions for Women' (1931), Woolf writes how it is a version of femininity embodied in this angel, the 'woman that men wished women to be', who hovers at the shoulder of the woman writer. It is the 'shadow of whose wing or the radiance of her halo upon my page' that Woolf must escape if she is to write. But once she has killed the angel, the woman writer is left not with truth, 'having rid herself of a falsehood' but with a question: '…what is herself …what is a woman?' For Woolf, the woman writer must not only kill the angel, but must find a way of accessing her unconscious and allowing her imagination to run freely, allowing her to write the truth about her body without falling prey to anxieties about shocking men.[2]

In Anne Sexton's poem, 'Consorting with Angels' (1963), from which this book borrows its title, the speaker of the poem has tired of what it means to be a woman. She is 'tired of the gender of things'. Sexton instead 'consorts with the angels', neither one thing nor the other, as she becomes, at the end of her poem, a divine and desiring creature. She has become herself, it might be argued, precisely in that way in which Woolf has suggested she must reimagine herself, her body androgynous, but nevertheless desiring; she has become the black woman of the *Song of Songs*; she has a voice that will allow her to sing her desires; but in finding that voice she has also had literally to reconfigure herself.

In *Consorting with Angels* I read the work of some of the most important women poets of the 20th century. In doing so, I examine the ways in which these women have attempted to explore and configure femininity in their texts. Such an image of femininity as Sexton's – or indeed Woolf's – is not held up as either prototype or strategic position for the woman poet here, but my title suggests more metaphorically that the women poets I discuss are constantly having to negotiate their gender as they negotiate the literary tradition, asking not just what is woman, but what it means to write their gender within the potentially confining roles of "poetess" or "woman poet".

Judith Butler's groundbreaking *Gender Trouble* (1990), which draws on both the work of Jacques Lacan and Michel Foucault to offer a 'performative theory of gender and sexuality', is an undercurrent to my understanding of the relationship between gender identity and the poetry by women discussed here. All gender is, according to Butler, not fixed:

> Words, acts, gestures, and desire produce the effect of an internal core or substance, but produce this *on the surface* of the body, through the play of signifying absences that suggest, but never reveal, the organising principle of identity as a cause. Such acts, gestures enactments, generally constructed, are *performative* in the sense that the essence or identity that they otherwise purport to express are fabrications manufactured and sustained through corporeal signs and other discursive means. That the gendered body is performative suggests that it has no ontological status apart from the various acts which constitute its reality. This also suggests that reality is fabricated as an interior essence, that its very interiority is an effect and function of a decidedly public and social discourse [3]

Or, as Jonathan Culler more simply states, 'the fundamental categories of identity are cultural and social productions, more likely to be the result of political cooperation than its condition of possibility. They create the effect of the natural...and by imposing norms... they threaten to exclude those who don't conform... Your gender is created by your acts, in the way that a promise is created by the act of promising.' [4] What separates the concept of gender performativity from performance of gender is the difference, Butler notes, between acts which constitute the self, and an idea of identity as 'interior essence' which can be expressed. But if gender performativity is important to my readings, so too is the idea of the performance of gender the text makes in relation to the poet. Edith Sitwell, Stevie Smith and Anne Sexton, whose work I discuss in the first section of the book, were all noted performers of their work, and their performances worked in varying ways to destabilise, question and negotiate their position as women poets, as well, ultimately as their gender. Sylvia Plath has also left us some powerful recordings of her reading her work which suggest that she too might have been a memorable live performer of her work.

As Terry Threadgold has remarked, it is important to bring together *performance* and *performativity* 'in trying to deal with the complex ways in which bodies and texts fold into one another, crafting and shaping the materiality of texts and of bodies. To perform in theatre contexts, or indeed in the contexts of everyday life, for which theatre becomes a metaphor, is always to struggle with substance, the matter, of the body.' [5] Poetry is not theatre, but the poet has a very different physical relationship to the poem than the novelist has to the novel because, despite its appropriation by the printed page, poetry has always been and remains an oral and performed art, and even at its most linguistically dense and "literary", poetry is written to be spoken, and heard, if only in the reader's head.

Performance of the poem, and performativity of the self, specifically a gendered self, must be read as part of a complex matrix between poet, text and speech, which is mediated through culture, intention, expression, language and the often prescriptive ideas of the woman poet and her role. Thus we see emerging a kind of double layering, and distinctions which can be made between the performativity of gender on the one hand, and the performance of woman as poet, on the other, who draws on her body as a site of display and struggle to affirm her gender as poet, whilst also attempting to question it. The importance of this presence of the physical (and gendered) body of the woman poet, in (and out of) her work is one which I explore variously in the first section of this book.

In this respect, the importance of the dramatic monologue to the woman poet's textual self-making is central. As Isobel Armstrong has argued, 19th-century women poets were central to the revitalisation of the dramatic form, although it was Robert Browning's influence on Ezra Pound and T.S. Eliot which brought the form to prominence at the beginning of the 20th century. The monologue is a form used extensively by women in the 20th century: Charlotte Mew, whose work I briefly discuss in my introduction to *Modern Women Poets*, and who is still a poet little read, made the 19th-century monologue modern with her use of free verse. And although, as I point out, both Sitwell and Smith use the monologue, the genre was brought back to prominent attention by Sexton's feminist reworkings of fairytales in her *Transformations* in 1971. In Britain, the poet U.A. Fanthorpe, a woman of the same generation as Sexton, began to use the form in the 1970s, and the subsequent monologues of Carol Ann Duffy and, to a lesser extent Liz Lochhead, have clearly been of great importance in popularising the form to a generation of women publishing in the 1990s.

The dramatic monologue sets up a potential for multiple ironies in its positioning of a complex relationship between writer, reader, persona and text as persona. The monologue's dependence on a listener who is sometimes also built in as a presence within the poem, and whose responses are often set up in parallel with the implied reader's, creates not just an intimacy with the speaker of the monologue, but frequently a sense of collusion. Such collusion works to bring reader and text closer than, for example, the 'I'/ 'you' dyad of the lyric which it overdetermines. But not only does the monologue allow the poet to speak in another voice, to take on a new register, accent, discourse, as a well a new personality, it may also accommodate a change of gender for the poet who may write not only as a woman who is other than herself, but also as man.

Crucially, and bound up with these shifts in gender that the monologue allows, the monologue seeks to embody the speaker while also saying that the presence of this body is *not* the poet's. Textually this embodiment may be signalled by reference to experiences which we know not to associate with the poet (especially if the monologue is spoken in the voice of an animal or an inanimate object!); in terms of gender, the poem might refer to clothes or body parts; and if we are present when the poet is reading such a poem, then there are obvious ironies which occur in the juxtaposition of the voice of the poem and the body of the poet. But even when the poet is not present, when a monologue works to its full effect, it demands that we construct for ourselves an imaginary body out of which the poem's voice speaks. The monologue, then, plays with ideas of embodiment and presence which, at the same time as representing a movement between self and other, also often figures its process.

The connection between performativity and performance in relation to the lyric, rather than the dramatic poem, is also of relevance here, specifically in relation to the confessional poem, a genre which is often performative in its promise of immediate revelation of the embodied self, and its effecting of catharsis and "forgiveness" for that self. Although the experiences of the confessional poem are of an intensely personal, and often extreme and transgressive nature – or at least purport to be – part of the confessional aesthetic demands that there must also be some kind of sympathetic union between poet and reader in the poet's presentation of that extreme state, and a collusion of belief. Such a union disturbs the usual boundaries between poet and reader as each poem produces its cathartic effect. This catharsis takes place in the act of telling, but also, and perhaps more strangely, in the act of listening, as the listener or reader takes on a dual role of one who identifies with the "sinner" but absolves, in their listening, the sin.

Confessional poetry as practised by men and women in the States, was an influential movement in relation to postwar poetics. Unlike autobiography, which purports to document factual and emotional truth, and which embeds its 'I' within a narrative, confessional poetry hovers in a hinterland between documentary experience and fiction, establishing itself as a mode which draws closer the borders of the relationship between the 'I' who speaks and the 'I' who is spoken about. If autobiography can be read as a narrative which fashions a truth about the history of the self, then surely we must read the confessional poem as an aesthetic of truth, the terms of its own nature determined exactly by its very authenticity – an authenticity which paradoxically is as subject to the 'tinkerings', as the American poet Robert Lowell called them, as of any other piece of creative writing. The dynamic set-up between autobiography and experience, and experience as mediated into an aesthetic, and the value of experience in relation to women's poetry, becomes a crucial issue, specifically within feminist debates concerning the value of the personal to the political.

As a way of defending against anxieties about the perceived precariousness of the lyric 'I', I also suggest that the surreal – itself an often both intertextual and performative strategy – has played an important part in the development of some women's poetry over the past century. While surrealism has in many ways been assimilated into a late 20th-century poetic postmodernism, some of the women I discuss here make recourse to the surreal as a way of defending against being positioned simply as a woman poet, while at the same time dramatising extreme anxieties about being a woman and what that gendering means both culturally and textually.

It is of course vital not to completely dehistoricise such an important 20th-century movement as surrealism. I am not, for example, arguing that the women I talk about here are influenced by a strictly Bretonian modernist surrealist practice. Although surrealist practices were many and various, as was the ideology behind them, the surreal, in its most general terms, is important because it gives a means through which to display aspects of the unconscious through an aesthetic, dramatising anxiety rather than explicitly articulating it. Surrealism in Britain never really took off as it did on the continent. But David Gascoyne's *Short Survey of Surrealism* was published in 1935, and the setting up of a London surrealist group gave a collective currency to the movement in Britain, for, as Steven Connor has noted, at least as long as the remainder of the decade. That the British poetic engagement with surrealism was an all-male affair is not surprising, given surrealism's problematic positioning of women as "other". As a series of poetic techniques, rather than a consistent aesthetic, however, surrealism filtered slowly through into the mainstream, often in an alliance with the gothic, and hand-in-hand with the development of postmodernism.

Michel Rémy, describing the surrealist poetry of David Gascoyne, astutely refers to 'the drama of meaning as it is celebrated by surrealism, the drama of transformation in the midst of self-making, of permanent decentering and derailing of every search after meaning ...the meeting of the subject with itself is thus deported and deferred in its initiate meeting with what is always other'.[6] For my purposes here, then, I will be thinking about surrealistic practices which have been absorbed by women poets as a performative strategy for projecting a self (or selves) outwards onto the world in a way that is not obviously or immediately identifiable with the *personal*. Whereas for some male poets the 'I' of personal experience resonates with authority, universality and importance, women speaking as 'I' articulate a personal experience too easily classified within literary tradition as minor, private, esoteric, unimportant and limited. Although in itself problematic in its equation of the irrational and the unconscious with the feminine other, the surreal as a more diluted poetic idiom of defamiliarisation offers an important strategy for women's narrations of self.

The final but equally important strategy I identify in the work of many of the women discussed here is an intertextuality which finds them drawing on texts by both men and women, engaging both with gender politics and the politics of that literary tradition in which – and against which – they write.

In one sense we cannot – as writers and readers – avoid intertextuality, whatever our gender. The theorist Michael Riffaterre, has, for example, suggested that in fact 'textuality is inseparable from and founded upon intertextuality'.[7] The dynamics operating in women's intertextual assimilations and appropriations have a particular quality, not least when they draw specifically on texts by men as a strategy of engagement with masculinity and the literary tradition, or look to women precursors as a way of accentuating and defining their own feminine aesthetic. Linda Hutcheon has seen intertextuality as 'authorised transgression' which she links to the parodic:

> postmodernist parody,...uses its historical memory, its aesthetic introversion, to signal that this kind of self-reflexive discourse is always inextricably bound to social discourse [8]

For Hutcheon, parody and intertextuality offer a liberating strategy for women writers, or anyone who is 'ex-centric':

> Parody seems to offer a perspective on the present and the past which allows an artist to speak *to* a discourse from *within* it, but without being totally recuperated by it. Parody appears to have become, for this reason, the mode of what I have called the 'ex-centric', of those who are

marginalised by a dominant ideology...parody has become a favorite
postmodern literary form of writers in places like Ireland and Canada,
working as they do from both inside and outside a culturally different
and dominant context. And parody has certainly become a favorite
postmodern literary form of the other ex-centrics – of black, ethnic,
gay, and feminist artists – trying to come to terms with and respond
critically and creatively, to the still predominantly white, heterosexual,
male culture in which they find themselves.[9]

Twentieth-century women's use of intertextuality, while not nec-
essarily always parodic, can almost always be read in terms of its
potential for subversion. In opening up a space between texts, even
as those texts overlay each other, intertextual strategies and our
reading of them demands that we think about how women's texts
relate to texts by both men and women. Examining the power and
nature of this space – which, it might be argued, is itself a perform-
ative space – is central to my readings of the poems in this study.

*   *   *

In Chapter One I look at the way Edith Sitwell literally attempts
to reconfigure herself as a woman poet. Sitwell's lifelong interest
in her self-presentation, and her transformation of herself into
stylised icon, has important implications not just for the develop-
ment of Sitwell's own aesthetics, but for literary and cultural con-
structions of the woman poet in the 20th century. Recognised in
the street, at Royal performances, and interviewed on the television,
Sitwell's prominence grew at a time when women's roles were under-
going a period of radical transformation after the First World War,
and her presence, increasingly overdetermined as the century pro-
gressed, continued to elicit strong responses until her death in 1964.
Throughout her life Sitwell was keen to resist idealisations of a
maternal femininity which emerged during the First World War
and at the same time also wanted to resist Victorian notions of the
"poetess"; she was keenly aware of her gender at a time when, in
spite of such distinguished friends and contemporaries such as
Marianne Moore, H.D. and Gertrude Stein, to be a woman and a
poet and taken seriously was still rare.[10]

Of aristocratic birth, Sitwell moved from her parents' family
estate of Renishaw in Derbyshire to London when she was in her
late 20s. Her first volume of poems *The Mother* was privately
printed in 1915; renting a flat with her former governess Helen
Rootham, she worked briefly as a secretary, and from 1917 to the
end of the war she worked in a munitions factory. But this did not
prevent her from cultivating a startling image of herself as poet as

she became prominent in London literary and artistic circles. Portraits of Sitwell in paintings, sculptures and photographs by some of the great 20th-century modern artists, are numerous, many of which can be found in the archives of the National Portrait Gallery. The photographs, in particular, allow us to see her assuming an increasingly stylised appearance, swiftly shaking off the image of Edwardian propriety we find in a formal domestic portrait taken when she was 17 which pictures her wearing a narrow, sashed dress typical of the period, her hair "frizzed" and in a fringe. In a series of photographs taken by Cecil Beaton in the 1920s and 1930s, when Sitwell was in her mid 30s and early 40s, her hair has been cut in a fashionable bob (*see below, page 54*, FIG.3), the starkness of which emphasises the austerity of her features. But in contrast to her fashionable hairstyle, she is wearing floor-length dresses of heavy brocade which in their design look back four hundred years. One of the most well-known of Beaton's photographs, taken in 1927, is of Sitwell, lying apparently in her tomb, eyes closed flanked by pre-Raphaelite lilies, and wearing a kimono, an image which takes this aestheticisation of her self, to which she was apparently more than compliant.

This was not the only photograph of Sitwell to be taken of her in a pose of death [11] and these photos heighten a quality in Sitwell's self-fashioning that is already present. For even when we see a photograph of Sitwell with her eyes open, the arrested quality of the pose constantly serves to aestheticise her, to make of her an art object, who, to quote Harold Acton 'possessed a distinction seldom seen outside the glass cases of certain museums'.[12] In the 1940s there are photographs of Sitwell wearing a sweeping black cape and an oversized fedora; in the famous photograph from 1948 of the Gotham Book Mart party, in which she sits with a queenly air at the centre of a room of poets that included W.H. Auden, Elizabeth Bishop, Marianne Moore and Randall Jarrell, she is wearing a hat which, with its glittering loops, doubles as a crown.[13] By the 1960s, when her appearance had become even more stylised, her hair, which we can occasionally see she was wearing in plaits wrapped round her head, is still almost always covered by elaborate feathered hats which give her a bird-like appearance, and her hands are festooned with jewels that are now, by some sort of poetic justice, part of an exhibit in the Victoria and Albert Museum.

It is hard when looking at these images not to see something of the dandy in Sitwell, as described in Baudelaire's essay 'The Painter of Modern Life'. For Baudelaire the dandy is described as having 'first and foremost the burning need to create for oneself a personal originality... It is a kind of cult of the self which can never-theless survive the pursuit of happiness to be found in someone else – in woman for example... It is the joy of astonishing others, and the proud satisfaction of never oneself being astonished.' [14] He continues:

> Dandyism appears above all in periods of transition, when democracy is not yet all-powerful, and aristocracy is only just beginning to totter and fall. In the disorder of these times, certain men who are socially, politically and financially ill at ease, but are all rich in native energy, may conceive the idea of establishing a new kind of aristocracy, all the more difficult to shatter as it will be based on the most precious, the most enduring faculties, and on the divine gifts which work and money are unable to bestow. (*Painter of Modern Life*, p.28)

Baudelaire's discussion focuses on the male dandy – a construct of artifice set up to directly escape the horror of the feminine "natural". But his description opens up a way of reading Sitwell by bringing to prominence first the inherent narcissism of the dandy's self-construction and secondly – and crucially – the idea that the man-ifestation of such self-display and originality emerges in at a time of political and cultural upheaval.

Sitwell was not, of course, the only modernist woman writer to be so concerned with dress. Sandra Gilbert and Susan Gubar have discussed the way in which dress has been an important component of modernist women's resistance to the constraints of a given pat-riarchal femininity, suggesting that 'for the woman poet a literal and figurative concern with clothing and make-up was often an enabling strategy'.[15] More recently, Laura Severin has argued that Sitwell, like Stevie Smith, was, 'in adopting a style that many would call ugly or at least shocking [...] able to interrogate concepts of normalcy that defined the feminine and poetic (male) identity'.[16]

Elizabeth Salter, in a memoir of her time spent working as Sit-well's secretary, tells how Sitwell was especially fond of the popular music hall comedienne Nellie Wallace (1870-1948), whose catch-phrase 'For God's Sake Hold together boys' Sitwell would often quote. Wallace's persona, as the spinster with terrible dress sense, allowed her to ignore conventional codes of feminine behaviour and speech in such bawdy songs as 'Let's have a Tiddly at the Milk Bar'. I am not suggesting that we must see Sitwell's dress sense as imitative of Wallace (although it is interesting that photographs of Wallace make her look very much like a man in drag); or that Sit-well's love of Wallace's performances saw her connecting her own work with popular culture. But Wallace represented one aspect of a woman's public performance, and while she didn't offer herself

as a role model *per se*, she certainly added a dimension to the spec-
trum of models of available femininity in a public capacity for Sitwell
as an early 20th-century woman poet.

Chapter Two examines the textual "performances" of Stevie
Smith. Born in Hull nearly 20 years after Sitwell, Smith was brought
up with her sister by her mother and her aunt in a middle-class
household in Palmers Green, London. Working as a secretary for
over 30 years, Smith was not just culturally and socially a part of
a different class from Sitwell, but of a more recognisably modern
generation. Like Sitwell, Smith devised a strategic self-presentation
which evolved as the century progressed; but rather than adopting
the highly-stylised and glittering carapace of Sitwell, Smith instead
chose to adopt a style of dress that is often considered in terms of
the childlike. As Severin has pointed out, Smith reviewed two books
on fashion in 1952, revealing her acute awareness of the politics of
fashion in relation to gender. In 'Clothes and the Woman', Smith
championed the more androgynous fashion of the 20s, directly
linking the revolution in women's clothing with women's changing
roles subsequent to the First World War. 'Smith's transformation
into a child,' Severin argues, which can be pinpointed to the 1950s,
'began when women's clothing was undergoing its own transforma-
tion in the direction of extreme femininity' (*Poetry Off the Page*, p.60).
Like Sitwell, Smith's construction of herself as a woman poet is
one which avoids any kind of sexualisation of her femininity, but
still demands that we look. And if the childlike clothes served to
androgynise Smith, they also identified her with the anarchic and
mischievous world of the child.

As in Sitwell's case the juxtaposition between clothing and the
poet became more extreme as Smith aged. But where Sitwell's
construction of herself was concerned with a Baudelairean artificiality,
Smith's imaging of femininity effects an uncanniness. The same
uncanny quality also inhabits her poetry. As Hermione Lee has
pointed out 'Smith's poems are about feeling funny, and they give
us funny feelings.'[17] Janet Montefiore has shown how reactionary
the constructions of the feminine were by the male poets of the
Auden generation, with whom Smith was contemporary. 'Older
women,' Montefiore writes,

> represent the deadly power of reactionary authority, either as mothers
> who give up their sons to death, or worse still as childless women who
> vent their frustration at their own barrenness in a death wish against
> young men. Young women, less threateningly, are expensive temptresses
> or, very occasionally brides... Auden's...malicious comic ballads which
> he wrote in the late thirties...all...gleefully culminate in the death of a

woman. Married women get killed by their husbands...single women destroy themselves out of boredom, or out of repression.[18]

The women depicted in Smith poems are also subject to the extreme pressures of a patriarchal culture, pressures which Smith examines in poems about love, religion and death. But Smith's rewritings of fairytale and myth, for example, are often comic and ironic in their analysis of women's oppression, though not always identifiably feminist. Not only was Smith taking on a challenging role in relation to constructions of femininity through her appearance, she was also dramatising, as do the accompanying illustrations to her poems, her anxieties about writing and the positioning of the woman poet.

Chapter Three looks at the work of Sylvia Plath. I discuss the various ways in which Plath continues to explore her femininity, and how that exploration feeds importantly into the development of her poetry. I show how Plath sets up masculine figures as a way of configuring a muse, and dramatises her anxieties about masculinity and femininity in her writing from the title-poem of her first collection *The Colossus* (1960) to the later poems of her posthumously published collection *Ariel* (1963). I also think briefly about Plath's recourse to surrealist models and techniques and the strategy surrealist imagery offers her as a way of negotiating gender assumptions and models.

To begin with, I look at the title-poem of Plath's first book, *The Colossus*. My primary focus in reading this poem is the way Plath makes intersections in her work between surrealist art and popular film as a way of attempting to construct and gender a viable muse, and to straddle a gender divide which endangers her sense of a writing self. The rather old-fashioned and heavily weighted term 'the muse' might seems anachronistic when discussing writing, especially that by women; nevertheless I use the term here because it corresponds to the setting-up of a monumental figure of otherness which Plath needs to do to establish a sense of self when she writes. In addition to this, the idea of the muse as promulgated by Robert Graves' *The White Goddess* (1948) was one that was important, in different ways, for both Plath and Ted Hughes. For Graves, the muse is a creative and yet simultaneously destructive female force, she is always 'other': 'Woman is not a poet: she is either a Muse or she is nothing.' When she becomes a domesticated woman and turns the poet into a domesticated man 'the Muse fades out, so does the poet': 'The White Goddess is anti-domestic; she is the perpetual "other woman".' [19] Such a framework seems nigh on impossible for Plath, to work, or even exist, within: as muse she must find muse; she must be alterity while in turn finding it for herself; she must resist the 'fade out' of domesticity as both poet and muse.

Graves' image of the muse was modelled on his partner the poet Laura Riding, and it is difficult not to imagine Plath seeing the relationship of Graves and Riding as some kind of model for poetic partnership when thinking about her own marriage to Hughes. My reading of 'The Colossus', which clusters round, and attempts to unpick, a series of documented and undocumented responses by Plath to high and popular culture that feed into the poem, offers no definitive genealogy. To make that claim for any poem would, of course, be impossible. But by focusing closely on the various prompts that texts and images might have been thrown up for Plath in the writing of the poem, I suggest the complex web of gender associations the act of writing presented Plath with at this pivotal point in her life. In establishing a connection between Stevie Smith and Sylvia Plath, and between Plath and Edith Sitwell, I offer a rereading of Plath's work through both male and female poetic models.

Plath's move to Britain was important not simply to her own development as a poet, but proved a significant influence on the work of the British women writing after her. As an American domiciled in England, first published in England, but also with strong associations with her American contemporaries of the period (Robert Lowell, Anne Sexton), Plath is never wholly recognised as being part of the British tradition – unlike T.S. Eliot, for example. She has nevertheless become an increasing presence in British poetry since the publication of her *Collected Poems* in 1981. As Jacqueline Rose remarks, one of the most important things we find in our reading of Plath is

> the constant overlapping of the most discomforting aspects of... [her] writing and her own status in the culture and the cultural phenomena of which she writes. Plath is a fantasy, she writes fantasy. She is a symptom, she writes the symptom. She anticipates, uncannily; she retaliates in advance...she haunts and is haunted by the culture. (*The Haunting of Sylvia Plath*, p.8)

In a survey of British poets in the 1980s, Plath and Larkin emerged as the two most influential – as represented by their volumes *Ariel* and *High Windows*.[20] Few contemporary women poets, however, until recently, have been willing to identify Plath as a major influence, and not surprisingly have shied away from being identified with an icon whose power as a poet has been so closely associated with madness and self-annihilation. Anne Stevenson, in her poetic dialogue with Plath, who was her contemporary, and later her biographer, writes in her poem 'Letter to Sylvia Plath' (1988), 'Because you were selfish and sad and died, / we have grown up on the other side / of a famous girl you didn't know';[21] Lavinia Greenlaw sees Plath as 'important and dangerous'[22] while Julia Copus (born 1969) writes: 'I've read other books since which have influenced me – probably far more usefully – but none that has provoked quite the same sort of exhilaration' (*MWP*, p.399). As a precursor to the women poets who follow her, Plath offers and embodies anxieties about the construction of the writing subject, emerging as she does from a history of women's exclusion or representation of distorted femininity in the literary tradition, and I will be arguing in the second section of the book that the perceived dangers of her influence contribute to some women looking towards poetic models which allowed them a constrastingly objective voice.

The first section of the book concludes in Chapter Four with a discussion of the work of another American poet, Anne Sexton. While the work of Sitwell, Smith and Plath seems quite tightly bound through intertextual connections, and their own readings and re-readings of each other, this is less evident in Sexton's case. As a presence, Sexton was important to Plath, as Plath was to Sexton, but perhaps not surprisingly, given that she is the only poet in the first part of my study not to have lived in Britain, Sexton has been less central to the development of a British poetic tradition. I argue for her place here, however, because her struggles are akin to that of the three earlier poets and are reflected in the work of British poets of the succeeding generation. One of the reasons that both Plath and Sexton are important to the British tradition is their inclusion in the revised version of A. Alvarez's *The New Poetry* (1966) – in which they were the only two women to appear. Alvarez argues in forceful terms in his introduction that poets must find a way of negotiating inner and outer lives:

> [T]he forceable recognition of a mass evil outside us has developed precisely in parallel with psychoanalysis; that is, with our recognition of the ways in which the same forces are at work within us...it is hard to live in an age of psychoanalysis and feel oneself wholly detached from the dominant public savagery...
> ...What poetry needs, in brief, is a new seriousness. I would define this seriousness simply as the poet's ability and willingness to face the full range of his experience with his full intelligence; not to take the easy exits of either the conventional response or choking incoherence.[23]

In her foreword to *The Complete Poems*, Maxine Kumin suggests that women readers often identified with the extremity of Sexton's

experience;[24] and that it was this graphic exposé of female experi-
ence with which the male reviewer could not identify that left them
uncomfortable or outraged:

> The facts of Anne Sexton's troubled and chaotic life are well known;
> no other American poet in our time has cried aloud publicly so many
> private details. While the frankness of these revelations attracted many
> readers, especially women, who identified strongly with the female aspect
> of the poems, a number of poets and critics – for the most part, although
> not exclusively male – took offense. For Louis Simpson, writing in
> *Harper's Magazine*, 'Menstruation at Forty' was 'the straw that broke
> this camel's back'. And years before he wrote his bestselling novel,
> *Deliverance*, which centers on a graphic scene of homosexual rape, James
> Dickey, writing in the *New York Times Book Review*, excoriated the
> poems in *All My Pretty Ones*, saying 'It would be hard to find a writer
> who dwells more insistently on the pathetic and disgusting aspects of
> bodily experience...' In a terse eulogy Robert Lowell declared, with
> considerable ambivalence it would seem, 'For a book or two, she grew
> more powerful. Then writing was too easy or too hard for her. She
> became meager and exaggerated. Many of her most embarrassing poems
> would have been fascinating if someone had put them in quotes, as the
> presentation of some character, not the author.'[25]

This issue of embarrassment highlights one of the crucial differences
between Sexton's work and the work of her male poetic confessing
contemporaries. For the male poet the act of confession may be
figured as a transgression against a preconceived notion of the
masculine as controlled, ordered and rational. For the woman poet,
however, this transgression works on a double model. On the one
hand it offers a liberation from stereotypical representations of
women (the angel in the house, the paragon of sexual and domestic
virtue) while on the other hand it may actually reinforce patriarchal
anxieties about women's fury and madness, desire and dirtiness,
and reinscribe them in the ostensible service of liberation. Without
negating or trivialising the anguish or difficulties of the male con-
fessional, or the powerfulness of their poetry, it does not seem unfair
to argue that the male confessional is radical precisely because he
can be seen to be exploring new territories of the male psyche; he
breaks down patriarchal notions of masculinity while at the same
time offering an extremity of experience as a testimony of suffering
that equates with prophecy and "strength". The male confessional
speaks as representative of the suffering of his time and his nation.
His pain is seen to be of both personal and global relevance. If this
confessing poet is Robert Lowell, a poet whose family is part of
the political ruling class, the implications are perhaps even more
extreme; and indeed the fact that Lowell served as a figurehead for
the so-called Confessional group serves to validate such conjectures.

The woman who confesses is, however, frequently read as testifying only to her own anguish and her own "weakness"; she is simply revealing the awfulness of femininity which was "known" to be there all along, and which, in the most simplistic terms, has led to her oppression in the first place. In speaking what she believes to be a personal truth she is making a spectacle of herself, throwing an already precarious subjectivity into a heightened state of prominence and vulnerability.

And it is here we see the exact nature of the problem: for if the woman poet *does* remain silent, if the awfulness of her confessional truth is such that it will serve only to oppress her further, she is left where she started, and cannot speak at all. Alternatively, she can speak a version of the self which also confirms a certain kind of femininity – that of beauty, passivity, orderliness and self-control – but which nevertheless fails to "tell it like it is". Diane Wood Middlebrook's controversial biography of Sexton, has shown, through its use of the tapes made during her psychoanalytic sessions from which some of the poems (which she referred to as her transference poems) are drawn, just how close some of the links are between poem and therapeutic material. Authenticity and related issues of truth are particularly charged in a reading of women's texts when an authenticity of actual bodily suffering becomes entangled with the quest for an establishment of a female writing identity. Sexton's mental illness and its expression in her poetry offers a simultaneously difficult but important representation of both women's experience and the woman poet, both for the reader and for the woman poet who writes after her.

While it is absolutely *not* my intention to create a pathology of the woman poet, the violence that figures in the work of all these women poets seems a central force behind their writing; that such violence sometimes becomes self-directed, that it seeks out the actual body as well being dramatised in the textual body, does demand that we ask difficult questions about women's relationship both to poetic language and to our culture. Stevie Smith attempted suicide in 1953, not long after she had written her best-known poem 'Not Waving but Drowning', an attempt which she later regretted, although her lifelong interest in death's ability to soothe and comfort in its nothingness is one of the most persistent themes in her work. Both Plath and Sexton made several attempts on their lives before their suicides. Edith Sitwell, on the other hand, although sometimes subject to depressions, lived until she was 77; the murderous impulse, however, is strong in her work and, as I will show, is early on directed towards images of the maternal; interestingly,

Sitwell also, throughout her life, had a morbid interest in murder mysteries and macabre details of true crime.

The legacy of the deaths of Plath and Sexton, who died when they were 30 and 46 respectively, has likewise, coupled with the interest in the work of Tsvetaeva and Akhmatova (read in translations), contributed to the deathly configuration of the woman poet. Likewise, Sitwell's and Smith's attempts to circumvent their femininity through a carapace of eccentricity also makes them difficult models for those women poets who write after them.

Germaine Greer, in her *Slipshod Sibyls*, gives a characteristically erudite and dogmatic account of women poets before 1900, before turning in her final chapter to the woman poet in the 20th century. 'Too many of the most conspicuous figures in women's poetry of the 20th century,' she writes, 'not only destroyed themselves in a variety of ways but are valued for poetry that documents that process. No woman now embarking on a career in poetry can be unaware of these terrible precedents.'[26] She continues: 'poetry as presented by the male literary establishment which Tsvetaeva, Plath and Sexton wooed all their lives, enticed the woman poet to dance upon a wire, to make an exhibition of herself and ultimately to come to grief.' (*Slipshod Sibyls*, p.422). In conclusion Greer suggests that

> [h]undreds of good women poets now travel the length and breadth of our world, performing their work with wit and style. Their verse does not incessantly vibrate at the highest frequency; they have other subjects beside themselves; they do not see themselves as outcast and solitary or unique in their capacity to be miserable. Because they fail to flay themselves alive, they will be called minor, and forgotten...until such a time as we come to prefer our poets of all sexes with the skin on. (p.424)

While I don't fully agree with Greer's unmodulated reflection on these women's deaths, or share her pessimism about the future of women's poetry, her suggestion that women poets need to see themselves as 'a woman poet, not the woman poet' is a concern central to my whole project – both in terms of this book and the anthology of poetry, *Modern Women Poets*, which accompanies it.

In the second section of *Consorting with Angels* I look more broadly at the work of women writing after the deaths of these prominent women poets, initially in the context of the burgeoning of the Women's Movement. In Chapter Five I look at the way in which Vicki Feaver (born 1943), Selima Hill (born 1945) and Carol Ann Duffy (born 1955) negotiate feminism as well as the feminine in their work. For Feaver and Duffy, recourse to myth and fairytale gives them access to a narrative, however much they then go on to destabilise the ideology that narrative upholds in their parodic revisioning. Whether they dramatise that narrative, or people it in a way that allows for a many-voiced rather than a univocal text, such engagements with storytelling allow for self-fabrication rather than self-presentation, for masquerade rather than unquestioned selfhood. I also look here at the tension in Duffy's work that arises between the voices of the dramatic poems and the way in which the body is figured in her lyrical poems. To conclude the chapter I examine Selima Hill's use of surrealist imagery, as well as touching on the way, in her extended dramatic and fragmented narratives, she writes about often extreme and difficult female experience.

By way of contrast, in Chapter Six I examine the work of recent women poets who construct versions of femininity in relation to national and "racial" identities, discussing the work of Medbh McGuckian (born in Northern Ireland in 1950), Moniza Alvi (born in Pakistan in 1954), Gwyneth Lewis (born in Wales in 1959), Kathleen Jamie (born in Scotland in 1962), Jackie Kay (born in Scotland in 1961) and Jo Shapcott (born in England 1953). This chapter draws together some of the central themes I have been exploring, but focuses at this point on the ways in which women poets in the 1980s and 1990s sought to problematise the medium of English through which they predominantly write. I think about how this is linked to their gender (and the ways in which they negotiate ideas of femininity) but also to their sense of national identities in Britain and Northern Ireland. Like the women I have discussed earlier in the book, all the poets examined here look for a way in which to place themselves within a literary tradition while simultaneously resisting its damage to femininity – whatever they perceive that to be – and the female body. Although it might well be argued that the wider aesthetic or political differences between the women are greater than the similarities between them, all are preoccupied thematically with destabilising essentialist notions and nationality and gender.

Finally, Chapter Seven looks at contemporary science and nature poetry by Jo Shapcott, Lavinia Greenlaw (born 1962) and Alice Oswald (born 1966). Both Shapcott and Greenlaw are strongly influenced by the American poet Elizabeth Bishop (1911-79), almost certainly the most influential and important poet to women writing in the 1980s and 1990s. In different ways both poets attempt to "take on", in every sense of the word, the discourse of science as a way of distancing themselves from areas traditionally deemed feminine. While Jo Shapcott makes use of the dramatic monologue, Lavinia Greenlaw consciously attempts to move away from models of poetry which are concerned with self-display and performance and, by contrast, looks to the paradigms of science to offer a model of objectivity which she can adopt in her writing. By contrast, in the second part of the chapter, I examine the nature poetry of Alice Oswald, exploring in particular her long poem *Dart* as well as her more recent and experimental lyrics. Here I also use Bishop as a touchstone. Although Bishop appears not to be an important poet for Oswald, her use of the dramatic poem to explore what Jonathan Bate has described as 'history-through-topography' bears interesting comparison with Bishop's own explorations of the self through geography. *Dart*, while clearly influenced by Ted Hughes, is also a poem which, at the same time as connecting with identifiable strategies in women's poetry of the 19th century, attempts to carve out for itself a multi-vocal feminine aesthetic for the 21st century.

The work of the many women poets not discussed here, as well as those who are, is included in *Modern Women Poets*. In compiling the anthology I have tried to include poems that can be read in the light of the strategies I identify here, but I have also attempted to show the range of poetries written women in the 20th century, in subject-matter and genre. So I include there poems about the body, sexuality, motherhood as well as religion, science, politics; I also include some extracts from longer narrative and dramatic poems, poems which show the continued engagement with myth and fairy-tale, as well as shorter more readily attributable autobiographical lyrics by women writing from the beginning of the century to its end. The pained cry of the anthologist is one which frequently testifies to the impossibility of including everyone who was worthy of inclusion. I am no exception here. *Modern Women Poets* sets out to chart one version of a history of women's poetry in the past hundred years. It is not all-inclusive but it is broad in its range, and my hope is that it provides a reference point for the general reader or student of contemporary women's poetry. Too often women poets have been read in isolation and to some extent fetishised as special cases. Seeing a publishing context for these women radically affects the way in which we read them. I also include at the end of this book a chronology of women's poetry so that the publication of texts can be easily seen across long writing careers.

Anxieties about the value and status of the female subject as well as the text, the relationship between women poets, poetry and the body were beautifully and cruelly summed up at the beginning of the 20th-century in Pound's famous throwaway remark to his "acolyte" Hilda Doolittle (H.D.) when he told her 'You are a poem but your poem's nought.' Such anxieties continue, for example, in

Harry Moore's more kindly meant but nonetheless revealing preface
to James D. Brophy's book on Edith Sitwell when he talks about
her 'plangently theatrical' recitals: 'Edith Sitwell was a spectacular
figure and a remarkable poet,' he writes. 'You could turn these
phrases around and still "catch" her: a remarkable figure and a
spectacular poet.' [27] Women's poetry is now very much a visible
part of contemporary poetry. It is the 'spectacularity' of the work
of these women poets – in all senses of the word – who wrote and
who have shaped the writing which succeeds them, which demands,
in every way, another and a different kind of look.

PART 1

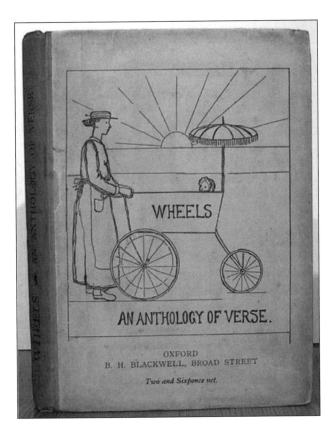

FIG 1: Cover *(above)* and title-page *(left)* of the first *Wheels* anthology, published by Blackwell's in 1916.

CHAPTER ONE

Wheels, Peacocks, Ghosts, Hambones and Hearts: Edith Sitwell's Self-Fashioning

I had a visit from Edith Sitwell whom I like. I like her appearance – in red cotton, many flounced, though it was blowing a gale. She has hands that shut up in one's own hands like fans – far more beautiful than mine. She is like a clean hare's bone that one finds on the moor with emeralds stuck about it. She is infinitely tapering, and distinguished and old maidish and hysterical and sensitive... I like talking to her about her poetry – she flutters about like a sea bird, crying so dismally.

VIRGINIA WOOLF, letter to Vita Sackville-West, 1927 [1]

As Woolf's typically incisive portrait of Edith Sitwell illustrates, Sitwell's remarkable appearance was central to the way in which she was perceived as both a woman and a poet in the London literary and artistic circles in which she swiftly became a well-known figure. Sitwell's first collection of poems, *The Mother*, was privately printed in 1915. In the following year she edited the first volume of *Wheels*, an annual anthology of poetry which was to appear for the next six years.

In a time of anthologies and manifestos – Edmund Marsh's Georgian anthologies which were published between 1912 and 1922, the Imagist manifestos of 1914-1917, and the Vorticist manifestos of 1914 and 1915, to name just a few – *Wheels* stands out. This is not for the quality of its writing, but for the unusual fact that the anthology does not declare itself explicitly. The first edition (or 'cycle' as they were to be known) had no introduction, no editorial comments, no manifesto, no biographies, no bibliographies. It included the work of nine poets: the three Sitwells, Edith, and her younger brothers Osbert and Sacheverell, Edith's former governess and companion, Helen Rootham, Victor Perowne, Arnold James, E. Wyndham Tennant, Iris Tree and Nancy Cunard.[2] It is only Nancy Cunard's poem 'Wheels', set in italics at the front of the book, and working in conjunction with the anthology's cover image of a woman pushing a pram with a baby in it, which creates, as it were, the poetic and ideological stage. The poem is often referred to and little seen, so I quote it in its entirety here:

I sometimes think that all our thoughts are wheels
Rolling forever through the painted world,
Moved by the cunning of a thousand clowns
Dressed paper-wise, with blatant rounded masks,
That take their multi-coloured caravans
From place to place, and act and leap and sing,
Catching the spinning hoops when cymbals clash.
And one is dressed as Fate, and one as Death,
The rest that represent Love, Joy and Sin,
Join hands in solemn stage-learnt ecstasy,
While Folly beats a drum with golden pegs,
And mocks that shrouded Jester called Despair.
The dwarves and other curious satellites,
Voluptuous-mouthed, with slyly-pointed steps,
Strut in the circus while the people stare. –
And some have sober faces white with chalk,
And roll the heavy wheels all through the streets
Of sleeping hearts, with ponderance and noise
Like weary armies on a solemn march. –
Now in the scented gardens of the night,
Where we are scattered like a pack of cards,
Our words are turned to spokes that thoughts may roll
And form a jangling chain around the world,
(Itself a fabulous wheel controlled by Time
Over the slow incline of centuries.)
So dreams and prayers and feelings born of sleep
As well as all the sun-gilt pageantry
Made out of summer breezes and hot noons,
Are in the great revolving of the spheres
Under the trampling of their chariot wheels.

Although each of the subsequent anthologies paraded an in-joke of
one sort or another on their covers, the line drawing on the cover
of the first edition (*see* FIG. 1, *page 32*) is especially provocative and
puzzling. James D. Brophy is almost certainly right to draw con-
nections between *Wheels* and Sitwell's poem 'Pedagogues' (pub-
lished in June 1916),[3] suggesting that the *Wheels* cover was also,
with its bright yellow cover, evoking the decadence of *The Yellow
Book* with its yellow covers and illustration by Aubrey Beardsley.[4]
In contrast to the erotic illustration of a woman on the cover of *The
Yellow Book*, however, the image of the woman and pram suggests
not just a matronly chastity, but that the anthology is the caretaker
of a new writing that in its infancy must be nurtured (the *New
Statesman* reviewer at the time noted the 'rather stupid' cover,
exclaiming 'None of the contributors can be as young as that.')[5] The
juxtaposition between historical cycles in Cunard's poem, and the
wheels which are part of the pram, sets up, in its dialogue between
text and drawing, a peculiar dynamic between the personal and

the universal. There seem also to be gender issues at stake, and the fact that the figure of the woman on the front looks more like a nursery maid than a mother in itself says much about class as well as suggesting a relation between nurturer and nurtured that is more to do with guardianship than ownership. It's impossible, however, to know how worked through such juxtapositions were, or indeed how ironically they were being used.[6] Dadaist use of machinery in artworks of the period – in turn working ironically against Futurist celebration of machinery – was common. For example, Marcel Duchamp's found object or 'ready-made' *Bicycle Wheel* (1913) was a sculpture which consisted of a bicycle wheel balanced on a painted wooden stool; the first issue of the French magazine *391* (1917) had as its cover an illustration which was variation on a bicycle wheel by Francis Picabia who 'enlisted the machinery of the modern world' to 'interpret ideas' or 'expose human characteristics'.[7] Whether or not it subscribed to them, and perhaps because it didn't it, *Wheels*, with its cover's invocation of the most female and domestic of machinery, was very much a part of avant-garde attempts in the period to 'make it new', even as it ironised and poked fun at them. And while Brophy argues particularly for a dialogue with Pound, it seems likely that Sitwell was also invoking and setting herself and her contributors against Vorticism and the journal *BLAST*, which had appeared in 1914 and 1915, and which was generated by Ezra Pound (whom she takes to task in the second edition of *Wheels*) and Wyndham Lewis, whom she was later to describe as her 'favourite enemy'.

In his rethinking of the development of Pound's imagism, Daniel Tiffany has convincingly argued that for Pound 'Decadent poems and theorising about "death-in-life" bear witness to a catastrophic loss of vitality in poetic language eventually matched by the spectre of mass death in World War I.'[8] An attempt to reconfigure the decadent aesthetic for a modern century, during and after the trauma of the war, is also very close to the heart of Sitwell's own poetics. But while there is a shared preoccupation with death within the anthology, the *Wheels* contributors are much more conventional in their sub-gothic reflections on death and decay than the Vorticists; their poetry is, in Wilfred Owen's terms, 'in the pity'. Sitwell included eight of her own poems in this first edition of *Wheels*. Two of these poems, 'The Drunkard' and 'The Mother' (*MWP*, pp.56-59) had been included in the five poems which made up Sitwell's first book. 'The Mother' is of particular interest to me here.

Working in deliberate juxtaposition with the image on the cover of *Wheels*, 'The Mother' is a poem frustrating and rewarding by turn. Despite its straightforward narrative and diction, its ambiguities demand that it be read on many and sometimes contradictory levels. The poem tells of a relationship between a mother and her son, who murders her. In baldly biographical terms it appears to be an attempt by Sitwell to transpose into art her violent and ambivalent feelings about her own mother. These feelings are surely also connected with her departure from the family home in 1915 at the age of 28 to live in London with her friend Helen Rootham, who, it has been suggested, had become a surrogate mother to her (see Victoria Glendinning, *A Unicorn Among Lions*, p.213). Sitwell's bid for independence not only coincided with the outbreak of the war but also with her mother's incarceration for six months in Holloway Prison for a debt which her father could have easily repaid. John Pearson, in his biography of the Sitwell siblings, relates that Sitwell told Geoffrey Gorer that 'the mother of her poem, with her compassion and her understanding of her child, was an idealisation of the sort of mother she had always wanted for herself, and never found in Lady Ida'.[9]

Such biographical details give some insight into the emotional charges the poem might have carried for Sitwell, but are, of course, never the whole story of a poem. Like the infant of Blake's 'Infant Sorrow', which 'The Mother', with its *aabb* quatrains, perhaps gestures towards, the child in Sitwell's poem has been brought into a 'dangerous world'. But unlike Blake's infant's world, Sitwell's is a world without fathers. Such an absence is interesting and unremarked on in the poem itself, and adds to the vulnerability of the portrayal of a mother whose goodness appears to depend on her capacity for self-sacrifice. Even before the son kills the mother, the relationship between mother and son is figured in terms of cannibalistic imagery as the child feeds off the mother's body, devouring her flesh and blood: 'We give them all we have of good / Our blood to drink, our hearts for food.' When the child reaches manhood he is ensnared by a vampiric woman: the shift in emphasis moves from a woman who is devoured to the devouring vamp: 'Her hungry, wicked lips were red / As that dark blood my son's hand shed.' That this gender drama is also later figured through a Christian iconography of sacrifice and redemption (to which Sitwell returns in her later work) complicates matters more, specifically because of the many ways the image of the nurturing and bleeding breast of the mother can be interpreted. For if the mother waiting at the foot of a tree for her son in some way recalls the Virgin Mary at the foot of the cross, the mother, drained by her child of blood not milk, who feeds her child with her 'heart for food' in a parodic eucharist, also herself figures as a pelican-like redemptive Christ with a bleeding breast, who sacrifices herself for her son's sins.

An iconography which angrily conflates the Great War with the feminine – as both mother and "vamp" – is not untypical of the period, as women were blamed for urging their sons and husbands to fight for their country.[10] In the image of the son hanging Christ-like, a flag-like emblem of disgraced nation, we see an image of male suffering and impotence set against the ghostly, but nevertheless present figure of the mother. Fantasies about male suffering and redemption in the context of the war were, like the displacement of fear and anger onto the feminine, not uncommon and it is certainly possible that Sitwell was recalling in the poem rumours of German crucifixions of soldiers and children which circulated throughout the war.[11]

Sitwell herself held strong pacifist views at this period, and it's tempting because of this to read the poem as an anti-war poem which offers, as an alternative to male aggression and greed, a model of maternal love and sacrifice. But if the poem is holding up the maternal as a positive model of femininity, such a model is clearly held in deep ambivalence – the mother does after all get killed. Furthermore, in its staging of a drama between mother and child, and its enactment of a fantasy of maternal constancy and benevo-lence and sacrifice, in contrast to an aggressive, manipulative and sexualised femininity, the poem at one level also appears to sanction and excuse male aggression and greed. The son's behaviour is seen by the mother as a direct consequence of her ability to love him 'enough'; the vamp character disappears from the narrative alto-gether, and the poem leaves, at its end, no possibility, for either ghostly mother or dead son, of peace, resurrection or redemption.

The poem is fascinating because of these ambiguities, but even more so because of the fact that Sitwell repeatedly returns to the poem throughout her life, reprinting it, reconfiguring it and revisit-ing its themes, most particularly its imagery which sets the material body up against a ghostly female. After its initial publication in 1915, and its reprint in *Wheels*, the text of 'The Mother', unaltered, reappears in Sitwell's *Rustic Elegies* of 1927 where it was published as part of a three-part dramatic monologue 'The Hambone and the Heart'. In the *Selected Poems*[12] of 1936 'The Mother' again appears under the title of 'The Hambone and the Heart', but this time with the addition of a fourth poem to the sequence in which it figures.

Even when the mother poem is dispensed with in the late 1930s, Sitwell still continues to write about mothers in relation to death in a way which suggests she was still using the poem as an emotional touchstone. *The Song of the Cold* (1945), for example, sees Sitwell returning to the poems of *Street Songs* (1942) and *Green Song and other Poems* (1944) where, she writes, the poems 'are now arranged in the sequence to which they belong'. In these reorderings we also find in *The Song of the Cold* poems which continue the maternal preoccupation: 'Eurydice', a new poem, turns up alongside 'A Mother to her Dead Child' and 'Anne Boleyn's Song' (Boleyn was of course the beheaded mother of Elizabeth I, with whom Sitwell shared a birthday, and from whom she claimed distant descent).

Sitwell frequently republished and rearranged poems under different titles and such a compulsion to publish and reorder was clearly more than a desire to simply make money (although this may ostensibly have been the impetus which directed the endless repackaging and republication of her texts). But the return and repeat of 'The Mother' poem is clearly no simple accident of economics. In the remainder of this chapter I want to suggest ways in which the poem, and maternal imagery more generally, become a trope through which we can see Sitwell exploring anxieties not just about her relationship with the maternal feminine in her poetry, but with language, and the body, and creativity itself.

*   *   *

It seems useful at this juncture to draw on the writings of the psychoanalyst Melanie Klein, who placed the relationship between mother and child as central to the development of our creative impulses. For Klein, the infant takes up one of two positions in relationship to the mother, and can also move between these positions. In the 'paranoid-schizoid' position the infant images the mother, through the metaphor of the breast, as aggressive and punishing. In contrast to this bad breast is the idealised good breast, bountiful, and always fulfilling of the infant's demands. The child, when it comes to perceive the mother as a person, not a part-object, fears that its powerful antagonistic feelings towards the bad breast have damaged the mother. It is from the desire to assuage guilt that the child takes up the depressive position and desires to 'make reparation', a reparation which for Klein is central to creativity. Or as Julia Kristeva neatly summarises Klein's depressive position, 'upon losing the mother...I retrieve her as sign, image word'. [13] In Kleinian terms, then, the relationship between mother and infant is, according to Elizabeth Wright,

[t]he prototype for the aesthetic interaction both as regards the artist to his medium and the audience to the art-object...the medium of the artist becomes the mother's body; the separating out of the bodily self from the primal object is the central mode of experience. The creative act repeats the experience of separating from the mother. [14]

Sitwell's 'The Mother' is a poem which recounts its narrative in the first person; the mother-child relationship is seen exclusively through the eyes of the mother. The fact that it is the mother of Sitwell's poem who tells her story in the first person disallows a straightforward or simplistic transposition of identification between Sitwell as child and poem as metaphorical mother. Yet it is still possible to read Sitwell's writing of the poem and the return of the poem, in her work, through Klein's model of creative activity. Sitwell's desire to assuage guilt, to leave the mother undamaged, and her powerful antagonism to her own mother, becomes transferred in terms of a compulsion to repeat maternal/child separation, and the poem's own refusal for that separation to occur – the mother is murdered, but returns as a ghost after her death, and remains in the poem after the child's death. Similarly the poem, which dramatises anxiety about maternal/child separation, refuses to die and continues to haunt Sitwell's work.

What is also important here, and which I have so far skirted around, is the fact that Sitwell begins her career as a poet with the publication of a dramatic monologue. My initial hesitation in using the term comes in part from the fact that 'The Mother', while technically a poem spoken in the voice of a character, doesn't have many dramatic qualities. Nor does it fully set up a dynamic between reader, character and poet, to develop fully the ironies which we might expect to find in a dramatic monologue. Such differences become immediately apparent if we compare 'The Mother' with dramatic poems by Sitwell's contemporary Margaret Sackville (1881-1963) or Charlotte Mew (see *MWP*, pp.25-28). So although Sitwell's poem is written in the first person, a first person identifiably not the unmarried and childless poet, we get none of the feeling when reading the poem of the dramatic monologue's ability to embody that first person 'I' of the mother – the poem may as well be a narrative written in the third person in the voice of a more objective narrator. Interesting, too, is the fact that in her reconfiguration of the poem over the years Sitwell is ever keen to construct the poem as a monologue, using framing devices of other monologues, and placing it in quotation marks as if recognising the poem's own dramatic failure. In my introduction, I mentioned that one of the appeals of the monologue to the woman poet is that it allows her to construct a body in the poem which is not identifiable as her own. What seems to be enacted in Sitwell's monologue, in the drama of the separation of the mother from the child, is more metaphorically also a deep anxiety for Sitwell about identifying herself not just with the mother's body, but with any body. Furthermore, the female hauntings which run throughout Sitwell's texts, and which to some extent must be read symbolically as a failure of the creative impulse, seem intricately bound up with the physical construction she was simultaneously making of herself as a woman and a woman poet outside them. Such poetic hauntings become a charged subtext to her aestheticisation of her own body with its elaborate costumes that stage the self, an aestheticisation which was to become increasingly deathly as the years progressed.[15]

* * *

Sitwell's most widely-known work, *Façade*, a collaboration with the 19-year-old composer William Walton, was first performed to an invited audience in the Sitwells' drawing-room in Carlyle Square in January 1922; the first printed version was published in the same year and *Façade* had its first public performance at the Aeolian Hall in June 1923. The title *Façade* made reference to the first modernist ballet, *Parade*, a collaboration between Satie, Cocteau and Picasso. *Parade* featured characters from some of the newly established circuses and had been performed by the Ballets Russes under the direction of Diaghilev in Paris in 1917. All three Sitwells were life long admirers of Diaghilev, and Sacheverell was in 1926 to collaborate with him on a staging of *The Triumph of Neptune*; Edith published a prose work, *Children's Tales from the Russian Ballet*, in 1928; and in the introduction to her *Collected Poems* (1957) she quotes Cocteau on *Parade* as 'the poetry of childhood overtaken by a technician'. (*CP*, p.xvii.) The first volume of *Wheels* had included in it some prose translations of Rimbaud by Helen Rootham who had initially introduced Sitwell to Rimbaud and the French Symbolists. It's interesting that in its turn, *Parade* seems to have been inspired by Rimbaud's prose poem, 'Parade', from *Les Illuminations*, which ends:

> O most violent Paradise of the maddened grimace! No comparison with your Fakirs or other theatrical buffooneries. Wearing improvised costumes in nightmarish taste they play romances and tragedies of brigands and demigods which are spirited as history and religions never were. Chinamen, Hottentots, gypsies, simpletons, hyenas, Molochs, old insanities, sinister demons, they mingle popular, homespun turns with bestial poses and caresses. They would [willingly] render new plays and sentimental songs. Master jugglers, they transmogrify place and person and have recourse to magnetic stagecraft. Eyes flame, blood sings, bones thicken, tears and red trickles run down. Their banter and their terror last a minute, or whole months.
> I am alone in possessing the key to this barbarous sideshow.[16]

Façade is, and has been, figured very much as a light entertainment; Sitwell herself described it as 'fun', and the nature of its entertainment is often considered in terms of pantomime (an accusation the creators of *Parade* were keen to avoid) and burlesque. John Lucas sees it enjoying its anti-Georgian stance, pointing out that 'Walton's witty inventive music plays teasingly with the more *outré* musical styles of the period and manages to be both knowing and in its way celebratory of the daring and the disreputable.' [17] But with its Rimbaudian invocation of 'improvised costumes in nightmarish taste' and its mingling of 'poplar homespun turns with bestial poses and caresses', *Façade* is clearly also working within what the theorist Mikhail Bakhtin would term the carnival-grotesque (which we have also seen, with its clowns, masked figures, dwarves and circus references, in Cunard's "manifesto" poem 'Wheels'). Julia Kristeva discusses the carnivalesque, in her analysis of Bahktin, as a desire to 'reduce the subject to nothingness':

> while the structure of *the author* emerges as anonymity that creates and sees itself created as self and other, as man and mask... The carnival first exteriorises the structure of reflective literary productivity, then inevitably brings to light this structure's underlying unconscious: sexuality and death. [18]

And although Sitwell hated the surrealists there is much to compare in *Façade* with the developing surrealist project in France, largely due to its own debt of influence to Symbolism and a celebration of the carnivalesque. Apollinaire had written the programme notes for *Parade*, describing it, in an early use of the term, as 'a sort of Sur-realisme'. [19] André Breton's *First Manifesto of Surrealism* puts great emphasis on Surrealism's ability to allow the mind to 'relive' 'with glowing excitement the best part of its childhood', [20] an emphasis to which Sitwell cannot have had too much antagonism. It is easy to see, too, how the poems which comprise *Façade* have much in common with cubist and surrealist collage technique, with their juxtaposition of texture and colour, and their emphasis on sound over sense. Even Sitwell's own lengthy description of *Façade* in her introduction to the *Collected Poems* gives it a wholly surreal feel:

> The poems appeared strange, sometimes because of the heightened imagery and sometimes because, to quote a phrase of the scientist Henri Poincaré, 'the accident of a rhyme can call forth a system'. To this I would add a planetary system.
> Some of these poems are about materialism and the world crumbling into dust; some have as protagonists shadows, or ghosts, moving, not

in my country world, but in a highly-mechanised universe; others have
beings moving
> To the small sound of Time's drum in the heart
– figures gesticulating against the darkness, from the warmth and
light of their little candle-show.
Some of the poems have a violent exhilaration, others have a veiled
melancholy, a sadness masked by gaiety. (*CP*, p.xvii)

Sitwell was not a surrealist, but the analogies are worth drawing
as they open up a dimension of the poem in relation not only to
the processes of *Façade*'s production, but also to the anonymous
positioning of the author and veiled sexuality and deathliness
Kristeva associates with the carnivalesque.

According to Pearson, the words to *Façade* were spoken by Edith
Sitwell through a

> Sengerphone – a large papier mâché megaphone with an elaborate mouth-
> piece that fitted round the speaker's face. It had been invented by one
> Herr Senger, a Swiss Opera singer, to enable him to sing the part of
> Fafner the dragon...it was Sacheverell's idea that the Sengerphone, the
> speaker and the orchestra should all be carefully concealed from the
> audience behind a painted curtain. (*Façades*, p.182)

The curtain, painted by the artist Frank Dobson, consisted of a
central image of a Greek mask with an open mouth, reminiscent
of the so-called death mask of Agamemnon, beside which was a
smaller African mask. Sitwell stood behind the larger mask to
recite her poems to the accompaniment of Walton's music, the
Sengerphone poking out through the mouth. Such an image of
Sitwell as disembodied poet is in extreme contrast to her later
assertion of presence, and one which Lewis was to satirise in his
account of *Façade* in *The Apes of God* (1930). Her positioning
behind the curtain was apparently meant to allow an "impersonal-
ity", but I also want to argue here that the projecting sengerphone
references the paraphernalia of 19th-century séances and returns
us again to an image of Sitwell, as she spoke the poems, not just
as a voice but as a kind of ghostly presence.

All three Sitwells had a lifelong interest in things ghostly. At
the death of their father, in what they deemed suspicious circum-
stances, Edith employed a medium to enquire about the nature of
the purported wrong-doings (particularly regarding their inheri-
tance). Later in her life, she spoke of Robert Lowell's poem 'The
Ghost', from his first collection, *Lord Weary's Castle* (1946), as one
of the great 20th-century poems, an anecdote which takes on more
resonance if we know Lowell's own 'versions' of Rimbaud and
Baudelaire. Sacheverell Sitwell was later to become the author of a

book on ghosts, *Poltergeists: An Introduction and Examination Followed by Chosen Instances*, a highly readable approach to ghostly phenomena, which was first published in 1940, and subsequently reprinted as a classic in its field in 1959 and 1988. In his introduction Sacheverell Sitwell draws a connection between art and the ghostly, drawing a parallel between 'the feeling in the pores of the skin' that is the ghostly visitation and the 'true communication...of music, poetry or painting'.[22] The connections between ghostliness and poetic voice deepen when we see that *Poltergeists* has as its epigraph a poem by Edith Sitwell, 'The Drum' (*The Narrative of the Demon of Teddworth*), first published in *Troy Park* (1925) and subsequently printed as the first of the *Façade* poems in Sitwell's *Collected Poems* (1957).

As Steven Connor has pointed out, '[i]t is routinely claimed that Victorian spiritualism is the expression of a widespread dissatisfaction with the materialism of 19th-century science, industry and social and political thoughts, an assertion that the transcendence of spirit, as a principle of moral, religious and even political renewal, in an objectified world of inert things and blindly mechanical processes'.[23] In his discussion of séances, Connor shows how somewhat paradoxically, 'spiritualism draws deeply on the experience of modern acoustic technologies...[and] attests and contributes to the ghostliness of these new technologies, even as it also deploys them in its strangely enthusiastic struggle against the supernatural' (*The Machine in the Ghost*, p.22). He describes how mediums would communicate with the dead using trumpets:

> [T]he spirits would employ a trumpet (resembling a speaking trumpet or megaphone rather than a musical instrument), or even a series of trumpets, which might be placed in the room at a distance from the medium. The trumpet served to amplify the voice, and to change its position: trumpets would be moved telekinetically through the air and round the room. The use of this property led to the mediums who specialised in this mode of manifestation becoming known as 'trumpet mediums'. (*The Machine in the Ghost*, pp.212-13)

Edith Sitwell – as far as we know – effected no telekinesis in her performance of *Façade*. But the parallels between Sitwell's use of the sengerphone to project her voice and the voices conjured by the trumpet mediums cannot have gone unnoticed by at least some of the members of *Façade*'s audience. If Sitwell figured herself as disembodied and impersonal in her recitation of the *Façade* poems, then in her use of the sengerphone she was also speaking her poems as a (ventriloqual?) medium for the dead.

The performances of the *Façade* poems did not adhere to a stable repertoire. Within the performance, the disembodied female voice

of Sitwell's poem, in its cataloguing of the grotesque antics, buffoon-
ery and romp, is constantly working alongside the music, and does
indeed in some ways become the music. Although it had initially
been proposed that Walton's music would be composed to accom-
pany the poems, Sitwell at times also wrote poems which were
rhythmically and texturally created to fit Walton's music. After
the first performance and publication in 1922, poems were written
and added until the last poem written with *Façade* in mind was
published in 1926. The last of the poems to be recited in perfor-
mances of *Façade* has always been 'Sir Beelzebub' (*CP*, p.158;
MWP, p.61), a poem which, ironically, was the first of the *Façade*
poems to be written. As such, the poem is a useful place to begin
to understand some of the themes and explore some of the poetic
techniques which were preoccupying Sitwell at the time.

In 'Sir Beelzebub' we see Sitwell again recalling Rimbaud, this
time his poem, 'Bal des pendus' ('Dance of the Hanged Men'), which
also features a 'Sir Beelzebub' and which begins:

> On the black gallows, one-armed friend, the paladins are dancing, dancing;
> the lean, the devil's, paladins; the skeletons of Saladins.
>   Sir Beelzebub pulls by the scruff his little black puppets who grin
> at the sky, and with a backhander in the head like a kick, makes them
> dance, dance to an old carol-tune![24]

Here the Sir Beelzebub of Sitwell's poem is transformed from
Rimbaud's demonic puppeteer of death to an image of bumbling
aristocracy. Beelzebub, demon, 'Lord of the Flies', was a Jewish
devil assimilated into the Christian tradition, used to represent the
fifth of the seven deadly sins, gluttony. The Sir Beelzebub of Sit-
well's poem finds himself transported into a pagan universe which is
also the louche world of the hotel barfly. *Façade* is in fact peopled
with such errant knights and 'gentlemen': Captain Fracasse, Don
Pasquito, Sir Bacchus, Old Sir Faulk, the admiral Sir Joshua Jebb,
in addition to stock *commedia dell'arte* figures such as Il Capitaneo,
Pierrot, Scaramouche, Il Dottore, and a handful of Kings and Queens:
James, Victoria, Priam. Just as Bakhtin describes, 'the diableries of
the medieval mysteries, in the parodical legends and the fabliaux'
so too is Sitwell's Beelzebub 'the gay ambivalent figure expressing
the unofficial point of view, the material bodily stratum'.[25]

The central joke of Sitwell's poem is its pun on the word 'bar'.
In Sitwell's poem the bar that is ostensibly crossed is the lounge
bar of a hotel. In Tennyson's poem 'Crossing the Bar' is of course
a crossing over into the afterlife. In Sitwell's poem such crossings
are predominantly intertextual. For while 'Sir Beelzebub' invokes

Rimbaud and the parodical devils of the medieval mysteries and 18th century, the poem also makes a series of satirical intertextual jabs at poems by the former laureate: 'The Charge of the Light Brigade' (its transformation of the Battle of Balaclava into a bala-clava), 'In Memoriam' (using the phrase *in memoriam*), and 'Crossing the Bar' (again directly quoting the words 'crossing the bar'). The reference to Proserpine also recalls one of Sitwell's favourite poets, Swinburne, and his poems 'The Garden of Proserpine' in which we see how Proserpina 'crushes for dead men deathly wine', and 'Hymn to Proserpina', 'a hymn to the Last Pagan of the Roman Empire'. Swinburne had himself parodied Tennyson and seems here, in his subtextual alliance with the feminine via Proserpina, to be set up as a touchstone for transgression. And just as the Sir Beelzebub of Rimbaud's poem pulls together his puppets to 'an old carol-tune', so too does Sitwell's Beelzebub pull together, and unite in its poetic body – gobbling them up even – the poems to which 'Sir Beelzebub' intertextually refers. The male poets invoked by the poem jostle and rub in dialogue with each other; parodied, imitated and admired figures their poems become simultaneously a part of Sit-well's poem's poetic textures.

Through its intertextual connections, Sitwell's poem also carries Tennyson's and Swinburne's poems' preoccupation with death: the death of Arthur Hallam, the death of six hundred in the Crimean war, and Proserpine's position as Queen of the Underworld, and wine goddess, who, carried off against her will and raped by Hades, is married to death for six months of the year.[26] In crossing the bar, then, it is not only Sir Beelzebub but the poem that steps over the mark, crosses the line, moves from one text to another, from male text to female text, from past to present, life to death, from sobriety to drunkenness, 'rocking and shocking' as the poem deter-minedly celebrates its 'nonsense' in its topsy-turvy universe.

Sitwell describes her own artistic practice in *Façade* as 'abstract... they are patterns in sound' , 'virtuoso excercises in technique':

> My experiments...consist of inquiries into the effect on rhythm and on speed of the use of rhymes, assonances, and dissonances, placed at the beginning and in the middle of lines, as well as at the end, and in most elaborate patterns. I experimented, too, with the effect upon speed of the use of equivalent syllables [...] assonances and dissonances put at different places within the lines and intermingled with equally skilfully placed internal rhymes have an immense effect upon rhythm and speed; and their effect on rhythm, and sometimes, but not always, on speed is different from that of lines containing elaborately schemed internal rhymes without assonances or dissonances (*CP*, p.xvi)

Sitwell also experimented with 'the subtle variations of thickness and thinness brought about in assonances' (*CP*, pp.xvi-xvii). Likewise the textual experiment sees her forging connections of meaning which arise from assonance and the semantic connections evoked by 'the softening from "apiaries" to "aviaries" ' (*CP*, p.xvii). These experiments with poetic texture are indebted, as much to Robert Graves's theories of poetic texture in his *Contemporary Techniques of Poetry*, whose influence Sitwell acknowledges, as they are to Swinburne's own habit of what Isobel Armstrong has described as 'dissolving the boundaries of language by coalescing distinctions of sound and meaning',[27] and, as I shall show in a moment, to Sitwell's readings of Mallarmé.[28] Although the *Façade* poems are meant to be heard initially for their sound rather than their sense, 'Sir Beelzebub' 's "nonsense" quality, as we have seen, disguises anxieties not only death and war, but also about Sitwell's positioning in relation to the male literary tradition and its 'classical meters'. To consider further the way in which Sitwell's use of texture works, it is worth looking briefly at two other closely related *Façade* poems, 'Waltz' (*CP*, p.144-45; *MWP*, p.59-60) and 'Popular Song' (*CP*, pp.146-47).

In contrast to the masculinity, imaged and textually incorporated in 'Sir Beelzebub', 'Waltz' has as its protagonists Daisy and Lily, two characters who are 'lazy and silly' as they idly 'walk by the shore of a wan grassy sea':

> They roam and determine
> What fashions have been and what fashions will be, –
> What tartan leaves born,
> What crinolines worn...

'Waltz' is constructed through the sounds of exotic fashions, the 'foam-bell of ermine', velours d'Afrande, tartaline, cashmere and barège: the poem is made up of fabrics, and their textures become the textures of language. Connections and meanings are made by the poem's rhymes which are not obviously interpretable or meaningful but which, in Sitwell's words, through an associative sound chain 'call forth a universe'. Like the waltz, the poem also "revolves", ending with the circular return to Daisy and Lily: 'Ladies, how vain, – hollow – / Gone is the sweet swallow, – Gone, Philomel'. The suggestion here, with the allusion to Philomel in juxtaposition to the talk of Daisy and Lily, is that of a transformation from silence (the woman with her tongue cut out becomes a bird). The unspoken subtext of the poem, then, is that of the woman who is forced to "sing" because of a rape (the parallels with Proserpine, again seem particularly pertinent here).

'Waltz' is followed in the *Collected Poems* by 'Popular Song', a
kind of Blakean response to 'Waltz', in which Lily O'Grady, who is
'silly and shady', longs to be like Daisy and Lily in their laziness,
and transforms into a 'negress'. Daisy and Lily are who they are,
Sitwell's poem suggests, because Daisy and lazy and silly and Lily
rhyme. Likewise Lily O'Grady is shady because of her name: or
perhaps she is named because of who she is. These verbal games
suggest the arbitrary nature of character and purpose. Lily O'Grady,
like the 'children gathering strawberries, who '[a]re changed by the
heat into Negresses' with fair hair, also becomes a 'Negress black
as the shade'. Just as her name in this fairytale world has made
her shady, her 'shadiness' has made her a 'negress'. Surreally, the
'negress' runs into the lake in which 'fish / Express a wish / For
mastic mantles and gowns with a swish' and Lily O'Grady achieves
her desire for transformation, through death: 'Silly and shady, / In
the deep shade is a lazy lady'. Like 'Waltz' the poem ends with a
silence, a silence in which even the nightingale is forbidden to
sing. Tellingly, in a discussion of *Façade* which is included in her
Selected Poems of 1936, Sitwell described the combination of sounds
made by vowels and consonants in *Façade* in terms of 'depth',
'shadow' and 'body'. Those, with 'neither depth nor body, are flat
and death-rotten'. By body, Sitwell presumably means here a full-
ness of sound, but it is significant that she chooses this word, and
that her polarisation of 'bodied' words and 'death-rotten' words
echoes the anxieties discussed earlier in this chapter concerning
the relationship between the maternal body and language.

*   *   *

I want now to think some more about the way in which this 'poetics
of embodiment' became implicated in Sitwell's construction and
staging of herself through her use of clothes. In an article 'Some
Observations on Women's Poetry', published in *Vogue* in 1925,
Sitwell urges that 'women's poems should above all things, be elo-
quent as a peacock, and that there should be a fantastic element, a
certain strangeness to their beauty'.[29] The peacock, a male bird,
exhibits, in the opening of its incredible tail feathers a beauty which
in the human world is always associated with feminine display and
adornment. This is not simply because women adorn their hair and
their bodies with its feathers but because the display and vanity
associated with the bird intrinsically associate it with stereotypes
of the feminine. In referring to the peacock's eloquence Sitwell is,
I think, not just referring to the sound of its voice, which Anthea

Trodd has suggested might recall Sitwell's own high-pitched voice, but also to the more metaphorical eloquence of its nature. For if the vanity and display of the peacock offer it as a feminised trope, then the phallic stiffening of its feathers which effect that display paradoxically also suggests male sexuality. For Sitwell, women's poetry is not seen in terms of a Woofian androgyny but becomes locked *across* constructions of femininity and masculinity and sexualised forms of display.

There are significant parallels to be drawn between the kind of writing Sitwell is suggesting a woman poet should aspire to and her own strategy of dress. Discussing Edna St Vincent Millay, Marianne Moore and, briefly, Edith Sitwell, Sandra Gilbert and Susan Gubar have suggested that in order to take on a public role these women, in different ways, 'adopted a mode of female female impersonation' [30] and that both Moore and Millay 'wrote as beings who impersonated "woman", in order to investigate both "female" costume and the very concept of "the feminine".' [31] And though of course Sitwell's elaborate costuming did not see her dressing as a man, her own construction of herself as woman poet might, in these terms, be seen as a kind of drag act which (like the female performance of Nellie Wallace, mentioned in my introduction) not only destabilises her femininity, as Gilbert and Gubar suggest, by ironically reinscribing it, but by performing femininity in terms of the transvestite's promise of a revelation of the something which it is not. Likewise, Sitwell's invocation of the image of the peacock sees the woman's poem as an extravagant and feminine display of gender which places the woman's poem as one which masquerades as the male poem that it is not. While acknowledging that such an analysis is 'risky' in her discussion of drag, Judith Butler has used the term 'gender melancholia' to suggest that 'gender performance allegorises a loss it cannot grieve, allegorises the incorporative fantasy of melancholia whereby an object is phantasmically taken in or on as a way of refusing to let it go':

> [F]or a "man" performing femininity or for a "woman" performing masculinity (the latter is always, in effect, to perform a little less, given that femininity is often cast as the spectacular gender) there is an attachment to and a loss and refusal of the figure of femininity by the man, or the figure of masculinity by the woman...drag is an effort to negotiate cross-gendered identification, ...[...] and allegorises some set of melancholic incorporative fantasies that stabilise gender. [32]

Poem and poet, in Sitwell's aesthetic, melancholically stage the presence of loss, which marks not only sexual difference, but the movement from the pre-linguistic relationship with the mother to language. In staging that loss Sitwell destabilises the gendering of both herself and her poetry.[35]

I am spending considerable time here in discussion of Sitwell's positioning of the woman poet in terms of that description of her being as 'eloquent as a peacock', but I want to continue to push the way in which we might use the analogy as a key to the gendering of Sitwell's work. The peacock feather, along with the sunflower and the lily, was a central icon of fin-de-siècle aestheticism, and strongly associated through its association with narcissism and display, with that iconic figure of fin-de-siècle sexuality and deathliness, Salome. Beardsley's famous illustrations to Oscar Wilde's play *Salome*, the first English edition of which was published in 1894, associate the peacock with the figure of Salome who is first imaged wearing a dress of peacock's feathers in the illustration for 'The Peacock Skirt' (*see* FIG. 2, *below*), as does, less obviously, Gustave Moreau's famous

painting *Salome Dancing Before Herod* (1876). As Elaine Showalter has discussed at some length, the figure of Salome was increasingly popular in the first quarter of the 20th century.[34] *The Dance of Salome* was performed in European music halls and set off a 'Salome Craze'. In the 1922 film version the Russian Alla Nazimova, who produced and starred in the film (at that time in her 40s), draws her inspiration from Beardsley's drawings, wearing elaborate oriental costumes and peacock feathers. That for Sitwell women's poetry might be seen in relation to the figure of Salome at this point in her life is highly suggestive when thinking about Sitwell's construction of gender. For, as Showalter comments, the dance of the veils performed by Salome was in fact 'the dance of gender, the delicacy and permeability of the veil separating masculine from feminine, licit from illicit desire' (*Sexual Anarchy*, p.152).

It is impossible to imagine that Sitwell did not know Wilde's play or Nazimova's role in the film, given both the play's and the film's notoriety, and indeed as we have seen there is equally good reason to assume that Sitwell was well aware of Beardsley's illustration (links with Beardsley are in fact often discussed in contemporary reviews of her work). Sitwell's manner of dress, as we have seen, sought to destabilise gender assumptions in the manner of drag. Marjorie Garber, drawing on Mallarmé's own description of the Salome story, points out that Salome in her dance 'delivers up to you through the ultimate veil that always remains, the nudity of your concepts and silently begins to write your vision in the manner of a Sign, which she is'.[35] Garber suggests that Salome herself is also a transvestic trope 'that the essence of the dance itself, its taboo border-crossing, is not only sensuality, but gender undecidability, and not only gender undecidability, but the paradox of gender identification...' (*Vested Interests*, p.343)

Flaubert, Huysmans, Gissmann and Maeterlinck all responded to the Salome story, all of whom had influenced Wilde, but it is Mallarmé's poetic drama, *Hérodiade* (1896), which seems to offer a kind of case history of the development of Sitwell's poetic in the *Façade* poems. In Mallarmé's *Hérodiade* the mother and daughter figures of the biblical story, Herodias and Salome, are conflated into one woman, Hérodiade, who is described by her nurse as a female narcissus: 'Sad flower that grows all alone / And, seeing its shadow reflected in a pool, feels nothing but anomie'.[36] In this respect Hérodiade comes to represent poetry itself, because for Mallarmé, poetry is a narcissistic activity: 'poetry stands in the place of love because it is in love with itself, and its pleasure in itself falls back deliciously in to my soul'.[37] Sitwell, as we have noted, was well-acquainted with French poetry.

Remembering Sitwell's murder of the mother in her earliest work, and the way in which 'The Mother' poem is very much connected with creativity for her, Mallarmé's merger of the cold and vengeful mother and the beautiful and seductive daughter into one figure who effects the decapitation of John the Baptist becomes highly charged. But for Sitwell to draw on, or align herself through association, with the techniques of this narcissistic aesthetic seems a precarious model for her poetic activity. As Peter Nicholls has pointed out, Mallarmé's poetry

> while subordinating local richness to a web of "musical" relations, is much preoccupied with the capacity of language to take the place of the object of desire...Inhibited sexual desire is...in some way compensated by the hermetic depth and materiality of the language: something of the self is extinguished so as to reappear in the "chastened" forms of artifice.[38]

Nicholls goes on in his discussion of Mallarmé, to draw on Rémy de Gourmont's essay 'Women and Language' (1901), which he offers as the model for subsequent 20th-century gendering which sees feminine language as musical, rhythmical 'tied to the repetitive and conservative rhythms of the oral tradition'. He concludes by citing Gourmont's assertion that 'All mimetic art is the work of women...The whole woman speaks. She is language incarnate.' (*Modernisms*, p.61). Decadence generally, and Mallarmé specifically, are dangerous models for Sitwell, as a woman writer, because the transformation of sexuality into textuality which they espouse for Sitwell is unmediated by the otherness of gender. Such a strategy of identification results not in a textuality that is "other" but in a process whereby the text and body – the potential object of desire – become not separated but entwined in the writer's own feminine body. As Nicholls suggests,

> That sense of language as falsely material and fetishistic was in turn closely bound up in its identification as feminine. However structured, the sadistic fantasies of the decadents almost always embodied a strong misogynistic drive, so there was a curious logic to the association of the dehumanised body of the female victim with the excessively material nature of a "feminine" language. (*Modernisms*, p.61)

Sitwell's own poem 'Herodiade' (*Selected Poems*, p.243), curiously separates mother from daughter again, giving us back Salome in a poem set in a spring in which flowers are as 'crisp' as the recently thawed snow, and which conflates writing with Salome's dance through its pun on the word 'page':

> The angels come as pages, show
> Salome how to touch the low
>
> Lute-notes and dance the sarabande,
> Leading the Princess by the hand,
>
> Until Salome's nurse appears,
> Harsh as the snow…

Part Salome, part Persephone, the woman at the poem's centre is figured both as child and innocent, at far remove from the figure of Salome as *femme fatale*. The poem ends with the angels leaving, realising that 'Theirs is no dance that she must learn'. For Salome has another kind of dance to perform; one which the poem itself seems to be saying it cannot interfere with and which the angels, those creatures of indeterminate sex, regard 'with shivering fears'. As such the poem appears to be a warning of the dangers of the narcissistic aesthetics of Mallarmé's *Hérodiade*, placing Salome in a kind of prelapsarian state of childhood, before she takes on the role of seductress and murderer. While Sitwell's own transformation into stylised icon allowed her to remove herself from the limiting definition of "poetess", her love of the decadents and their ' "chastened" form of artifice' also saw her locked within an aesthetic which configured femininity with language and death, a deathliness to which she repeatedly, even compulsively, returned.

*   *   *

Sitwell's *Troy Park* (1925) [39] includes her thinly veiled autobiographical poem about the ghost 'Colonel Fantock' and again figures a fictionalised Edith, who is described in the poem as looking as if she were drowned. In the volume, in which characters drift through the Renishaw estate, renamed as Troy, we also see Sitwell's continuing preoccupation with the female body and disembodiment in the image of the ghost, as well as a renewed interest in the use of the dramatic monologue. 'The Little Ghost who Died for Love' (*CP*, pp.178-80) is spoken in the voice of Deborah Churchill, 'born 1678…hanged in 1708 for shielding her lover in a duel'. Throughout the poem a tension is drawn up between the speaker's voice, 'quivering', 'a little nightingale that grieves' (echoes of Philomel here) and her physical appearance in her 'long cloak of brown'. 'The Mirror' is a monologue in the voice of a lady's maid (we are explicitly told this in a framing sentence at the beginning of the poem) who sees a ghost in the moonlight of her mistress's chamber, only to realise that this 'ghost' is her 'lady's image' in the mirror:

> Her too-gaily coifed flower-crowned head
> Was trembling slightly as with secret glee
> Upon the frail and bitter vertebrae

But the mirror also cries out to the maid to the effect that the lady's reflection and the maid's reflection are one and the same:

> The mirror said, 'your lady's or your own.
> When youthful petulance is worn away
> To that eternal smile so wide and gay
>
> Where lovers of the Flesh at last may see
> Where is the deathless sole reality.'

Although the dynamic set up in this poem is quite brilliant in the way it suggests complex lines of identification between reflection and recognition of self and other, Sitwell is still not wholly successful in these monologues in adopting the voice of 'another'; she cannot quite let go of a sense of self enough to transform that self into something recognisably not her, pushing the text away from her own body to create another textual body. The voices in the poems still continue, as in 'The Mother', to rely on the rather clunking artifice of the poem's rhyme scheme – a rhyme scheme it shares with 'The Mother' – against the (albeit constructed) spontaneity of the monologue's direct speech. This problem is, however, also the problem of which the poem speaks, that is the inability to remove the female self from a narcissistic and deathly relationship with language. This move towards the dramatic monologue at the same time as she was continuing to write the experimental *Façade* poems seems symptomatic of Sitwell's awareness of the problems that the decadent aesthetic presented her as a woman poet.

Troy Park also includes poems which we would now recognise as belonging to *Façade*. In 1926, however, although still composing *Façade* poems, Sitwell relinquished the performance of *Façade* to the family friend and composer Constant Lambert. This seems an important departure, coupled with the fact that *Rustic Elegies*,[40] her next volume, published in 1927, was the first and only of Sitwell's books to include a portrait of her as a frontispiece (*see over*, FIG. 3, *page 54*), and as such was an important marker in her self-fashioning. The photograph of Sitwell, taken by Cecil Beaton in 1926, is seldom reproduced. This image of Sitwell, which suggests beauty rather than grotesquerie, sees her looking knowingly at the camera, but there is less of a self-conscious or arrested quality to the portrait than in many of the pictures we have come to associate with Sitwell. Her hair is worn in a fashionable bob, her face seems lightly made up, her eyebrows are arched and defined, and her dress, made

FIG 3: Edith Sitwell photographed by Cecil Beaton in 1926 (COURTESY SOTHEBY'S)

of what looks like heavy textured brocade, with its square neck and wide sleeves, though marking out a female form in its contours, is not figure-hugging; there is no suggestion that the clothes are moulding her figure in the way in which the corsets and stays of the previous centuries constricted and contorted the female body. The painted foliage on the backdrop to the photo contrasts with the plastic (or silk?) which catches the light to the side of the picture. This portrait of Sitwell figures her some way between the natural and the artificial, concepts highly gendered in decadent thinking which saw woman as a kind of abhorrent nature. In *Rustic Elegies*, a volume which was pivotal to her development, Sitwell continued in her exploration of the relationship between language, fashion, and the body, in imaging herself, and on the page.

Rustic Elegies is comprised of three sections, 'Elegy on Dead Fashion' (*CP*, pp.197-209), 'The Hambone and the Heart' (*CP*, pp.181-86) and 'Prelude to a Fairy Tale'. 'Elegy on Dead Fashion' is a long poem which elegises a lost bucolic world, 'that forgotten tomb that was our heart', 'The sound fountains / Weeps swan-soft elegies to the deep mountains, – / Repeats their laughter, mournful now and slow, To the dead nymph Echo.' (*CP*, p.203) It is tempting in its drawing together of landscape and voice to read the poem as setting up an idyllic, pre-lapsarian maternal landscape, a paradise that consists of 'the ancient bliss of Venus' and which might be compared with H.D.'s Hellenic maternal landscapes (Helen, it has been pointed out, was H.D.'s mother's name) as we see the fashionable women replace the mythic goddesses and nymphs of a bucolic pre-lapsarian idyll. In his *Arcades Project*, Walter Benjamin argues that fashion becomes a paradigm for modernity marking an 'emporium for exchange between woman and commodity'. In one important section, written in 1935, he suggests that it is fashion which brings together the past and the present, the living and the dead:

> Not the body but the corpse is the perfect object for [fashion's] practice. Fashion marries off the living to the inorganic. Hair and nails, midway between the inorganic and the organic, always have been subjected to its action...Fashion is sworn to the inorganic world. Yet, on the other hand, it is fashion alone that overcomes death. It incorporates the isolated into the present. Fashion is contemporary to each past.[41]

If Sitwell's poem is an extended elegy to the maternal body, which the poem, in its overlay of past and present, is reluctant to lose, it is also an evocation of a lost paradise where fashion is associated with corruption and decadence. It is a world where 'the gods' are 'no larger than ourselves' and, as she pointedly reveals her class allegiances, where 'Psyche has become a kitchen maid'. (*CP*, p.208).

'Elegy on Dead Fashion', with its emphasis on material textures, sets up a contrast to the other images in the poems in *Rustic Elegies*, of disembodiment, and of a ghastly inanimate fleshliness. The nymphs and goddesses of its bucolic idyll drift in a scene which has been overlaid by the deathliness and decay of the modern world:

> Rich as a tomb each dress! oh, pity these!
> I think the rich died young, and no one sees
> The young loved face show for a fading while
> Through that death-mask, the sad cynic smile.
>
> .   .   .   .   .
>
> These living skeletons blown by the wind
> Were Cleopatra, Thaïs... age unkind
> Has shrunken them so feeble and so small
> That Death will never comfort them at all.
>
> They are so poor they seem to have put by
> The outworn fashion of the flesh! They lie
> Naked and bare in their mortality
> Waiting for Death to warm them, childishly.
>
> (*CP*, p.209)

The second section of *Rustic Elegies* consists of a reworking of 'The Mother', this time now figured as a dramatic exchange, 'The Hambone and the Heart', a poem dedicated to the homosexual Russian painter Pavel Tchelitchev, with whom Sitwell had a long, and deeply painful romantic friendship from the late 1920s to the 1950s. It is too simplistic to suggest that the mourning for the mother is displaced by the melancholic mourning for the desired but unattainable Tchelitchev. But it is certainly worth reflecting on how maternal and erotic love and loss become combined in this sequence of poems which describes (somewhat comically to the modern reader) a hambone in the hands of a Clown in dialogue with the heart of the mother whose son has killed her. The first part of the monologue is spoken in the voice of a girl from a 'great house in the barrack square' who announces to 'the dust of all the dead':

> ...my heart has known
> That terrible Gehenna of the bone
> Deserted by the flesh, – with Death alone!
>
> Could we foretell the worm within the heart,
> That holds the households and the parks of heaven,
> Could we foretell that land was only earth,
> Would it be worth the pain of death and birth,
> Would it be worth the soul from body riven?
>
> (*CP*, p.181)

The girl returns, after 'The Mother' poem has been rehearsed:

> For underneath the lime-tree's golden town
> Of Heaven, where he stood, the tattered Clown
> Holding the screaming Heart and the Hambone,
> You saw the Clown's thick hambone, life-pink carrion,
> That Venus perfuming the summer air.
> Old pigs, starved dogs, and the long worms of the grave
> Were rooting at it, nosing at it there:
> Then you, my sun, left me and ran to it
> Through pigs, dogs, grave-worms' ramparted tall waves.
>
> (*CP*, p.185)

With its melodrama and overblown use of gothic, this is not Sitwell at her best. But the parallel she draws (as 'lost son' becomes rather clumsily 'lost sun') between the girl who is grieving ('the worm where once the kiss clung') and the mother who mourns her child, is notable.

Why then, at this point, does Sitwell choose to reintroduce 'The Mother', a poem twelve years old, for the third time back into her work? In July 1923 Sitwell read and reviewed the American poet Gertrude Stein's *Geography and Plays* (1922) [42] and in the following year, having been introduced by Dorothy Todd, who was the current editor of *Vogue* for whom Sitwell often wrote, had met Stein in Paris. As Cyrena Pondrom points out in an essay exploring the connections between the two poets, Sitwell, in early reviews of Stein's *Geography and Plays*, had shown some initial ambivalence about Stein's writing. But by 1925, as Pondrom points out, she was holding up Stein as a model for modernist practice; and by 1926 she was praising *Geography and Plays*, as 'one of the most exciting books of our time'.[43] In *Bucolic Comedies* (1923) Sitwell had included a poem, dedicated to Dorothy Todd, 'Country Cousins', which is three variations on a line of Stein's, 'A coral neck and a little song, so very extra, so very Susie' from her poem 'Sacred Emily' (1913) also first published in *Geography and Plays*. 'Sacred Emily' includes Stein's most quoted line 'Rose is a rose is a rose is a rose' and is a long poem which links a coded sexuality with creativity, and the urge to 'Put something down some day in my handwriting'.

It is impossible to know the extent to which Sitwell was reading and reinventing Stein's 'Sacred Emily' as a sexual or a lesbian poem. Sitwell hated the explicit heterosexual sex of Lawrence's *Lady Chatterley's Lover* which she described as 'a very dirty and completely worthless book' (*Unicorn Among Lions*, p.127) – and whether the coded sexuality of Stein was "read" by her is unclear.

Her interest in Stein as poetic "mother" appears first and foremost to have been focused in the sympathetic connection of stylistic innovation which for Sitwell, in its non-grammatical baby talk, also seems to have evoked the childhood paradise for which she mourns in so many of the bucolic poems. Sitwell rather literalises Stein's piece in her first tragi-comic re-writing of a poem about a hen laying an egg. Sitwell's poems also recall, with their named characters Liz and Jeanie, and celebration of sisterhood, Christina Rossetti's 'Goblin Market' – a poem which she wrote was 'perhaps the most perfect poem written by a woman in the English language'.[44] Bringing together the influence of Rossetti and Stein sees Sitwell calling on female literary models to establish a female poetic born out of assimilation and improvisation: curiously the libidinal energy so present in the Rossetti in Sitwell's poems has been absorbed by the style. 'Centaurs and Centauresses' ('Jodelling Song', *CP*, pp.142-43), composed in the same year as 'Country Cousins' (which is placed as number 25, immediately prior to 'Waltz and 'Popular Song' in the *Façade* section of the *Collected Poems*) is, as Sitwell points out in a footnote, also a reworking of Stein, this time here 'Accents in Alsace: A Reasonable Tragedy' (1919) from *Geography and Plays*.

In the context of attempting to read Sitwell in terms of the creation of a female poetics, Sitwell's interest in Stein, particularly at this point in her writing, is clearly significant. It is worth quoting Sitwell's poem and the quotation from Stein she cites, in full:

Jodelling Song

'We bear velvet cream,
Green and babyish
Small leaves seem; each stream
Horses' tails that swish,

And the chimes remind
Us of sweet birds singing,
Like the jangling bells
On rose-trees ringing.

Man must say farewell
To parents now,
And to William Tell,
And Mrs Cow.

Man must say farewells
To storks and Bettes,
And to roses' bells,
And statuettes.

Forests white and black
In spring are blue
With forget-me-nots,
And to lovers true

Still the sweet bird begs
And tries to cozen
Them: "Buy angels' eggs
Sold by the dozen."

Gone are clouds like inns
On the gardens' brinks,
And the mountain djinns, –
Ganymede sells drinks;

While the days seem grey,
And his heart of ice,
Grey as chamois, or
The edelweiss,

And the mountain streams
Like cowbells sound –
Tirra lira, drowned
In the waiter's dreams

Who has gone beyond
The forest waves,
While his true and fond
Ones seek their graves'

The section of Stein's 'Accents in Alsace' (The Watch on the Rhine) which Sitwell quotes, at slight variance and delineation from the Stein original, which uses no quotation marks, in her footnote to the poem, reads as follows:

'Sweeter than water or cream or ice. Sweeter than bells of roses. Sweeter than winter or summer or spring. Sweeter than pretty posies. Sweeter than anything is my queen and loving is her nature.
    'Loving and good and delighted and best is her little King and Sire whose devotion is entire, who has but one desire to express the love which is hers to inspire.
    'In the photograph the Rhine hardly showed.
    'In what way do chimes remind you of singing? In what ways do birds sing? In what way are forests black or white?
    'We saw them blue.
    'With forget-me-nots.
    'In the midst of our happiness we were very pleased.'

Although 'Jodelling Song' was first performed as part of *Façade* in 1923, Sitwell chose not to publish the poem in *Troy Park* in 1925 and we can only imagine that thematically or technically it did not fit in with the collection. Stein's 'Accents in Alsace' also appears to have influenced Sitwell's nostalgic poem 'Yesterday' (*TP*, pp.30-32), dedicated to Helen Rootham, which *was* published in *Troy Park*. In this poem, which begins 'Sweet was my childish life to me' there is no direct acknowledgment of the Stein 'play', but the influence is patently there. Compare for example Stein's lines 'In what way do chimes remind you of singing? In what ways / do birds sing? In what way are forests black or white?' with Sitwell's 'words / Grow into lands unknown where birds / Are singing in an unknown tongue / Of loveliness for ever young'; the 'crystal eggs as hard as the air' in Sitwell's poem seem to recall Stein's angel's eggs, which also appear in 'Jodelling Song'. 'Yesterday' is a lament in a winter (which is also an emotional winter) for the spring of childhood (which is a metaphor for creativity), spoken by an old blind crone:

> But my heart still dreams that the warmth of spring
> Will stir in its thickets, begin to sing
> In the lonely crystal egg of my head –
> Though it seems all the lovely wings are dead
> And only pity and love are left...

It is not until Sitwell again draws on the poem in 'Jodelling Song' printed under the title 'Centaurs and Centauresses' in *Rustic Elegies*, that she brings our attention to her poem's antecedent in a foot-note. Sitwell also draws heavily on the vocabulary of the preceding section of the 'play', 'Alsace and Alsatians', as Pondrom also points out: angels eggs, storks, forests, forget-me-nots, bells all appear. Sitwell picks up here on the pastoral aspect of Stein's 'play'. White storks, the symbol of Alsace, return from Africa to herald the beginning of spring, which the 'play' celebrates through an image of youth, innocence, fecundity: 'All the leaves are green and babyish'. The section of 'Accents in Alsace' that Sitwell cites bears little stylistic relation, on first inspection, to her own poem, written as it is in quatrains rhyming *abab*. In her eloquent discussion of the relationship between the two poems Pondrom suggests that

> [t]he poem is not in any conventional sense an imitation....It can be fairly understood as a transportation of the linguistic practices of Stein, however, in some ways which are not apparent in Sitwell's earlier poems. One of the most important disruptions of conventional linguistic prac-tice in Stein's style derives from a conflict between the propositional form of the sentence and its semantic content. For example, even where the conventional subject–verb–object structure is preserved, and the appropriate part of speech is selected in each position, the lexical con-tent of some of the words is such that the proposition is nonsense. The reader is forced to displace the proposition in ways that enable its lexical meanings to make sense. Because these displacements result in incomplete

verbal structures, possible meanings proliferate and a single meaning never emerges as final and complete....

An analogous practice is clearly evident in Sitwell's 'Jodelling Song'...

The images and incidences which succeed each other seem to have symbolic psychic significance. But coherent meaning may be achieved only if we presume a hidden story, of which we see only interrupted surfaces, deformed and displaced as in the dream-work.

(*Influence and Intertextuality*, p.215)

One clear difference between the poems, despite their shared vocabulary, is this hidden story. While Stein's poems are celebratory of the fresh potential fertility and creativity of Spring, and new love, Sitwell's poem, which begins with language homonymically suggestive of birth (bear), and marriage (the chiming of bells), is much more, as it progresses, concerned with men and loss, specifically a reununciation of familial bonds: William Tell the national hero of Switzerland as father, Mrs Cow as mother. Using the name Mrs Cow again connects Sitwell to Stein – cow is a recurrent noun in her erotics the meaning of which critics have variously seen as symbolising orgasm or defecation – but also symbolically seems to draw attention to the male as speaker (tell), the woman as wife (Mrs) and female body (cow). Sitwell's poem is noticeably also concerned with a narrative of masculine love between older men and younger boys, paternal (Tell and his son) or sexual (Ganymede, the beautiful youth abducted by Zeus to become his lover and cupbearer to the gods, who in Sitwell's poem is a waiter). Under its title 'Centaurs and Centauresses' potential splits and hybridities in the poem become emphasised. The title, in another intertextual allusion, also refers to the painting by the 19th-century painter, Eugène Fromentin, 'Centaurs and Centauresses Exercise by Shooting the Bow', a painting which sees these creatures, half-human, half-horse, in a rural scene with their children. Is, then, Sitwell suggesting that the text of her poem is also a kind of centaur, half hers, half Stein's; and in some way, is she gendering that divide, setting her own poetry up in terms of the "masculinity" of the homosexual, and Stein's as the "femininity" of the lesbian? How then do we read the poem in the light of her comments made in 1925 in relation to the woman's poem being as 'eloquent as a peacock'?

Stein's work clearly offered Sitwell a crucial marker in her writing career as an experimental woman writer and saw her temporarily changing poetic tack as her response to a female poetic model can be seen first obliquely and then directly. Crucially in 'Jodelling Song' / 'Centaurs and Centauresses' we see Sitwell moving away from the narcissistic Mallarméan technique to what might be seen as a textual regeneration of the mother through the echoing of a woman writer – the jodel, after all, is a song which resounds and repeats itself through an echo. *Rustic Elegies* as a whole dramatises a debt to female inspiration. In its dedication 'to HR who has taught me all she knows' and in its ordering of the poems throughout the volume, Sitwell constructs a narrative which symbolically kills the mother of the earlier work, in favour of the "body" of the new poetic "mother", Stein. In the final section of the book we see Sitwell dramatising a fairytale of 'snow-white Anne' who is eventually poisoned by a witch and 'melts quite away'. With its title 'Proserpine' it is impossible to know whether this is in fact meant to be Proserpine speaking, or whether Sitwell is reconfiguring the myth in terms of a murderous older woman and her daughter. But the final longer and more philosophical poem of *Rustic Elegies* becomes conciliatory in its relation to the death. In a meditation on poetry and poetic process, Sitwell now spells out the connection between the materiality of the mother's body and the 'buds of poems' which lie, foetus like, 'curled / Waiting for us to bring them to their birth':

> There is a terrible groping animal
> Consciousness that lumbers to appal
> The heart...this only knows the flowering dire
> And urge of its hot blood and earth desire,
>
> And through this, its relationship to other
> Material aspects of the world its mother, –
> The dark earth purring in its sleep.

Sitwell's transfer of aesthetic allegiance from Mallarméan decadence to Stein at this juncture begs many interesting questions about the importance of gendered role models for female and well as male writers. Such a transfer is not after all a final and premeditated, or exclusive choice. Though Sitwell had abandoned the experiment of *Façade* by the 1940s, she does not apparently continue to use Stein as a model any later either, than the publication of 'Centaurs and Centauresses'/'Jodelling Song' in 1926. Mallarmé was himself important for Stein, and indeed, Stein's own commentary on her modern technique compares interestingly with Mallarmé's narcissistic poetics. Stein writes:

> I began to wonder at about this time just what one saw when one looked at anything really looked at anything. Did one see sound, and what was the relation between color and sound, did it make itself by description by a word that meant it or did it make itself by a word in itself...I became more and more excited about how words which were the words that made whatever I looked at look like itself were not the words that had in them any quality of description.[45]

As we have seen decadent language is very much connected to a bodily feminine. Stein, Nicholls argues, like H.D.,

> shares…the desire to move beyond an object-based poetics which derives its force from a repudiation of the feminine, and to discover in its place a form of writing that reveals continuities between self and world…H.D. remarks of the mother that 'If one could stay near her always, there would be no break in consciousness', and once the feminine is no longer marked as 'other', the way is open to a use of language which does not require it to represent what is absent. (*Modernisms*, p.202)

Such a poetics as Stein and H.D. were constructing, which works in parallel to Sitwell's, puts into perspective the depth of the anxieties felt by Sitwell which were strategically and defensively "solved" in *Façade* by moving away from the language of objects to the music of feminine bodily language. Mallarmé's decadence, and his "femininity" (as Swinburne's), ostensibly and with many dangers, had offered Sitwell a feminine space from which to write, but one which, in order to progress with her writing and embrace modernity, Sitwell had ultimately to reject. The culmination of her poetic experiments in search of that space, and her rejection of them, was her *Gold Coast Customs* (1929).[46]

In her introduction to her *Selected Poems* of 1936, in which *Gold Coast Customs* is the last poem to be included, Sitwell describes how it was 'written with anguish…I would not willingly re-live that birth' (*Selected Poems*, p.47). A long sequence, dedicated again to Rootham, the 'customs' that the poem refers to are burial ceremonies 'during which', Sitwell writes, 'the utmost licence prevailed, and slaves and poor persons were killed that the bones of the deceased might be washed with human blood' (*CP*, p.237). The poem is set in Ashantee and draws on Hegel's *Philosophy of History* and Georg Schweinfurth's *The Heart of Africa* to give a portrait of a cannibalistic society set up in parallel with a contemporary London society, figured through the image of a Lady Bamburgher:

> Lady Bamburgher rolls where the foul news-sheet
> And the shambles for souls are set in the street.
>
> And stuck in front
> Of this world-tall Worm,
> Stuck in front
> Of this world's confession –
> Like something rolled
> Before a procession,
> Is the face, a flimsy worm-skin thing
> That someone has raked
> From the low plague-pit
> As a figure-head

> For Corruption dead,
> And a mask for the universal Worm.
>
> Her ape-skin yellow
> Tails of hair
> Clung about her bone-white bare
> Eyeless mask that cackled there...
>   (*CP*, p.241)

In her notes to the poem Sitwell is concerned to point out that when she cites Hegel describing how 'Negroes' have 'no knowledge of the immortality of the soul' and an Africa where 'cannibalism is looked upon as quite customary and proper' she intends 'no reflection whatever upon the African races of our time'. Her quotation of the Hegel, she writes 'no more casts a reflection upon them than a passage offering to the cruelties of the Tudor age casts a reflection upon the English of our present age' (*CP*, p.426). Sitwell invokes the African throughout her work as part of a not unproblematic symbolic association between light and shade, but here, despite the excuse that the poem is a satire, Sitwell's depiction of the Africans in *Gold Coast Customs* depends too easily on unpleasant caricatures and stereotypes of blackness, while also drawing on unpleasant stereotypes of femininity.[47]

In her attack on London, Sitwell sets up the nature/culture divide between the Africans and Lady Bamburgher in a way which continues to dramatise her anxieties about the maternal. The parallel set up in the poem between the 'godless' Africans and the corrupt English aristocracy, which is of course deeply problematic despite Sitwell's protestations, is one which figures the rich and idle generation of party-goers in terms of a devouring class whose pleasures are also at the expense of human life and suffering. Lady Bamburgher, 'her soul the cannibal / Amazon's mart', is compared with 'the Amazon queen / With a bone-black face' who 'Wears a mask with an ape-skin beard' and 'grinds / Her male child's bones in a mortar, binds / Him for food, and the people buy' (*CP*, pp.241-42). The poem is a far remove from the bucolic idylls of the earliest poems, the comic underworld of *Façade*, even the lost idylls of *Elegy on Dead Fashion*. But in a reversal of the baby's cannibalising of the mother in 'The Mother', here is a mother who is devouring and not being devoured. The poem appears uncensored in its unleashing of its venom, and the desire of its narrator to abject herself: 'Perhaps if I too lie down in the mud,' Sitwell writes, 'Beneath tumbrils rolling / And mad skulls galloping' 'I shall forget the shrunken souls, / The eyeless mud squealing "God is dead"':

> Starved men (bags of wind) and the harlot's tread,
> The heaven turned into monkey-hide
> By Lady Bamburgher's dancing fleas,
> Her rotting parties and death-slack ease...

In her *Powers of Horror*, Kristeva defines abjection – the breaking down of barriers between subject and object we see in vomit, faeces, the corpse, as preserving 'what existed in the archaism of pre-objectal relationship, in the immemorial violence with which a body becomes separated from another body in order to be'.[48] Abjection marks the moment of separation from the mother:

> as in true theater [sic], without makeup or masks, refuse and corpses show me what I permanently thrust aside in order to live. These body fluids, this defilement, this shit are what life withstands, hardly and with difficulty, on the part of death. There, I am at the border of my condition as a living being. (*Powers of Horror*, p.3)

In *Gold Coast Customs* we see a creative performance of that separation from the mother that allows the emergence of individual subjectivity. Twice in her introduction to the *Selected* Sitwell remarks on her inability and unwillingness to talk about the poem's 'implicit meanings' and it is perhaps not surprising that Sitwell fell silent as a poet after such a violent breach, spending a decade writing prose and assembling anthologies.

Sitwell's own mother died in 1937; Helen Rootham, nursed by Sitwell after a long and unpleasant illness, died in 1938. Sitwell marks the move away from 'experiment' in the *Collected Poems* as 1940, and it is not until the poems of 1942 that we see any kind of reconciliation with maternal figures. In the monologue 'Eurydice' (*CP*, pp.267-70), spoken in Eurydice's voice, the poem testifies to poetry's potential – but in this story, stalled – ability to return people from the dead. At Orpheus's song, Sitwell writes, it was

> ...as if a lump of gold had changed to corn
> So did my Life rise from my Death. I cast the grandeur of Death away
> And homeward came to the small things of Love, the building of the
>   hearth, the kneading of daily bread,
> The cries of birth, and all the weight of light
> Shaping our bodies and our souls.

Symbolically the poems of this period, when Sitwell was in her late 50s, all signal a new lease of life and energy and the poems appear to work reparatively in relation to the maternal relationship. 'A Mother to a Dead Child' (*CP*, pp.286-87) is a tender lament for a lost infant:

> Return from your new mother
> The earth: she is too old for your little body,
> Too old for the small tendernesses, the kissings
> In the soft tendrils of your hair. The earth is so old
> She can only think of darkness and sleep, forgetting

Unlike the earlier mother poems, the haunting is not figured as "real" return, but as a subjective manifestation of the mother's inability to deal with the loss of the child. In 'Anne Boleyn's Song' (*CP*, pp.303-04) the maternal is again figured as restorative figure who brings life to death:

> But I who grew in the heart as the bird-song
> Grows in the heart of Spring...I, terrible Angel
> Of the emeralds in the blood of man and tree,
> How could I know how cold the nights of Spring would be?
>
> When my grey littering King –
> Old amorous Death – grew acclimatised to my coldness?
> His age sleeps on my breast,
> My veins, like branches where the first peach-blossom
> Trembles, bring the Spring's warmth to his greyness.

It would perhaps be too much to ask that Sitwell's work remained imaginatively and chronologically coherent in its transformation of maternal imagery. Yet in Sitwell's later – and two most anthologised poems – 'Still Falls the Rain' (1940) (*CP*, pp.272-73; *MWP*, pp.61-62) and 'Dirge for a New Sunrise' (1945) (*CP*, pp.368-69) – imagery from 'The Mother' subtly reappears. In 'Still Falls the Rain' the return to 'The Mother' is only tangentially figured in the image of Christ, the son who hangs from the tree. Christ's suffering is figured as the horror of war, just as the horror of war is seen as the suffering of the 'self-murdered heart'. Susan Kavaler Adler, a not wholly reliable but nevertheless interesting reader of Sitwell's poems, suggests that 'Still Falls the Rain' is 'symptomatic of the pathological mourning state'.[49] What such an assertion misses is the fact that Sitwell's poem is attempting to voice collective trauma in the face of the war; and that out of this state, which is perhaps paralleled by or reflects a state of personal melancholy, rises the cry for mercy, the desire to 'leape up to my God: who pulles me doune'. These cries, taken from Marlowe's *Dr Faustus*, cries which for Faustus remain unanswered, in Sitwell's poem are answered by a benevolent God who 'was once a child among whom beasts has lain'. It's interesting here that reparation can only take place through the figure of an all-powerful God who transcends the fleshly suffering of the human, as we see Sitwell setting up Christ as a divine muse. In 'Dirge for a New Sunrise', a poem written in response the horror of the bombing of Hiroshima, the maternal imagery is being more explicitly worked through, again though the image of the crucifixion, and the murdering of the mother. Here it is the matricide of Nero who: 'conceived the death / Of his mother Earth, and tore / Her womb, to know the place where she was conceived'. 'Mother or Murderer,' Sitwell writes, 'you have given or taken life − / Now all is one!'

In *A Survey of Modernist Poetry* (1926) Laura (Riding) Jackson and Robert Graves argue their case for the modernist poem in a paragraph which bears interesting parallels to Sitwell's own implicit definition of her modernist project manifest in *Wheels*:

> The most striking characteristic of modernist poetry is that it declares the independence of the poem. This implies a new sense of the poem's rights comparable with the originality of the poem as for the originality of the child. It is no longer considered proper to keep a child in its place by repressing its personality or laughing down its strange questions until it turns into a rather dull and ineffectual version of the parent; the modernist poet is similarly freeing the poem of repressive nursery rules and, instead of telling it exactly what to do, encouraging it to do things, even queer things, by itself. He pledges himself to take them seriously on the principle that the poem, being a new and mysterious form of life has more to teach him than he it. It is a popular superstition that the poet is the child; really the child is the poem and the most that the poet can be is a wise, experimenting parent.
>
> (*Modernism: An Anthology*, pp.434-35)

Sitwell's desire to write a new poetry, to recast decadent aesthetics, saw her continually struggling to construct a place for herself as a woman poet. In doing so she had to negotiate what was to her a deathly femininity, as well as the poetic dominance of the masculine and impersonal modernism of Pound and Eliot. In a letter to the soldier poet Robert Nichols in 1918 Sitwell had expressed her frustration about the positioning of women's poetry by male reviewers. 'They grumble,' she wrote,

> because they say that women will try to write like men and can't − then if a woman tries to invent a female poetry, and uses every feminine characteristic for the making of it, she is called trivial. It has made me furious, not because it is myself, but because it is unjust.
>
> (*Façades*, p.132)

Sitwell again returned to the question of women's poetry, writing to Maurice Bowra nearly 30 years later. Here, however, her ire is directed against the women poets themselves whom she deems to have failed to create a technique that allows a female poetry:

Women's poetry, with the exception of Sappho (I have no Greek and speak with great humility on that subject) and with the exception of 'Goblin Market' and a few deep and concentrated, but fearfully incompetent poems of Emily Dickinson, is simply *awful* – incompetent, floppy, whining, arch, trivial, self-pitying – and any woman learning to write, if she is going to be any good at all, would, until she had made a technique for herself (and one has to forge it for oneself, there is no help to be got) write in as hard and glittering a manner as possible, and with as strange images as possible – strange, but believed in. Anything to avoid that ghastly wallowing. (*Selected Letters*, pp.253-54)

This is a voice which, in its antipathy to women poets, is hard to reconcile with the voice in letters of the same period to her friend the poet Hilda Doolittle, to whom she writes, for example, in 1940, praising her for having come through personal difficulty 'as the woman and the poet you are...' (*Selected Letters*, p.218); or which later, in 1945, saw her praising Doolittle's *Trilogy* poems: 'I know this book so well, and yet print has given it even a finer body...I shall never forget the day when I saw those poems first, but the feeling remains exactly the same. I shall never see any flowering tree again without thinking of that revelation.' (*Selected Letters*, p.274) And yet, as can be seen in the passage I quote at the end of my introduction to *Modern Women Poets*, in which she bemoans the lack of women poets 'to point the way', it is clear that Sitwell did come to realise that part of her struggles as a poet were to do with the lack of, or we might consider her lack of ability to fully read, her women poetic predecessors. The contemporary women poets of formidable stature, with whom she had literary friendships – Moore, Stein, Doolittle – and with whose work she was familiar, were perhaps too close, too much the potential rivals, to fully sustain her work. Joanne Feit Diehl, in her reading of the relationships between women poets suggests a model of poetic influence which centres around Klein's theories of envy and gratitude, arguing that

Klein's emphasis on the importance of envy in terms of creativeness beyond the originatory feeding situation is pertinent not only to questions of literary production in general but to influence relations in particular. Klein's assertion that 'at bottom, envy is directed against creativeness: what the envied breast has to offer is unconsciously felt as the prototype of creativeness, because the breast and the milk it gives is felt to be the source of life' illuminates our understanding of the anxieties a woman writer may experience as she turns to her female literary precursor for inspiration and at the same time senses the fragility of her female predecessor's position *vis-à-vis* the dominant tradition of male authorship. A desire to do damage to the "mother" who is already at risk becomes yet another factor in the vexed situation of the woman writer who would align herself with an alternative female tradition because she simultaneously wishes to be endowed with the power associated with masculine-identified literary authority.[50]

Anxious not be considered in terms of the "weakness" and sentiment of the "poetesses" of the previous century, Sitwell largely distanced herself – in her dislike of Barrett Browning, for example, and her pointed admiration of only one of Rossetti's poems, 'Goblin Market' – from any historical female poetic lineage. Her poem 'The Mother' was not addressed, as far as I am aware, to another woman poet, implicitly or explicitly, but the desire for a female poetic role model, and the potential for ambivalence in relating to the female tradition about which Diehl talks, seem especially pertinent to a reading of Sitwell's poem which both sets up and assassinates its female protagonist, wanting her and also wanting to do her damage, reluctant to let her go. Sitwell continued to write and publish, both poetry and prose, until her death in 1964. If Sitwell had difficulties in relating to female role models, her own defensive and self-preserving construction of herself did not make her or her work an easy poetic model to follow. Her struggles with what it meant to be a woman and a poet, and her relationship both to her own body as well as to her textual one, were, however, of vital importance to a later generation of women who were presented, even before they reached the poems, with such a strong and perhaps equally strange, and glittering image of the woman poet.

CHAPTER TWO

'Tirry-Lirry-Lirry All the Same':
The Poetry and Performance
of Stevie Smith

'Oh talking voice that is so sweet, how hold you alive in captivity, how point you with commas, semi-colons, dashes, pauses and paragraphs?'

STEVIE SMITH, *Novel on Yellow Paper* (1936)

Like Edith Sitwell, Stevie Smith increasingly came to use the way she dressed to construct for herself a persona as woman poet. In comparison with Sitwell's presentation of herself as the hard and glittering monolith, Smith's later adoption of a "costume" made her simultaneously vulnerable and challenging. Michael Horovitz has described the 'frail figure she cut, her delicacy exaggerated by the dolly-bird frocks and bar-strapped shoes she still donned, all through her sixties, for any sort of outing'.[1] In a similar vein, Jeni Couzyn describes first seeing Smith 'trembling like a frail bird on the stage of London's Festival Hall, in her tweed skirt and ankle socks'.[2] Elsewhere, in her biography of Smith, Frances Spalding, describes her eclectic style of dress: 'Hats she bought at church jumble sales or Help the Aged shops, dresses, in C. & A. children's departments or from the trend-setting boutique, Bus Stop, in Church Street Kensington'[3] and quotes a description of her given in her memorial address: 'The old-fashioned strap shoes and knitted stockings; the broad headband; the little girl's white dress: she might look – did, indeed, look – so simple that from a back view you might wonder what so young a person was doing at an adult gathering.' In this chapter I want to look closely at the drawings which accompany Smith's poems. There is nothing new in emphasising the importance of such a dialogue between text and image in Smith's work *per se*, but I want also to suggest that we must read the drawings, in conjunction with the novels, as well as Smith's ways of dressing and performing, as part of a complex strategy through which we see Smith, like Sitwell, attempting to negotiate a relationship for herself between her body and the body of the poetic text.

Philip Larkin, a fan of Smith's poems, described the drawings as 'a mixture of "cute" and "crazy"', they have an amateurishness reminiscent of Lear, Waugh, and Thurber without much compensating

felicity'.[4] Smith herself was ambiguous in her statements about the
status of the drawings, explaining that 'the drawings are so much a
part of the verses that they must be published with them' and 'Oh,
I've got a boxful of drawings...The Drawings don't really have any-
thing to do with the poems.'[5] Perhaps because of the drawings,
which were generally added to the poems at a later date, Smith has
often been marked out as an eccentric writer whose work is hard
to take seriously. Critics who do want to read Smith seriously have
often returned to establishing a connection between Smith and the
Blake of *Songs of Innocence and Experience*, not just because of Blake's
obvious influence on Smith and the intertextual allusions to Blake's
poems, but also because of the dialogue that occurs between text
and illustration in her work, the nursery rhyme quality of the rhymes
and rhythms, and because of the fact that Blake would often sing his
poems, as Smith would keen and intone hers.[6] Seeing the drawings
in the context of other women's poetic practice of the period, how-
ever, seems equally important. As Janet Montefiore has pointed out,
'the typography and layout' of women's poetic writing in the
1930s, when Smith published her first collection, 'are often dis-
tinctive, many of them being illustrated with wood engravings, an
art which flourished between the Wars, especially among women
artists'. Montefiore continues:

> This use of black-and-white engravings is a distinctive feature of
> women's poetry, which is not found among male poets of the period –
> perhaps because Faber, the firm which published most of the latter,
> was not interested in graphic art. Some of these engravings are
> straightforward illustrations, but most of the books suggest complex
> and interesting relations between text and picture.[7]

There is certainly a decorative element to some of Smith's draw-
ings, and an interest in the patterns of wallpapers and fabrics in
the drawings which accompany poems like 'Croft',[8] 'The Castle'
(*CP*, p.228) (*see* FIG 4 *below, page 72*) and 'The River Humber'
(*CP*, p.133). The drawings are surrounded by a single line which
serves to frame it, as might the inked background and frame of an
engraving or print. These drawings are not the norm, however,
and in general, Smith's drawings frequently work in contrast to
the painstakingly engraved illustrations of either Blake or the other
women poets of the 1930s, who published their work with accom-
panying woodcuts, often by other artists. Not only the artistic
process involved, but the depth and solidity of the woodcut, make
these images a very different presence to the 'amateurishness' of
Smith's drawings to which Larkin alludes. With their thinly inked
lines, their presence is very much connected with the creation of a

FIG 4: Drawing by Stevie
Smith which accompanies
'The Castle'

sense of provisionality. Such a gesture towards provisionality, which sometimes suggests irony, sometimes collusion with the poem, is never monologic in its meaning or authoritarian in its direction of the reader. Coupled with this provisionality is also a frequent suggestion of movement in the drawings themselves, so that movement occurs both in the drawings and in constant dialogue with the text, creating, as it were, a reading narrative as the eye moves from one to the other.

While there are undoubtedly many artistic, economic and cultural reasons why women should choose to illustrate their texts at this period, and it is necessary to note that the woodcut served to illustrate prose works as well (and was also used, but less extensively it appears, by men), there is however a more general connection to be made — although I do it tentatively — between the "adornment" of the text and the adornment of the female body as a strategy of gender performativity. The childish quality of Smith's drawings strongly prefigures the development of Smith's adoption of a childlike attire and the two strategies seem obviously connected. Moreover, Smith's use of the pictures also runs in parallel with the writing of her novels and the construction of a sense of self which they create. For if Pompey, the heroine of Smith's first novel, *Novel on Yellow Paper* (1936), is a veiled Stevie (Smith was known to her immediate family and friends as Peggy up until the mid-1920s when she started to write poems), then the construction of Stevie as "woman poet" is also filtered and constructed through the narrative of the 'talking voice that runs on' of the novels.[9] As Frances Spalding has suggested, the success of Smith's early poems in the *New Statesman and Nation* provided a good base of interest for her novel. Similarly, the publication of the *Novel on Yellow Paper* in 1936 (written over a two-month period at the instigation of the publisher who wanted the novel before he would consider the poems he had already seen) offered Smith's readers a way into the mindset of the poems. Such a route of entry into the poems is not, of course, necessary, but the poems of *A Good Time Was Had by All*, published in 1937, would surely have been read at the time of publication as being as much *Novel on Yellow Paper*'s protagonist Pompey's poems as Stevie's. The publication of the novels and the poems subsequently went hand in hand. Smith's second volume of poems, *Tender Only to One*, was published in 1938, the same year as her second novel, *Over the Frontier*; the volume of poems, *Mother, What is Man?* was published in 1942, and her final novel *The Holiday* (1949) preceded the poems of *Harold's Leap* (1950).

Fiction has always been more hospitable to the female voice in the way in which is allows splittings and versions of the self which are not directly attributable to its author, furnishing the self with a narrative context and a rooted worldly existence. Although Smith's novels are all written in the first person, embedding the 'I' that speaks in a narrative puts that 'I' in a much less precarious position than the lyric 'I', which always carries with it an impulse to exist out of time. The novels perform an important initial function for Smith in her earlier work, "fleshing out" an image of the poet behind the poem, offering Smith a place from which to write which simultaneously displays a strong sense of self, whilst also disguising it. Smith's pictures serve a similar but not identical function, instead sublimating Smith's anxieties about the body and the presence of the female poet, embodying them visually in the poetic texts. (Curiously, the two strategies become closely linked in her radio play in 1959, *A Turn Outside*, when, because Smith cannot for obvious reasons use pictures to work in dialogue with the poems she includes in the play, she instead replaces them with accompanying short prose narratives.) It seems highly likely that the presence of the pictures and Smith's adoption of a "costume" are also connected. Both Romana Huk and Laura Severin, the two most recent commentators on Smith's work, have pointed out that Smith's transformation into a child through her choice of clothing did not occur until the 1950s. It seems unlikely to be coincidental that the cessation of co-publication of novels and poems – and perhaps also the later move to the performing of the poems in the late 1950s – coincided and overlapped with such a radical transformation of herself.[10]

Smith's awareness and engagement with gender and the connection between body and voice in her poetry is, not surprisingly, complex, and I want to focus here on the poems which, throughout her *oeuvre*, explicitly or implicitly present the woman poet or use an image of the performer, which I read as a cipher for the woman poet. In 'Too Tired for Words' (1956),[11] a piece essentially about depression, we see Smith engaging directly with the idea of a woman poet as performer in her discussion of her poem 'The Actress' which concludes with the couplet 'I have a poet's mind, but a poor exterior, / What goes on inside me is superior.' Smith discusses the poem at some length:

> Here is an actress, a middle-aged actress. Look at her! She is walking a tightrope, tears roll down her cheeks, she carries a spangled wand and wears a crown. She is quite sure she is superior and wishes other people could see it, but my word, she looks pretty awful...But this feeling of superiority is a thick cloak. It drops, and one sees loneliness as something to be despised and condemned... (*Me Again*, p.115)

This depiction of the split between inner feeling and outer presentation presents the woman performer as a tragic figure, full of self-delusion. Smith suggests that there is an unbridgeable gap between interior feeling and exterior presentation of the self, between inner voice and external body. The actress's costume as a tightrope walker performs a role which dramatises the nature of that split, which in the poem becomes configured as a split between high and low art, the poetic soul, and the actress who fails to adequately represent it. Any reading of the poem and the prose discussion of the poem must negotiate the multiple ironies and slippages of Smith's voice as the inner feeling of superiority transforms into an external disguise in the image of the cloak, which itself slips to reveal the actress's inner loneliness. What Smith seems to be suggesting, however, is that even as she destabilises the sense of the superiority of the poetic mind, the poet's nature is one of cloaked performance, a performance of both internal and external display.

'The Songster' (*CP*, p.30), a single quatrain, which was published in *A Good Time Was Had By All* (1937), is an interesting place to begin reading Smith's own dialogue with her sense of the woman poet:

The Songster

Miss Pauncefort sang at the top of her voice
(Sing tirry-lirry-lirry down the lane)
And nobody knew what she sang about
(Sing tirry-lirry-lirry all the same).

Beneath the title of the poem, not fully embedded in the text, but heralding it and more a part of it than it would be if it were beside the text, is a drawing (FIG 5, *above*) of a straight-haired, plain and be-hatted woman. The woman is wearing the square shoulders and closely-cut dress typical of 1930s daywear and is noticeably large-bosomed.[12] Her arms are clasped nervously behind her, her mouth a wide open o, her gaze not meeting the eye of the reader. 'The Songster' parodies ideas of invocation which have been prominent from Homer to Milton. 'Sing muse' the poetic tradition demands, and yet even as Miss Pauncefort does sing in the poem, she evokes an anxiety in the reader about her place in the world; her very presence has to be asserted by its embodiment in the drawing on the page, but it is her embodied presence which also creates anxiety and difficulty about the status of her words. Placed as it is between title and poem, the drawing of Miss Pauncefort stands on top of her own poem: a poem which both she (in the second line) and the poet sing (the whole quatrain, but in unison with Miss Pauncefort in the final line). At the same time as she sings, Miss Pauncefort, positioned as she is beneath the title, is also physically a part of the poem, although unlike a poem which compares interestingly with 'The Songster', 'Mrs Simpkins' (*CP*, p.21), whose

subject is placed between the first and second stanzas, she is still
somewhat liminal and has not been fully incorporated into the
poem by her presence. Potential ironies therefore are drawn up
between the speaker of the poem, the poem as text, and the reader
who reads and speaks simultaneously as narrative voice and Miss
Pauncefort. Miss Pauncefort, who does, of course, literally 'pour
forth', appears to be on trial, or on stage, perhaps singing as part
of a competition or an audition. The audience's blatant refusal to
care about the way in which the woman's song is interpreted (and
as reader we are made complicit in that refusal) contrasts with the
sly satirisation of this unmarried woman with the vaguely ridiculous
name, a name which, broken into two – pansy (paunce) and strength
(fort) – carries intimations of a traditional femininity associated
with the flower, and strength. It is almost in spite of herself, the
drawing suggests, that Miss Pauncefort stands up to sing.

What is especially interesting is that without the illustration the
poem reads very differently: it has a devil-may-care bravura. Yet
with the picture of Miss Pauncefort, we are made immediately
uncertain about the status of women's speech or song. While my
feelings about Smith's costuming are not as positive, Severin has
suggested that Smith's own adoption of the dress of the 1920s, with
the button shoes and Peter Pan collars 'allowed Smith to create an
outside space from which to challenge her cultures' restrictive
definitions of femininity'.[13] Although Smith's performance persona
strikes me, like the actress's, as symptomatic of more painful 'inner
feelings', Severin's noticing that Smith adopts the dress not simply
of the child, but of an androgynous fashion associated with the
1920s, allows us to read the figure of Miss Pauncefort, with its
uncomfortably emphasised bosomy curves, as embodying anxieties
about a too easily identifiable feminine voice. What the drawing of
Miss Pauncefort does is embarrass us, and that embarrassment
comes from her own self-consciousness and enthusiasm, coupled
with the ungainliness of her excessive femininity. Nobody can blame
us for not understanding this woman, the poem seems to say. The
phrase 'sing tirry-lirry-lirry' becomes a marker for that which is
nonsense, and which we as reader are told we cannot interpret. It
is all the same, the poem tells us, nothing has changed, the singing
can make no difference to us anyway.

An interesting contrast to 'The Songster' in the same collection
is the poem 'Mrs Simpkins'. This is not a poem about a poet or a
performer in the conventional sense, but about a woman who
develops an interest in spiritualism. But the poem is clearly linked
to 'The Songster' in the way in which it presents an image of a

woman incorporated into a poetic text, and links with another later "named" women poet performer in Smith's work, Mrs Arbuthnot, to whom I will turn in a moment. The woman in the poem 'Mrs Simpkins' is this time dressed in the extravagant and glamorous costume of the 1920s with her high heels, knee-length tassle-fringed dress, fox fur, veiled hat and painted, ring-adorned fingers. As in 'The Songster' there is a clearly demarcated floor beneath the woman's feet which acts to "stage" this character. The woman looks out from the poem wearing an expression which we can read in many ways, but which predominantly seems to evoke feelings of dislike (it is an unhappy, corpulent and unpleasant face), and pity (it is a fearful face). The specific positioning of this female character is central, quite literally, to our reading of the poem. Mrs Simpkins stands between the end of stanza one and the beginning of stanza two, creating a hiatus within the poem which works to create a comic pause as we read. The last line of the first stanza, 'Things had moved very far since the days of her youth', hovers above the drawing of the woman we assume is Mrs Simpkins, and is followed by a textual silence, a silence in which the poem demands that the reader let his or her eyes see for themselves the result of that move from youth to age. Here, as our eyes move across the body of Mrs Simpkins, we are asked to evaluate an older woman who, the poem is suggesting to us through both word and picture, is mutton dressed as lamb.

The second stanza begins 'So she became a spiritualist'. By the time we reach that second stanza we have acceded with the narrator of the poem that indeed things have 'moved far'. Our reading of Mrs Simpkins' female body in its elaborate dress must find it unsatisfactory, just as it is intimated that Mrs Simpkins' found her own self and her life unsatisfactory. As reader, like spirit and medium, we must literally cross over from one side of the poem to the other, over the body of Mrs Simpkins, where we are greeted by the 'hearty' spirit who assured us that since *his* 'crossing over' he is 'no different to what I was before'. Although the nature of the spirit's return is not made explicit in the poem (and in some ways, in the fiction of the poem the spirit can come to Mrs Simpkins in any way it likes, we do not have to seek a "realist" explanation of the how), in its speaking of its 'garbled truth' there is a strong suggestion that the voice of the spirit speaks through the body and voice of Mrs Simpkins herself, in her act of mediumship.

If we do read the poem this way – and I want to – then the hearty homily that the spirit gives us is both Mrs Simpkins and the spirit, just as the poem is both its narrator and the poet, separate, but connected through the body as its vehicle of transmission.

Unpicking the complex way in which Smith seems to be address-
ing issues of the relationship between body and voice, and her
presentation of the material self in relation to the spirit, is not easy.
The poem appears intent on ridiculing the woman who, bored with
the Trinity, turns away from Christianity as Smith's negotiation of
body and voice/spirit also dramatises anxieties of a theological
nature. But typically in a Smith poem, such a single-voiced thing as
blame becomes double-edged, for if the woman's turn to spiritual-
ism is due to her gullibility it is also due to the church's failure to
sustain her. Spiritualism was a movement (founded, it is interest-
ing to remember, by Blake's contemporary Swedenborg) which
historically attracted women, almost certainly because of the voice
it gave them in comparison to their silenced position within the
hierarchies and patriarchal structures of orthodox Christianity.
The spiritualist in Smith's poem can in some ways be compared
with both the poet and the actress in the way in which she per-
forms as medium for the language and her ambiguous position –
depending on whether we believe in the ability to commune with
spirits or not – sets her up as either creator or performer, or both.
Steven Connor is especially interesting here in his analysis of the
relationship between the female body and the séance:

> The primary purpose of the séance was not to evoke beings from
> another world, but to enact the hypothesis of a different kind of body
> in this world. The excited passivity of the scéance characteristically
> produced sensory intensification, a condition in which...thoughts were
> on the point of becoming things... With this intensification came a
> sense of the enlargement of the body's forms and limits. This is centred
> on the body of the medium, whose role was not so much to provide a
> channel for other entities, as to exemplify a bodily condition of fluidity
> and transmissibility as such.[14]

Smith's Mrs Simpkins becomes a spiritualist because, the poem
seems to suggest, of her awareness of the limits not just of the
female body, but also of the limits of the power of the female voice.
And it is no accident that the spirit who appears in the poem is
male. The humour and the horror of the poem comes in the moment
of dialogue between Mrs Simpkins and her husband when we dis-
cover, at the same time as Mr Simpkins, that in fact 'there is no
separation', that there is no cessation of domestic and familial
relations. Such a discovery, in Smith's world, in which death offers
a sweet release from the suffering of the material world, is a truly
awful discovery. And the full irony of Mr Simpkins' suicide is of
course that in his despair about never being able to be free of his

relatives and his wife, his resorting to the drastic measure of suicide only serves to bring him closer to that which he fears. Nevertheless, by the end of the poem Mr Simpkins *has* been separated from his wife; we are not told of his fate, only the fate of his wife who is now reduced to a 'financial tightness' from which only the spirit world can relieve her. Whereas – if we follow the logic of Mrs Simpkins' spiritualist homily – Mr Simpkins has gone to a place where he is 'no different than he was before', the circumstances of Mrs Simpkins' life have changed radically. Her spiritualist interests have indirectly caused the death of her husband at the same time as reducing her to poverty. But neither her belief in the spirit world, nor her grief at separation from her husband, is apparently so strong that it sees her attempting to reach it on any permanent basis. Mrs Simpkins' material situation could be escaped, and, if she believes in the spirit world such an escape would be no sacrifice. The joke here is on both of the poem's unfortunate characters; the gullibility of both has drastically changed their lives. But Smith's interest in the poem is as much to do with the relationship of the woman to language and the body as it is to questions of theology. Mrs Simpkins is punished in and by the poem for believing in the possibility of separation between the body and the spirit/voice, a punishment which also seems to hover in the background as a threat to the woman poet.

Smith returns to a named female character with a poem about a poet in 'Mrs Arbuthnot' (*CP*, p.492) published 20 years later in *Not Waving but Drowning* (1957). The poem also dramatises another kind of separation, this time between the self and the natural world. The name 'Mrs Arbuthnot', like Miss Pauncefort, smacks in its sounds, of comedy, but importantly too reminds us of Pope's 'Epistle to Dr Arbuthnot', a verse satire, itself reminiscent of Horace, about the number of bad poets writing ('Bedlam or Parnassus, is let out: Fire in each eye, and papers in each hand / They rave, recite and madden round the land').[15] Smith's poem is not about any old performer, it is instead about a 'poet of high degree' whose 'talent left her':

> For her lost talent she weeps,
> Crying: I should write a poem,
> Can I look a wave in the face
> If I do not write a poem about a sea-wave,
> Putting the words in place.

In contrast to the drawing of Miss Pauncefort or Mrs Simpkins, the drawing accompanying 'Mrs Arbuthnot' is of a disembodied, and somewhat ravaged looking head (*see* FIG 6 *below*). It is placed outside the poem and the outline of the face is heavily scored.

Although her mouth is open as if to speak, her head, like that of
Miss Pauncefort, is slightly turned to one side away from the direct
gaze of the reader. The refusal of the direct gaze in the drawing
works in dialogue with the woman poet's anxiety in the poem,
'Can I look a wave in the face / If I do not write a poem about a
sea-wave', a phrase which also plays with the phrase 'to look death
in the face'. But the poem also seems to suggest that the poet's
anxiety about connecting the poet to the world of natural things,
and the inevitable disjuncture between word and thing ('wave' and
her representation of it, 'sea-wave') is dangerous. It is only through
death that Mrs Arbuthnot's struggle with her desire to 'look a wave
in the face' is abated, but her struggle is not resolved through writing,
rather it is resolved by her actually becoming, in death, the thing
she writes about:

> She has gone to heaven
> She is one with the heavenly combers now
> And need not write about them.
>
> Cry: She is a heavenly comber,
> She runs with a comb of fire,
> Nobody writes or wishes to
> Who is one with their desire.

The phrase 'comb of fire' reminds us simultaneously of the Fool's
coxcomb and the wheel of fire in Act Four of *King Lear* when
Lear, awakening from sleep thinks he is in Hell and that Cordelia
is an angel. It also recalls the 'fire in each eye' of the Pope poem.
Mrs Arbuthnot is not in hell, she is in heaven; but it is a heaven
in which she has merged with her subject, not written about it.
The poet who cannot write about the comber – the long, curling
wave which is mimicked in Mrs Arbuthnot's headware – becomes
it. Mrs Arbuthnot's desire to write about the wave was, suggests
the poem, a futile wish to write a certain kind of poetry. In death
the poet has found her wish, to find a unison with the long curl-
ing wave which in life, language would not allow her. It is only
death which has given her a truly transcendent experience.

The poem's speaker retains an ironic distance from its subject,
but as in 'The Songster' there are moments when the relationship
between poet, poem and speaker in the poem begin to collapse in
on each other through Smith's use of direct and indirect free
speech. As in the previous poem there is no straightforward moral
judgement being made, but rather a snappish assertion that Mrs
Arbuthnot 'need not write' now she is dead (note the fact that
'need' stands in the place of 'can'). The final two lines of the

poem place the writer as conflicted and neurotic, but in the context of the poem, the desire that is unconflicted is equated with the ability to connect the mind of the poet to the thing. And such Romantic connections, the poem suggests, do not serve the woman writer. In heaven, having become a wave, a heavenly comber, Mrs Arbuthnot has also become the fool.

It is important to remember the cultural anxieties which were still prevalent, even in the 1950s, in relation to women writing poetry and the figure of the "poetess", and that those anxieties continued through the configuration of the term *poetess* well into the 1970s. Such anxieties transmit in Smith's writing into poems not just about women poets, but elicit numerous poems about the muse, and writing itself. 'The Word' (1972) (*CP*, p.542; *MWP*, p.84), to take one example, is accompanied by a drawing which gestures, more than any of the other drawings discussed, towards an image we might identify with Smith herself: childlike, with her hair bobbed and in a clip. In contrast to the previous poems discussed, the female character of the drawing is not performing to an audience; instead she sits reflectively. Again this character does not direct her gaze at the reader and the drawing positions the seated woman as if she were contemplating the text of the poem beside her.

'The Word' begins with a quotation from Wordsworth's short lyric 'My heart leaps up when I behold',[16] a poem in which Wordsworth celebrates the importance of childhood experience in the life of the adult, at the same time establishing a paternal lineage of humanity:

> My heart leaps up when I behold
>   A Rainbow in the sky:
> So it was when my life began;
> So it is now I am a Man;
> So be it when I shall grow old,
>   Or let me die!
> The Child is Father of the Man;
> And I could wish my days to be
> Bound each to each by natural piety.

In 'The Word' we see Smith directly questioning this lineage, a lineage which we might also read as the paternal succession of the literary tradition. This point is further emphasised by the fact that Wordsworth's well-known statement 'The Child is Father of the Man' is violently rebutted by Gerard Manley Hopkins with a poem of his own, 'The Child is Father to the Man'.[17] 'The words are wild!' exclaims Hopkins in his poem, simultaneously suggesting that the language of poetry is not simply rooted in the child's experiences or the poet's subjectivity; in Hopkins' poem Wordsworth's words are themselves wild (and wrong). But just as Hopkins reacts against his predecessor, so too does he establish a dialogue with the male poetic tradition in invoking him. Such connections are, for this woman writer, much more complex: she fears the word and 'all that is brought to birth and born'. The metaphor of creation through lineage and its 'natural piety' can't work for Smith's speaker as she plays around with the expression 'my heart is in my mouth'. This time the mouth on the drawing is a dot of surprise and consternation, not an open mouth of speech.

Although Smith has male poets in her poems (in 'The Poet Hin' [*CP*, 551-52], for example, the male poet imaged like Miss Pauncefort in the body of the poem is anxious not about his verse but its status; in 'Thoughts about the Person from Porlock' [*CP*, pp.385-86] the male poet positively seeks distraction from his art), none share the anxiety about writing as the women; their anxieties are not about writing *per se* but about their writing's reception in the world. In this vein, but in relation to a woman poet, is 'Pearl' (*CP*, p.457).

Pearl

To an American lady committing suicide because of not being appreciated enough

Then cried the American poet where she lay supine:
'My name is Purrel; I was caast before swine.'

Because of its dedication to the American lady poet, and its publication date, we would not be blamed in supposing that the poem refers to Sylvia Plath, who died in 1962, and with whom Smith had a single but friendly correspondence when Plath wrote to her suggesting a meeting after the publication of Smith's *Selected Poems*. 'Pearl' is a curious poem to write *in memoriam*, particularly in the light of Smith's own preponderance for death's seductive charm. The satirical imitation of the American accent, the allusion to drowning, when of course Plath famously gassed herself, open up the poem to resonances which go beyond the circumstances of an individual life. The image of drowning in the accompanying drawing links the poem to Smith's own frequently used metaphor for union with death and perhaps sees Smith effecting an identification between her own life and Plath's. (Interestingly, Smith does have a four-line poem, 'Mabel' [*Me Again*, p.221], about the suicide of a woman who gasses herself and finds 'dying / Sublime' which is accompanied by an untypically smudgy portrait of a long-haired young woman who bears passing resemblance to Plath.)

'Pearl' is only a couplet, but the illustration (FIG 7, *opposite*) takes up the whole page, and appears to have a much more complex, if enigmatic, allegorical narrative. The poem sits in between the two landscapes – perhaps they are, in their upperness and lowerness, heaven and hell. Or perhaps they work as a kind of "thought bubble" for the woman character at the bottom of the page. At the top of the poem, above the title type, lying in the middle of a road between trees is a hairless figure, who appears more male than androgynous, although his maleness is not qualified by the addition of any distinguishably male costume or features. The figure's mouth is open in what seems to be a shocked expression. Ahead, the sun is either rising or setting, though its situation to the left of the picture suggests that the sun is in the west and therefore setting. Beneath the poem is a woman lying beside a river; she has her hand in the water. The way she is lying suggests contemplation rather than shock. The reference to pearls and swine comes from the Sermon on the Mount (Matthew 7.6) when Jesus says 'Do not give what is holy to dogs, and do not cast your pearls before swine or they will trample them under their feet and turn and tear you to pieces.' In the context of the Bible, the saying is most often interpreted as being about the sharing of the gospel. But here the divine word is the poetic word. In a merger similar to that seen at the end of 'Mrs Arbuthnot', the American Lady poet has become the word, the pearls, the woman Pearl, but by contrast, even in death this poet gets to say her name, to speak her pearls of great price, in her own voice.

The uncollected poem 'Miss Snooks, Poetess' (*Me Again*, p.226) continues Smith's exploration of the figure of the woman poet. In contrast to the figures we have seen who struggle with both writing and performance, the poem satirises the complacency of the woman writer who fails to challenge any givens. In using the word 'poetess' Smith deliberately estranges herself from this gendered notion of the poet. The poem is an attack on a kind of middle-class conservatism and acutely diagnoses the difficulty of propriety facing the woman poet. This 'poetess' is the 'good girl' who receives accolade from her peers but is unchallenging and does what is expected of her sex:

> Miss Snooks was really awfully nice
> And never wrote a poem
> That was not really awfully nice
> And fitted to a woman,
>
> She therefore made no enemies
> And gave no sad surprises
> But went on being awfully nice
> And took a lot of prizes

In Smith's work the woman poet or her coded figuring as the woman performer, does not, as we have seen, get an easy ride. Her images of woman as poet or performer and her anxieties about them seem little changed from the late 1930s to the 1960s, despite the many changes in women's domestic, social and cultural situation. In terms of their attempts to write, or to perform, Smith's women characters appear to be battling constantly against personal unhappiness, silence, embarrassment, and the expectations of their sex. In dramatising Smith's anxieties about the relation of the body to the voice, these poems compare usefully with Smith's increased use of the dramatic monologue. I will return to Smith's use of the monologue at the end of this chapter, but to conclude this section I want to offer a reading of the most well-known of Smith's poems, 'Not Waving but Drowning' (1953) (*CP*, p.303; *MWP*, p.81-82).

'Not Waving but Drowning' is a poem which focuses on a death, both real and metaphorical, in a complex interplay of gender and intertextual reference. Specifically, however, it dramatises a split between body and voice which not only sets up a dialogue between male and female, but through its intertextual appropriation, between women poets. 'Not Waving but Drowning' was written only weeks after the death of Queen Mary, several months prior to the coronation of Elizabeth II and to Smith's suicide attempt. It is interesting to speculate whether in Smith's mind the death of the old queen and the impending coronation of the new monarch in some way drew a line under the experiences of the 1930s and 1940s, bringing two decades of anticipated war and war to an end. The poem certainly bears useful comparison with 'Come on, Come back' (*CP*, pp.333-34) which also appeared in *Not Waving but Drowning* and which is, so the poem's subtitle tells us, an 'Incident set in a future war'. In this poem a 'girl soldier Vaudevue' swims out until a treacherous undercurrent 'Seizing her in an icy-embrace / Dives with her, swiftly severing / The waters which close above her head'.

In a letter to her friend Kay Dick on 25 April 1953, Smith wrote how she was feeling 'too low for words' but 'worked it off...in a poem & *Punch* like it, think it funny I suppose, it was most touching I thought' (*Me Again*, p.294). The words 'funny' and 'touching' bring together an important nexus of strategies within the poem, and allow me to focus again on this difficult relationship Smith sets up between voice and body in her work. Smith's use of the word 'touching' in her letter to her friend evokes a world of sentiment, even sentimentality, rather than the tragedy with its huge sense of irony that the misinterpretation of the drowning man's signalling involves. But it also makes me want to ask in what way the poem is touching to Smith, implying as it does an emotional connection which in some way is brought to bear on the physical. The drowning man in the poem calls to be touched, to be physically rescued, but is misunderstood, just as the speaker of the poem remains 'untouched' in her position 'too far out'. The poem, too, asks that we as readers are 'touched', simultaneously allowing and refusing us such sentiment and connection, pushing us, as Smith supposes it will the readers of *Punch*, to read it as 'funny'. In identifying the fact that the poem both asks for and resists 'touch', Smith is also alerting us to the anxieties between body and voice, and the bringing together and separating of body and voice, which the poem performs.

'Not Waving but Drowning' is constructed around a central paradox, that of a dead man who is moaning. And it is around this speaking dead man that the poem's funniness, its uncanniness, resides. For if the poem is about a dead man moaning, it is also a dialogue between its speaker and the moaning man whose tale it tells. The cries of the dead man thus become an objective correlative for the deadness of the other voice of the poem as the 'no no no' of the third stanza echo and enact the sound of the word 'moans'. The male voice speaks the famous lines: 'I was much further out than you thought / And not waving but drowning', although as we read and reread the poem we realise that to speak those lines would of course be an impossibility. The 'dead one' cannot moan, but the narrator can, and, so the logic of the poem suggests, must also in some metaphorical way be dead. When the lines 'I was much further out than you thought / And not waving but drowning' are repeated in the final stanza, however, the dead one's moans are bracketed off, and, in their proximity to the image of the figure in the drawing, the lines that follow now become spoken by another voice, perhaps the figure in the drawing, perhaps the speaker of the poem.

The uncanny feeling the poem produces comes not just from the situation itself, but is buried in the etymology of the word, from Smith's use of the word 'larking' which occur in the middle stanza. According to the OED the slang word 'lark' means 'to frolic' or 'to play tricks'; but the word is also associated with riding a horse across country, an etymology which bears greater relevance than might be assumed when read in conjunction with Smith's repeated use in both her prose and poetry of the image of the rider as one riding out to death.[18] The colloquialism, 'his heart gave way' serves to reduce the tragedy of the incident. But in doing so it also importantly makes the poem less about the drowned man's tragedy than about the empathy and identification felt by the poem's speaker, whose heart we begin to surmise, is also metaphorically giving way. The waving man's death becomes subsumed in its metaphorical quality, and his refusal (although he is already dead) to die.

As Romana Huk has remarked, there is not always a straightforward alignment of gender between the speakers of the poems or their subjects and the illustrations. The drawing that accompanies 'Not Waving but Drowning' (*see* FIG 8 *below*) is central to our under-

standing of the dialogues occurring in the poem between speaker, subject and author, but its gender is ambiguous. With its arched eyebrow and heavily defined eyes which peer from behind a veil of hair, its partly hidden face is distinctly feminine. And yet with its shoulders, which have a masculine thickness, and its straight body, the figure is actually quite androgynous, carrying no element of the female decoration we often find in other images of women and girls in Smith's drawings. Crucially to the poem and these internal dialogues are the lines 'I was too far out all my life'. These lines echo lines from Edith Sitwell's poem 'Colonel Fantock' (1925), discussed briefly in the previous chapter, a loosely-veiled autobiographical poem about the Sitwells' childhood. In the poem Sitwell writes (and note again that word 'touch'):

> I was always a little outside life –
> And so the things we touch could comfort me;
> I loved the shy dreams we could hear and see –
> For I was like one dead, like a small ghost,
> A little cold air wandering and lost.

Spalding has pointed out that Smith's poems 'The Bereaved Swan' (CP, p.40),[19] 'Spanish School' (CP, p.27), 'Bag-Snatching in Dublin' (CP, p.47) and 'The Man Saul' (CP, p.132) are almost certainly indebted to the Sitwell of the Façade poems, and that Smith went to hear Sitwell read during the Second World War on at least one occasion. Smith had also copied out four lines from Sacheverell Sitwell's Doctor Donne and Gargantua in one of her reading notebooks, the first lines of which she quotes uncited in Novel on Yellow Paper:

> Pompey is an arrogant high hollow fateful rider
> In noisy triumph to the trumpet's mouth,
> Doomed to a clown's death, laughing into old age,
> Never pricked by Brutus in the statue's shade.[20]

In 'Colonel Fantock' Sitwell figures herself not only as a ghost, but a drowned woman when she describes her childish self, a description which is uncannily like the drawing that accompanies Smith's poem when Sitwell writes of a 'body flat and strange, whose pale straight hair / Made me appear as though I had been drowned'. In Sitwell's idyllic world of Troy Park the siblings listen to the sound of Peregrine's (Sacheverell Sitwell's) voice; they are 'like Ophelia drowned in blond / And fluid hair, beneath stag-antlered trees'. Here then is Smith's ghostly female subtext to the poem: the lines by another woman poet and the conflation of her with her brother (Osbert/Dagobert) into an image of a mad woman who speaks 'nonsense' and who famously drowns herself. Like the moaning voice of the poem, the drawing which accompanies the poem, is both present and absent; the feature's of the character's face are covered by hair which is also in effect a scribbly erasure. Importantly, though, 'Not Waving but Drowning' is not a poem about suicide, and though it clearly connects with recurrent images of death through drowning in Smith's work, it is a poem which stages a resistance to death, using the words of another woman poet in that resistance.[21]

*   *   *

I want to end my discussion of Smith by looking at some more of the dramatic monologues. In the title-poem of her third book, 'Harold's Leap' (*SS*, p.111), Smith draws attention to the performed nature of the poetic voice by her inclusion of a female figure who stands at the top left hand side of the poem, almost as if she has parted an invisible curtain to reveal the text of the poem. The relationship between poem, text and poet are all clearly demarcated to form a visual triumvirate. The female figure's arms "present" and frame the scene narrated in the poem which is represented by a drawing which occurs lower down the page and which sees Harold in his attempt to commit suicide. In the later poem from *Not Waving but Drowning*, 'Farewell' (*CP*, p.381), we see that the poem is accompanied by a figure (*see* FIG 9 *below*) with arms raised in a stylised gesturing which, at the same time as smacking of an Elizabethan style of theatrical declamation, serves to ironise the reader's response to the declamation and which is being signalled as, if not histrionic, then certainly a staged performance.

The figuring of female bodies as both spectators to textual per-
formance and actual performers of texts contrasts interestingly with
poems in which Smith makes use of the dramatic monologue to
speak as women characters from myth. The combination of the
monologue with a mythic narrative sees a doubling of fictions which
serve to draw the poet and the reader away from a dependence on
the lyric 'I'. Alicia Ostriker has argued that the use of

> myth, folktales, legend and Scripture...confers on the writer the sort
> of authority unavailable to someone who writes "merely" of the private
> self. Myth belongs to "high" culture and is handed "down" through
> the ages by religious, literary, and educational authority. At the same
> time, myth is quintessentially intimate material, the stuff of dream life.
> Forbidden desire, inexplicable motivation – everything in the psyche
> that to rational consciousness is unreal, crazed, abominable.[22]

For Ostriker, female versions of myths and legends and fairytales
'are corrections...representations of what women find divine and
demonic in themselves; they are retrieved images of what women
have collectively and historically suffered; in some cases they are
instructions for survival' (*Stealing the Language*, p.215). Smith is
not so concerned with writing about these characters to straight-
forwardly feminist or political ends, or in using them as corrections
or revisions as later women poets have done, but instead uses them
as a way of interrogating the way we relate to those characters to
tell us stories about ourselves. What seems most important in Smith's
use of myth and fairytale is the sophisticated manner in which she
suggests that such characters from mythic or fairytale narratives
are in themselves as subject to ambiguities and ambivalences as
any other character. The characters Smith recreates, therefore,
must be seen as both fallible in themselves as well as fallible as
fictions, just as we are fallible as both storyteller and listener in
the way in which we relate to them.

'The Afterthought' (*CP*, p.256; *MWP*, p.81) retells the story of
Rapunzel from the point of view of the overly reflective prince
who has come to rescue her. It plays directly with the idea of the
tensions and connections set up in the monologue between speaker,
and the implied addressees of audience and other characters with-
in the poem at its end when the prince asks anxiously 'What is that
darling? You cannot hear me? / That's odd. I can hear you quite
distinctly.' The monologue here also sets up tensions between male
and female, slyly asking us to rethink whether Rapunzel who, as
imaged addressee is also the reader/listener (is she bored, frustrated,
pretending not to hear?) wants to be rescued. But the poem also
asks of its reader whether or not he or she wants complicity in the

fairytale romance; a refusal to hear is a refusal to uphold both the integrity of the prince and the ideology of courtly love. Smith's adoption of a male voice here sets up multiple dynamics between reader and poet. Our hearing of the poem (actual or imaginary, as we read) finds us constructing a male persona spoken through the female voice of the poet, adding a further dimension of irony to the final lines. For as well as the voice of the prince we too can hear the voice of the woman poet whose mimicry (and it is a gently satirical mimicry here, I think, rather than an attempt at a convincing adoption of voice) allows him to speak, quite distinctly.

'I had a dream...' (*CP*, p.421-23) perhaps recalls Alexander Korda's 1927 film *The Private Life of Helen of Troy*. The poem is, as the figures alongside the poem at beginning and end suggest, also a performance (*see* FIG. 10 *below*). At the beginning of the poem the

FIG 10: Drawings
accompanying
Stevie Smith's
'I had a dream...'
at the beginning (*left*)
and end (*right*)
of the poem.

speaker lays bare the device of the dramatic monologue in its first lines, lines that usually in a dramatic monologue would create and hold in tension the framework of relationships and ironies between speaker, poet and audience. Here we see Smith adding a fourth dimension to the equation which works to construct meaning when she writes 'I had a dream I was Helen of Troy / In looks, age and circumstance, / But otherwise I was myself.' Smith's poem is, unusually for a dramatic monologue, written in the past tense. It works by bringing to prominence the relationship between the poet and the poem rather than in conventional monologues which focus their energies on the relationship between reader and character. The speaker of the poem is self-aware and the irony of the dramatic monologue is thus also reduced. The central speaking character knows that she is in a story but does not know '...which of the

Helen legends I was, / The phantom, with the real Helen in Egypt, / Or the flesh-and-blood one here / That Menelaus would take back to Sparta. / Remembering this, that there was still some uncertainty, / Raised my spirits.' Trapped as the character Helen of Troy, the speaker identifies herself as caught in 'an ominous eternal moment' 'always / This heavy weather, these colours, and the smell of the dead men. / It is curious to be caught in a moment of pause like this, / As a river pauses before it plunges in a great waterfall.' The character cannot quite fit her own monologue, she is aware of her own construction, of the kinds of femininity that represent her, but with which she feels unable to identify:

> ...But oh, Cassandra, I said, catching hold of her
> For she was running away, I shall never make
> That mischievous laughing Helen, who goes home with Menelaus
> And over her needlework, in the quiet palace, laughs,
> Telling her story, and cries: Oh shameful me. I am only at home
> In this moment of pause, where feelings, colours and spirits are substantial,
> But people are ghosts. When the pause finishes
> I shall wake.

If the dramatic monologue offers a form which promotes identification with otherness, the dreamer who attempts to identify herself with Helen fails in her identification. Moreover her at-homeness is in a world of disembodiment where 'people are ghosts'. There is an echoing of Pirandello as well as a foreshadowing of Beckett in these monologues where characters search for unity with their identity and get lost in the space between their selves and construction of the self they are meant to be. In 'Phèdre' (*CP*, p.426-28), Smith plays both with the idea of rewriting a male text to the benefit of the female characters as well as exposing the "truth" behind these female characters:

> Poor Phèdre
> Not only to be shamed by her own behaviour,
> Enforced by that disgusting goddess,
> Ancient enemy
> Of her family,
> But nowadays to have to be played
> By actresses like Marie Bell
> In awful ancient agonising, something painful

Marie Bell had made her name in French cinema in the 1930s, and was in fact to make a film version of *Phèdre*, directed by Pierre Jourdan in 1968 when she was 68 years old. Smith's main objection to Bell's performance seems to be her age (she was only two years older than Smith herself), an objection which heightens the humour and which makes a game out of the fact that Phèdre is a "real" person who might object to the people who take on her voice (including Smith). Smith's analysis of the plot of *Phèdre* sees her desiring a conclusive family romance although not without a sharp sense of ambivalence about the happiness of marriage ('one would have to be pretty simple / To be happy with a prig like Hippolytus'). Here we see Smith comparing the marriage of Phèdre and Hippolytus with her own equally compromised simplicity in rewriting the tale:

> But she was simple.
> I think it might have been a go,
> If I were writing the story
> I should have made it a go.

Not only do we see in these lines how Smith was interested in re-visiting and retelling narratives, but how they sometimes became an important part of the performance of herself. The last line here serves to conflate the image of Phèdre with the speaker of the poem. Not only is the marriage made a go of, but so too is the narrative.

Seamus Heaney, in a short appreciation of Smith's poems in 1976, described hers as a memorable voice, 'her voice pitching between querulousness and keening, her quizzical presence at once inviting the audience to yield her their affection and keeping them at bay':

> She chanted her poems in an artfully off-key, in a beautifully flawed plainsong that suggested two kinds of auditory experience: an embarrassed party-piece by a child half-way between tears and giggles, and a deliberate faux-naif rendition by a virtuoso.
>
> (*In Search of Stevie Smith*, p.211)

Smith's reputation as a performer of her work grew in the 1960s with the development of the *New Departures* readings run by Michael Horovitz. It's interesting to note that at the same time as Smith was becoming well known as a performer of her work, Edith Sitwell's presence as a woman poet, in performance and on television, was also becoming prominent. The connections to be drawn between the two poets, who never, as far as I know, met, are fruitful. Both are identified through their eccentricity, an eccentricity which is also tied up with their femininity and their Englishness. Both, in their anxieties about the relationship between the poetic 'I' and the 'I' of the poet, focus those anxieties on the body, as well as the possibilities of creating complex and gendered relations between body and text. Both, as we will see, were to prove fascinating and important influences on Sylvia Plath, to whose work I now turn.

CHAPTER THREE

Liberty Belles and Founding Fathers: Sylvia Plath and the Search for a Gendered Writing Self

Femininity – what it is and its construction in relation to a writing "self" – preoccupied Sylvia Plath throughout her life. Her anxieties about writing were intricately bound up with issues concerning not only the ways in which to write, but about how to combine the roles of woman, wife and mother with the equally precarious role of writer. In a journal entry from 1959 she writes:

> How many girls go to sleep on marrying after college: see them twenty-five years later with their dew-eyes turned ice, same look, no growing except in outside accretions, like the shell of a barnacle. Beware.[1]

While such difficulties may be read as symptomatic of wider cultural anxieties about the role of woman in society in the 1950s and 1960s, for Plath the anxieties became overdetermined by personal circumstance: her marriage to Ted Hughes, whom she set up as a figure of masculine strength and alterity, coupled with the concomitant mythologising of the loss of her own "masculinity" embodied in the figure of her dead father.

Plath and Hughes left England for America in 1957, where they lived for two and a half years. In 1959 Plath conceived their daughter, born, after her return to England, on 1 April 1960. The last years of the decade were, we might conjecture, a period of transition, one where Plath was forced to assess her relationship with her nationality, her relationship with her husband, and her femininity in relation to her writing, a process which had perhaps begun in the mid 1950s. Perhaps most importantly, this period saw Plath moving towards the completion of a first book of poems, *The Colossus*, her search for a publisher, and her attempt to find for herself a public place in the world at the same time as securing a domestic future with her husband and child. In 1958 we find Plath writing in the *Journals*

> What to do with fear of writing: why fear? Fear of not being a success? Fear of the world casually saying we're wrong in rejections? Ideas of maleness: conservation of creative power (sex and writing). Why do I freeze in fear my mind and writing; say, look: no head, what can you expect of a girl with no head? (*Journals*, p.437)

Plath's anxieties about her ability to write as a woman are worked through in her prose writing of the mid to late 1950s. 'Superman and Paula Brown's New Snowsuit' (1955), 'The Wishing Box' (1956) and 'Johnny Panic and the Bible of Dreams' (1958) all focus on the loss of female creativity. All three show women in conflict with a masculine authority, all three equate dreaming with creativity, and all three end with a female death. In 'Superman and Paula Brown's New Snowsuit', femininity, as it is acquired in puberty, entails the relinquishing of masculine energy associated with creativity. In 'The Wishing Box', which charts the decline of a woman in a marriage, the loss of her creative imagination, and her death, femininity is placed in direct opposition to masculine creativity, and suffers directly because of it. Only in 'Johnny Panic and the Bible of Dreams', a short story about a bored secretary in a psychiatric hospital, is the division between male and female, and masculine and feminine, more difficult to discern. Here the female narrator who attempts to create is punished by death.[2]

All three short stories reflect not only general social anxieties about gender and creativity, but point specifically to anxieties about the woman writer. Not only, then, was Plath consumed by anxieties about sexual difference in relation to creativity, there was a strong sense for her, as well as for her contemporaries, of an absence of poetry by women that dealt well or interestingly with female experience.[3] In the *Journals* in 1958 we find Plath looking to women poets as both role models and rivals, expressing a desperate desire to position her aesthetic, and its implicit construction of female subjectivity, in relation to the work of other women. She writes:

> Arrogant, I think I have written lines which qualify me to be The Poetess of America... Who rivals? Well, in history – Sappho, Elizabeth Barrett Browning, Christina Rossetti, Amy Lowell, Emily Dickinson, Edna St Vincent Millay – all dead. Now: Edith Sitwell & Marianne Moore, the ageing giantesses & poetic godmothers. Phyllis McGinley is out – light verse: she's sold herself. Rather: May Swenson, Isabella Gardner, & most close, Adrienne Cecile Rich... (*Journals*, p.360)

It's interesting that at this point Plath makes no mention of Stevie Smith, of whose work she was a little later to become a devoted fan. It's notable, too, that Plath rejects the American McGinley on the grounds that she writes 'light verse'. Neither does Plath mention Elizabeth Bishop, whose *North and South* was published in 1946. And though there are later entries in the journals which describe Bishop in terms that position her as a more 'feminine' Marianne Moore,[4] Plath remained ambivalent about Bishop's sexuality.[5] Of the three poets Plath identifies as rivals to her title, Swenson, Gardner and Rich, two are now less well-known in Britain. May Swenson, who was born in Logan, Utah in 1919, taught poetry at Bryn Mawr, the University of North Carolina, the University of California at Riverside, Purdue University and Utah State University and was an editor at New Directions publishers from 1959 to 1966. At the time when Plath was writing, Swenson's two published books were *Another Animal* (1954) and *A Cage of Spines* (1958). A cousin of Robert Lowell, and for some years a professional actress, Gardner, born in 1915, was an associate editor of *Poetry* from 1952 to 1956. Her first collection, *Birthdays from the Ocean*, appeared in 1955, when she was 40. Read alongside the work of the young Sylvia Plath, their work now seems both emotionally and stylistically that of a different century. Adrienne Rich – the most important of the three 'rivals' – had at this stage in her career published two collections, *A Change of World* (1951) and *The Diamond Cutters and Other Poems* (1955), although Plath may well have seen poems which later appeared in *Snapshots of a Daughter-in-Law: Poems 1954-1962*. In a journal entry of 1957 Plath refers to Rich as dull (*Journals*, p.295). Her importance to Plath at this stage can perhaps best be marked by Plath's description of Rich's *The Diamond Cutters* as 'easy yet professional, full of infelicities and numb gesturings at something, but instinct with "philosophy", what I need' (*Journals*, p.466).

This desire for a more instinctive poetics is picked up later when we find Plath reflecting on her relationship with Anne Sexton, with whom she studied under Robert Lowell. In an entry from the journals in 1958 Plath praises Sexton's work: 'she has very good things, and they get better, though there is a lot of loose stuff' (*Journals*, p.475); and then in a later entry notes: 'Must do justice to my father's grave. Have rejected the Electra poem from my book. Too forced and rhetorical. A leaf from Ann [sic] Sexton's book would do here. She has none of my clenches and an ease of phrase, honesty.' (*Journals*, p.478). That Plath is here eliding her need to resolve her relationship with her dead father with her need to find for herself a new style is crucial to the complex strategy of gender identification Plath makes in her poem 'The Colossus',[6] the poem that was to give her the title of her first collection. Before looking in depth at this poem, which is central to understanding the development of Plath's work, I will turn briefly to Plath's configurations of femininity in her early poems.

In 'Female Author' (CP, p.301), Plath parodies the bourgeois decadence of the woman writer who 'plays at chess with the bones of the world' as 'she lies on cushions curled / And nibbles an occasional bonbon of sin':

> Prim, pink-breasted, feminine, she nurses
> Chocolate fancies in rose-papered rooms
> Where polished highboys whisper creaking curses
> And hothouse roses shed immoral blooms.
>
> The garnets on her fingers twinkle quick
> And blood reflects across the manuscript;
> She muses on the odor, sweet and sick,
> Of festering gardenias in a crypt,
>
> And lost in subtle metaphor, retreats
> From gray child faces crying in the streets.

Blood and roses – two images traditionally associated with the feminine because of the symbolic connection with menstrual blood and the female genitals – are equated with decay and sickness as the female author (Miranda waiting for her Ferdinand?) [7] evades the concerns of the outside world in favour of 'subtle metaphor'. The author is associated with the colours red and pink: she herself becomes the metaphor which is in fact her own femininity, and which she must escape if she is to write about the outside world. For Plath, writing about her own experience as a woman was something that was full of pitfalls as was finding a way to write about that experience in a language which was different from the ways in which she perceived women had written in the past. Several years after writing 'Female Author' we find Plath writing proudly in a letter to her mother that the poet Ted Hughes considers her unlike any other female poet:

> Ted says he never read poems by a woman like mine; they are strong and full and rich – not quailing and whining like Teasdale or simple lyrics like Millay; they are working, sweating, heaving poems born out the way words should be said... [8]

Such a description of Plath's poems is indeed telling in its merging of both "masculine" and "feminine" elements: the poems are associated with the male, they work, they sweat, but they also heave and are born. Here the discourse becomes much more to do with maternal imagery, even though the word *born* suggests that it is the mother who gives them forth, rather than is them. In fact Plath often equated the writing of poems with fecundity: maternity and motherhood becomes closely intertwined in poems such as 'Poems, Potatoes' (1958, *CP*, p.106), 'Stillborn' (1960, *CP*, p.142), and 'Barren Woman' (1961, *CP*, p.157) and certainly motherhood became equated with an ultimate version of femininity to which she aspired. She wrote in 1957: 'I will write until I begin to speak my deep self, and then have children, and speak deeper still.' (*Journals*, p.286).

And in a journal entry for 1959, when she is trying to conceive, she writes despairingly of her failure to ovulate:

> Suddenly everything is ominous, ironic, deadly. If I could not have children – – – and if I do not ovulate how can I? – – – how can they make me – – – I would be dead. Dead to my woman's body. Intercourse would be dead, a dead-end. My pleasure no pleasure, a mockery. My writing a hollow and failing substitute for real life, real feeling, instead of a pleasant extra a bonus, a flowering and fruiting...This is the one thing in the world I can't face. It is worse than a horrible disease. Esther has multiple sclerosis, but she has children. Jan is crazy, raped, but she has children. Carol is unmarried, sick, but she has a child. (*Journals*, pp.500-01)

Plath's equation of the infertile body, steeped as it is in cultural notions of valuable femininity, is clearly problematic. It is important to remember, however, as several commentators have pointed out, that the material we have now in the journals was never intended for publication, and that it is the nature of the journal to act as a sounding board, a place for the private working through of difficult emotions or ideas. Nevertheless, Plath's anxiety about childlessness, her ability to be an 'earth-mother' and for Ted to be a 'patriarch', seem central to her thinking at the time. And for Hughes, writing in *Birthday Letters*, the decision to have children becomes deeply connected with Plath's decision to try to leave the difficulties of her relationship with her dead father.[9] In a much later poem, 'Childless Woman' (1 December 1962) (*CP*, p.259), which obviously refers, at least on one level, to Hughes' new and childless mistress, Plath equates childlessness with narcissism, latent violence, and death ('Spiderlike, I spin mirrors, / Loyal to my image, // Uttering nothing but blood'). We see Plath here at her most conservative. Yet paradoxically, we see that she is simultaneously and painfully aware of the need to somehow find a strategy that will allow her to escape such positioning. One way of doing this was from her interest in surrealism.

Plath's anxiety about her desire to write and her need to circumvent cultural constructions of femininity, and its translation into surrealist practices, seems to emerge organically from an interest in dreams and psychoanalysis – an interest that is clearly documented in her journals. But Plath also has an abiding interest in the work of the surrealists themselves: Buñuel, Giorgio de Chirico and the primitivist Henri Rousseau. Plath's work is also influenced by her readings of Aldous Huxley. Huxley's interest in hallucinogenics showed Plath a way in which it was possible both to reconstruct ideas of the self and transform realist representations of the world. In the journals we find Plath's account of her eagerly reading

Huxley's recently published *Heaven and Hell* (1956), which she describes as being concerned with 'antipodes in mind' (*Journals*, p.231). Similarly, Plath's violent projection of self into extreme emotional states or positions within the text, which, in its breakdown of the boundaries between conscious and the unconscious, the rational and irrational, pleasure and pain, has the power to effect a radical transformation of the self.

While the work of Sitwell and Smith can be fruitfully compared with surrealist practice, neither poets draw specifically or directly on any surrealist work. Plath's interest in surrealism is, however, marked explicitly in her work by two poems written in 1957: 'The Disquieting Muses' (*CP*, pp.74-76), which is based on the painting by Giorgio de Chirico, and her poem 'Yadwhiga, on a Red Couch, Among Lilies' (*CP*, pp.85-86), based on a painting by Henri 'le Douanier' Rousseau. In a commentary for a radio programme on her poem 'The Disquieting Muses' – which takes its title from the De Chirico painting of the same name – Plath describes the muses:

> All through the poem I have in mind the enigmatic figures in this painting – three terrible faceless dressmaker's dummies in classical gowns, seated and standing in a weird, clear light that casts the long strong shadows characteristic of de Chirico's early work. The dummies suggest a 20th-century version of other sinister trios of women – the Three Fates, the witches in *Macbeth*, de Quincey's sisters of madness. (*CP*, p.276).

In the poem, the muses are indeed described very much in the De Chirican mode, '[w]ith head like darning eggs to nod' who sit around the narrator's bed:

> Mother, who made to order stories
> Of Mixie Blackshort the heroic bear,
> Mother, whose witches always
> Got baked into gingerbread, I wonder
> Whether you saw them, whether you said
> Words to rid me of those three ladies
> Nodding by night around my bed,
> Mouthless eyeless, with stitched bald head.

The muses, however, bring us to the moment of naming, reminding us of the story of the Sleeping Beauty who is surrounded by fairies who will each give her a gift or blessing.[10] The female muses of Plath's poem, however, have both sight and speech denied them; their powers are more sinister, and as representations of femininity offer an image of a-sexuality and powerlessness. 'The Disquieting Muses' is a poem that addresses issues of naming (the muses are present at a christening) and the movement towards the assertion of an individual identity. Within the framework of the poem this self-assertion is achieved through the rejection of the mother. But this rejection of the guidance of the mother represents also a rejection of an adequate model of female creativity:

> Mother, you sent me to piano lessons
> And praised my arabesques and trills
> Although each teacher found my touch
> Oddly wooden in spite of scales
> And the hours of practicing, my ear
> Tone-deaf and yes, unteachable.
> I learned, I learned, I learned elsewhere,
> From muses unhired by you, dear mother.

'Learning elsewhere', I would argue, in Plath's case, means learning from a model of masculinity. The disquieting muses, representative of a mutilated femininity, are her guardians in a landscape of exile that represents a limbo in gender terms:

> Day now, night now, at head, side, feet,
> They stand their vigil in gowns of stone,
> Faces blank as the day I was born,
> Their shadows long in the setting sun
> That never brightens or goes down.
> And this is the kingdom you bore me to,
> Mother, mother. But no frown of mine
> Will betray the company I keep.

De Chirico's *The Disquieting Muses* is itself rooted in the memory and loss of the father. Explaining a dream about his father that inspired the painting, De Chirico writes

> I struggle in vain with the man whose eyes are suspicious and very gentle. Each time I grasp him, he frees himself by quietly spreading his arms which have an unbelievable strength, an incalculable power … It is my father who thus appears to me in my dreams…
>   The struggle ends with my surrender: I give up: then the images become confused.[11]

In a text from 1913, 'Mystery and Creation', De Chirico describes the moment of creativity which is clearly linked not only with the paintings of the immediate period (from which 'The Colossus' may take its inspiration in part also – for example *Enigma of an Autumn Afternoon* in which a notably headless statue is gazed at beside an ocean), but with its classical statues and column, is clearly also connected thematically with De Chirico's *The Disquieting Muses*, and, by association, with Plath's poem:

> Everything gazed at me with mysterious, questioning eyes and then I realised that every corner of the place, every column, every window possessed a spirit, an impenetrable soul. I looked around at the marble

heroes, motionless in the lucid air, beneath the frozen rays of that winter
sun which pours down on us without love... At that moment I grew
aware of the mystery which urges men to create certain forms. And the
creation appeared more extraordinary than the creators.[12]

The similarities between both De Chirico's and Plath's desire to
compulsively play out the father's loss are potent, and in her jour-
nals she copies out quotations from De Chirico which she says
'have unique power to move me' (*Journals*, p.359). One of the
quotations she places as an epigraph to her poem 'On the Decline
of Oracles' (1957) (*CP*, p.78): 'inside a ruined temple the broken
statue of a god spoke a mysterious language'. Here the memory of
her Prospero-like father is constantly with her:

> My father died, and when he died
> He willed his books and shell away.
> The books burned up, sea took the shell,
> But I, I keep the voices he
> Set in my ear, and in my eye.

The ability to write becomes closely bound up not just in the father,
but in his loss. Note the double 'I' in the penultimate line which
is both stutter and pause, overdetermined keeping and preserving
of the self as well as rhetorical pose.

'The Colossus' (1959) (*CP*, pp.129-30) may also owe its classical
imagery to De Chirico's *The Archaeologists* (1927-28). Certainly,
the journal entry of 19 October, which obliquely describes the
poem's genesis, does so in terms which may be easily equated with
the surrealist technique of automatic writing:

> Most of my trouble is a recession of my old audacity, unselfconscious
> brazenness. A self-hypnotic state of boldness and vigor annihilates my
> lugubrious oozings of top-of-the-head matter. I tried Ted's "exercise":
> deep-breathing, concentration on stream-of-conscious objects, these last
> days and wrote two poems that pleased me. One a poem to Nicholas,
> and one the old father-worship subject. But different. Wierder [sic]. I
> see a picture, a weather, in these poems.' (*Journals*, p.518)

In 'The Archaeologists' the faceless mannequins are dressed in
togas and the drapes are comprised of classical architecture. They
are studying a tablet with Greek lettering. In her journal, Plath
quotes another passage from De Chirico that this time seems most
relevant to 'The Colossus':

> Day is breaking. This is the hour of the enigma. This is also the hour
> of prehistory. The fancied song, the revelatory song of the last, morn-
> ing dream of the prophet asleep at the foot of the sacred column, near
> the cold, white simulacrum of god. (*Journals*, p.359)

Plath adopts De Chirico's imagery and the sentiments behind them (which appear to bear close parallels to her own feelings about her father) to dramatise the construction of a female self, showing the process of creativity acting in conjunction with the process of mourning. But 'The Colossus' is a poem as much about the literal reconstruction of a feminine self as about the physical reconstitution of the Father who is pieced together through myth and memory with 'glue and Lysol', and its enigmatic quality comes in part from the dialectic being set up between such presence and absence. The narrator of the poem, small as an ant, crawls over the enormity of the construction that is her father. The poem juxtaposes images of speaking against images of listening. So we see in the first stanza how reconstruction becomes a metaphorical articulation:

> Pieced, glued, and properly jointed.
> Mule-bray, pig-grunt and bawdy cackles
> Proceed from your great lips.

Yet it is the enormity of the narrator's grief and longing which asserts presence, even if that presence seems on one level at least to mourn the loss of its being. The narrator 'squats in the cornu-copia' of the Colossus' 'left ear', but by the end of the poem the narrator, dissolved in both time and space ('My hours are married to shadow'), does not care to listen any longer for the 'proper' return of her father.

As trope for both absence and presence, it is tempting to see the construction of the colossus as an attempt to reconstruct the lost phallus through the creation of a fetish object. For little boys castration anxiety vacillates between two contradictory notions, and, writes Naomi Schor, 'the mark of fetishism is a perpetual oscillation between two logically incompatible beliefs: woman is and is not castrated'.[13] For Elizabeth Grosz the female fetishist's castration anxiety figures a disavowal which is different from that of little boys. For the female fetishist the castration that is refused acknowledgement is not the absence of the *mother's* phallus, but a refusal to acknowledge the absence of the daughter's – that is, her own.[14] In drawing up a metaphorical analogy between the narrator and Electra – the poem is set under a 'blue sky out of the Oresteia' – who desires and is frustrated in her desires for her father, Plath creates a fetish which, as well as giving her a power to create her father, and her self as her father (she becomes phallic, she can create), also allows her to enact a separation from that phallic body. Plath writes in her journals:

> Read Freud's 'Mourning and Melancholia' this morning... An almost
> exact description of my feelings and reasons for suicide: a transferred
> murderous impulse from my mother onto myself: the 'vampire' meta-
> phor Freud uses, 'draining the ego': that is exactly the feeling I have
> getting in the way of my writing: Mother's clutch. I mask my self-
> abasement (a transferred hate of her) and weave it with my own real
> dissatisfactions in myself. (*Journals*, p.447)

As a poem that enacts mourning, 'The Colossus' deals with the
loss of a literally small pre-adolescent self and both the loss of the
father and the phallus, a necessary act if self-integration is to be
achieved. Melanie Klein, in 'Some Reflections on the Oresteia'
(1963) writes:

> It is particularly in grief and in the process of mourning that the indi-
> vidual struggles to preserve the good relations which previously existed
> and to feel strength and comfort through this internal companionship.
> When mourning fails...it is because this internalisation cannot succeed
> and helpful indications are interfered with. The appeal of Electra and
> Orestes for the dead father under the mound to support and strengthen
> them corresponds to the wish to be united with the good object who
> has been lost externally through death and has to be established inter-
> nally. This good object whose help is implored, is part of the super-
> ego in its guiding and helping aspects. This good relation to the inter-
> nalised object is the basis for an identification which proves of great
> importance for the stability of the individual.
>   ...the phantasy that the dead internalised object, when it is loved,
> keeps a life of its own – helpful comforting, guiding – is in keeping
> with the conviction of Orestes and Electra that they will be helped by
> the revived dead father.[15]

With its setting under 'a blue sky out of the Oresteia', 'The Col-
ossus' becomes placed clearly within the tragedy of vengeance for
the lost father. Furthermore, the figure of Electra is also a charged
one for Plath. Her poem, also written in 1959, 'Electra on Azalea
Path' (*CP*, pp.116-17), is a dramatic monologue written in the voice
of a woman who is haunted by the similarities between her own
life and the story of Electra. The monologist is both Electra and
herself. Plath is punning on her mother's name, Aurelia Plath in
the title of the poem transforming her into a landscape of death,
the Azalea Path:

> A field of burdock opens to the south.
> Six feet of yellow gravel cover you.
> The artificial red sage does not stir
> In the basket of plastic evergreens they put
> At the headstone next to yours, nor does it rot,
> Although the rains dissolve a bloody dye:
> The ersatz petals drip, and they drip red.

Plath's desperate attempt to locate a place for the creative female self acts out a rejection of her mother, but also recreates the landscape that comes to represent the tragedy of both the loss of her father, and the loss of the masculinity that she sees as vital to her creativity.

In her reading of Plath's later poem, 'Daddy' (1962), Tracy Brain presents a convincing argument that 'Daddy'

> is also the American continent itself, and the geography in the poem is important. Daddy's American spelled 'gray' toe is 'Big as Friscoe seal': an image of the hugeness of Daddy himself, coloured and shaped like an animal in one of Plath's visual similes, and of his swollen toe. Through his association with San Francisco, and his likening to seals, Daddy stretches from the north coast of California where his toe bathes in the Pacific, to the easternmost tip of Cape Cod or 'Nauset', where his head lies in the freakish Atlantic. Given the poem's irony about the cross breeding of identity, it is difficult to resist seeing this picture of Daddy's gray largeness, capped by that head in the Atlantic, as an image also of the Statue of Liberty, that great symbol of America as a melting pot.[16]

This is certainly an interesting take on the poem, and helps us reflect also on the double-figuring of Plath's colossus as a figure of both male and female identification. Marina Warner's poetic description of the Statue of Liberty, at the beginning of her book *Monuments and Maidens*, is telling in its depiction of the statue, and worth quoting at length:

> Climb inside her head and look out of one of the jewels in her crown, and you will see a helicopter hovering opposite, and the stargazing bowls of camera lenses staring back at you. The passengers are waving, delighted by human puniness beside the looming face of the colossus. But unlike them, you are inside her and you cannot tell how small you seem. Instead you find yourself in a confined space that resembles the bridge of an old pilot boat, camped, uneven in shape, and coated in institution green gloss paint against corrosion. A sequence of grimy panes provide limited visibility, and are so tight-fitting and small that the kind of craft they might most appropriately belong to would be an old diving bell, an altogether inappropriate association in the radiant, exalted and upright head of Liberty Enlightening the World.
>
> The notices at the bottom of the one hundred and seventy-one steps warn that the view is best from Liberty's pedestal and that far above, inside her seven-pointed crown, vision is restricted. But everyone swarms up to the top inside her, for the voyage obeys imagination's logic and requires ascent into the heart and mind of Liberty. Departure, sailing across an ocean, docking at a small leafy haven, gazing up at the colossus who is benign and approachable, and then, to enter her, to find that she is enfolding, even pregnable: these are the phases of the common dream of bliss.[17]

To read the image of the colossus of Plath's poem as being simultaneously the Statue of Liberty (an image of a woman holding a burning torch with the chains of tyranny at her feet) does not seem an impossible transformation. The figure who squats in the ear of the colossus in the poem may well be inhabiting a powerful metaphor, that of Liberty herself. At the time of writing 'The Colossus', Plath was only two months away from leaving America for the last time. She was also three months pregnant, leaving her own mother, about whom she had strongly ambivalent feelings, and soon to become a mother herself. Marina Warner's description of the statue is again invaluable when drawing links between the statue and Plath's 'The Colossus':

> To modern eyes, trained to enjoy self-revelation and inner structures, the interior of Liberty is more beautiful than the exterior. She is mechanical, strong, even though, as one engineer working on the restoration pointed out, the structure Eiffel designed was not properly assembled by the workmen who erected the statue three years after it had been crated in France for transport to America. They began attaching the copper sheets to the frame and found, as amateur paperhangers do, that the drapery did not meet as it should have done in the region of Liberty's right arm, which she raises to hold her torch. The facing of the statue had shifted round her body. So a few extra struts were added just under her armpit, to accommodate the fault.
>
> Visitors are no longer allowed to climb up the ladder in her arm to the torch... (*Monuments and Maidens*, p.9)

It's no giant leap of the imagination to connect this description of the statue with Plath's description of the figure scaling the colossus with pots of glue and Lysol, or squatting in the cornucopia of its ear. While the colossus of Plath's poem is clearly a representation of the exploration of the male god/father figure, we may also read it as being about the construction of a female figure, escaping from chains, which has inscribed on its base the words of a woman poet, the anarchist Emma Lazarus. That Lazarus's poem is called 'The New Colossus' further compounds the connections between the statue and the poem. Lazarus's work deplores anti-racist, in particular, anti-Jewish sentiment, and it is hard to imagine that her name did not carry for Plath a huge emotional charge.[18] And of course the statue, in association with Lazarus's poem, represents not only woman, but the mother of exiles. The connections between both the later poem 'Daddy' and 'The Colossus' in relation to the Statue of Liberty seem strong, and I want now to probe the associations of the poem further, by thinking about the other great monument of America, Mount Rushmore, which, I want to argue, Plath uses indirectly when thinking about the poem and Hitchcock's film, *North by Northwest*, which premièred in the United States in July 1959.

If the Statue of Liberty is a symbol of maternal authority, then the faces of the Presidents on Mount Rushmore are a clear paternal one. It is a neat coincidence that the sculptor of the Mount Rushmore figure, Gutzon Borglum, was responsible for 'perfecting Liberty's torch after years of difficulty' (*Monuments and Maidens*, p.9). Alfred Hitchcock had used the image of a figure crawling down the Statue of Liberty in his film, *Saboteur* (1942), one of the first anti-Nazi propaganda films to be released before America entered the war. The figure who crawls 'small as an ant' down the face in 'The Colossus' can also be compared productively with the figures who crawl down the faces of the American presidents at Mount Rushmore as they appear in *North by Northwest*. Whether or not Plath saw the film (she records having seen *To Catch a Thief* in her journals) it would have been hard for her to have missed the multiple advertisements that appeared in *Life*, *Time*, *McCalls*, *Cosmopolitan*, *Look*, *Redbook*, *Saturday Evening Post*, *Seventeen* and *True Story*, or the ten-second trailers that ran on television in the States as part of the programme 'Alfred Hitchcock presents' throughout the summer.[19]

There are several points of connection to be drawn between the film, Plath's poem 'The Colossus' and Plath's continuing personal mythology. Hitchcock's film is a Cold War comedy thriller about identity and mistaken identity. The action takes place in a flight across America during which time both the male, Roger Thornhill (played by Cary Grant) and female double agent, Eve Kendall (Eva Marie Saint) "grow up". The male figure leaves his mother's protection and there are quips about being little boys and little girls. 'I'm a big girl,' says Kendall to Thornhill. 'Yes,' he answers, 'and in all the right places.' Towards the end of the film Kendall shoots Thornhill with a fake gun allowing him to die and return Lazarus-like back to life. The film takes its title from the line in *Hamlet* 'I am but mad north-north-west. When the wind is southerly, I know a hawk from a handsaw' (Act 2, scene 2). This allusion to *Hamlet*, who is, of course, obsessed with the ghost of his dead father, would surely have not gone unnoticed by Plath. Nor, too, could she have failed to notice the uncanny resemblance between Grant and Eva Marie Saint on the rockface and Plath and Hughes themselves,[20] which becomes even more marked in the stylised film posters. If we place *North by Northwest* alongside 'The Colossus' not only, then, does it show us a way in which 'The Colossus' explores Plath's identification and resurrection of the father, at a time when she has returned to her country of birth, but it points up how the poem is exploring the relationship Plath has between her male and female integrated self, her English and American self, playing out both on screen and in still images, part of her continuing mythology of her relationships with men. If we follow a rather complex chain of identifications that Plath is Thornhill (played by Grant, an Englishman) who is in turn Hamlet, but that she is also Eve Kendall (an American who will marry her other English self, Hughes, who in 'The Rabbit Catcher' she identifies as Adam) we see Plath struggling to assume not simply a gender identity, but a national one.[21]

In a fascinating essay on the faces at Mount Rushmore, Simon Schama discusses the campaign of Rose Arnold Powell to have the face of the campaigner for women's suffrage, Susan B. Anthony, carved alongside those of the presidents, a campaign which she began in the late 1920s, which she continued even after the death of Borglum in 1939 until the end of her life in the 1960s.[22] Given such a history, the site takes on a symbolic resonance of the refusal of the American nation to include women important to its history as part of a public commemoration. Yet as Stanley Cavell has remarked on Hitchcock's use of the presidents at Rushmore in his essay 'North by Northwest':

> Even if this monument exemplifies competition and domination as much as it does commemoration, still it is about founding fathers, a wish, however culturally expressed, to get back to origins. (*A Hitchcock Reader*, p.260)

Reading *North by Northwest* as 'an American comedy of remarriage', Cavell goes on to suggest that the proposal by Thornhill to Kendall is 'the legitimising of marriage, the declaring that happiness is still to be won there, and that America is still a fit place...in which happiness can be found', noting finally that the proposal represents an 'achieving of a new innocence and the establishing or re-establishing of an identity' (*A Hitchcock Reader*, p.261). This might perhaps be an optimistic reading of Hitchcock's film, though it is certainly not an untenable one. Like the film, perhaps for Plath the image of the man and woman, who at the very end of the film, rather than falling from the rock face, fall into bed on a train as a newly married couple, offers an image of union, independence and hope. In her movements of association between ancient Greek colossus and modern image of liberty and independence, to the faces of Jefferson, Roosevelt, Washington and Lincoln, Plath may therefore be seen to be working out the drama of her bid to write via both personal and public images of male and female power. The collection *The Colossus* as a whole marks beginnings and endings. We find a beginning in its publication in Britain in October 1960 when Plath is settled in England with her husband and daughter; there is a drawing to a close at its publication in the States in May 1962 before her separation from Hughes in the December. The multiple associations called to mind, perhaps from the stream of conscious technique Plath practises in order to write the poem, show her exploring ways of mourning her father and celebrating her marriage to Hughes and their impending parenthood, setting up figures which are simultaneously totem and muse, both male and female, symbols of loss and reparation, independence and freedom.

*   *   *

As we have seen, Plath's early interest in surrealism offered her a place from and through which to explore anxieties about femininity. In 'An Appearance' (4 April 1962) (*CP*, p.189) [23] we find Plath addressing a conflict between creative desire and socially given female roles in one of her most explicitly surreal poems:

An Appearance

The smile of iceboxes annihilates me.
Such blue currents in the veins of my loved one!
I hear her great heart purr.

From her lips ampersands and percent signs
Exit like kisses.
It is Monday in her mind: morals

Launder and present themselves.
What am I to make of these contradictions?
I wear white cuffs, I bow.

Is this love, then, this red material
Issuing from the steel needle that flies so blindingly?
It will make little dresses and coats,

It will cover a dynasty.
How her body opens and shuts –
A Swiss watch, jeweled in the hinges!

O heart, such disorganisation!
The stars are flashing like terrible numerals.
ABC, her eyelids say.

The poem extravagantly displays its narrator's failure to resolve her desire to write on the one hand, which she associates with the

masculine, and an equally strong pressure for her to fulfil a pre-
scribed and socially desirable nurturing female role. The conflation
of the typewriter and the sewing-machine become an image for
such tensions, as her own body too transforms into a machine. As
Hal Foster points out: 'often in surrealism mechanical-commodified
figures parody the capitalist object with its own ambitions, as when
the body is rearticulated as a machine or commodity' (*Compulsive
Beauty*, p.127). Machines are there to help the subject of Plath's
poem create – to sew, to write, two potent and culturally gendered
forms of creativity. But the subject of the poem is also portrayed
as machine and commodity. Plath presents us with an image of
the body which both services need, and is literally in service. The
subject of 'An Appearance' articulates a failure to resolve herself
with either gender or her creativity. As early as 1950 we find Plath
writing in the *Journals* about her ambivalence over the female body:

> I am at odds. I dislike being a girl, because as such I must come to
> realise that I cannot be a man. In other words, I must pour my ener-
> gies through the direction and force of my mate. My only free act is
> choosing or refusing that mate. (*Journals*, p.54)

Plath sees her only freedom being to achieve through an embodi-
ment of her own desire in the form of a chosen masculine other.
The entry continues, then, with Plath still trying to situate herself
within a matrix of sex and gender differentiations:

> I am part man, and I notice women's breasts and thighs with the cal-
> culation of a man choosing a mistress....but that is the artist and the
> analytical attitude toward the female body...for I am more woman;
> even as I long for full breasts and a beautiful body, so do I abhor the
> sensuousness which they bring... I desire the things which will destroy
> me in the end... (*Journals*, p.55)

Here the feminine is viewed from the masculine position, as Plath
considers herself as object. Intellect, analytical ability and artistry
are marked as masculine in her schema as she alienates herself from
her femininity as it is constructed through the maternal and the
sensuous body, whilst also recognising the annihilating dangers of
such conflicts. In Freud's 'Hysterical phantasies and their relation
to bisexuality' (1908) he records an example of hysteria's 'bisexual
meaning': 'the patient pressed her dress up against her body with
one hand (as the woman), while she tried to tear it off with the other
(as the man).'[24] This image seems to encapsulate perfectly the tension
in the poem which acts on the dichotomisation of male/female
roles and the dilemma of making a choice of identification. In her
reading of Plath's poem, 'The Rabbit-Catcher' (21 May 1962)

(*CP*, pp.193-94), Jacqueline Rose points out a struggle similar to the one we see in 'An Appearance'. The fact that 'The Rabbit Catcher' was written only a month later than 'An Appearance' is obviously important and shows Plath still working through this anxiety about constructing a sexualised identity that allows her, as a woman, artistic creativity. The first five lines of the poem echo the anxiety of identification we find in 'An Appearance'

> It was a place of force –
> The wind gagging my mouth with my own blown hair,
> Tearing off my voice, and the sea
> Blinding me with its lights, the lives of the dead
> Unreeling it, spreading like oil.

The self is turned against self. Subjectivity is compromised; it is blinded by her environment, the narrator is silenced by her own hair, trying to legitimate herself in a genre where femininity is not legitimate.

Like 'The Colossus' and 'An Appearance', 'Daddy' (*CP*, pp.222-24), which was completed on 12 October 1962, is a poem about the reconstruction of the self both in and through the power of language, and in relation to a powerful male figure. The poem begins with the line 'You do not do, you do not do / Any more, black shoe', a construction which, while being the speaker of the poem's assertion of inadequacy about the shoe, can be read also as a statement of inadequacy about the self that speaks it, embedding within it ideas of both doing and not doing. The lines do, of course, echo the nursery rhyme 'There was an old woman who lived in a shoe / She had so many children she didn't know what to do.' The identical end-rhymes of 'do' and 'shoe' have been swapped round. The old woman who lived in the shoe was bound to repro-duce, and implicit then in these first two lines is a rejection of the role of housewife and mother. The lines act simultaneously to reject patriarchal positioning of woman as mother – the shoe, the role, no longer does – while at the same time associatively linking the poem with a nursery rhyme, an oral tradition of poetry which has traditionally been passed from mother to child.

I'd like to suggest, too, that in addition to recalling Anne Sexton's poem 'My Friend, My Friend', first published in 1959,[25] Plath at some level is recalling two poems by Edith Sitwell which she writes about in a long and detailed undergraduate essay on the develop-ment of Sitwell's work in 1953.[26] Sitwell was clearly an important poet to Plath at this period. In an extempore burst of enthusiasm, before she continues in her professional analysis of the writing,

Plath states that 'I do not know when I have been so struck and
entranced by any poet; it is as if my life had been a twilit room,
and suddenly the walls had fallen away...transfiguring and perme-
ating the ordinary day-by-day world until the whole universe sang
with vibrant undercurrents of meaning!' ('Edith Sitwell', p.23).
Plath returns on several occasions during the essay to discussing
Sitwell's use of nursery rhyme, discussing in some detail Sitwell's
poem 'Lullaby'. 'Lullaby' follows Sitwell's famous and most antho-
logised poem, 'Still Falls the Rain', in a twelve-part sequence in
the *Collected Poems*. As 'Still Falls the Rain' ends with the voice
of God: 'Still do I love, still shed my innocent light, my Blood,
for thee', 'Lullaby' picks up this attestation of love in its refrain.
As it is little read, the poem is worth quoting in full:

Lullaby

Though the world has slipped and gone,
Sounds my loud discordant cry
Like the steel birds' song on high:
'Still one thing is left – the Bone!'
Then out danced the Babioun.

She sat in the hollow of the sea –
A socket whence the eye's put out –
She sang to the child a lullaby
(The steel birds' nest was thereabout).

'Do, do, do, do –
Thy mother's hied to the vaster race:
The Pterodactyl made its nest
And laid a steel egg in her breast –
Under the Judas-coloured sun.
She'll work no more, nor dance, nor moan,
And I am come to take her place.
Do, do.

There's nothing left but earth's low bed –
(The Pterodactyl fouls its nest):
But steel wings fan thee to thy rest,
And wingless truth and larvae lie
And eyeless hope and handless fear –
All these for thee as toys are spread,
Do – do –

Red is the bed of Poland, Spain,
And thy mother's breast, who has grown wise
In that fouled nest. If she could rise,
Give birth again,

In wolfish pelt she'd hide thy bones
To shield thee from the world's long cold,

And down on all fours shouldst thou crawl
For thus from no height canst thou fall –
Do, do.

She'd give no hands: there's naught to hold
And naught to make: there's dust to sift,
But no food for the hands to lift.
Do, do.

Heed my ragged lullaby,
Fear not living, fear not chance;
All is equal – blindness, sight,
There is no depth, three is no height:
Do, do.

The Judas-coloured sun is gone,
And with the Ape thou art alone –
Do,
    Do.'

In response to Sitwell's poem, Plath writes:

> In the nightmarish 'Lullaby', the Ape is seen as mother, teacher and
> protector, where the world is a modern one of pterodactyl airplane-
> birds that lay steel eggs. There is a light chilling horror in the lilting
> lullaby that sings of a meaningless metallic future...
>   ...In this new world there are no distinctions, all is the same, mass-
> produced, another Death-in-Life, where sight and blindness are equal.
> The sun, traitorous, is gone, and all that is left is the Ape in this shat-
> tering regression to a steel-age, exceedingly more terrible than any
> stone age could have been. (An added irony is gained by the lullaby
> since it contains echoes of the lovely lyric in 'The Sleeping Beauty':
> 'Do, do / Princess, do / Like a tree that drips with gold you flow.')
> ('Edith Sitwell', pp.20-21)

Plath is acutely aware of the double irony of writing about horror
in the lullaby refrain, and as aware, too, of the twofold irony of
recalling Sitwell's earlier poem. Parts 4 and 15 of the sequence of
Sitwell's Sleeping Beauty poems do, indeed, as Plath points out,
carry the refrain 'Do, do, / Princess, do', an incantation which is
set up against the spell cast by the bad fairy in the tale who curses
the infant princess. While Sexton's poem is a cry for forgiveness
from a state of religious emptiness and guilt, and is a poem which
agonises at the narrator's mother's death, the refrain works in
Sitwell's earlier poem to mitigate against death. It, too, is a lullaby,
but one which turns death to sleep. But, in a further irony, the
performative 'I do' of the marriage vow becomes the 'do' of a
sleep which will refuse a sexual awakening. 'Lullaby', like 'Daddy',
recalls the invasion of Poland; like 'Daddy' the war is seen in terms
of an adulterous male (the Pterodactyl has fouled his nest). If the

'do' refrain works in Sitwell's 'The Sleeping Beauty' as a hypnotic call in the world of repression and silence, as does perhaps the fairytale, and in 'Lullaby' as an affirmation of maternal comfort in the face a terrifying universe, Plath's use of it in 'Daddy' transforms it to a cry reawakening anger and violence.

In throwing off the oppression of enforced reproduction and mothering that the 'do' of the nursery rhyme suggests, in addition to recalling both the failure of the sleeping girl to be sexually awakened in 'The Sleeping Beauty', and its specifically female grieving in the face of the war, 'Daddy' is a clear and multi-layered assault on patriarchy and war. Perhaps – and extraordinarily – because of Plath's comments when she introduced the reading of 'Daddy' on the radio, the poem has been read largely in terms of its autobiographical resonance:

> Here is a poem spoken by a girl with an Electra complex. Her father died while she thought he was God. Her case is complicated by the fact that her father was also a Nazi and her mother very possibly part Jewish. In the daughter the two strains marry and paralyse each other – she has to act out the awful little allegory once over before she is free of it. (*CP*, p.293)

Yet Plath's statement about the poem does several things: it places it very firmly in the realm of the fantastic. This is an allegory, she seems to be saying; it is a dramatic monologue. The figures in the poem are not "real" but a part of another character's psychic fantasy. But we may also read them as metaphorical figures. The Nazi father and the mother who may possibly be part Jew can be read as condensed and displaced tropes. The obvious link between the role of the authoritarian father and the role of the authoritarian state are pointed out by Wilhelm Reich:

> The political and economic position of the father is reflected in his patriarchal relationship to the remainder of the family. In the figure of the father the authoritarian state has its representative in every family, so that the family becomes its most important instrument of power. [27]

The resurgence of fascist organisations in Britain – in particular the mass rally in Trafalgar Square of the National Socialist Movement on 1 July 1962 – may well have kindled Plath's interest in Nazi imagery. In 1958 several journal entries show her preoccupation with imagery from the holocaust: a dream which assimilates her reading an article she had read in *The Times* 'about tortures & black trains bearing victims to the furnace' (*Journals*, p.330); a recording of an afternoon 'reading magazines in the library at Smith which always sickens me...cremation fires burning in the dead eyes of

Anne Frank: horror on horror, injustice on cruelty – all accessible, various – how can the soul keep from flying to fragments – disintegrating, in one wild dispersal' (*Journals*, p.414); and a journal entry for the last day of the year sees her working on a short story, the 'present theme' being 'the awareness of a complicated guilt system whereby Germans in a Jewish and Catholic community are made to feel, in a scapegoat fashion, the pain, psychically, the Jews are made to feel in Germany by Germans without religion' (*Journals*, p.453).

But Plath is also using Fascism as a metaphor that works to highlight the horror of patriarchy through Fascism, by reminding us of the degree to which Nazi ideology was obsessed with the veneration of the woman as biological receptacle for the future "master race". Without leaning to heavily on biographical evidence, it is also quite fruitful to compare Reich's statement with what Aurelia Plath, Sylvia's mother, writes about her marriage to her husband, Otto Plath, in the introduction to *Letters Home*:

> Despite the fact that he was only sixteen when he arrived in the United States, the Germanic theory that the man should be *der Herr des Hauses* (head of house) persisted, contrary to Otto's earlier claims that the then modern aim of "fifty-fifty" appealed to him...
>
> The age difference between us (twenty-one years), Otto's superior education, his long years of living in college dormitories or rooming by himself, our former teacher-student relationship, all made this sudden change to home and family life difficult for him, and led to an attitude of "rightful" dominance on his part. He had never known the free flow of communication that characterised my relationship with my family, and talking things out, reasoning together just didn't operate. At the end of my first year of marriage, I realised that if I wanted a peaceful home – and I did – I would simply have to become submissive, although it was not in my nature to be so. (*Letters Home*, p.13)

In her critique of patriarchy and Fascism, Plath is also, it seems certain, recalling the psychoanalyst Erich Fromm's *Escape from Freedom* (1941), a book she owned two copies of, in which Fromm discusses 'those dynamic factors in the character structure of modern man, which made him give up his freedom in fascist countries'.[28] Fromm explores at length the masochistic tendency, 'the submission under the "leader" in Fascist ideology' (*Escape from Freedom*, p.154) as the desire 'to get rid of the individual self with all its shortcoming, conflicts, risks, doubts, and unbearable aloneness' (*Escape from Freedom*, p.153).

In 'Daddy' we see an attempt to break down oppressive patriarchal/fascistic structures; we see simultaneously a desire for the reconstruction of the self in language. In stanzas 5 and 6 we see how the narrator's relationship with the father has acted as silencer:

> I never could talk to you
> The tongue stuck in my jaw
>
> It stuck in a barb wire snare.
> Ich, ich, ich, ich
> I could hardly speak.
> I thought every German was you.
> And the language obscene.

Responding to these stanzas, Jacqueline Rose draws on a passage from Plath's diary:

> I; how firm a letter; how reassuring the three strokes: one vertical, proud and assertive, and then the two short horizontal lines in quick smug succession. The pen scratches the paper. I... I... I... I... I...I... I
> (*The Haunting of Sylvia Plath*, p.226)

Commenting on the repetitive 'I'/'ich' in 'Daddy', Rose continues: 'The effect, of course, if you read it aloud, is not one of assertion, but of the word sticking in the throat.' Thus identity is denied even as it is asserted: the narrator cannot claim even her own subjectivity. But as well as being what Plath called in a letter 'the gag in the throat of the happy housewife' the 'ich' sound is also the sound of sickness, of retching and disgust. The narrator cannot speak the language of the father: literally it is foreign to her. In an earlier poem, 'Little Fugue' (2 April 1962) (*CP*, p.187), Plath writes:

> Such a dark funnel, my father!
> I see your voice
> Black and leafy as in my childhood,
>
> A yew hedge of orders,
> Gothic and barbarous, pure German

And it is the father, who at the blackboard, with his cleft chin, teaches the language. Daddy speaks 'gobbledygoo'; what the OED defines under gobbledegook as 'pompous official or professional jargon' – a language, in other words, which attempts to seize power by exclusion.

In a letter to her brother, written on the same day as she wrote 'Daddy', Plath seems to contradict the voice of the poem: the 'obscene language' becomes as heady and mellifluous as mulled wine. But in this letter to her brother and her sister-in-law a startling process of transformation seems to be taking place. Plath writes:

> I wish you would both consider going on a holiday to Germany and Austria when you come [to Europe]. You should know some lovely places in the Tyrol, and I would love to go with you! I just dread ever

going on holiday alone... Just now I am a bit of a wreck, bones literally sticking out all over and great, black shadows under my eyes from sleeping pills, a smoker's hack... Tell me you'll consider taking (I mean escorting! I'll have the money!) me to Austria with you, even if you don't, so I'll have that to look forward to. I've had nothing to look forward to for so long! The half year ahead seems like a lifetime, and the half behind an endless hell. Your letters are *glühwein* to me (I really must learn German. I want above all to speak it.) (*Letters Home*, p.468)

There is an almost bathetic resonance here between the horror of emotion being expressed in the poem and the almost simultaneous façade of enthusiasm she presents in her letter home. Even more interesting and more provoking is that Plath seems to have taken on board an identification of self which tallies horrifically with pictures of emaciated inmates from the concentration camps: 'Bones literally sticking out all over and great, black shadows under my eyes'. Plath becomes horror, the gap between self and the other that is the poem becomes blurred. The process of self-alignment with the Jew is also, of course, drawn in 'Daddy':

> An engine, an engine
> Chuffing me off like a Jew.
> A Jew to Dachau, Auschwitz, Belsen.
> I began to talk like a Jew.
> I think I may well be a Jew.

Both Plath and the narrator of 'Daddy' are allying themselves and their situations with the inmate of a concentration camp, something which, as has been noted many times, is a disturbing and potentially offensive parallel to draw. Plath's comparison, however, seems to foreshadow a growing feminist iconography of female suffering. Betty Friedan's *The Feminine Mystique*, published in 1963, a year after 'Daddy' was written, was an important book for the small community of women writers and scholars at Radcliffe College, who included Plath's acquaintance, Anne Sexton, and Tillie Olsen and Maxine Kumin, and it is likely that it would have been equally resonant, with its feminist readings of Freud, for Plath. In *The Feminine Mystique*, Friedan (who, like Plath, was a graduate of Smith College) also aligns the dehumanisation of prisoners in the camp with the situation of the housewife in the 1950s and 1960s who had, she claimed, also undergone a similar process which undermined the sense of self. She writes:

In the concentration camps the prisoners were forced to adopt child-like behavior, forced to give up their individuality and merge themselves in an amorphous mass. Their capacity for self-determination, their ability to predict the future and to prepare for it was systematically destroyed. It was a gradual process which occurred in virtually imperceptible stages – but at the end, with the destruction of adult self-respect, of an adult frame of reference, the dehumanising effect was complete...

...American women are not, of course, being readied for mass extinction, but they are suffering a slow death of mind and spirit. Just as with the prisoners in the concentration camps, there are American women who have resisted that death, who have managed to return to a core of self, who have not lost touch with the outside world, who use their abilities to some creative purpose. They are women of spirit who have refused to "adjust" as housewives.[29]

Plath's own refusal to 'adjust' was a refusal which underwent a series of vacillations. The split between the culturally enforced role of housewife and creative urge were, when rubbing up against each other, inevitably going to provoke a deep-seated anxiety. Hannah Gavron, in her book *The Captive Wife* (1966), records the question of a Radcliffe College in 1963 which dramatises this anxiety almost perfectly:

What should I study so that whoever I marry I can continue to have an interesting and responsible job on a part-time basis so that I can look after the children without fear of growing stale?[30]

Friedan's analogies are difficult and often uncomfortable ones to make. But I would argue that Plath's narrator is not simply becoming 'the Jew', or simply saying that she identifies with the position of Jewishness, and its representation of exile, suffering, or even as Friedan argues, as a metaphor for the 'deadening of spirit' and the 'slow death of the mind' that is the result of oppression. Plath rather seems to become the poem she is writing, surrendering to the text, blurring boundaries between textual and non-textual subjectivities, becoming the suffering the poem enacts – which is the suffering of Jewishness – rather than aligning herself with Jewish suffering herself. For the poem clearly considers its subject in terms of simile, and supposition: 'I began to talk like a Jew. / I think I may well be a Jew', and 'I may be a bit of a Jew'. Hence the poem enacts an actual loss of identity, which is only found or renegotiated within the poem. We find the metaphor for this self-same loss of identity in stanza ten:

Every woman adores a Fascist,
The boot in the face, the brute
Brute heart of a brute like you.

The connection between the constraining shoe and the boot which the Fascist kicks in the woman's face seems clearly apparent. The bruised, distorted face becomes representative of the bruised and distorted individuality: the facelessness of the women whose identity is distorted, brutalised by patriarchy into something which no longer even exists.

In the poem's narrative, suicide then figures as means for a reconstruction of the self which rather unhappily echoes an attempt to reconstruct an absent paternal authority in 'The Colossus'. It is in these final three stanzas that the poem becomes more patently autobiographical in its severing of relations with Plath's by now estranged husband, Ted Hughes, and her father. 'Daddy' was written only four days after she had decided to divorce Hughes officially. Communications breakdown – the 'Black telephone is off at the root' and all male symbols of patriarchy (which have now simultaneously become intensely personal) – are murdered with a suitably parodic phallic stake.

*   *   *

With 'Poppies in October' (*CP*, p.203), 'Ariel' (*CP*, p.239) was one of two poems written on Plath's birthday on 27 October 1962. Drawing on an article by Mary Kurtzman, Linda Wagner-Martin draws on a convincing argument about the cabalistic influence on the poem which

> depends, line by line, on those beliefs as generated from Tarot card 14, Art or Temperance, on which a black-white woman is doing alchemical work over a cauldron, with a lion and an eagle at her feet. Associated with this iconography is the number 60, the Hebrew letter S, the sign Sagittarius, the God Jupiter, the Goddess Diana, the color blue, the horse, the Arrow, the hips and thighs, the centaur, and the Path of union with one's Higher Self or Holy Guardian Angel, symbolised by the sun.[31]

But the title 'Ariel' carries multiple connotations. Meaning 'lion of God', Ariel is referred to as an angel in Ezra, and presented with a lion's head in a number of magical tracts; for Jewish mystics Ariel was Jerusalem; biblically he was a man, an altar, and an angel who helped Raphael cure disease. According to the Testament of Solomon he controlled demons, and in some occult writings as well as Gnostic lore, he was the 'ruler of the winds'. He is referred to as a rebel angel by Milton, who is overcome by the seraph Abdiel, features in Pope's *The Rape of the Lock*, is Shelley's alter ego, and, most famously, he is the 'tricksy spirit' of Prospero in Shakespeare's *The Tempest*, a play to which Plath's poems repeatedly refer.[32] When introducing the poem, Plath described it purely in terms of the

biographical: Ariel was a horse she used to ride. But 'Ariel', con-
jured by the multiple resonances of the images of angels and spirits,
is a 'muse' poem that sees her, in Gravesian terms, meeting the
'goddess'. This image is not so far from the imagery of the muse
we have seen Smith exploring in the image of Hermes in the pre-
vious chapter. It is worth noting, too, that Plath had listened to a
broadcast Laura (Riding) Jackson gave on the radio in 1962, which
promoted her poem, 'Little Fugue'. (Riding) Jackson's 'The Tiger'
(MWP, pp.73-76), a poem about a woman finding her 'inner animal',
also seems relevant to any reading of 'Ariel', particularly the lines
'Not to be image of the beast in me, / I press the tiger forward. /
I crash through. / Now we are two. One rides.'

Equally important, however, is the fact that 'Ariel', written on
Plath's 30th birthday, recalls the poem of Plath's earlier hero, Dylan
Thomas, whose birthday Plath shared. Plath had also written an
earlier poem about rebirth, 'Poem for a Birthday', which was
completed on 4 November 1959, when she was three-months-
pregnant. Influenced by Roethke's Greenhouse poems, the seven-
part poem ends with an image of reconstruction: 'My mendings
itch. There is nothing to do / I shall be as good as new', lines
which in their rhythms certainly anticipate the later poem 'Daddy'.
Thomas's two poems were also written on or for his own birthday:
'Poem in October' (written in his 30th year) and 'Poem on His
Birthday' written on the occasion of his 35th birthday.[33] The latter
poem in particular would have held resonances for Plath and con-
tains not only shared 'Ariel' imagery: fire, berries, angel, riding, but
seems to link in with Plath's growing mythologising of the drown-
ing father we see most clearly in 'Lorelei' (CP, p.94).[34] Thomas's
final stanza reads:

> I hear the bouncing hills
> Grow larked and greener at berry brown
>   Fall and the dew larks sing
> Taller this thunderclap spring, and how
>   More spanned with angels ride
> The mansouled fiery islands! Oh,
>   Holier then their eyes,
> And my shining men no more alone
>   As I sail out to die.

In its use of the lion imagery, 'Ariel' also prefigures the poem
written two days later, 'Purdah', which alludes to Clytemnestra
through the lines 'The shriek in the bath / The cloak of holes'. In
a journal entry from 1958, Plath writes of her decision to memo-
rise the work of poets – Eliot, Yeats, Dunbar…Ransome [sic],

Shakespeare, Blake and Thomas and Hopkins:

> all those who said to words 'stand stable here' and made of the moment, of the hustle and jostle of grey, anonymous and sliding words a vocabulary to staunch wounds, to bind up broken limbs and 'set the skull back about the head' – my own husband-in-poetry's words... (*Journals*, p.341)

We must surely read Plath's desire to associate herself intertextually with Thomas's birthday poem differently from the way we read her interaction with the work of Sitwell, Smith or (Riding) Jackson. We see Plath viewing language, specifically what she constructs as male poetic language, as an agent for healing or reconstructing the damaged self, or even, we might argue, the inevitably damaged castrated female self. In looking for 'a vocabulary to staunch wounds', Plath's integration of Thomas's poem in 'Ariel' suggests we read the poem as a regeneration of self through the act of writing, the speaker of the poem growing one with the horse which is ridden reflecting the alliance of male and female. The significance of the shared birthday for Plath sets up a sense of poetic reincarnation; repeating the act of writing the poem for the birthday Plath literally recalls Thomas. Furthermore, the tendency to read the word suicide literally in a Plath poem blinds us to the metaphorical power of the word. The sun is the cauldron, the pot in which things are melted down as the rider becomes one with the other in the dawn. That this is a becoming one with a male poet who died in 1953 when he was 39, and at a time when Plath was beginning, through imitation, to find herself a voice through the practice of her craft, is surely of equal relevance to any foreshadowing of Plath's own self-annihilation. Plath here is moving beyond the sphere of Thomas's "influence" or imitation; she is not quoting him directly, just as she is not quoting Smith or (Riding) Jackson directly. But consciously or unconsciously her 'invocation' seeks to ally her with both female and male writers in a literary tradition into which she feels she is being reborn.

The autumn of 1962 was a period of intense creativity for Plath, as she elaborates in a letter to the poet Ruth Fainlight: 'I am fascinated by the polarities of muse-poet and mother housewife. When I was happy domestically I felt a gag in my throat.'[35] 'Lady Lazarus' is dated 23-29 October. Over this period Plath also had completed 'Cut', 'By Candlelight', 'The Tour', 'Ariel', 'Poppies in October', 'Nick and the Candlestick' and 'Purdah'. We might then usefully see this poem as a culmination of poems written in less than a week, such a run of poems suggesting a mining or working through of ideas, lines from one poem peeling off, generating one another. In its dissection of the body it recalls the slightly earlier poem 'The Applicant' (11 October), but the Lazarus of the title may also recall Emma Lazarus, whose *Songs of a Semite* were published in 1882, and to whom we have already seen Plath making implicit reference in 'The Colossus'. Tracy Brain has drawn interesting connections between the poem and a 16th-century painting by Sebastiano del Piombo, *The Raising of Lazarus*, which was hung in the National Gallery when Plath visited London before moving there in 1962 (*The Other Sylvia Plath*, p.138). Whatever the prompt – and the prompts and allusions are in fact likely to be many – the primary tension in the poem results in the dynamic between the victim and protagonist: suicide and murdered. As a figure who returns from the dead (John 11: 1-44), Lazarus is the brother of Martha and Mary, Mary who is also sometimes presumed to be Mary Magdalene, the sinner who annointed Jesus' feet (Luke 7: 37). When Plath writes in the poem 'I am only thirty' she is surely anticipating her own birthday and the sense of looking forward and back that the anniversary of the birthday brings. The speaker of the poem works as a palimpsest of personas which circle around the personal one for Plath who is recalling her own brushes with death. This figure becomes superimposed by the holocaust victim, who in turn becomes an image of the risen Christ. The poem vacillates between these figures in a performance of resurrection, 'The big strip tease' before the 'peanut-crunching crowd'.

Tim Kendall is perceptive when discussing both 'Daddy' and 'Lady Lazarus' when he remarks that

> The gulf between poet and persona, cold-blooded technique and blood-hot emotion, analyst and victim, seems unbridgeable. If these divisions can be successfully reconciled, it is through Plath's emphasis on performance and repetition. Freud's account of repetition compulsion shares with Plath's description of 'Daddy' a crucial verb: just as Plath's persona must 'act out the awful little allegory', so Freud notes that the Oedipus complex and its derivatives are 'invariably acted out in the sphere of transference'. Repetition guarantees performance, and performance requires an audience. Freud notes, as if glossing 'Daddy', that 'the artistic play and artistic imitation carried out by adults, which, unlike children's, are aimed at an audience, do not spare the spectators (for instance in tragedy) the most painful experiences and can yet be felt by them as highly enjoyable'. Plath categorised 'Daddy' as light verse, a genre which W.H. Auden considered to be 'written for performance'.[36]

It is in the context of Plath's explorations of the qualities of the dramatic monologue that Plath wrote to Stevie Smith on 19 November that same year, requesting an appointment to meet her having spent the week listening to the British Council's recordings of

Smith reading her poetry, and proclaiming herself 'an addict of your poetry, a desperate Smith addict'. Plath's letter continues:

> I have wanted for ages to get hold of *A Novel on Yellow Paper* (I am jealous of that title, it is beautiful, I've just finished my first, on pink, but that's no help to the title I fear). (*Me Again*, p.6)

The novel to which Plath refers, was of course, *The Bell Jar*, which was written on the back of old drafts of Ted Hughes' poetry – a utilitarian response to paper shortage, no doubt, but also in the light of the points I have been making about Plath's attempt to place herself in relation to male creativity, a symbolic juxtaposition between male poetic and the female writer's semi-autobiographical coming into being in its context.

Why did Smith hold such a fascination for Plath? Previously Plath's relationship to women poets had, as we have seen, been one that was largely rivalrous or dismissive. Perhaps certain resemblances between the two women's biographies were a strong factor. Like Plath, Smith also grew up without a father. Smith's poem 'Papa Love Baby' (*CP*, p.16) is a curiously melancholy and threatening poem about family relations and domestic abandonment. Thematically, Smith's interest in things German, and her poems about the release of Death must also have hit a particularly resonant note for Plath. There is a strong sense in Plath's letter that through listening to recordings of Stevie Smith (it seems vital that her enthusiasm stems initially from hearing Smith, rather than reading her: she gets to know Smith as voice, not through public performance, nor through her books and their accompanying drawings) Plath found for herself a means of liberating herself from an 'I' that demanded the verification of the identity of suffering. Smith's particular use of the dramatic monologue, and the influence of nonsense verse which in some ways connects her to the surrealists, cannot fail to have interested Plath. Combined with the public persona which Plath must later have seen Smith adopting as a defence against "femininity", Smith offered Plath one route out of the personal which immediately gendered her poetry and gave her a position from which to begin to talk about public and political issues. The distinctions made here by Freud in the quotation from Kendall above, between the child's and the adult's performance, perhaps allows us draw a neat, if artificial line, between the poetic perfor-mances of Stevie Smith and Plath. This, of course, begs the ques-tion as to who Plath's audience was, one which in a way is already answered in Kendall's assertion that Plath's monologues place her as both performer and listener, a strategy we can see also re-enacted

within the narrative of the fairytale in the work of Anne Sexton.
It is in this way that these, surely Plath's most painful poems, reflect
back on the self whilst at the same time attempting not to be, in her
words, 'mirror-looking and narcissistic'. Smith's illustrations, in
their turn, create a listener who while being a part of the poem is
also ironically apart from it. The poem is not directed at the illus-
tration, but the illustration becomes, to continue Freud's analogy,
part of the child's game, self-aware and nevertheless complicit in it.

It is the performed self which eventually predominates in *Ariel*.
In 'Lesbos' (*CP*, pp.227-30) Plath compares the performance of
the Hollywood star with her own performance, as the speaker of
the poem and as wife: 'You acted, acted, acted for the thrill.' Plath's
recognition that the particular kind of way in which Smith trans-
forms the dramatic monologue into a performance of the self, was
clearly a vital element in her approach to the later poems. Plath's
experimentation with the dramatic monologue, which we see most
notably in 'Three Women' (1962) (*CP*, p.176) which she later dram-
atised as a radio play, as well as in such poems as 'The Detective'
(*CP*, p.208) and 'Purdah' (*CP*, p.242), sees her moving between
the desire to establish both a dramatised and performed self, a
distinction clearly made in the latter two poems mentioned. In the
dramatic monologue of 'The Detective' Plath uses a voice which
overlays and vacillates between what appears to be a semi-autobio-
graphical narrative, in which a woman is discussed in the third
person, and the voice of Sherlock Holmes talking to Watson. 'The
Detective' is an extraordinary poem in its ability to suspend its
multiple dramas and narratives, to give Plath access to a voice which
allows her to know herself in otherness, to inspect herself from a
male and a female perspective. In the poem the woman discussed
is both alive and dead, only present in her absence. The irony of
the poem is that in attributing blame to a murderer there must be
someone who has been murdered. The "who dunnit" of the poem
cannot be solved unless there is a someone to whom things have
been done. But what is done in the poem's terrifying analysis of
the trap of women's domestification cannot be identified because
the victim has herself evaporated before her death:

> This is a case without a body.
> The body does not come into it at all.
>
> It is a case of vaporisation.
> The mouth first, its absence reported
> In the second year. It has been insatiable
> And in punishment was hung out like brown fruit
> To wrinkle and dry.

> The breasts next.
> These were harder, two white stones.
> The milk came yellow, then blue and sweet as water.
> There was no absence of lips, there were two children,
> But their bones showed, and the moon smiled.

Whereas the female body in 'The Detective' is held up as a potential
site for resistance, albeit a lost one, in 'Purdah' we see Plath using
the segregated and veiled female body to set up a complex dynamic
of gender, between female poet, herself veiled behind the dramatic
monologue, and between theatrical performer (the male actor who
takes on the female role of Clytemnestra); between language which
asserts a bodily presence ('I smile', 'I gleam', 'I breathe', 'I revolve',
and the threat and promise of the lines, repeated three times, 'I
shall unloose') and an awareness of the performativity of gender in
the text:

> Veil stirs its curtain.
> My eye
> Veil is
>
> A concatenation of rainbows.
> I am his.
> Even in his
>
> Absence, I revolve in my
> Sheath of impossibles,

Christina Britzolakis reads the poem as

> poised in the moment preceding the denouement of its own narrative:
> the breaking of purdah, the unleashing of revenge, the shattering of the
> illusion created by language, and the abrogation of formal control...
> The male-created images and representations which imprisoned the
> speaker in a state of "purdah" are converted into a form of symbolic
> revenge, culminating in the invocation of the husband-murderer Cly-
> temnestra, borrowed from Aeschylus's *Agamemnon*.[37]

Plath's choice of an oriental woman through whom to dramatise this
murderous unveiling of femininity is little commented on; neither
is the fact that the promise of an unveiling of femininity is never
actually provided by the poem. The speaker of the poem is sur-
rounded by parakeets and macaws and her symbolic 'unloosening'
is figured as the losing of a feather which links her speech to their
chatter. It is hard not to think back to Sitwell here again and the
dance of Salome, that other deathly unveiling of gender, and Sitwell's
own configuration of the idle chatter of the parakeets. But more
obviously, in its veiling and unveiling, the poem also importantly
recalls Canto 6 of Byron's *Don Juan*, in which the 16-year-old Juan

enters a Turkish harem in disguise as a woman, Juanna (to clinch the argument, Plath's and Byron's poems share that unusual word 'concatenation'). Marjorie Garber discusses this famous episode in Byron's poem, suggesting that

> The extraordinary transvestic materials of the poem clearly reflect upon Byron's own construction of "masculine" and "feminine" roles, as well as upon his fascination with the possibility of breaching or destabilising them... By locating transvestism, strategically, in an Eastern locale, Byron deploys the chic of Araby, its sexual and sartorial destabilisation, as a powerful fantasy as well as a social critique...his supporting cast of eunuchs, fops, and epicenes personify the very real power of transvestism not as a carnivalised stage elsewhere, an exotic other, but rather as a reminder of the repressed that always returns. (*Vested Interests*, pp.320-21)

Once the intertextual joke is unveiled, we must read Plath's poem in a double way. On the one hand, as Britzolakis does, we can read it in terms of a straightforwardly feminist unleashing of repressed femininity. At the same time it is impossible not to see that the poem questions exactly what that unveiling might reveal. Clytemnestra, played in Greek tragedy by a man, in a play written by a man, performs the role of murderous woman. Don Juan, as Juanna, performs as woman, again in a text written by a man. Both Aeschylus's and Byron's texts may be unveiled in Plath's own performance of the promised revelation of gender, a promise which would, if it were allowed, show us what we do not, perhaps, expect to see. Behind the threatened unveiling of the female body lie men who are disguised as women; behind the female text, lies the male poem.

*   *   *

Throughout my readings of Plath what is clear is that the establishment of a female writing self must be done with recourse to writers of both sexes: Plath needs literary models of both genders. In her struggle to work in both genres, in the high art of poetry and the short story writing which she associated with popular culture, she constructs a gender divide that designates poetry as masculine, and prose as feminine. Transgressing the genre divide also for Plath becomes a transgression of cultural constructions of gender. In 'A Comparison', published in 1962, Plath attempts to illustrate the difference between poetry and prose. She writes:

> How I envy the novelist!
>   I imagine him, better say her, for it is the women I look to for a parallel – I imagine her, then, pruning a rosebush with a large pair of shears, adjusting her spectacles, shuffling about among the teacups,

humming, arranging ashtrays or babies, absorbing a slant of light, a fresh edge to the weather and piercing, with a kind of modest, beautiful X-ray vision, the psychic interiors of her neighbours... Her business is time, the way it shoots forward, shunts back, blooms, decays and double exposes itself. Her business is people in Time. And she, it seems to me, has all the time in the world. She can take a century if she likes, a generation, a whole summer. (*JP*, p.56)

Containing echoes of Virginia Woolf's essays in its tone as well as its content (Woolf writes 'A novel is the least concentrated form of art'), Plath's essay allows us several important insights. 'A Comparison' is first of all an expression of anxiety about the appropriateness of genre, with poetry and prose being placed within a complexly gendered framework. Rather than being engaged in an accumulative process in which the novelist has both the time and space of narrative, the poet, on the other hand, writes Plath 'can take about a minute'. Poems, instant, explosive immediate, are like 'round glass Victorian paperweights':

[A] clear globe, self-complete, very pure, with a forest or village or family group within it. You turn it upside down, then back. It snows. Everything is changed in a minute. It will never be the same in there – not the fir trees, nor the gables, nor the faces. (*JP*, p.56)

This description of the poem sounds very much in line with imagist aesthetics, the presentation of an image which is 'hard and clear, never blurred not indefinite'. And indeed elsewhere in the essay Plath cites Pound's famous Imagist poem, 'In a Station of the Metro'. For Pound, the image 'presents an intellectual and emotional complex in an instant of time'; it is for Plath

The presentation of such a 'complex' instantaneously which gives that sense of sudden liberation; that sense of freedom from time limits and space limits; that sense of sudden growth. (*JP*, p.57)

Where 'A Comparison' becomes most interesting is in its description of the violence which the act of generating the poem, and the indeed the violence which the poem itself contains:

If a poem is concentrated, a closed fist, then a novel is relaxed and expansive, an open hand; it has road, detours, destinations; a heart line, a head line; morals and money come into it. Where the fist excludes and stuns, the open hand can touch and encompass a great deal in its travels. (*JP*, p.57)

Plath, by placing herself as the poet, in contrast to the feminised novelist, only by afterthought a woman, who seems captured in a strange domesticity which includes children and gardening, seems to be suggesting that either gender can fit within this paradigm.

But the image of the fist which 'excludes and stuns' seems cultur-
ally male, and we would not be wholly misled if we were to draw
the conclusion that on taking up the role of poet Plath must also
model her creative self in terms of masculinity. 'A Comparison'
ends: 'The door of the novel, like the door of the poem, also shuts.
But not so fast, nor with such manic, unanswerable finality.' Poetry
by implication is amoral, irrational. It is equated with death. It is,
I want to suggest, to this 'violent pleasure' to use the surrealist
Georges Bataille's description of poetry that she turns to work
through and experience as a way to avoid self-annihilation.

That the establishment of a viable feminine self is always figured
precariously between life and death says as much about the threat
of being overwhelmed by the culture's patriarchal impulse as it
does about Plath's personal pathology. Surrealist splitting of the
feminine into the realm of the unconscious and irrational, and her
positioning as *femme-enfant* and muse, as many commentators have
pointed out, while ostensibly and passionately in favour of the lib-
eration of women from "hearth and home", was nevertheless a
problematic construction for those women who wanted to create
within such a schema, and not that far removed from the kind of
female muse so dangerously espoused by Robert Graves. Plath's
working through of her ownership of creativity *in spite of* her gender,
seems key not only to Plath's work, but pivotal for the women
writers who come after her. The anxieties Plath experiences are
shared in various ways by her female predecessors as well as her
successors. They are made more complex not only because of cul-
tural and historical changes in the value and configuration of the
feminine, but also because the most famous and talented of their
predecessors casts a strong shadow on their own conception of the
woman poet as victim and on creativity as self-annihilating, some-
thing Plath herself throughout her life was, ironically, struggling
to resist. Shortly after Plath's death in 1963, A. Alvarez published
four poems in *The Observer*: 'Edge', 'The Fearful', 'Kindness' and
'Contusion' with a note that Plath

> was systematically probing that narrow and violent area between the
> viable and the impossible, between experience which can be transmuted
> into poetry and that which is overwhelming. It represents a totally new
> breakthrough in modern verse and established her, I think, as the most
> gifted woman poet of her time.[38]

Plath herself had noted this sense of a remarkable 'new break-
through' in modern poetry in her discussion of Robert Lowell's
Life Studies:

These peculiar private and taboo subjects I feel have been explored in recent American poetry – I think particularly of poetess Anne Sexton, who writes also about her experience as a mother; as a mother who's had a nervous breakdown, as an extremely emotional and feeling young woman. And her poems are wonderfully craftsmanlike poems, and yet they have a kind of emotional and psychological depth which I think is quite new and exciting.[39]

Yet even here, Alvarez's final statement identifies Plath as 'the most gifted woman poet of our time'. She is not 'the most gifted poet' and for Alvarez a recognition of her difference seems important both in his reading and understanding of her work, and ultimately his evaluation of it. For Plath, Anne Sexton is referred to as a 'poetess' (a term which she also uses in relation to herself when talking about her poetic rivals), and yet she seems anxious to assure that her poems are crafts*man*like. Womanhood and motherhood are placed at odds with each other. Creation – and that which is valid and good – is masculinised.

How we place Plath, then, is crucial not only to our reading of her work but to our assessment of her influence on the women writing after her death. Throughout Plath's *oeuvre* we see her vacillating between masculine and feminine identification, unwilling to fall into constrictions of an identity that she fears will fix her in a role that freezes her creative impulse. Like Smith, the poet is figured as performer. Plath's anxieties about the balancing act the woman poet must perform, are almost uncannily anticipated in an early poem, 'Aerialiste' (*CP*, p.331), where she writes:

> Each night, this adroit young lady
> Lies among sheets
> Shredded fine as snowflakes
>   Until dream takes her body
> From bed to strict tryouts
> In tightrope acrobatics.

Such signals of her own awareness of the dangers of her enterprise, become a part – not always easy to negotiate – of the way she genders herself as much as she constructs an image of a woman poet.

CHAPTER FOUR

Consorting with Angels:
Anne Sexton and the Art of Confession

Anxieties about the way in which she looked when she performed to an audience constantly recur in Anne Sexton's letters and it is clear that Sexton's sense of herself as a poet as well as a woman was being both asserted and constructed during her poetry readings, for which she became well-known. In the early 1970s Sexton's interest in performing her poetry culminated in a tour of America with a jazz-rock band called, after one of her early poems, 'Her Kind'. 'Anne Sexton and Her Kind' included a guitarist, flute and saxophone, electric keyboards and a drummer, and later bass players. As Diane Wood Middlebrook comments in her biography of Sexton, 'the musicians were to write back-up rhythms and song motifs to already existing poems... Sexton learned to deliver words in an acoustical envelope formed by the instruments.'[1] Sexton had started her working life as a model, and unlike Sitwell's and Smith's performances, Sexton's presentation of herself, as powerfully sexy and conventionally glamorous, did not see her adopting a persona which obviously worked to destabilise assumptions about femininity and the woman poet. The often taboo-breaking content of her poems worked alongside and in juxtaposition with the image of desirable femininity she was also projecting, and as Elisabeth Bronfen has pointed out, although 'her gestures were...calculated, controlled, and self-reflexive, they did not come from the position of one who could ironically distance herself from the discourse that constructed her, but rather from one who could only make explicit her implication within this discourse...'[2] Like all of the women discussed so far, Sexton held complex feelings about her women poet contemporaries, and the relationship of her gender to her poetry. Asked in interview in 1961 whether she had 'ever felt at a disadvantage' as a woman poet, Sexton replied

> That's a very big subject. Oh Terrific. Yes. Definitely...There are so many lady poets and they're almost all so bad...[...] There are whole clubs of women poets: it's all right to be a poet if you're a woman. Therefore you can be a bad one. [...] Women don't strive to make anything real out of it. They just dabble in it. (*Anne Sexton*, p.151)

In this chapter I explore the relationship Anne Sexton has with the confessional genre, and the space it offers the woman poet in its invocation of the female body as a site of experience and truth.

More than in any other genre, the confessional poem demands a dynamic of belief between reader or listener and poet. The belief in the authenticity of the 'I' that speaks the poem that exists both during and after the poem has been read conflates the poet's experience with the dramatised textual experience. As we have seen, in the dramatic monologue the reader must suspend his or her disbelief when reading or listening to the poem. While Plath's 'Lady Lazarus' and 'Daddy', for example, perform extreme psychic states, they do so from within a dramatised monologue that establishes the presence of a masked poet, whose embodiment is always at a remove from the persona it creates. In the case of the confessional poem there is often no ironic gap placed between reader, listener and text. We must believe in Sexton's body, and its experiences, of abortion, masturbation, menstruation, her suicide attempts, her pill taking, outside the poem, just as the poem invokes it as text. And although there is often slippage and movement in the matrix between poet, persona and poem in the dramatic monologue, strictly, the confessional poem sets out to invoke a unity between poet and poem, the present and authentic body of the poet presented in its text, however ambivalent or ravaged, or damaged the presence of the poetic body may be.

In Sexton's early work, her poems veer between those which dramatise the self and those which employ a monologue. But if the early poems are much more dependent on a voice of otherness, from her 1962 collection *All My Pretty Ones* onwards we see a gradual movement towards the establishment of an unmediated self. This movement culminates in *Live or Die* (1966) in which all the poems are fixed not only to an account of a personal experience, but are dated as if to emphasise the importance of ascribing them to a particular person at a particular time, to make them immediate responses to the moment. It is a sudden change of tack when, with the publication of *Transformations* (1971), arguably her most sustained and successful work, we see Sexton returning to use the dramatic monologue in her versions of Grimm. These movements back and forth to the dramatic monologue, which see Sexton essentially reconstructing a sense of the relationship between the monologist and the poet, seem to me symptomatic of a continuing struggle for Sexton to circumlocute the difficulties of writing the purely personal as a woman poet. Sexton begins in her work, as a cipher for this continuing negotiation, to look for a figure of alterity which she finds in the figure of the angel. The angel works for Sexton as a muse who can move between objective and subjective experience while still allowing her a voice of anguish and suffering, but adds to it a dimension of androgyny which removes it directly from being simply an expression of her female self. The angel is both her and not her, the good self and the bad self, the human and the transcendent. From writing to a 'you' who listens – frequently a male figure of authority, the teacher, the psychiatrist, the doctor, or even the lover – Sexton shifts her muse from the external, her necessary other, to an internal muse who dramatises her dilemma, and who offers an imago which allows her to speak both to and about herself.

The poem 'Music Swims Back to Me'[3] is an interesting example of an early poem in which we see Sexton setting up a persona which may or may not be identifiable as the poet. The poem, which was published in *To Bedlam and Part Way Back* (1960), is written in the first person, spoken by a character, who we learn is a patient in a 'private institution on a hill'. Without any other prompts, without the quotations marks that we saw Lowell urging Sexton to use as a distancing device, we in all likelihood identify the speaker of the poem with Anne Sexton at the same time as attributing the speaker – deluded, confined, forgetful – as being an Anne Sexton not of the present but of the past. She must be an Anne of the past, the logics of the poem suggest, as the poet who is lost in dreamy unison with the radio's music could not have written the poem. An important part of the poem's dynamic is established with the speaker's attempts to engage a 'Mister' in conversation in the first line of the poem, as she asks the way home. This patient, it transpires, is locked in a dark room with 'four ladies, over eighty, / in diapers every one of them'. The patient remembers dancing to the music she now hears, and the first night she was brought to the institution, 'the strangle cold of November' when 'even the stars were strapped to the sky'. The poem moves from the present to the past tense, to conclude again in the final stanza with the speaker of the poem locked in what might be described as the past's continuous present:

> They lock me in this chair at eight a.m.
> and there are no signs to tell the way,
> just the radio beating to itself
> and the song that remembers
> more than I. Oh, la la la,
> this music swims back to me.

The final line of the poem again invokes 'Mister'. Mister, who is, of course also the reader, must wait and listen; his presence becomes a guarantee of the narrator's existence. The relationship set up between female speaker and male listener in 'Music Swims Back to Me' occurs in other poems in the collection which depend on the creation of a dynamic between male listener and female speaker, such as 'You, Doctor Martin' (*CP*, pp.3-4) or 'Said the Poet to Her Analyst' (*CP*, pp.12-13) and 'To John, Who Begs Me Not to Enquire Further' (*CP*, pp.34-35). In this latter poem Sexton addresses what it means to write a confessional poem:

> I tapped my own head;
> it was a glass, an inverted bowl.
> It is a small thing
> to rage in your own bowl.
> At first it was private.
> Then it was more than myself;
> it was you, or your house
> or your kitchen.
> And if you turn away
> because there is no lesson here
> I will hold my awkward bowl,
> with all its cracked stars shining
> like a complicated lie,
> and fasten a new skin around it
> as if I were dressing an orange,
> or a strange sun.
> Not that it was beautiful,
> but that I found some order there.[4]

The poem, addressed to John Holmes, who ran the creative writing class which she, Maxine Kumin and others attended in 1957, is an eloquent plea for the 'complicated lie' of the confession. Echoing Blake's 'Thel's Motto',[4] and obliquely engaging with some of the images of shadowy femininity which appear in the book of Thel, the poem also links up with the epigraph Sexton uses for the volume, a letter of Schopenhauer to Goethe, dated November 1815, which reads :

> It is the courage to make a clean breast of it in the face of every question that makes the philosopher. He must be like Sophocles's Oedipus, who, seeing enlightenment concerning his terrible fate, pursues his indefatigable enquiry, even when he divines that appalling horror waits him in the answer. But most of us carry in our heart the Jocasta who begs Oedipus for God's sake not to inquire further... (*CP*, p.2)

In this strange reversal of genders, Sexton positions herself as Oedipus, her mentor as Jocasta. Writing, Sexton seems to be pointing out, is about taking oneself to the horror of one's own fate. But what exactly is that fate – one of finding one's identity in what had seemed a certain world, to be not what one had thought? To discover that sexual relations between men and women are not what had been previously assumed? Or is it to submit to some predestined tragedy of gender identity? In *Powers of Horror*, Julia Kristeva sees Oedipus as a scapegoat figure:

> Entering an impure city – a miasma – he turns himself into *agos*, defilement, in order to purify it and to become *katharmos*. He is thus a purifier by the very fact of being *agos*. (*Powers of Horror*, p.84)

Might then the confessing poet, who transgresses the borders of the spoken, also in performing that confession, speak for and cleanse, the generation for which it speaks? Sexton's poem, however, testifies to the recreation of something other than the self that testifies. The 'complicated lie' involves the construction of another self. But it also allows for a making sense of suffering on a wider scale than the purely personal, to an exchange of experience between men and women, Oedipus and Jocasta. As 'To John, Who Begs Me Not to Enquire Further' ends:

> ...your fear is anyone's fear,
> like an invisible veil between us all...
> and sometimes in private,
> my kitchen, your kitchen,
> my face, your face.

The image of the angel first appears alongside these poems in her first collection. In 'The Waiting Head' (*CP*, pp.31-32) it is a glanced image of a figure who becomes an alter ego:

> Surely I remember the hooks
>
> of her fingers curled on mine, though even now
> will not admit the times I did avoid this street,
> where she lived on and on like a beached fig
> and forgot us anyhow;
> visiting the pulp of her kiss, bending to repeat
> each favor trying to comb out her mossy wig
> and forcing love to last. Now she is always dead
> and the leather books are mine. Today I see the head
>
> move like some pitted angel, in that high window.

This representation of a self who is both the poet and not the poet sets the ground for later poems in which the angel acts as a figure of otherness. But perhaps Sexton's most difficult and pivotal use of the angel is to be found in her poem, 'Consorting with Angels' (*CP*, pp.111-12), which appeared in 1963. This enigmatic poem sees the speaker of the poem interrogating gender constructions in relation to her own sexuality, and ultimately rejecting stereotypical masculine or feminine gender constructions in favour of a mutilated and limbless but nevertheless desiring subject. The creature with whom we are left is left with nothing but the bodily parts which define her difference (the breasts, the vagina); and the points of similarity between genders (the legs, arms, hands, feet) are sacrificed in favour of a fish-like skin. The speaker of the poem is tired of the feminine masquerade, 'the cosmetics and the silks' as well as the mouth and breasts. (This mutilation of the body might be compared to a later poem by Lowell, 'Seals', in which the speaker of the poem offers a kind of prayer that 'If we must live again, not us; we might / go into seals'. Like the torso, the seals are virtually limbless and fishy, yet the image of the seal, though androgynous, is one which seems less ambiguously positive: 'we'd handle ourselves better: / able to dawdle, able to torpedo, / all at home in our three elements, / ledge, water and heaven'.) [5] Accordingly the speaker of the poem also rejects stereotypical woman's adoption of "masculine" behaviour (as figured by Joan of Arc who is put to death in a man's clothes in the city of chains), but she also rejects the masculine – the husband and the potentially abusive father with his threatening 'white bone'. Instead the speaker of the poem identifies her gender with the angels, which in the poem seem to mark difference itself – there are 'no two in the same species'. Here the 'I' of the poem has 'lost' her 'common gender and my final aspect'; she is not a 'woman anymore / not one thing or the other.' The poem also makes direct allusion to Blake's *Marriage of Heaven and Hell*:

[S]oon we saw seven houses of brick: one we entered; in it were a number of monkeys, baboons, & all of that species, chaind by the middle, grinning and snatching at one another, but withheld by the shortness of their chains: However, I saw that they sometimes grew numerous; and then the weak were caught by the strong, and with a grinning aspect, first coupled with & then devourd, by plucking off first one limb and then another, till the body was left a helpless trunk. This after grinning & kissing it with seeming fondness, they devourd too. (*Blake's Poetry*, p.97)

Sexton is clearly allying herself with a visionary, mystical tradition, yet one which, like Blake's interrogational and satirical approach to the writings of Swedenborg, takes on a stance against texts which inscribe masculinity to the exclusion of the feminine. Blake's scenario, however, offers a much more horrific and grotesque vision than Sexton's. The trunk or torso that Sexton leaves us with is not finally devoured: what is left is an image of woman as orifice – the mouth, the vagina, and the anus – orifices that ingest, engulf, expel. Yet, unlike Lowell's image in the poem 'Seals' included in *Notebook*, this figure does not represent the freedom of androgyny in the sense of a merger of masculine and feminine sexual characteristics; rather it represents a vision of an all encompassing or even engorging sexuality.

The speaker of the poem defines herself in terms which link her directly to the woman speaker of the *Song of Songs*, depending heavily as it does on its intertextual reference to the *Songs*. Sexton's figure is clearly sexual, and clearly powerful, and is interestingly echoed by Lowell's 'Mermaid Emerging' in *The Dolphin* (1973):

> Mermaid, why are you another species?
> 'Because, you, I, everyone is unique.'
> Does anyone ever make you do anything?
> 'Do this, do that, do nothing; you're not chained.
> I am a woman or I am a dolphin,
> the only animal man really loves,
> I spout the smarting waters of joy in your face –
> rough-weather fish, who cuts your nets and chains.'
> (Lowell: *Collected Poems*, p.684)

The interplay between Sexton and Lowell here is an interesting one, and it is worth pointing out that although Lowell is an important figure to Sexton, she is equally as important to him as a poet. What connects these images, one mutilated, one transformed, the other a mythical creature which is both one thing and another, is that they seem to represent for both poets an escape from the fixity of sex roles. But although the speaker of Sexton's poem places herself in between Adam and Eve, we are ultimately left with a figure who is simultaneously and paradoxically identifying with a woman's sexuality (at the expense of a mutilation of her 'human characteristics – her arms and her legs) through her identification with the speaker of the *Song of Songs*; a figure who is both 'black and beautiful', but who also denies that she is female: 'I am no more a woman / than Christ was a man'.[6] Sexton's use of the line break is neatly juxtaposed by a final image of the woman who, Christ-like, achieves an in-between state, between the male and the female, the human and the divine through the act of suffering. Clearly, then, 'Consorting with Angels' cannot be simply read as a confessional poem: its surreal, apocalyptic vision, its biblical stealing, all serve to destabilise any sense of a straightforwardly "authentic" self who is examined in the retelling of a "true" event.

'Consorting with Angels' was published in Sexton's *Live or Die* (1966), a volume which includes some of her most raw and personal work. 'Flee on Your Donkey' (*CP*, pp.97-105), for example, takes as its epigraph two lines from Rimbaud's poem 'Fêtes de la faim', '*Ma faim, Anne, Anne, / Fuis sur ton âne*'. The poem underpins Sexton's poem with its references to hunger and the figuring of eating up the world – ingesting it – as a kind of unhappiness. Sexton's use of the epigraph works cleverly to both identify the poem with a speaker 'Anne', an identification which brings the 'I' that speaks close to Anne Sexton the poet, but at the same time setting up that Anne as the fiction of another poet with whom the poet is in dialogue. 'Flee on Your Donkey' is about the return to a psychiatric hospital, and is again initially addressed to a doctor: 'you, my doctor, my enthusiast, / were better than Christ; / you promised me another world / to tell me who / I was'. The body that the 'I' of the poem invokes is a body which is inspected by doctors for reflexes, but mostly becomes eradicated in dreams and trances, trances in which the speaker testifies 'I could be any age, / voice, gesture – all turned backward / like a drugstore clock'. The narrator of the poem is herself distanced from the ill body which performs its illness, 'pretending dead', or later, eating God's finger 'like a white flower' as she anticipates the electroconvulsive therapy: 'Is this the old trick, the wasting away, / the skull that waits for its dose / of electric power?' But rather than seeing the sick body (as the Decadents might) as a site of transformation and transcendence, the split between the sense of the self and the body figures a desire for a removal from the difficulties of body, such as we have seen in 'Consorting with Angels'. At the end of the poem the narrator invokes 'Anne', both Anne the poet and the Anne of the Rimbaud poem, urging her to flee on her donkey out of the hospital. The poem ends with the lines 'In this place everyone talks to his own mouth. / That's what it means to be crazy. / Those I loved best died of it – / the fool's disease.' By this stage the poem has moved in its address from the doctor to the self / poet. This final image, then, suggests the establishment of a split between seeing the self as both subject and object (a strategy particularly reminiscent of Plath's 'An Appearance'). Here Anne Sexton the poet talks to Anne who is both herself and not herself, who is also addressing a male poet, who, in invoking her name, talks to her. But mouths of course can't listen and the poem ends placing madness as that which can be told by the self, but not heard.

What's perhaps most interesting about the movements between the confessional poem and the dramatic monologues which also offer a confession in another voice, and the in-between place that the angel poems offer Sexton, is the fluidity in which Sexton moves between these different ways of "confessing". In *Transformations* (1971), a volume which brings together 17 retellings of Grimms' fairytales, the confessional element is partially projected onto the characters of the fairytales whose stories are retold and dramatised. The book as a whole is dedicated to Sexton's daughter, 'who reads Hesse and drinks clam chowder' and thus appears to vacillate between the intimacy of the kind of tale that a mother might tell to a daughter as bestowal of wisdom and cautionary tale, and the positioning of the audience who still must find ways of learning the 'lessons' each tale might perhaps bring. In the poems Sexton invokes children as her implicit listener – 'all of you: / Alice, Samuel, Kurt, Eleanor, / Jane, Brian, Maryel', making of the reader or listener also a child. The dynamic of the first poem, 'The Gold Key' (*CP*, pp.223-24), sets the speaker of the poems up as

> ...a middle-aged witch, me –
> tangled on my two great arms,
> my face in a book
> and my mouth wide,
> ready to tell you a story or two.

The layers of irony working in the poems are several and dependent on the dynamic set up between an audience of different ages and the narrator who sometimes appears complicit with her audience, sometimes desires to teach them a lesson. Each fairytale is introduced by a preliminary contextualisation as if to make the fairytale relevant in some way to contemporary issues, or issues that in some way reflect on the audience's lives. The nature of transformation, between Grimm tale and contemporary fable, sets individual experience alongside archetypal ones, destabilising myths about femininity in the process. It might also be argued that the establishment of Sexton's narrator and her prefacing of the poems sets up a parodic relationship between analyst and analysand as we see Sexton's narrator becoming spectator to, and commentator on her own fantasies.

In many ways the poems of Sexton's *Transformations* offer a place of reflection and revision of powerful narratives that dramatise very real anxieties about the family and sexuality and relationships within it. Throughout her tales Sexton repeatedly undercuts the heterosexual romance. Thus we see in 'Rapunzel' that the happy union between Rapunzel and the prince is to be set against the abandonment of Mother Gothel, who dreams of Rapunzel's yellow hair, her 'heart shrunk to a pin'. The princess at the end of 'The White Snake' (*CP*, pp.229-32) gets her man only to find in marriage a kind of living death:

> They played house, little charmers,
> exceptionally well.

> So, of course,
> they were placed in a box
> and painted identically blue
> and thus passed their days
> living happily ever after –
> a kind of blue coffin,
> a kind of blue funk.
> Is it not?

Perhaps the most disturbing aspect of these transformations, however, is the actual failure to effect change. The events of the original tale may have been given a contemporary parallel (Rumpelstiltskin with a voice like Harry Truman, Snow White wearing a piece of lace, tight as an Ace bandage, for example), but the damage inherent in the relations between men and women has only been highlighted, not subverted or healed.

Sexton's need for a mediating figure, that we have seen effected in the image of the angel, in these stories becomes a narrator who is full of anger and distaste, who is implicated in all the narratives but ultimately powerless. This is seen most disturbingly in the final poem of the book, 'Briar Rose (Sleeping Beauty)' (*CP*, pp.290-95). Of all the poems Sexton's 'Briar Rose' is the most mobile in terms of the transposition and slippage between fairytale and first person account of suffering and mental illness. The narrative of the fairytale is preceded by the story of a girl 'who keeps slipping off', 'speaking with the gift of tongues /…stuck in the time machine, / suddenly two years old sucking her thumb, / as inward as a snail, / learning to talk again'. Sexton's story does not end with the prince's kiss, however, but continues to explore the illness of the princess who cannot sleep without sleeping pills and whose traumatic awakening at the kiss of the prince recalls her abuse at the hands of her father. In Sexton's poem the 'trance girl' princess can only awake to presence of her father's kiss, and the last stanza of the poem then reverts to a voice which apparently conflates the narrator's voice with the voice of the princess. Sexton's story sees her Sleeping Beauty locked in a "between" world. The prince's kiss has taken her out of her trance, but has left her instead suffering a Christlike but excruciating redemption:

> Each night I am nailed into place
> and I forget who I am.
> Daddy?
> That's another kind of prison.
> It's not the prince at all,
> but my father
> drunkenly bent over my bed,

circling the abyss like a shark,
my father thick upon me
like some sleeping jellyfish.

What voyage this, little girl?
This coming out of prison?
God help –
this life after death.

Elisabeth Bronfen argues that in the poem

Anne Sexton from the start...self-consciously addresses her role as
poet. For it is equally true of the author of these transformations that
she performs different roles, having become the medium of other voic-
es and other stories, and she lingers between past and present, crossing
psychic discontent with poetic gift. (*The Knotted Subject*, p.311)

Such 'mediumship' as Bronfen suggests perhaps also returns us too
to Stevie Smith's poem, 'Mrs Arbuthnot'. But where the voice that
tells Smith's poem works at a satirical remove to dramatise an anxiety
about the relationship between body and voice, in the *Transformations*
poems Sexton takes on that voice or voices through the voice of
her narrator, to become them at the same time as they become her.
It's interesting too in this context to remember that Edith Sitwell's
poem *The Sleeping Beauty* (1924) also dramatises this condition of
deathly removal, and that in her poem the princess is never allowed
to be woken, instead remaining in what Bruno Bettelheim, in his
reading of the original fairytales, has termed a 'state of narcissistic
withdrawal' which does not allow for 'harmony within oneself, but
also with the other'.[7]

The contrast between the poems of *Transformations* (1971) and
The Book of Folly (1972) could not be greater. By *The Book of
Folly* angels are becoming an increasing preoccupation, as Sexton's
six poem sonnet sequence 'Angels of the Love Affair' reveals.
Written in the May and June of 1971, the title of the collection is
taken from Ecclesiastes 1.17:

I gave my heart to know wisdom, and to know madness and folly: I
perceived that this also is a vexation of the spirit. For in much wis-
dom is much grief and he that increaseth knowledge increaseth sorrow.

Again Sexton is using a biblical source to present a critique of
patriarchal restrictions on femininity, but as much as she offers a
criticism of religion, she is also representing it, through the figure
of the angel, as a source of solace. The epigraph to the 'Angels of
the Love Affair' sequence asks 'angels of the love affair, do you
know that other, the dark one, that other me?' With their setting
up of Contraries, rather than binary oppositions, these poems are

influenced not only by Blake, but by the work of the Chilean poet Pablo Neruda, whom Sexton met in London in 1967, and whose work she had been reading for a considerable time.[8] With often shockingly graphic detail, that charts mental illness, bodily disease, desperation, these are poems about the horrors of the genesis of the self. The angels of the poem look both to Blake's 'The Angel that presided oer my birth'[9] and, certainly in the first poem, Neruda's 'Ode to Fire'.[10] Using prayers or invocations, Sexton maintains the binary opposition established in previous angel poems, between black and white, in a progressive exploration of the establishment of a female identity. This time, however, it is an opposition between heat and cold and red and white: images of fire and ice and red and white stitch themselves throughout the sequence, as blood, as rubies, as raspberries, a mouth, blizzards, sugar, a face. Both of these colours are represented ambiguously – for if white is representative of the clean sheets of the second sonnet, it is also the blizzard of the fifth; if red is the 'little bits of dried blood' or the blood that 'buzzes like a hornet's nest' it is also the fruit of childhood and the red mouth of the kiss. Like Blake's use of Contraries, Sexton is clearly here using opposites in order to deconstruct them in a way that is reminiscent of her deconstruction of fixed gender roles.

In 'Angels of Fire and Genitals' (*CP*, pp.332-33), the first poem of 'Angels of the Love Affair', the speaker asks

> do you know slime,
> that green mama who first forced me to sing,
> who put me first in the latrine, that pantomime
> of brown where I was beggar and she was king?

The first sonnet introduces elemental imagery, in this case fire, which is followed in the next three sonnets of 'Angels of the Love Affair' by earth and then wind and water imagery. The Angel of Fire might refer in particular to two angels: the seraph who placed burning coals on Isaiah's lips to relieve him of his silence, and Uriel, whose name means 'Fire of God' and who is thought to be the angel who stands outside the garden of Eden with his sword of flames. These two powerful images are suggestive of the connection between speech, and saying the right thing (Isaiah was punished for not naming his child the name that God had wanted) and sexuality (the angel was placed outside Eden once Adam and Eve, having eaten of the Tree of Knowledge, had been exiled). Uniting these two images at the beginning of the sequence sets up these two preoccupations between speech and sexuality, and traces the continuing anxiety Sexton has with the representation of herself as a woman who 'speaks the poem'.

Throughout the sequence there is a repetition of the word 'hole', clearly here associated with feminine sexuality. Homophonically 'hole', which is also 'whole', denotes a sense both of emptiness and completeness. The angel leaves her sense of self in a position of liminality which both refutes and embraces the female sex. This sense of liminality, of dilemma and anxiety about the positioning of the self, also potentially offers a position of power. Being neither one thing nor the other, it might be said that one also creates for oneself the possibility of continual freedom, the stasis implicit in this position also offers the continual possibility of movement. Yet the first four of the six angel sonnets end on images of stasis or petrifaction 'Mother of fire, let me stand at your devouring gate'; 'I have known the tuck-in of a child / but inside my hair waits the night I was defiled'; 'I stand in stone shoes as the world's bicycle goes by'; 'Your arms are cut and bound by bands // of wire. Your voice is out there. Your voice is strange. / There are no prayers here. Here there is no change.'

The angels seem to offer an escape from this stasis, each poem offered up to the angel like a prayer. And yet it is as if this is a prayer that will never be answered. Sexton writes in the third sonnet, 'Angel of Flight and Sleigh Bells' (*CP*, pp.333-34):

> Angel of flight, you soarer, you flapper, you floater,
> you gull that grows out of my back in the dreams I prefer,
>
> stay near. But give me the totem. Give me the shut eye
> where I stand in stone shoes as the world's bicycle goes by.

And in the sixth, 'Angel of Beach Houses and Picnics (*CP*, pp.335 -36):

> ...I hear my lungs fill and expel
> as in an operation. But I have no one left to tell.

These painful and difficult poems nevertheless seem to indicate some kind of progression from the images of abjection in the earlier poems, so that the body of the complete woman in 'Angel of Beach Houses and Picnics', sunbathing nude at the end of the sequence, offers some semblance of hope for a return to this lean, young, healthy and politicised self:

> Once I sunbathed in the buff, all brown and lean,
> watching the toy sloops go by, holding court
> for busloads of tourists. Once I called breakfast the sexiest
> meal of the day. Once I invited arrest
>
> at the peace march in Washington. Once I was young and bold
> and left hundreds of unmatched people out in the cold.

Increasingly, Sexton's experimentation with the figure of the angel allows her direct access to 'the word' of other male poets, as well as to the power of divinity itself. Sexton's use of the angel, like Blake's, gives her access to powerful images from Christian iconography. The angel acts as a powerful muse which allows her to 'consort', with all the ambiguities of pleasure and collusion that that word contains. In 'The Fallen Angels' (*CP*, pp.430-31), included in posthumously published *The Awful Rowing Towards God* (1975), the angel has become a metaphor for writing itself:

> They come on to my clean
> sheet of paper and leave a Rorschach blot.
> They do not do this to be mean,
> they do it to give me a sign
> they want me, as Aubrey Beardsley once said,
> to shove it around till something comes.
> Clumsy as I am,
> I do it.
> For I am like them –
> both saved and lost,
> tumbling downward like Humpty Dumpty
> off the alphabet.

In 'Talking to Sheep' (*CP*, pp.484-86), a poem that appeared in the posthumous collection *45 Mercy Street* (1976), and which has strong echoes of 'Consorting with Angels', Sexton seems to sum up her career as a confessional. Her poem begins:

> My life
> has appeared unclothed in court,
> detail by detail,
> death-bone witness by death-bone witness,
> and I was shamed at the verdict
> and given a cut penny
> and the entrails of a cat.
> But nevertheless I went on
> to the invisible priests,
> confessing, confessing
> through the wire of hell
> and they wet upon me in that phone booth

The father's white bone from 'Consorting with Angels' has become a death-bone. The invisible priests of the poem seem to represent a disembodied male who metamorphoses into the faceless person at the end of the telephone to whom she confesses her poems? As Kumin writes, the telephone played an important part in Sexton's writing process:

During the workshop years we began to communicate more and more
frequently by telephone…a working method which does much to train
the ear to hear line breaks, internal rhymes, intentional or unwanted
musical devices, and so forth. We did this comfortably and over such an
extended period of time that indeed when we met we were somewhat
shy of each other's poems as they appeared on the page. (*CP*, p.xxv)

Perhaps the telephone here works as symbolic umbilicus, the curly
loop which acts as life line of communication between the two
women, the poems arising out of long and intimate, and faceless
conversations almost as if taking place between priest and confes-
sor: 'Whoever God is,' explains Sexton, 'I keep making telephone
calls to him. I'm not sure that's religion. More desperation than
faith in such things.' (*Anne Sexton*, p.355). Such a comment seems
to set in flux both the idea of the speaker and listener of the lyric.
And yet we see Sexton again looking to a male poet in order to
establish a poetic self, for her poem 'Talking to Sheep' (*CP*, pp.484–
86) also appears to echo James Dickey's 'The Sheep Child' (1966)
which, while again addressing her problematic relationship with
confessional writing, sets up a dynamic between the author's own
(albeit heavily intertextually plundering) work, and that of a male
writer. Dickey (as we have heard) had been a fierce critic of Sexton's
work, and had written several searing reviews of her past collections.
The two poets met for the first time in December 1965, and formed
an intense friendship which, on Dickey's part at least, bordered on
infatuation, and Sexton is clearly addressing Dickey via his poem.
'The Sheep Child', with humour and tenderness, gives voice to
the child of a union between a man and a sheep 'this thing that's
only half / Sheep   like a woolly baby / Pickled in alcohol   because /
Those things can't live   his eyes / Are open   but you can't stand to
look'. In Sexton's poem she is representing the poetic self as much
as a hybrid as Lowell's mermaid, or Dickey's sheep, as she is a
Jesus, the good shepherd, who suffers so that others may be redeemed.
Yet writing as a woman involves a necessary mutilation of herself in
public, and she becomes a circus freak, neither woman nor man:

> *…My breasts are off me.*
> The transvestite whispering to me,
> over and over, *My legs are disappearing.*
> My mother, her voice like water,
> saying *Fish are cut out of me.*
> My father,
> his voice thrown into a cigar,
> *A marble of blood rolls into my heart.*
> My great aunt,
> her voice,

> thrown into a lost child at the freaks' circus,
> *I am the flame swallower*
> *but turn me over in bed*
> *and I am the fat lady.*

The poem's positioning of the woman poet is oddly reminiscent of the positioning of the hysteric at one of Charcot's Tuesday gatherings at the Salpêtrière in Paris, in which his "patients" were hypnotised and asked to perform a variety of tricks. Is this, Sexton seems to be questioning, her status as performer of her work? [11]

As I have argued, for Sexton the role of the woman poet and the confessional, is a difficult one. And yet the speaker of the poem – the woman who writes – appears to have few alternatives:

> It was wise, the medical men said,
> wise to cry *Baa* and be smiling into your mongoloid hood,
> while you simply tended the sheep.
> Or else to sew your lips shut
> and not let a word or a deadstone sneak out.

Clearly, reading Sexton presents a difficult case. In crying *'baa'*, rather than identifying with the mother or the father, the 'ma' or the 'pa', but also refusing its simple-mindedness, by becoming the black sheep, Sexton embraces the most difficult alternative. She attempts to speak the horror in which she finds herself, but also tries 'to push around' that horror on the page in a way which may make it relevant to others, and in particular relevant to a generation of women suffering, to various degrees, the effects of patriarchy. Increasingly for Sexton the poem is not simply an expression of suffering, but aims to purge, to disinherit her experience. Whereas Lowell remembers, and places the self he describes within the bounds of specific time and specific history, merging the boundaries between public and private experience, and while John Berryman fabularises and dramatises, for Sexton as her work progresses, the confessional works as a compulsive repetition and reenactment of suffering, which hauls trauma into the moment of writing itself. As she herself acknowledges in 'Talking to Sheep', 'I keep making statues / of my acts, carving them with my sleep'. Because of this it might be tempting to read Sexton's writing as a solely therapeutic act, a reading which indeed ties in with the direct relationship that can be drawn between her writing and her psychiatric treatment and ensuing therapy. Yet Sexton's poetic is so much more than this. Her interrogation of femininity and gender in relation to her writing, her desire to transform the horror of personal experience into wider realms – the relations between men and women, male

and female, the human and the divine – is an ambitious one that
prefigures, and, in a sense, allows much of the poetry arising from
the women's movement in the 1970s, paving the way for a poet
like Sharon Olds who in turn has influenced a new generation of
poets. Sexton's poetry does not always, perhaps, offer a clearly
positive feminist model, yet her bravery, her erratic power, suggests
a model of confession which is about the desire and impossibility
of cleansing and atonement in a secular context; it is one that works
on the borders of existence, and sometimes even on the borders of
poetry itself. Sexton's work attempts to refigure the self as a model
of power that moves her from the horror of silence to the horror
of suffering at a mythic level as well as a personal one; a suffering
which in *Powers of Horror*, Kristeva describes as

> ...the place of the subject. Where it emerges, where it is differentiated
> from chaos. An incandescent, unbearable limit between inside and out-
> side, ego and other. The initial, fleeting grasp: "suffering", "fear",
> ultimate words sighting the crest where sense topples over into the
> senses, the "intimate" into "nerves". (*Powers of Horror*, p.141)

FIG 10 (*opposite page*): Drawing by Stevie Smith
which accompanies her poem 'No Categories'

PART 2

CHAPTER FIVE

Myth, Fairytale and Feminism after the Women's Movement

In the 1970s, when I started on the circuit, I was called a poetess. Older
male poets, the Larkin generation, were both incredibly patronising and
incredibly randy. If they weren't patting you on the head, they were
patting you on the bum.
CAROL ANN DUFFY, interview with Jeanette Winterson,
The Times, 3 September 2005

A useful touchstone for thinking about feminism's relationship to
poetry is Lilian Mohin's *One Foot on the Mountain: An Anthology
of British Feminist Poetry 1969-1979* (1979).[1] The anthology includes
the work of 55 women, their work arranged in alphabetical order of
first names, each entry prefaced by a photograph, or other visual
representation, and an autobiographical statement. One of the anth-
ology's aims, Mohin writes in her introduction, was to 'seek to
describe the horror of our oppression' (*OFOTM*, p.3). Some of the
women included in the anthology – Alison Fell, Judith Kazantzis,
Gillian Allnutt, Stef Pixner, Astra, Michelene Wandor and Michèle
Roberts – went on to publish individual poetry collections, but in
the main, the poets included were writing as a form of activism
and self-expression. Claire Buck sees the anthology directly taking
'the confessional model inherited from Plath and Anne Sexton' but
'reformulating' it 'as a poetics of consciousness raising in which
women's personal experience becomes central to the poetry, but
only in so far as its status as private and individual experience is
challenged by means of a feminist political perspective'.[2] Such
feminist consciousness-raising sets up not only experience as a
source of truth, but also, Mohin suggests in her introduction (drawing
on the work of Mary Daly's *Gyn/Ecology*), locates poetic language
as a radical medium of truth:

To begin to write from within female experience is still a new task – we
are all unsure, not able to trust that our perceptions are not infiltrated by
the pervading present patriarchal culture. Challenging every assumption,
and then finding assumptions so old and deep we had not noticed them
and challenging those too, has left us with little time for disseminating
our work. This book is an attempt to remedy that. Nearly all our per-
ceptions 'are implanted through language – the all pervasive language

of myth, conveyed overtly and subliminally through religion, "great art", literature, the dogmas of professionalism, the media, grammar. Indeed deception is embedded in the very texture of the words we use, and here is where our exorcism can begin.' (*OFOTM*, p.2)

Nearly 20 years after the publication of *One Foot on the Mountain*, Vicki Feaver (born 1943), Carol Ann Duffy (born 1955) and Selima Hill (born 1945) were all writing a poetry still recognisably feminist in its politics which often sought an identification with a largely female audience, and which continued in the vein of Mohin's urge in her introduction 'to tell each other everything we can, every secret, because we know this intimate, difficult exchange makes a difference, is the process of change' (*OFOTM*, pp.5-6). All three poets, however, were publishing not with feminist presses but with mainstream publishing houses or well-distributed poetry independents (*The World's Wife* was in fact Duffy's first volume with a major commercial publisher not supported by Arts Council funding). All three had developed strategies for writing about the "intimacy" of female experience which deflected a direct relationship between the 'I' of the poet and the poetic 'I'. In the poems discussed here we see both Feaver and Duffy making use of myth and fairytale in combination with the dramatic monologue. By contrast, rather than investing in the narratives of myth and fairytale as a poetic landscape, I look at the way Selima Hill turned instead to surrealism, dream imagery and the dramatic narrative as a vehicle for those explorations.

VICKI FEAVER

As we have seen so far in this book, women's subversive use of myth and fairytale is not simply a late 20th-century phenomenon. In her *Feminism and Poetry*, Janet Montefiore cites a catalogue of work by women poets, feminist theorists and writers drawing on such narratives, including H.D.'s *Trilogy* (1944) and *Helen in Egypt* (1961), Margaret Atwood's 'Circe / Mud' sequence; Judith Kazantzis's *The Wicked Queen* (1980), Michelene Wandor's *Gardens of Eden* (1984), Anne Sexton's *Transformations* (1971), Liz Lochhead's *The Grimm Sisters* (1981), Monique Wittig's *Le Corps lesbien* (1973), Luce Irigaray's *Speculum* (1974), and a whole list of books by women novelists, including Angela Carter's *The Bloody Chamber* (1981).[3]

Both Duffy's and Feaver's poems explore ways in which such a strategy of 'revision', as Alicia Ostriker calls it, offers, as it did Smith and Sexton, an embodying narrative as well as a means of exploring a feminist politics. In her analysis of myth and fairytale in fiction by contemporary writers, Susan Sellers gives a comprehensive analysis of the history of understanding the functions of these stories. Drawing on the writing of Roland Barthes, Marina Warner and Bruno Bettelheim among others, she suggests that 'the communal process of telling and retelling a myth until it contains the input of many in a pared down form has the paradoxical effect of reflecting our experiences more powerfully than if we were to retain a profusion of personal details'.[4] As such, the mythic narrative and the fairytale, as well as the recovery of prominent and usually neglected female figures from history, offer useful vehicles for writing about the personal, distancing in the process, the teller from the tale.

Feaver's first book-length collection, now out of print, *Close Relatives*, was published by the mainstream London publishing house Secker & Warburg in 1981. The book is about family life and its disillusionments. Feaver writes:

> The strengths are the unpretentiousness and clarity of the voice and visual quality of the poems. The weakness is mostly in the form and the limitations of language (it's often just too simple) and in the use of abstract metaphors...the poems are more straightforwardly autobiographical. I think, too, they're fairly one-dimensional.[5]

Feaver's second collection of poems, *The Handless Maiden*, was published by another commercial London publisher, Jonathan Cape, in 1994 after a gap of 13 years. In both volumes Feaver explores the body as a site of power and difference in a way which connects her work with the work of women writing out of the Women's Movement in the 1970s. In *The Handless Maiden*, however, in order to move away from what she perceived as the 'straightforwardly autobiographical' and 'one-dimensional' we see Feaver turning to myth and fairytale in juxtaposition with more personal poems about women in her family and childhood, and her relationships with men. The back cover blurb to *The Handless Maiden* contains comments – all by men – which are telling in the way they position our reading of Feaver's femininity, none more so than the astute comment by Matthew Sweeney, a friend and champion of Feaver, who describes her work as 'domestic gothic', adding: 'These are powerfully distinctive women's poems that don't shut out men.' What's interesting is the way the comments on the cover attempt to validate the potentially disruptive exploration of female violence and women's bodily experiences, signalling a potential anxiety in the male reader.

While using myths and fairytale, Feaver does not always do so as a dramatic monologue; her blend of myth, fairytale and personal history offers both fertile subject-matter and a shielded position from which to write. Feaver places the narratives of female experience as part of a continuum, where the lyric 'I' and the 'I' that speaks the monologues of the volume are barely distinguishable. Although her poems are not performances in the way Stevie Smith's are, she has spoken of Smith's importance to her in becoming a poet, and the way that Smith mixed 'the magical and the practical', and the use she made of 'myths and fairytales and the collective store of female wit and fantasy'.[6] And like Smith, on whom she did doctoral research, Feaver repeatedly returns to images of death in her work. But if death for Smith came to represent a release of the self into nothingness, for Feaver death is always the product of a furious female vengeance. Feaver is also much more interested in the female body than Smith, and throughout *The Handless Maiden* images of menstrual blood, which become thematically associated with female power and metaphorical male castration, are set alongside images of spurned and murderous women. Feaver gives an insight into the way she was drawing up for herself a poetic lineage of women writers as well as to how she was thinking about the relationship between the body and the poems when she writes

> I had read Lorca's lecture on *duende*...and found exciting the idea of art originating in a power 'that has to be roused in the very cells of blood'. I made a conscious decision to try and draw on this energy in my writing...Lorca's identification of *duende* with death and suffering: 'The *duende* does not appear if it sees no possibility of death... [It] likes the edge of things, the wound.'
> But women have also identified with the need for violence and ferocity in their writing. Virginia Woolf felt that she had to 'kill' the Angel in the House before she could write uncensored. Sylvia Plath spoke of the 'blood jet' of poetry, Emily Dickinson of a 'loaded gun', and Stevie Smith, in the most violent images she could muster, of 'an explosion in the sky...a mushroom shape of terror', of the human creature 'alone in its carapace' forcing a passage out 'in splinters covered with blood'. Poetry she wrote, 'never has any kindness at all.'[7]

'The Handless Maiden' (*THM*, p.12) is a monologue which reworks a Russian version of a tale from Grimm about a blameless maiden who is the victim of her father's greed.[8] A footnote to the poem emphasises the fact that the maiden's hands grow back at the end of the narrative not because the woman has been good, as in the Grimm version, but because she saves her child. In Feaver's poem, which I quote here in full, the narrative focuses on the relationship between mother and child, and on the physicality of

that relationship. Importantly here, the child is not a son, as in the
Grimm, but a daughter:

The Handless Maiden

When all the water had run from her mouth,
and I'd rubbed her arms and legs,
and chest and belly and back,
with clumps of dried moss;
and I'd put her to sleep in a nest of grass,
and spread her dripping clothes on a bush,
and held her again – her heat passing
into my breast and shoulder,
the breath I couldn't believe in
like a tickling feather on my neck,
I let myself cry. I cried for my hands
my father cut off; for the lumpy, itching scars
of my stumps; for the silver hands –
my husband gave me – that spun and wove
but had no feeling; and for my handless arms
that let my baby drop – unwinding
from the tight swaddling cloth
as I drank from the brimming river.
And I cried for my hands that sprouted
in the red-orange mud – the hands
that write this, grasping
her curled fists.

There is an implicit connection made in the poem between the
hands of the Handless Maiden and the hands of the poet in a rare
moment of self-reflexivity when the speaker/writer of the poem
draws attention to 'the hands / that write this'. Not only has the
monologist become the poet but the poet has become the mono-
logist and we see, despite the distancing effect of the fairytale's
narrative and the use of the monologue, a close identification between
poet and poetic 'I'. In a journal entry published as part of an essay
written about her creative processes, Feaver does in fact explain
how she came to identify extremely closely with the character of
her poem: 'I am the handless maiden, writing my story with my
new grown hands,' she writes, continuing: '...the typewriter is a
distraction. I want poems to come out of my own hand, my body.'
(*How Poets Work*, p.150)

The hands which regrow in Feaver's poem become an image of
the powerless and wrongly-punished female who is regenerated in
her resuscitation of her daughter with her 'curled fists'. Hands in
the poem become a specifically female symbol for Feaver, not simply
because of their connection with the maternal, but because they
come to represent something "natural" and "authentic" by way of

juxtaposition with the silver man-made hands the Maiden's husband gives her (for which we might parallel Feaver's desire not to use a typewriter). Importantly, too, it is the bond of love between mother and daughter which sees the mother's damaged limbs restored and this restoration occurs in another feminised space in the poem, the river's 'red-orange mud' that holds echoes of the red jelly or the menstrual blood that is threaded throughout the collection.

In my earlier discussions of Edith Sitwell and Anne Sexton I touched briefly on Julia Kristeva's notion of abjection and its relation to the establishment of an 'I'. For Kristeva, 'corporeal waste, menstrual blood and excrement, or everything that is assimilated to them, from nail-parings to decay, represent – like a metaphor that would have become incarnate – the objective frailty of the symbolic order'.[9] Menstrual blood specifically

> ...stands for the danger issuing from within the identity (social or sexual); it threatens the relationship between the sexes within a social aggregate and, through internalisation, the identity of each sex in the face of sexual difference. (*Powers of Horror*, p.71)

In 'The Handless Maiden' Feaver uses the red-orange mud as symbolic both of the maiden's metaphorical castration and as an image of power in which a specifically maternal nurture restores the completeness of her body. In using bloodiness as a running trope throughout *The Handless Maiden* volume (as well, presumably, in her next collection, *The Book of Blood*), Feaver situates her writing, like the blood, on the boundaries of the body at the same time as offering a metaphorical engagement with sexual difference and a construction of the subject who narrates the poems as well perhaps as the poet who writes them. In 'Women's Blood' (*THM*, p.19; *MWP*, pp.217-18), menstruation is seen in the context of three generations of women – the granddaughter is plotting to murder the grandmother before she murders her mother, or her mother murders her. The menstrual blood is repeatedly hoarded and hidden in the poem, because it represents the narrator's 'wickedness oozing out' of her. These images of menstrual blood are also connected with other brightly coloured red and orange gelatinous substances in the volume, with the jams and jellies that are a product of women's work, or the syrups and jellies that Circe feeds Ulysses to allow him 'to keep up with a goddess' ('Circe', *THM*, pp.2-3). In 'Crab Apple Jelly' (*THM*, p.13), for example, the crab apple jelly made by the mother of the poem transforms into an image of a severed head in its muslin cloth: 'brown-stained, horrible', a pouch / of sourness, of all that went wrong / in that house of women'.

Counter to these images of abjection are images of water, often water figured at the edge of experiences. If water is seen as a purification (we remember that in the tale of the Handless Maiden the maiden was saved from the devil because of her cleanliness; even when her hands were cut off her tears served to clean her body), it also works as a site of transformation. Images of drowning and resuscitation seen in 'The Handless Maiden' recur somewhat differently in 'Lily Pond' (*THM*, p.38), in which Feaver writes of perpetrating a murder through drowning, playing with the idea of real and fantasised death, which recalls Smith's poem 'Not Waving but Drowning' in its playing with ideas of the undead dead. Feaver writes: 'Thinking of new ways to kill you / and bring you back from the dead, / I try drowning you...'

The poem reads like a straightforward lyric, and because we are given no other mythic embodiment for the speaker, it is hard for us to read the narrative of murder without in some way attributing its agency to the poet. So although the poem announces itself as fantasy and metaphor (the beloved is psychically lost and dead), there is still an ambiguity about how we allow ourselves as reader to identify with this murderous woman, and the 'I' of the poem unsettles the divide between the monologues of mythic women and the lyric poems of an apparently more personal nature. The poem ends with the speaker 'covering / your green algae-stained corpse / with a white sheet' under which she climbs with the eroticised final lines: 'thumping your chest, / breathing into your mouth'. As well as being an attempt to recover the lost love object, the poem, as its speaker breathes into the corpse's mouth, also dramatises a resuscitation of the creative self.

In 'Right Hand' (*THM*, p.23) Feaver dramatises the conflict of the relationship between the exterior and the interior body again using the image of the hand as one of creativity. The separation of the hand's will from the speaker's becomes allied with the acts of writing poetry itself. The right hand of the poem is a kind of phallic companion and acts as a counter to the handlessness of the maiden: 'Ever since, in an act of reckless / middle-age, I broke my wrist / learning to skate, my right hand // refuses to sleep with me.' In its subtle allusions to hands in other literary texts – Auden's poem 'As I walked out one Evening' and the scene in Hardy's *Tess of the d'Urbervilles* in which Tess is washing up – the hand becomes a symbol for the self who writes, and sleeps, with the literary tradition.

Three other poems in the collection draw on iconic female figures, the monologue 'Circe' (the only woman from myth), and poems on two women of prominence in the Jewish tradition, 'Judith'

(*THM*, p.41), another monologue, and 'Esther' (*THM*, p.42), whose
story is written in the third person. Circe, the enchantress from the
Odyssey who turns Odysseus's men into pigs, and seduces Odysseus
for a year, holding him captive on her magical island, is figured as
a woman who 'always falls for cold men' and who grieves for the
loss of her lover. Judith also mourns for her lost husband, but
rather than giving up her powers at the end of the poem, enacts a
murder. The figure of Judith, from the Old Testament Apocrypha,
is one which has been frequently represented in art and literature,
and, as Margarita Stocker has commented in her book-length study
of Judith, her 'story has multiple meanings and many faces, each
reflecting something to our culture'.[10] Judith is connected with other
biblical female icons, but as Stocker points out, where Salome and
Delilah, who shears off Samson's hair, are *femmes fatales*, Esther is
a figure who also foreshadows the iconography of the Virgin Mary,
although she is less powerful than Judith in her position as 'a
domesticated consort and trophy wife' (*Judith, Sexual Warrior*, p.12).

Stocker's analysis of the figure of Judith is comprehensive and
fascinating. Initially she argues that 'the book of Judith was delib-
erately written as an exemplary moral tale...a deliberately constructed
consoling story written to address the concerns of the Jewish people
in the 2nd century BC after the Babylonian captivity', and that '[a]t
one level, the Book is a parable of what it means to be Jewish'
(*Judith, Sexual Warrior*, p.5). In reflecting cultural concerns, how-
ever, Judith in the 16th century was, for example, connected with
Elizabeth I, as a way of stressing her militancy and celibacy, and
'[d]uring the early modern age – between 1500 and 1800 – Judith's
icon became a sign of death inextricably linked with rituals and
power. Her myth was a template for the primitive rituals underlying
public spectacles that were designed to manifest the power of the
state' (*Judith, Sexual Warrior*, p.87). Freud, in his use of the Judith
tale, sees her beheading of Holofernes as a symbolic castration, but
as Stocker points out, where the story of Oedipus 'mythologises
Western culture's central convictions about family, sex and power...
Judith's deploys them in order to ultimately contest them' (*Judith,
Sexual Warrior*, p.21).

Feaver's own description of the processes by which she wrote
'Judith' are illuminating here in terms of the way in which they
reveal the importance of her own identification with the story, its
contestation of power relations, and in particular how she felt her-
self "becoming" the character about whom she was writing:

> I kept asking myself questions in my notebook and trying to answer
> them. 'How can a woman be capable of violence? How be the opposite

of everything she'd been brought up to be? What is the motive? Rage?
What rage? The rage of grief.' I tried to imagine Judith's state of mind,
rather like an actress does to get into a part. ('She has to keep him
believing that she's fallen in love with him, that she's going to let him
sleep with her – she has to bring out his best instincts; and in that
moment when she does, she almost falls in love with him'...'I think she
must have come to love the man she was going to kill, or she could not
have done it.') In the end I think I almost became Judith; though I was
obviously ambivalent about this close personal identification because the
early drafts of the poem veer between a first person voice and a safe,
more distant, third person narration... It is obvious to me now that the
poem was a vehicle for the grief and rage I was feeling when I wrote
it. The story is Judith's but the emotions are mine.[11]

Feaver's use of the story follows the narrative from the point at
which Judith enters Holofernes' tent, reflecting back on the death
of her husband during the harvest. The murder of Holofernes is
seen against a backdrop of her mourning her husband, and, when
seeing the warrior Holofernes, her desire

> to lie
> sheltered and safe in a warrior's
> fumy sweat, under the emerald stars
> of his purple and gold canopy,
> to melt like a sweet on his tongue
> to nothing.

Ruth Padel has suggested that here the poem reverses the conven-
tions of the male love poem in which the male 'I' of the poem
watches and eroticises a woman. In choosing to remain with the
first person and to make the poem a monologue, Feaver establishes
a clear and owned self in the poem to voice that desire 'to melt like
a sweet on his tongue'. There is also a poetic justice in the fact that
the murder Judith enacts becomes domestic in its configuration as
she slices off the head of Holofernes as she might cut off the head
of a fish.

The poem asks us to rethink the configuration of an iconic woman;
contrastingly, 'Esther' shows another dimension to Feaver's pre-
occupation with the severing of body parts, and the abject body
(Judith needed to roll 'in the ash of the fire / just to be touched
and dirtied / by something' to assuage her sense of emptiness). In
'Esther' the heroic Jewish queen cuts off her own hair, filled as it
is with the smell and semen of her lover, and, making a paste fills
the orifices of her body with it:

> She mixes a paste
> of hair and stinking mud, stuffs
> her ears, mouth, the crevice

> in her body's soft rock
> he turned inside-out
> like a purse, the tide
> in her rising, spilling over
> like boiling mare's milk.

The ambiguities of the poem's final five lines create an interesting intersection between images of male and female. Esther has been turned 'inside out', and once again we see an image of a woman made powerful – even phallic – through her suffering. The tide of anger which rises like milk also mimics an ejaculation as Esther becomes at once a male and female body: the penis which ejaculates the mother's milk. Feaver writes:

> I came to want to write about her because of Hardy's quote…in *Jude*… 'And she humbled her body greatly, and all the places of her joy she filled with her torn hair'…I wouldn't think it one of my best poems: but it connected with my sense of being sexually abandoned, with an almost witch-like ritual of abasement/power.[12]

Feaver's allusion to Sue Bridehead here in relation to the poem is an interesting one, representing as she does a woman in denial of her own physicality and sexuality, the 'intellectualised, emancipated, bundle of nerves', who is described in terms of a repression of femininity: 'that which was female in her she wanted to consume within the male force.' In Feaver's poem that male force is reinscribed in the poem as an image of the body's mutation.

In both 'Judith' and 'Esther' Feaver is rethinking ways in which women respond to male sexuality, and resisting narratives of heterosexual romance in both the first and third person. In an essay on the work of Elizabeth Bishop, Feaver praises Bishop's ability to 'blur the boundaries of male and female space and of masculine and feminine characteristics and subvert phallocentric divisions of gender'.[13] An exploration of such gender boundaries is at heart of her poem 'Hemingway's Hat' (*MWP*, pp.220-21), which also invokes Bishop as a touchstone to its 'transvestite twist'. Although 'Hemingway's Hat' is not really classifiable as a dramatic monologue, its speaker tries on the roles of gender much as the poet might in the monologue. Rather than using fairytale and myth, the drama played out in the poem is focused through the iconic figure of Ernest Hemingway as it attempts to deconstruct cultural myths and constructions of masculinity. Taking Hemingway as a focal point for the poem is interesting both in its allusion to Hemingway's own creation of himself as 'Papa', and to his work, much of which, particularly in the posthumously published work, explores to some degree notions of male and female role-play, set against the backdrop of war.

In the poem Feaver explores the social conflicts inherent in stereotypical masculine and feminine behaviour. Three generations of men are represented. Hemingway, a literary father who fought in the First World War and in the Spanish Civil War, and who was on one of the tanks which liberated Paris and also wrote accounts of these events; an 'actual' father who fought in Burma; and a male lover who has fought in or documented events in Vietnam, a war which has come to represent a crisis of American masculinity.[14] The poem questions the cultural displays of masculinity as represented by Hemingway, his peaked cap a symbol of patriarchal authority. On the head of a man this hat makes the male character look 'dashing, nerveless'; on the head of the woman speaker, it makes her 'feel / like a Shakespearean heroine / dressed as and played by a boy'. The speaker's image of herself as a woman playing a boy who plays a girl sees Feaver playing essentialist notions of gender, and suggesting its performative nature. While the men of the poem suffer in their adoption of socially and culturally acceptable models of masculinity, the woman speaker who has 'tried' to be a son by cutting her hair, subsequently also participates in a performance of femininity:

> Then, while you raced stolen cars
> for the thrill, I changed myself
> into a girl – stilettos, stiff
> nylon petticoats, a perm.

In the final two stanzas of the poem the changing of hats becomes a metaphor for a release from limiting gender roles, and sees Feaver alluding to Elizabeth Bishop's poem 'Exchanging Hats'[15] in her 'game of changing hats'. In Feaver's poem the sexual act is one in which the participants 'float free' of prescribed gender roles just as the dead rise 'above the field of battle' at Plei Mei. At the end of the poem male and female share the penis, 'a glistening pillar / sliding between us' as making love they become neither male or female. The poem ends by attributing to the man 'a woman's tenderness', an ironic comment and salutary reminder of the ways in which gender ascriptions define human acts. If fixed gender roles have dissolved in the bedroom, outside the bedroom gender roles and the ways in which we describe behaviour are still so much a part of our culture that the swapping which takes place does so within a framework of stereotypical descriptions of femininity, creating in the telling of this 'woman's tenderness' an added poignancy.

CAROL ANN DUFFY

These myths going round, these legends, fairytales,
I'll put them straight; so when you stare
into my face – Helen's face, Cleopatra's,
Queen of Sheba's, Juliet's – then deeper,
gaze into my eyes – Nefertiti's, Mona Lisa's,
Garbo's eyes – think again.[16]

CAROL ANN DUFFY

As I have discussed elsewhere, the dramatic monologue has perhaps appealed to women because of the way it emphasises an artificiality that women already sense in constructions of their own subjectivity.[17] Whereas all of Feaver's monologues are in the voices of women from myth or fairytale or history, it's notable that Carol Ann Duffy moves between genders in her early monologues, where she identifies with "ordinary" people, before finally settling in *The World's Wife* (1999) on a book-length collection of iconic female monologists from myth and fairytales. As a 'putting straight', a revisionary strategy of recasting myth, Duffy's women monologists are frequently powerful, vengeful women whose assertiveness, violence and aggression parodies stereotypes of male behaviour.

Like Feaver's monologues, Duffy's work both as a way of identifying with other women's experience, and as vehicle for exploring her own feelings through a persona that splits off the poet from the 'I' of the poem. However, whereas Feaver uses the narratives and lives of female characters as a way of exploring aspects of her own psychology, Duffy uses the stories in tangent with autobiographical narratives, so that myth and fairytale become ways of reading and mythologising her own life, just as they offer a personal and collective fantasy of avenging through violence male power and its prohibitions. Strikingly, Duffy is much less interested in *The World's Wife* than in her previous work in the "individual case"; rather we find her looking to voice collective feelings about the way women relate to men, exposing that 'shared horror' Mohin talks about in her anthology's introduction. By the late 1990s, however, Duffy's poems are as much shared secrets and fantasies as they are shared jokes at the expense of men, and their cruelty is always thrown into relief by their humour.

The poems of *The World's Wife* split between tales of women who already have named positions of their own in narratives – Eurydice, Circe, Salome, Medusa, Delilah, for example – and the creation of new ways into myths, fairytales and history through characters who are the wives of famous husbands whose lives they expose and demythologise. The poems frequently bring mythic experience to the level of personal experience. 'Thetis', for example, is a poem spoken in the voice of the shapeshifting goddess of war (whom Stevie Smith compares to poetry itself, and about whom Jo Shapcott also has a poem). Here the speaker of the monologue is always at risk from dangerous men. The speaker concludes

> So I changed, I learned,
> turned inside out – or that's
> how it felt when the child burst out.

Here we see how mythical shapeshifting runs in parallel to the shapeshifting of a woman's pregnancy: the mythical woman has become the ordinary woman doing the extraordinary thing of child-birth. A similar strategy can be seen at work in 'Salome' (*TWW*, pp.56-57) where we are given a narrative of 'the morning after the night before' which works to give a kind of realist account of a hangover, and the surprise of finding a man whose name you don't know in your bed. But then, as in 'Thetis', the narrative twists so that women who might have identified with the story in their recognition of the behaviour, or their fantasy about behaving in such a way, then become implicated in the fact that Salome is not the world-weary apologist she initially presents herself as. For actually the head on the pillow is *only* a head:

> In the mirror, I saw my eyes glitter.
> I flung back the sticky red sheets,
> and there, like I said – and ain't life a bitch –
> was his head on a platter.

The monologue ties into all sorts of contemporary "myths" about the dangerousness of female sexuality, and the still-resonant taboos around female promiscuity. It also carries with it a sense of revenge, of turning the tables for the women in history and fiction who have been murdered by men, or punished for their excessive sexuality. Duffy's 'Salome' and Feaver's poem 'Judith', though both about murderous women, are, however, very different in the responses they evoke. The implication in Duffy's tale is that Salome has committed the murder herself, whereas in the biblical story the severing of John the Baptist's head is only caused by Salome. Judith, however, has always been the murderer, and she does so in the context of war. Whereas Feaver is exploring the ways in which such a murder as Judith's might be moral, as well as in other ways using the poem as a way of talking about grief and loss, Duffy simply, it seems, wants to use Salome as a figure of jubilant and amoral power. So whereas in an earlier monologue, 'Psychopath'

(1987), written in the voice of a male killer, Duffy was interested
in her character's individual psychology and at pains to present
his behaviour as arising from painful childhood experiences, and
wider patriarchal pressures on men, the Salome monologue un-
apologetically celebrates a behaviour which transgresses moral,
social and legal codes. Her behaviour is in effect licensed by its
mythic quality.

'Mrs Tiresias' (*TWW*, pp.14–17) sees Duffy addressing explicitly
the relationship between gender and the body, exploring the per-
formances which make up gender, and also, potentially, decon-
structing them. Tiresias was the man, in Greek myth, who lived for
seven years as a woman and seven years as a man. In Sophocles'
Oedipus he is famously the blind seer who foretells the downfall of
Oedipus; in Eliot's *The Waste Land*, Tiresias is the visionary 'throb-
bing between two lives' who has, as both man and woman, 'fore-
suffered all / Enacted on this same divan or bed'. In her poem Duffy
uses the character of Tiresias's wife to narrate the tale of a man
who is mysteriously transformed into a woman when he returns
from a morning walk. It is for Mrs Tiresias to teach him feminin-
ity, for although Tiresias has a woman's body, he is not able to
assume femininity in some "natural" way:

> …at first I tried to be kind;
> blow-drying his hair till he learnt how to do it himself,
> lending him clothes till he started to shop for his own,
> sisterly, holding his soft new shape in my arms all night.

We learn, too, from Mrs Tiresias that although he becomes an expert
in women's issues, Tiresias remains resolutely conservative in his
sexuality. He considers himself a heterosexual male even when he
has lost his male body. The relationship between husband and
wife becomes chaste once he is transformed. Mrs Tiresias 'put it
about that he was a twin'. Tiresias won't kiss his wife in public
anymore because he doesn't want to be considered lesbian; but
neither, Mrs Tiresias suggests, even though he goes about 'on the
arms of powerful men', would there be any sexual relations with
men: she 'knew for sure / there'd be nothing of *that* / going on'.

Tiresias's female body and essential inner maleness upholds the
cultural taboo of lesbianism which could be enacted in the public
sphere with his legal wife. He also upholds the taboo of male homo-
sexuality, which, in spite of his exterior female body, as an inner
male would also offend or repulse him. All this, of course, is played
to great humour, but at the end of the poem Tiresias meets his wife
again, this time with her new female lover at 'a glittering ball',

and the two characters – the man masquerading as a woman in a woman's body – and the woman who is a lesbian, shake hands:

> ...I noticed then his hands, her hands,
> the clash of their sparkling rings and their painted nails.

The bodies of both women are the same, and yet one is not an "authentic" woman. Both women represent their femininity, however, in terms which, with their adorned hands, highlights the artificiality of femininity. In his masquerade, it is only, and crucially, the female voice which Tiresias cannot get right. It is 'A cling-peach slithering out from its tin', a syrupy, processed fruit which is contrasted with the fruit of his wife's lips when she makes love with her girlfriend. What then is Duffy saying here about the relationship between anatomy and gender? And how does that relate to her own constructing of monologues as a woman poet, and her attempt to "get right" a male voice.

Throughout 'Mrs Tiresias', Tiresias is represented by the narrator as a man in a female body. His masculinity is constituted by his clothes as well as by his ridiculous actions. Firstly, as a man, this involves his writing letters to *The Times*. When he is a woman he continues to write letters, not to announce as formerly having heard the first cuckoo, but to demand 'full-paid menstrual leave twelve weeks per year'. Unlike Foucault's Herculine, the hermaphrodite who, with his indeterminate sex and confused gender, enjoys 'a multiplicity of pleasures' (*Gender Trouble*, p.97), or Woolf's Orlando who, having become a woman, enjoys her relationships with men, Tiresias is unable to reconcile male inner feelings with the female surface of the body. Nor has Tiresias's change from male to female resulted in any change from his selfish and self-regarding behaviour, behaviour Duffy implicitly posits as "masculine".

The acknowledgement at the end of the poem of the similarity between the lesbian and the masquerading woman can be read several ways, some more positively than others. Duffy's narrator seems to be arguing for an essential masculinity or femininity until the end of the poem when questions about those gender identities get thrown open in the similarity of the surface bodies of the husband and the lover. In this twist Duffy seems to be suggesting that all gender is, as Judith Butler has argued, 'an act...a performance that is repeated...a re-enactment and reexperiencing of a set of meanings already socially established' (*Gender Trouble*, p.140). But it's hard to pin down exactly the poem's political intention here. Is Mrs Tiresias pondering, for example, whether her husband's capacity for exploitative and "false" behaviour is not intrinsically

male but is also a capacity her lover has as a woman? In drawing a
parallel between the two women, is she offering a critique of women's
display of femininity which can be seen as a collusion with patri-
archy's subjection of women? Butler's analysis of drag is useful here:

> The performance of drag plays upon the distinction between the anatomy
> of the performer and the gender that is being performed. But we are
> actually in the presence of three contingent dimensions of significant
> corporeality: anatomical sex, gender identity, and gender performance. If
> the anatomy of the performer is already distinct from the gender of the
> performer, and both of those are distinct from the gender of the per-
> formance, then the performance suggests a dissonance not only between
> sex and performance, but sex and gender, and gender and performance.
> As much as drag creates a unified picture of "woman" (what its critics
> often oppose), it also reveals the distinctness of those aspects of gen-
> dered experience which are falsely naturalised as a unity through the
> regulatory fiction of heterosexual coherence. *In imitating gender, drag
> implicitly reveals the imitative structure of gender itself – as well as its
> contingency*...we see sex and gender denaturalised by means of a per-
> formance which avows their distinctiveness and dramatises the cultural
> mechanism of their fabricated unity. (*Gender Trouble*, pp.137-38)

Tiresias is not of course in drag in the world in which he inhabits,
living as a woman, because his physical body has changed from
male to female, but to all intents and purposes the poem positions
him to the reader, who sees only his masquerading of femininity,
as a man in drag. Even though, or perhaps because Tiresias's
anatomy has changed, there is no "dissonance" between sex and
performance in Tiresias's performance of gender.

It's especially hard to fully tease out the implications of that
final identification between authentic and inauthentic woman at
the end of the poem because of the monologue's ability to present
us with a wholly unreliable narrator. When Duffy's poems are
written in the voice of a man, there is often an internal dialogue
between the voice of the speaker and another voice which we
identify as the voice of the female poet. In *The World's Wife*, how-
ever, the gap between the voice of the poet and the monologist
has been narrowed. It can't be eliminated because of the other
narrative structures, the myth, fairytale, history, which it wants to
draw on as a strategy of collective experience with other women.
And anyway, the whole point of the dramatic monologue is in set-
ting up a text that removes the poet from the poetic 'I'. What is
crucial in reading the poem is that the bodily presence of the nar-
rator remains ungendered – she mentions the backs of her knees,
her gritted teeth, her lips and her neck, but *her* performance of
femininity is never actively displayed. At the end of the poem she

becomes spectator to the femininity of her past and present lovers, a femininity which in some way is alien to her, and which implicitly sets both narrator, and by implication, the poet, up at a remove from such performances, as neither masculine or feminine. Yet rather than gleefully deconstructing fixed notions of gender identity for all its characters, as Woolf's *Orlando* arguably does, Duffy's poem appears to offer its readers in the voice of the monologist, a fixed and stable femininity, which, while not dependent on anatomy, is dependent on notions of an interior essence, even as it makes jokes about the ridiculousness of Tiresias's sense of a fixed interior masculinity.

Throughout *The World's Wife* volume men are figured as boring, selfish, faithless "jerks" and Duffy treads a difficult line between a crude anti-male perspective and the adoption of irony and a know-ingness that arises from a postfeminist awareness that social and cultural conditions (for some women at least) have, since the 1970s, changed radically.[18] Because of these changes, the audience of Duffy's poems are being asked and allowed to laugh at male behaviour, and the poems carry less of a sense of consciousness-raising, of a rallying cry for change, working instead as poems which aim to draw a sense of recognition from readers (who are prompted to exclaim *Men!*), and to locate all impetus for change in the realm of fantasy. This is not a criticism of the poems as such, but the comic-grotesque figures in *The World's Wife* who murder, lampoon and piss, deliberately function very differently from Feaver's more subtly delineated explorations of an individual psyche. Duffy's 'Circe' (*TWW*, pp.47-48), for example, is a monologue which is triumphant in its dismissal of men, and its discussion of the vari-ous ways to cook pig. The pigs in the poem are not just Ulysses' men whom Circle turned into pigs, but the "male chauvinist pigs" of the contemporary world. Circe's devouring of pork in the poem is highly sexualised, and there is a strong sense that this symbolic eating of men is revenge for their sexual mistreatment of women when she exclaims: 'When the heart of a pig has hardened, dice it small':

> One way or another, all pigs have been mine –
> under my thumb, the bristling, salty skin of their backs,
> in my nostrils here, their yobby, porky colognes.

The double embodiment provided by both myth and fairytale and the monologue clearly offers Duffy safe ground for the exploration – however parodically – of the most explicit, and only, anti-male politics in her most popular work to date.

'Mrs Beast' (*TWW*, pp.72-73), the penultimate poem in the book, stages a poker game in which, in a kind of gothic fancy dress, a smoking trail of iconic women from the near and distant as well as mythic past appear. It is in this poem that Duffy suggests her motivation for the poems, when, towards the end of the poem Mrs Beast prays

> thumbing my pearls, the tears of Mary, one by one,
> like a rosary – words for the lost, the captive beautiful,
> the wives, those less fortunate than we.

Avril Horner has argued that *The World's Wife* moves in its first poem, 'Little Red-Cap' (*TWW*, pp.3-4), to a rejection of 'heterosexuality in pursuit of poetic female integrity, to the final poem 'Demeter' (*TWW*, p.76), which 'celebrates the mother-daughter bond and, by implication, a community of women'.[19] Duffy's seventh collection, *Rapture*,[20] is the first of her books to fully explore a lesbian sexuality and to embody a female lover in any sustained way (frequently her love lyrics are androgynous in their gendering). *Rapture* is also her first collection not to include dramatic monologues. Perhaps because of this, *Rapture* is suffused with anxiety about the representation of both the narrator's as well as the beloved's body, which later appears more as absence than presence in the sequence of 52 poems, suggesting that for Duffy such "naked" use of the lyric must still carry with it some kind of protective distance. In 'You' (*Rapture*, p.1), the beloved lies 'on the bed, like a gift, like a touchable dream', and by the end of the love affair in 'Art' (*Rapture*, p.60), the lover's body as well as the lover exist only in language:

> Only art now – our bodies, brushstroke, pigment, motif;
> our story, figment, suspension of disbelief;
> the thrum of our blood, percussion;
> chords, minor, for the music of our grief.

As part of the book's launch, Duffy has been performing the poems with a jazz group, with some of the poems set to music and sung by Eliana Tomkins. If this brings us back to the performances of Anne Sexton in the 1970s – although, unlike Sexton's, in these performances Duffy's readings remain discretely separate from the musical versions – it does so in a way which suggests the need for a device to stand in the place of the monologue's protective distancing, highlighting the fact that the poems are a performance and not to be readily identified with the 'I' who is linked to the poet's body.

SELIMA HILL

> I wanted to write something like 'the first person narrator is not neces-
> sarily the same as,' and I got myself into terrible tangles. In the end
> Andrew [Motion, then her editor] said 'well, you're just drawing attention
> to it more than anything. You can't disclaim something just by dis-
> claiming it really!' [21]

On at least two occasions in interview in the last 15 years, Selima
Hill has described herself as having 'a man's brain in a woman's
body';[22] her sense of herself as a poet thus depends upon a gen-
dering which draws on stereotypical divisions between masculinity
and femininity and the setting up of a gendered conflict between the
mind and the body. Such a construction perhaps feeds into her
acute anxieties about the relationship between the construction of
her poetic 'I' and its relation to her own bodily self. In the devel-
opment of Hill's work there is an increasing use of surrealist imagery
that she uses to deflect and dramatise anxieties about her own status
as both woman and woman poet. Like Feaver, Hill writes explicitly
about the female body but her use of surrealism's extravagant per-
formances depends not on myth or fairytales, but works increasingly
through the construction of selves through extended narratives
and through an endless replication of dream images which are set
up to display and shield the psyche. Like Sitwell, Hill has stated
that she 'hates' the surrealists, and although Sitwell was to rather
sheepishly admit that when she wrote she did so as a kind of
automatic writing, Hill is the most identifiably surrealist of all the
women I discuss in this book. Her aesthetic increasingly depends
on the creation of visually provocative imagery and an associative
way of linking those images, techniques which are also, if not in
their process, then in their effect, very much allied to the surrender
to the unconscious of automatic writing.

In the 'Manifesto of Surrealism' of 1924, André Breton defines
surrealism in the following way:

> SURREALISM, *n.* Psychic automatism in its pure state, by which one
> proposes to express – verbally, by means of the written word, or in
> any other manner – the actual functioning of thought. Dictated by
> thought, in the absence of any control exercised by reason, exempt
> form any aesthetic or moral concern.

> ENCYCLOPEDIA. *Philosophy.* Surrealism is based on the belief in the
> superior reality of certain forms of previously neglected associations, in
> the omnipotence of dream, in the disinterested play of thought. It tends
> to ruin once and for all all other psychic mechanisms and to substitute
> itself for them in solving all the principal problems of life.[23]

Not only then does surrealism operate outside aesthetic considera-
tion and restrictions, but being purportedly outside literary and
artistic traditions, it also acts as an assault on tradition. In its prizing
of the dream – repressed images, memories, and thoughts which
are then displaced and condensed – it also, and importantly for
the woman poet, seems to offer a coded place from which to
work. Surrealism's construction of the feminine reveals its strongest
roots in the early psychiatric experiments of Charcot and Janet
with hysterical women at the Salpêtrière. For the surrealists, the
hysterics' embodiment and re-membering of trauma was seen not
as a 'pathological condition' but as a 'supreme form of expression',
a 'mental state that is more or less irreducible and that is charac-
terised by the subversion of the relations between the subject and
the world of morality, with which it takes issue'.[24] The surrealists
revered the body as a means of expression: the Dadaist Arthur
Cravan declared as early as 1914 that 'genius is the extravagant
manifestation of the body'.[25] In *Clair de Terre*, published in 1923,
Breton's female muse is invoked, objectified and transformed
through his desire as her body becomes language: 'If only in the
depths of the Opera two breasts dazzlingly clear / would ornament
the word love with the most marvellously living letter.'[26]

   This idea of the body working as an instrument against repres-
sion through non-verbal expression figures strongly in the work of
the theorist Hélène Cixous. In Cixous' writings the body is fêted
as emancipatory, and her aesthetics of *écriture féminine* seem inti-
mately bound up with surrealist desires to assimilate neglected or
repressed "feminine" qualities, with the female body figured as
carnivalesque in its subversive potential. In a collaborative work,
The Newly Born Woman, Cixous writes, with Catherine Clément,
how 'the sorceress and the hysteric manifest the festival of their
bodies, do impossible flips, making it possible to see what cannot
be represented, figures of inversion'.[27] Famously Cixous and Clément
cite the example of Dora, on whom Freud wrote his case history,
constructing the hysterical woman as an exemplary female figure
and urging a return to the body as a way of unleashing desire:

> At first, individually, on two separate levels: – woman, writing herself,
> will go back to this body that has been worse than confiscated, a body
> replaced with a disturbing stranger, sick or dead, who so often is a bad
> influence, the cause and place of inhibitions. By censoring the body,
> breath and speech are censored at the same time…
>   Write yourself: your body must make itself heard. Then the huge
> resources of the unconscious will burst out. Finally, the inexhaustible
> feminine Imaginary is going to be deployed. (*The Newly Born Woman*,
> p.97)

Like Cixous – and, as Woolf suggests, the woman writer who kills
the angel must – Hill seems in the poems to be putting the female
body at the centre of her work. In her first collection, *Saying Hello
at the Station* (1984),[28] rather than using surreal images, Hill depends
more frequently on imagery from ancient Egypt. In 'Questioning
Mr Bonnet' (*THIBD*, pp.12-13; *MWP*, pp.237-38), this imagery –
of Thoth, 'on a lotus flower, the blue baboon', the inventor of
writing, and his nine baboon musicians – becomes set up in a
dynamic that sees her identifying anxieties about the value of her
own writing as she waits the judgement of the (male) Egyptian god:

> Mr Bonnet, did you meet him, and will I,
> when I step on board the silver barque?
> Will he be saying *Pleased to meet you,*
> *Mrs Hill, and how's the writing going?*
> as we descend the corridors of night
> into the Judgment Hall. Will he pat me
> on the shoulder with his cracked
> avuncular hand and, tucking my book
> inside his sky-blue cape, will he wink
> before he picks his tail up and climbs
> onto his special perch above the scales?

However, by Hill's third collection, *The Accumulation of Small
Acts of Kindness* (1989), we see her moving from the self-contained
lyric to poems which would subsequently contain a narrative line,
or work as accumulated fragments which work as meditations on a
single theme. *The Accum-ulation* tells the story of a young woman
with schizophrenia who is in a psychiatric hospital and her eventual
move towards recovery and release. Drawing on Hill's own experi-
ences of a breakdown as well as time spent visiting the Maudsley
Hospital in South London where she was a volunteer, the poem
jostles with the debris of language, fragments of remembered texts
and phrases, in its attempt to represent the associative thinking of
schizophrenia, and remains the most experimental of her works.
The sheer energy at which the images are thrown out at the reader,
the shifts in tempo, the way in which the patient's thoughts and
the comments of those who surround her are juxtaposed, shows
the processes through which the patient, alienated from herself and
disoriented, gets to know herself, body and voice, in language:

> See me see me see me in the garden.
> I'm made of ants.
> Whose voice is that?
> *It's hers.*
> Feel between my legs two lips like lollies,
> or like a blood-hound on the verge of tears.
>   (*THIBD*, p.76; *MWP*, p.240)

As an attempt at fictionalised autobiography the poem carried an initial disclaimer. The first section was originally written in a fully worked out and crackable code, a code which Hill has spoken of as wishing she had retained.[29] This vacillation in Hill's work between fear of exposure of the self and its dramatic and dramatised expression is a tension that runs throughout her work.

Hill's anxieties about her bodily identification with the poetic voice become more obviously solved in *A Little Book of Meat* (1993).[30] There she establishes a more obviously fictionalised narrative framework which holds together a series of interlinked lyrics which form an atemporal, non-linear exploration of a young woman's consciousness. The volume begins by acknowledging the debt of Thomas Merton, Thich Nhat Hanh and Flannery O'Connor, while the "disclaimer" on the back cover tells us that the poems are

> Written in the voice of a woman growing up on a remote cattle farm with her mother, a devout Catholic, and her much-loved assortment of animals. She is already nearly thirty, knows little of the outside world, and walks with a slight limp. One day a stranger calls, a travelling slaughterman...

This scenario draws its inspiration, at least in part, from the life of Flannery O'Connor, who from the early 1950s to her premature death in 1964, lived with her mother on a dairy farm. The sequence addresses the nature of desire as an irresistible force which cannot be controlled by religious structures. In 'Desire's a Desire' (*LBOM*, p.59), the narrator cannot 'eat or sleep', her 'only desire's a desire / to be free from desire':

> It taunts me
> like the muzzle of a gun;
> it sinks into my soul like chilled honey
> packed into the depths of treacherous wounds;
> it wraps me up in cold green sheets
> like Indian squaws
> who wrap their babies in the soft green sheaths of irises
> that smell of starch...

Images of penetration and enclosure, the interior and exterior body, the penis and the vagina, are placed in relation to each other but interact rather than oppose each other. As Ian Gregson points out

> Characteristically in those lines the exotic (Indian squaws) and the domestic (the smell of starch) are juxtaposed in a way that produces disorientation sharpened by the extent to which the predominant womb/enclosure references are paradoxically linked to coldness...sexual longing [is] implied both by images from traditional love poetry (honey, wounds, flowers) and by the Freudian genital symbolism (the gun, the sheaths)[31]

'Do It Again' (*LBOM*, p.60) dramatises anxieties about the way in which women are trapped in prescriptive female roles which demand that they be silent, neat and beautiful, and which do not allow them to express bodily desires. The narrator's desire, which is figured as a product of the interior body, contrasts with "appropriate" forms of female desire, which are bleached, sanitised, and inhumane, and which depend on the power of attraction of the exterior body:

> but all we're allowed's anxiety like fishbones
> lodged in our throats
> as beauty parlours hum;
> all we're allowed is having pretty faces
> and cold and glittery hearts like water-ices.
> Mine's more like a centrally-heated boiler-room
> evil and warm;
> like kidneys on a plate.
>
> But all we're allowed's the dry hum of the driers;
> all we're allowed's one word,
> like darkness
> *No.*

The shock of these images comes again from the juxtaposition of temperatures and textures – 'the glittery hearts like water-ices' – dissolving, appetising, and the 'kidneys on a plate', which by contrast are 'evil and warm', both animal and human, and wholly unappetising.

In 'Being a Wife', from her collection *Aeroplanes of the World* (1994) (*THIBD*, p.92), Hill addresses the way in which women take on social roles in a masquerade of identity as the poem's speaker remembers a formative sexual experience, 'The body I remember feeling as big as America in, / the thighs so far away / his hand had to ride in an aeroplane to get there' and 'the feeling of being on the edge of something'. This early sexual experience is 'somehow authentic and right', and the poem concludes with lines which suggest that gendered roles are a performance and that there is a core female self which can be recovered:

> Being a wife is like acting being a wife,
> and the me that was her with him in the past is still me.

Although Hill's anxiety about the role of woman can be as explicitly recorded in this poem, elsewhere in the collection she still continues to use surrealism as a way of signalling rather than baldly stating her anxiety. In 'The Villa' (*THIBD*, p.142) for example, her female protagonist escapes from a male domain of sadism to a female (or perhaps simply feminised) lover, 'breathing gently / like a giant flower / smelling of custard / being stirred, / and licked':

> His famous cock
> that he goes on about's
> about as much fun
> as a frozen lamb,
> and I just ran away
> across the heath
> one night;
> I left the moonlit villa
> far behind,
> the helicopters, chainsaws,
> parrots, knives,
> and little maids who specialise
> (he gives them sweets)
> in screaming
> at the parrots...

These are not monologues, but the lyric 'I' in these poems is sent to a realm at a remove from the poet's own. The images mix the domestic with the sexual, the gestures towards the romantic or romanticised (the heath, the moonlit villa) with accoutrements that would sound more at home in a slasher movie are combined with a debunking humour. In 'The Island' (*THIBD*, p.129), Hill seems to be proposing social organisation in terms of a gender separatism and green economics:

> We don't use cars, or electricity,
> and men especially seem to find that hard.
> Another thing – we feel healthier.
> We work the horses, bear much fewer children;
> and eat and dress and live very simply.
> We shepherd sheep. We scale trees for fruit.
> We abseil cliffs for samphire and fresh eggs;
> and some of us, as you have pointed out,
> migrating to the cities, abseil glass.

By pushing the imagery in this direction Hill is employing a strategy not unconnected to myth and fairytale in the use made by images that arise from the unconscious and the dream and which look to a collective experience achieved through fantasy.

In 'The Veil' (*THIBD*, p.138), a poem set in a darkened room which is pervaded by the smell 'of blood and bleeding', Hill seems to be playing with ideas of gender and sexual difference. In the poem a woman servant sits, unmoving, 'her face...sullen' and beside her, also unmoving is a 'rigid man-shaped veil'. The whole scene conjured is evocative of a piece of performance art:

> ...I came back every day,
> until at last my patience was rewarded.
> The veil moved – as if some furtive moths

> were arguing among themselves like thieves.
> As morning broke, I crept a little closer;
> then, just as I was leaning down to speak,
> the servant gave me one of those bleak looks
> the neighbours have been paralysed by lately.
> Not only you, my friends. The whole area.

The poem begs as many questions as it answers. Who is bleeding? Is the blood of the poem menstrual, or has some other mutilation – a metaphorical or real castration – taken place? If the veil that covers the 'man-shaped veil' is removed, what will we find?

For Hill, like Feaver, the domestic is not a secure place, but rather one of dramatic confrontations and invasions. Hill's sixth collection, *Violet* (1997),[32] splits into two "meditations", one on the narrator's relationship with her sister (it is hard to discern if she is real or imaginary), and the other on the narrator's relationship with an ex-husband and his girlfriend. In *My Sister's Sister*, the sequence, like a series of photographs, follows images of the two sisters as they grow up. Taboos about the female body are explored in these addresses to the sister who also functions as a kind of alter ego. In the *My Husband's Wife* sequence, the preoccupation with being a "good girl" is transposed to the wife who has been left by her husband, and who must deal with her rage and jealousy. The short fragmentary poems offer glimpses of the coming into being of a new self. In both halves of the book, Hill sets up a female alter ego (the sister, the husband's lover) through whom she can ask: 'And what do I feel? And what do I think?' (*Violet*, p.27). *Bunny* (2001), like *Lou-Lou* (2004), returns to the charting the consciousness of a young girl. Whereas *Lou-Lou* is a conscious return to the events of *An Accumulation*, *Bunny* operates a kind of parallel narrative, telling the story of a young girl's move into adulthood in the 1950s, and how, brought up by aunts, perhaps abused by the male lodger, she also ends up in a psychiatric hospital.

It is these explorations of desire and madness that have led Sean O'Brien to describe Hill as 'one of the least *embarrassed* poets ever to have found publication':

> There is a sense in which it is not part of Hill's work to ask the reader to agree to the possible validity of her way of seeing things, for if the poet is a discoverer, her imagination is already landed on a new continent, already *there*, even if its whereabouts are not yet clear... And that may help to account for the feelings of disorientation and irritation initially experienced by some male readers who find themselves turning back at the border to face the possibility that their vocabulary is simply not equipped for the job of reading the resulting poems.[33]

Although O'Brien clearly admires Hill's work, such a passage gives great insight into the way her work might be read by men. The issue of embarrassment which Lowell raised in relation to Sexton's work again returns, begging the question, of course, as to exactly who is embarrassed and why. For if Hill is taboo-breaking, the taboos she breaks are all around aspects of women's experience which are often otherwise unspoken or unnamed. Unlike Duffy in her monologues, Hill does not share the joke of the difficulty of relationships between men and women, rather she seeks to identify a shared trauma, both real and metaphorical, a sharing made possible through the surreal imagery which both displays itself as product of a subjective 'I', but which has become objective in its coding as dream image.

Hill's dramatised confessions, which are difficult to otherwise contextualise, have seen her variously compared to Smith, Plath, and even Christopher Smart.[34] If Hill's later work reads as if it has much in common with the confessionals, hers is a confession in which the individual who confesses does so from a fragmented and sometimes chaotic consciousness. Whereas the confession can sometimes make coherent a self who is nevertheless ambivalent, Hill's female characters, while they change and grow in their narratives, are not in the individual poems which make up aspects of their lives, ever fixed. Their consciousness is always exploratory and evolving, the "truth" they speak creating a space for the shared catharsis of suffering.

*   *   *

None of the women discussed here would welcome the label "feminist poet", nor, I suspect, would any want to be thought of simply as a "woman poet". The gender politics of Duffy, Feaver and Hill do, however, and in various ways, if not always conclusively, see them all committed to the explorations not just of the place of the female body but to an awareness of the constructedness of gender roles, and a desire to "tell" the difficulty of relationships between men and women. Duffy's work of the last six years sees a comparison with the poetry of Anne Sexton becoming increasingly evident, although the comparison works best in terms of an analysis of strategy rather than a comparison of poetic technique.

In terms of poetic role models it is Duffy who is most frequently cited as a central influence for a new generation of women writing. A major part of her importance has been her explorations of the monologue's potential to use the demotic and to allow access to

kinds of different female experience. That her first full-length col-
lection, *Standing Female Nude* (1985), has as its title-poem a mono-
logue which focuses on the tensions between male representations
of the female body and the dramatisation of her voice is indicative
of the centrality of anxieties in this respect. Despite Duffy's wide
popularity and prominence, the work of all three women has, how-
ever, been crucial to mapping a place for the exploration of female
experience and a feminist politics in contemporary women's poetry
that does not seek to limit or reduce experience we identify as
women's.

   Theoretically, culturally, women's relationship to their bodies
was very much on the agenda in the 1970s. The Women's Movement
did much to bring the subject of women's body as a marker of
difference and oppression to wider political attention. The wide
and free availability of contraception, the Abortion Act of 1967
meant that technically women's relationship to their bodies in the
public and private sphere was undergoing radical change. Hand in
hand with the control of fertility came the rapid commercialisation
of the female body and the increase in representations of that body
that saw a move towards the transformation of the female body into
an increasingly commodified, androgynous and muscular form. In
my next chapter I turn to look at the way a slightly later genera-
tion of women poets have negotiated national identities, with the
body once more at the forefront of their explorations.

CHAPTER SIX

Motherlands and Mothertongues: Writing the Poetry of Nation

The relationship between body, poet and text is, as we have seen, a complex one for women. I look here at the ways women poets in the 1980s and 1990s began to explore the manner in which their countries of origin and cultural differences impinged on the way they represented femininity in their poems. David Kennedy has remarked that for poetry in the 1980s

> [t]he lack of an identifiable, populated locale or of an easily identifiable speaker is...typical. The inhabitants of the early poems of Hofmann, Didsbury, O'Brien and [Geoffrey] Hill for example, are usually isolated or separated individuals...a new generation of poets no longer felt obliged, or perhaps, no longer felt able to write as citizens of 'the society of the poem'. As the decade progressed this resulted not only in the voice speaking a poem being left open to question but to that voice being placed, as it were, in inverted commas.[1]

While Kennedy cites Jo Shapcott's poem 'Phrase Book', which I will discuss in detail at the end of this chapter, as an example of such a postmodern trend, the relationship women have to an identification with society and nation is more complicated than Kennedy would suggest, particularly when it defines itself through nation figured in resistance to English and Englishness. In grouping these women together I am not suggesting that they adhere to any coherent ideological position, but the legacy of British Imperialism, and the divisions and difficulties set up within notions of Britishness in relation to both Black and Asian as well as Northern Irish, Scottish and Welsh identities, obviously plays a large part in the connections that can be drawn between them.

In their poetry the women I discuss explore how writing becomes bound up in cultural anxieties about their relationship to language and experience as women, as well perhaps as psychic ones which dramatise anxieties about sexual difference. National literature's repeated adoption of the feminine as a trope for nation – as motherland, mother tongue – is in this respect clearly problematic for many women writers, and all of the women included here actively resist configurations that straightforwardly equate the female body with nation. None of the women suggest in their writing that there is something intrinsic or essential about their gender or their nationality; rather, they question both gender and nation as fixed entities in order to explore the tensions which arise between them. Such tensions suggest, of course, not only patriarchy's part in the construction of national discourse, but also the force by which such discourse can at times become concentrated, and resisted, in the female body in its "double" otherness.

MEDBH McGUCKIAN

> On the secret shelves of the weather
> With its few rhymes, in a purse
> Of blood, I closed the top
> Of my lesson-filled inkwell
> A she-thing called a poetess...[2]

I begin here by discussing the work of the Northern Irish poet Medbh McGuckian. Born in 1950, McGuckian first came to prominence when she won the National Poetry Competition in 1979. Her first full-length collection was published by Oxford University Press in 1982, and since then she has published a further ten volumes of poetry. Although a resident of Belfast during the civil rights marches of 1969 prior to the establishment of Direct Rule in 1974, and having chosen to remain in Belfast throughout the period of 'the Troubles', McGuckian rarely makes direct reference to public or historical events in her early poetry. Eamon Grennan reads McGuckian's writing as one which 'makes and inhabits a world of elided borders, a world of language seeking some approximation to the fluctuating ripple-and-glitter-world of feeling itself', suggesting that 'such a radically lyrical destabilising of conventional assumptions' is not only 'a mimetic rendering of the fluid and fluctuating nature of consciousness itself, but would also be both a response to and an expression of a sense of responsibility in the idiosyncratic environment of Northern Ireland'.[3] A response to such national instabilities must also, given women's positioning by the state, be gendered. Clair Wills reminds us that

> women (the female body, sexuality, and reproduction) are at the centre of public policy and legislation. Indeed as the figure of the motherland should alert us, in certain ways the body of the Irish woman (and her analogue in conservative nationalist discourse, the home) is the very ground – both figural and material – of national enterprise [...] representations of the female body in Ireland are not the arena of the private or the personal, but precisely the place of interpenetration of public political discourse, and notions of private ownership and personal identity [...]

When the nation is represented by one version of femininity, the mother-
land, when the dispossession of the Irish is figured in terms of exile
from the mother's body, the mother's tongue, what access to legitimis-
ing roles, what means of "possessing" a history or a tradition do Irish
women have? The desire to legitimise oneself (all too often confounded
with the process of legalising one's position), to submit to an authority
(that of the father) in order to accede it, presupposes acceptance of the
supremacy of tradition. The process of legitimisation asks us to fit our-
selves in to a familial narrative in which goods, and the authority to
own them, pass from father to son. But the daughter's inheritance
requires not simply a diversion of familial chattels; it necessitates a
disruption (an evolution) of tradition. In the literary system it performs
a mutation of genre.[4]

I quote Wills at length here because while her comments are specific
– and importantly so – to the work of Irish women, many of the
points she raises, particularly in relation to private and public dis-
course, will have more general resonance in my discussions of the
other women I discuss, and the relationship of body and nation
which they attempt to reconfigure.

As we have seen, attempts to make the 'mutation of genre' that
Wills identifies for women poets have often involved a reconfiguration
of the relationship between text and body, and sometimes a drama-
tisation of the female and poetic body in the process. McGuckian's
own aesthetic relies heavily on her linguistic attempts to map an
idea of the unconscious, whether it is the unconscious of a text, or
the poem, or the poet herself, and much has been made of reading
her poetic strategy alongside or complicit with so-called French fem-
inist theorists of the body such as Luce Irigaray and Hélène Cixous.[5]
Irigaray's description of patriarchy's positioning of the feminine
for example, might almost read like an analysis of McGuckian's
poetics:

Hers are contradictory words, somewhat mad from the standpoint of
reason, inaudible for whoever listens to them with ready-made grids,
with a fully-elaborated code in hand… One would have to listen with
another ear, as if hearing an "other meaning" always in the process of
weaving itself, of embracing itself with words, but also of getting rid
of words in order not to become fixed, congealed in them.[6]

Making such a connection, however, useful as it is in many ways,
falls victim to taking the Irishness – and the particularity of her
resistance to writing in English – out of McGuckian's work. It is
highly relevant, for example, that McGuckian wrote her Masters
dissertation on Irish Gothic, drawing particular attention to the
ways in which Irish characters spoke 'nonsense' as a direct resis-
tance to English colonialism. She writes:

The Gothic mode was the only acceptable form providing scope for the expression of...ambivalence. It allowed for the confrontation of truth alongside its evasion, the indulgence of the sentiment of the past with the realisation of the present degradation.[7]

Perhaps because of the instability and thus inherent danger of dreams, McGuckian very often situates dreams and the dreaming self within the stable and restraining, constraining and containing environment of the house. In an interview with Kevin Smith in 1985, McGuckian explained:

The house is probably the poem itself, often or a symbol for the world of the poem. I feel a house is a very secure place, especially in Belfast – I do think that if I didn't live in Belfast I wouldn't have this... I'm for houses. They're protective – the protectiveness a woman feels about her personal life and her body and her history.[8]

Crucially, too, the 'fluctuations' of a McGuckian poem, as Grennan calls them, must be read against and alongside the sense of literary and historical time when she appropriates and makes intertextual reference to numerous source texts in her poems. Such intertextual 'slips' or steals (what her contemporary Paul Muldoon elsewhere has referred to as the Irish writer's tendency towards the 'slip' and 'slop' of language) see McGuckian attempting to reconcile, redis-cover, rewrite, to literally incorporate the feminine body into the body of the text as texts, often by canonical male authors, become intimately woven into the female textual body, intersecting with her 'own' writing, like warp to weft.[9]

'Slips' (*MWP*, pp.272-73; *The Flower Master and Other Poems*, p.21) was published in McGuckian's first collection in 1982.[10] I want to focus on this poem because it exemplifies the strategy at work in many of McGuckian's poems and as such offers a case history of her poetics. 'Slips' is composed almost entirely from a series of assembled footnotes from Freud's *Psychopathology of Everyday Life: Forgetting, Slips of the Tongue, Bungled Actions Superstitions and Errors*, his 1901 treatise which was published a year after the *Interpretation of Dreams*. In my reading of 'Slips' I look closely at the way McGuckian uses Freud as a source book for the interpretation of her own dreams and memories, transforming the text into a series of notes and prompts which give her access to her to an elusive narrative of femininity (itself without recourse to footnote). This narrative is also, in its displacements and elisions, a narrative of the feminine in relation to nation as well as the feminised nation.

In his paper, 'Screen Memories' (1899), Freud outlined ideas which were to become the underpinning of his later theory of the unconscious' dream-work in which, through personal reminiscence, he shows how unsuspected meanings could lie beneath seemingly mundane memories of childhood. Elaborating these ideas in *The Psychopathology of Everyday Life* he writes:

> I started from the striking fact that a person's earliest childhood memories seem frequently to have preserved what is indifferent and unimportant, whereas (frequently, though certainly not universally) no trace is found in an adult's memory of impressions dating from that time which are important, impressive and rich in affect... The indifferent memories of childhood owe their existence to a process of displacement: they are substitutes, in [mnemic] reproduction, for other impressions which are really significant... As the indifferent memories owe their preservation not to their own content but to an associative relation between their content and another which is repressed, they have some claim to be called 'screen memories'...[11]

The Freudian slip, as Paul Keegan has pointed out, 'is, among other things, an act of pointing, a communication. It says: "I want you to know that I am hiding something from myself," as if it takes two to make a mistake.'[12] The images in McGuckian's 'Slips' are set up as a series of screen memories in an appropriation which transforms Freud's psychoanalytic treatise into a poetic text which recounts the erasures and losses of a woman's personal history, making a commentary not just on Freud's elisions of femininity in his work, but also making a wider statement about the relationship of personal history to the public sphere. The hiddenness of femininity, hidden from the self but also urgently searched for, thus becomes displayed in the poem at the same time it is concealed in a way similar to surrealism's use of the dream image.

As far as I am aware the first two lines of 'Slips', 'The studied poverty of a moon roof, / The earthenware of dairies cooled by apple trees', are not directly traceable to a literary text, and seem to begin the poem with memories or evocations of memories of a private and personal nature. They possess their own secret narrative at which the reader must work, teasing out contextual associations, balancing the visual imagery at the same time as making wider associations. The first line is in fact a typical McGuckian line in its conflation of images which are drawn together by a coherent grammar and syntax, but which linguistically, once they are unpacked, demand that huge associative leaps be made in the process of attempting to "understand" them. A 'moon roof', a term used more frequently in the 70s, is similar to a sun roof, but is concerned with letting light in rather than blocking sunlight. It would be fixed in the roof of a car. But the poem seems to suggest that we must read its moon roof metaphorically rather than literally and the subsequent contextualising of the dairies and the orchard suggest not the metal and glass of the late 20th century, but perhaps the roof (or absence of roof) of the farm building. Metaphorically then, perhaps a moon roof is a roof which is open to the elements, hence its poverty. Dairy farming has been a central part of the 20th-century Irish agricultural economy, focussed particularly in the northern counties. Here then we are presented with a rural Irish farming scene, the economics of which may be tough but which, in its "studied" poverty, nevertheless evokes nostalgic images of a pastoral scene before the introduction of modern technology. Neil Corcoran suggests that the apple imagery 'inevitably drags along in its wake Genesis-motifs of Eve, temptation and fall'.[13] If this is the case then we see how in just two lines McGuckian is suggesting complex relations between the national economy and a woman's sexual economy. I would like to suggest, however, that McGuckian is also drawing on very specific trees in Freud which again return us to issues of nation.

Once we realise, reading and interpreting 'Slips' retrospectively, that the remaining stanzas of the poem are constructed from Freud's text, it is possible to associate an anecdote Freud recounts with the image of the apple trees, which also provides a key to the way in which we must read the screen memories of McGuckian's poems. Often, in its bid to evoke meaning through association, and its impulse to shift the reader away from definitive interpretations, reading a McGuckian poem seems to push the reader towards over-interpretation. For example, how tenuous is the connection made between the image of the apple trees and the trees Freud recounts in his earlier paper, 'Screen Memories', which occur in a man's memory '[o]f a child breaking off a branch from a tree while he is on a walk and of his being helped to do it with someone'.[14] In a sense, the poems seem to say, it doesn't matter. Here, it seems possible that McGuckian is recalling the Freud, because she already *has* done. The intertextuality is such that it may only itself be a tangential intertextuality rather than the kind of direct intertexual lifting which I want to go on to show creates the poem. Risking the tangential, however, and because it also sheds light on the manner in which a reader might learn to read McGuckian's poems, I want to suggest that the reference to the Freud is indeed there. Here is the passage in question (which might easily be an excerpt from a conversation between Conan Doyle's Sherlock Holmes and Doctor Watson), in which we see Freud subjecting the memory of the tree to the same kind of scrutiny we must the poem if we are to reveal the process of the dream-work:

He reflected for a little and then answered: 'I can make nothing of the first one. It is most probably a case of displacement at work; but the intermediate steps are beyond guessing. As for the second case, I should be prepared to give an interpretation, if only the person concerned had not been a Frenchman.'

'I cannot follow you there. What difference would that make?'

'A great deal of difference, since what provides the intermediate step between a screen memory and what it conceals is likely to be a verbal expression. In German "to pull one out" is a very common vulgar term for masturbation – someone was helping him do it – which in fact occurred at a later period. But even so, it does not fit, for in childhood scenes there were a number of other people present.' (*Screen Memories*, p.319)

Pointedly, Freud's interpretation does not work because of the particular nature of national difference. And it is here, in the overlaying of the imagery, that we reach a resonant impasse in McGuckian's poem. In the last line of this stanza there is a sudden stumble for the reader as the poem works syntactically and grammatically, but semantically, as in the moon roof's poverty, errs towards the nonsensical (how can an apple tree, which is inanimate, 'make a wash'?). Is this a reference to the falling of appleblossoms? to ejaculation? The slippage into the memory of a washing powder slogan – '*Persil* makes the whitest wash' – has begun to interfere with the process of remembering this scene, and it is from this point that the poem begins to "pick up" its Freudian texts.

In his essay 'Soap Powders and Detergents', included in his book *Mythologies* (1957), Roland Barthes discusses the techniques employed in selling washing powder, and the importance of 'the art of having disguised the abrasive function of the detergent under the delicious image of a substance at once deep and airy which can govern the molecular order of the material without damaging it'.[15] In McGuckian's poem we have perhaps 'the delicious image'; the molecular order of Freud's source material has been changed but also remains undamaged. 'Slips', in its airing of her clean washing is a 'white wash', an attempt to present femininity with bias and concealment, as the OED informs us; the underclothes of woman become the underclothes of the feminine psyche. Ironically the multiplication of texts create a text about lost memories, proliferate to examine women's experience and refilling the white space on the page.

Once – if – we realise that by the second stanza that the poem is composed of Freud's text, that the slips of the poem are not just underclothes that are hanging out to dry, several associative links spring forth which also seem to impress themselves as important. The reference to apple trees may tangentially link the poem back to Freud's masturbation memory in 'Screen Memories', as the poem puns on the idea of ejaculation. But just as powerfully, the poem makes another 'slip' into a literary text and an intertextual connection with the reference to washing in two well-known poems by another Northern Irish poet, Louis MacNeice, 'Snow' (1935)[16] and 'Soap Suds' (1961) (*CP*, p.517). Whereas 'Snow', with its incorrigible plurality, its celebration of the 'drunkenness of things being various' (the name Medbh translated literally means intoxicated), seems to have more of a general stylistic influence on McGuckian's aesthetic, in 'Soap Suds', it is soap which acts synaesthetically to conjure childhood memory:

> This brand of soap has the same smell as once in the big
> House he visited when he was eight: the walls of the bathroom open
> To reveal a lawn where a great yellow ball rolls back through a hoop
> To rest at the head of a mallet held in the hands of a child.

If MacNeice's 'Soap Suds' conjure, in this somewhat Proustian moment, the recollection of the big house (emblem of Anglo-Irish colonialism), it also recalls, as Edna Longley has argued, *Alice in Wonderland*, a narrative in which of course a young girl falls underground to encounter a dream-like world.[17] Longley has drawn convincing comparison between Louis MacNeice's analysis of what he calls 'double-level writing...sleight of hand' in his Clark Lectures, published as *Varieties of Parable* in 1965, and to the importance of the development of MacNeice's disruption of syntax in creating connections between time and perception. (*Poetry in the Wars*, p.211; pp.219-43). In her invocation of MacNeice, then, McGuckian is drawing as much on an aesthetic as she is on a theme, although in both cases for the two poets the two become inextricably linked. This knot of references and associations at the beginning of the poem then, not only locates the poem in an exploration of the psyche, but places it in the context of a Northern Irish literary tradition.

After this complex beginning, the intertextual references become much easier to trace. Stanza two begins with a direct allusion to Freud's chapter in *The Psychopathology of Everyday Life*, 'The Forgetting of Proper Names' where Freud remarks that frequently 'a name is not only forgotten but wrongly remembered'. The 'town in France like a woman's Christian name'. The line also refers to Freud's discussion of the

> name of a town in Italy [which] escaped the subject's memory as a consequence of its great similarity in sound to a woman's first name, with which a number of memories charged with effect were connected...
> (*Psychopathology*, p.67)

Veronika (the Hungarian would be Verona), who is a house servant, is disliked because of

> her repulsive looks, her shrill, raucous voice and her insufferable asser-
> tiveness, to which she believed herself entitled by her length of service.
> At the same time the tyrannical way in which she used to treat the
> children of the house was intolerable...
>   ...My antipathy was at one time so violent that I found Veronika
> positively nauseating, and I had more than once expressed my aston-
> ishment that all the same it was possible for her to have an erotic life
> and be loved by someone. (*Psychopathology*, p.68)

The forgetting of the woman's Christian name in 'Slips' seems to imply that the poem will also forget any 'unpleasant' aspects of femininity which are here a trouble for Freud, in particular in relation to female assertiveness.[18]

In stanza three, McGuckian moves on to draw her text from Freud's chapter on screen memories which picks up on points from his earlier paper on screen memories. The key phrase to the poem, which appears at the beginning of stanza three is the line 'My childhood is preserved as a nation's history'. As far as I am aware, this is the one line in the poem which isn't a directly stolen line. Instead it encapsulates some of the points made in Freud's chapter on screen memories. Here then is the crux of the poem: the idea that these screen memories not only speak of the life of the private individual, but that private life is also a record of a whole nation. McGuckian's stolen lines are from here onwards straight-forward, as in the lines 'My favourite fairytales the shells / Leased by the hermit crab.' In Freud's interleaved copy of the 1904 edition the following notes are to be found. 'Dr. B- showed very neatly one Wednesday (i.e. at a meeting of the 'Vienna Psycho-Analytic Society' that fairytales can be made use of as screen memories in the same kind of way that empty shells are used as a home by the hermit crab. These fairytales then become favourites, without the reasons being known.' (*Psychopathology*, p.90). Freud's note con-tinues to re-address the memory of the 'grandmother's death as a piece of ice', an image which also appears in 'Slips':

> From a dream of P's it appears that ice is in fact a symbol by antithesis
> for an erection; i.e. something that becomes hard in the cold instead of
> – like a penis – in heat (in excitation). The two antithetical concepts of
> sexuality and death are frequently linked through the idea that death
> makes things stiff. One of the Henri's informants instanced a piece of ice
> as a screen memory for his grandmother's death. (*Psychopathology*, p.90)

The second line in stanza four, 'my mother's slimness restored to her', refers to an incident remembered by Freud and which he discusses in his chapter on childhood and screen memories:

> When I began in my forty-third year to direct my interest to what was
> left of my memory of my own childhood there came to my mind a scene
> which had for a long while back (from the remotest point, as it seemed to
> me) come into consciousness from time to time... I saw myself standing
> in front of a cupboard ['*Kasten*'] demanding something and screaming,
> while my half-brother, my senior by twenty years, held it open. Then
> suddenly my mother, looking beautiful and slim, walked into the room
> as if she had come in from the street. (*Psychopathology*, p.90)

Although I'm not aware of the edition of Freud used by McGuckian
in her composition of the poem, it's interesting to note that the
editor's note in the Penguin edition concerned with fairytales and
the bowl of ice actually appears on the same page as this memory.
Freud later analyses this screen memory by recounting two incidents,
the first of which refers to a patient, a 'man severely inhibited in
his erotic life, and who is now over 40, is the eldest of nine chil-
dren'. The man claims that, although he was 15 when the youngest
members of the family were born, he had not noticed any of his
mother's pregnancies:

> Under pressure from my scepticism a memory presented itself to him;
> once at the age of eleven or twelve he had seen his mother hurriedly un-
> fasten her skirt in front of the mirror. He now added of his own accord
> that she had come in from the street and had been overcome by unex-
> pected labour pains. The unfastening ['*Aufbinden*'] of the skirt was a screen
> memory for the confinement ['*Entbindung*']. (*Psychopathology*, pp.89-90)

Freud then goes on to devote the rest of this chapter with the
relation of his own childhood memory, as previously recounted to
Fleiss, of the 'plastic picture' of his young self standing before the
'wardrobe':

> When...my naughty brother had done the same thing to her that he
> had done to the nurse and I forced him to open the cupboard ['*Kasten*']
> for me. I now understand too, why in the translation of this visual
> childhood scene my mother's slimness was emphasised: it must have
> struck me as having just been restored to her. I am two and a half
> years older than the sister who was born at that time, and when I was
> three years old my half-brother and I ceased living in the same place.
> (*Psychopathology*, p.92)

Freud's footnote, added in 1924 reads:

> The child of not yet three had understood that has little sister who had
> recently arrived had grown inside his mother. He was very far from
> approving of this addition to the family, and was full of mistrust and
> anxiety that his mother's inside might conceal still more children. The
> wardrobe or cupboard was a symbol for him of his mother's inside. So
> he insisted on looking into this cupboard, and turned for this to his big

brother, who (as is clear from other material) had taken his father's place as the child's rival. Besides the well-founded suspicion that his brother had had the lost nurse boxed up, there was a further suspicion against him – namely that he had in some way introduced the recently born baby into his mother's inside. The effect of disappointment when the cupboard was found to be empty derived therefore, from the superficial motivation for the child's demand. As regards the deeper trend of thought, the affect was in the wrong place. On the other hand, his great satisfaction over his mother's slimness on her return can only be fully understood in the light of this deeper layer. (*Psychopathology*, pp.92-93)

Line three of stanza four refers quite explicitly to several anecdotes recounted in Freud's chapter on 'bungled actions' in which he cites various incidents reported by Maeder, Jones and Sachs in which keys are fitted in the wrong locks. McGuckian's line, 'My own key slotted in your door', in this context, not excluding its highly charged sexual symbolism, refers to his colleague Maeder's comments that:

> everyone has had the experience of taking out his bunch of keys on reaching the door of a particularly dear friend, of catching himself, as it were in the act of opening it with his key just as if he were at home. This causes a delay, as he has to ring the bell in the long run, but it is a sign that he feels – or would like to feel – at home with this friend. (*Psychopathology*, pp.216-17)

The final stanza of 'Slips' takes up references from several of Freud's other chapters in *The Psychopathology*: chapter six is divided into two halves, the first is concerned with 'misreading' and the second to 'slips of the pen'. In chapter nine, Freud deals with the losing of objects. A propelling pencil is cited as being lost as a direct result of the owner's anger resulting from a letter sent by his brother-in-law, the original giver of the pen:

> It is often only an expression of the low estimation in which the lost object is held, or of a secret antipathy towards it or towards the person that it came from; or else the inclination to lose the object has been transferred to it from other more important objects by symbolic association of thoughts. Losing objects of value serves to express a variety of impulses; it may either be acting as a symbolic representation of a repressed thought – that is, it may be repeating a warning that one would be glad to ignore – or (most commonly of all) it may be offering a sacrifice to the obscure powers of destiny to whom homage is still paid among us today. (*Psychopathology*, pp.264-65)

The final line of McGuckian's poem refers much more directly to a brief paragraph of Freud's:

> Girls who are proud of having beautiful hair are able to manage their combs and hairpins in such a way that their hair comes down in the middle of a conversation. (*Psychopathology*, pp.272-73)

This example of a 'symptomatic or chance action' Freud claims as being found in 'healthy and neurotic people', and McGuckian uses the image not simply to signal sexual provocation, but also perhaps to end the poem with a symbol of undoing as if the meaning of the poem has finally been unravelled and slipped into consciousness.

If unpicking all the textual references seems to suggest a deeply complex and complicated poem, as a lyric, the poem is in fact startling in its uniformity and simplicity. Unpicking the intertextual relationship between poem and "ur-text" lets us see how McGuckian has appropriated Freud's text in order to recoup a specifically female experiences concerning matrilineal lines, sexuality and pregnancy. What is so remarkable about the poem is the way McGuckian so seamlessly (so to speak) allows Freud to speak so lyrically in her poem as a *feminine* voice, with so little alteration of his text. The poem, in fact, could be said to be a "mistake" – it slips into the public arena from Freud's text in which it was marginalised (in footnotes) or repressed, to reveal something about women, perhaps as the underslip erotically appears from beneath the layer of the woman's exterior clothing, promising an intimacy that is closer to the woman's body than her outer clothing allows. All the voices McGuckian appropriates from within Freud's text are male voices; not only is she "stealing" Freud's text, but the male voices and experiences which his text carries. The text she steals is also in a way "stolen", at one remove from Freud's own text by virtue of the fact that it has already been translated.

Such 'palimpsestic double writing', which Michael Davidson terms the 'palimtext', performs the act of writing itself. The strategy of the poem is one remove on from the process of the surrealist cut-up in that the reassemblage of text is not governed by chance. It is, Davidson suggests 'a writing-in-process', which 'retains vestiges of prior writing out of which it emerges'; more importantly, 'it is the still-visible record of responses to those early texts'.[19] Thus McGuckian's poem enacts transgression by becoming part of a dominant discourse in its own right, and the otherness of female experience is made central: ideas of nation, myth and identity are all brought into play, and constructed in relation to the feminine. The absence of women's sexuality and her relation to it is one which McGuckian seeks to recover in this process – and it is no small irony that we find that the reissued edition of *The Flower Master* contains poems specifically about women – poems entitled 'Aunts' (*TFM*, p.22) and 'My Mother' (*TFM*, p.23), as well as 'Faith' (*TFM*, p.12), which is about a grandmother – which in the original Oxford edition of 1982 had (presumably) been edited out.

As Wills argues, throughout McGuckian's work, she uses

> images of reproduction, and specifically the authority a mother has
> over her children, to construct alternatives to the control of the
> Catholic Church and its representation of perfect motherhood. The
> Catholic ideal of femininity is in turn related to the nationalist myth of
> Mother Ireland, and McGuckian undercuts both by translating the
> public image into the "private" discourse of the changing contours of
> her body. (*Improprieties*, p.159)

That body here is of course also the textual body. While I have been
arguing throughout these chapters that this use of intertextuality
to recast women's engagement with gender is a dominant feature of
women's poetic writing in the 20th century, McGuckian's strategic
use of intertextuality is the most extreme of all the poets I discuss
in that it has become her dominant *modus operandi*. McGuckian's
poetics has done much to show that a woman's poetic writing could
focus on the female body without fixing experience to that body in
a reductive or essentialising way, and that the privacy of the female
body and its poetic exploration does not have to remain outside a
public discourse. For McGuckian, the boundaries between public
and private are highly charged when she writes 'I feel that you're
going public – by writing the poem you're becoming a whore.
You're selling your soul which is worse than any prostitution – in
a sense you're vilifying your mind. I do feel that must be under-
taken with the greatest possible fastidiousness.' [20] In becoming the
whore, in writing the private publicly, McGuckian also destabilises
the public/private boundary as well as the relations between tex-
tual and poetic body. In interview, McGuckian has discussed the
gendering of the poet. She writes:

> I basically see the role of the poet as a male role which I have adopted.
> I chose it for that reason. I didn't choose it because there were any
> female examples, because I didn't know about them then. I wanted to
> do something that would make me into a man, or give me the status
> of a man. And I'm proud of it for that reason, which is probably com-
> pletely wrong...the motivation behind it was to gain status; I couldn't
> see how I was going to gain in any other field. [21]

What seems of utmost importance here is that the 'mutation of
genre' Wills speaks of occurs on a textual level, and that despite
the extremity of circumstance of McGuckian's situation in Belfast,
she is able to allow the text to work as a poetic body, without
apparently needing to perform that resistance – like Sitwell, Smith
– in and through her physical body.

GWYNETH LEWIS

What would it be to move beyond
our need for angels? Just to relax
might take us a century. To like
that sensation, longer. We'd understand
and calculate the logarithms of grace
to easy solutions in our sleep.
Not to need messages about
but to be, instead, a literal place

we have a map for? [22]

The mid-1990s saw an upsurge in the publishing of women's poetry, in particular the priorities of a younger generation of women who had an interest in exploring their sense of themselves as women at the same time as addressing their position in relation to their national identity. The difficulties in the configuration of nation in terms of the female, most specifically in relation to ideas of a "mother country" and a "mother tongue", are explored by the bilingual Welsh poet Gwyneth Lewis (born 1959) with increasing urgency in her English writing. Debates about the status and currency of the Welsh language reached new prominence in the debate about Welsh devolution in the late 1970s, a debate concluded in the vote for devolution in 1997, and the establishment of the Welsh Assembly in 1999. It is worth here recording some important statistics. According to census information provided by the Office of National Statistics in 1891, 54% of the Welsh population spoke Welsh. At the census in 1981 and 1991 that percentage had fallen to 19%. The Welsh language television station S4C was not launched until 1982, and it was not until 1993 that the Welsh Language Act of 1967 was amended to place the Welsh and English languages on an equal footing.[24]

Having Welsh as her first language, and growing up bilingual, Lewis has made the difficult and unusual choice to write and publish in both Welsh and English. Poets such as Menna Elfyn (see *MWP*, pp.285-89) in Wales or Nuala Ní Dhomhnaill (see *MWP*, pp.297-303) in the south of Ireland, or Meg Bateman (see *MWP*, pp.349-52) in Scotland, for example, choose to write exclusively in Welsh or Gaelic for political as well as aesthetic and creative reasons; and the majority of the Welsh-language poets included in the recent *Bloodaxe Book of Modern Welsh Poetry* (2003) write exclusively in Welsh.[24] Lewis, however, resists a monoglot poetics, and to some extent her Welsh writing is kept "private" to those outside Wales, her Welsh poems, with a few exceptions, remaining, through choice, largely untranslated into English.[25] In the preface to *Keeping Mum*, her third English-language collection, which is in fact a partial translation of Lewis's Welsh book *Y Llofrudd Iaith* [The Language Murderer] (1999),[27] she discusses her feelings about this decision:

> One of my survival tactics until now has been to keep both sides of my linguistic family apart for as long as possible. I publish one book in Welsh, the next in English. Translating my own work from Welsh into English has held little appeal, simply because the audience and concerns addressed are distinct and, often, mutually antagonistic... (*Chaotic Angels*, p.143)

Lewis's decision to give equal priority to both the languages she speaks creates an interesting divergence in her work and in fact dramatises an often painful splitting of the self. 'Half' (*Modern Welsh Poetry*, p.368) is the second part of 'Wholeness' which was published as part of *Y Llofrudd Iaith*, and is one of the few Welsh poems Lewis herself has translated – something which is significant in itself. While ostensibly being a metaphor for the finding of self achieved in a Platonic union, the poem might also be read as a metaphor for a desire for union between her bilingual selves. Such a union in Lewis's work however, remains at the level of fantasy, the conflicts between her Welsh and English voices being invariably violent and increasingly the subject of her later work.

Unlike many Welsh English-language poets who transport Welsh words and phrases into their English poems (see, for example, Gillian Clarke's fine poem 'Translation' in *MWP*, p.194), with one exception, which I will turn to in a moment, it is only recently, and in the context of her poem about the death of the Welsh language, that Lewis uses Welsh words in her English poems. In their essay on the relationship between language and culture in post-colonial contexts, Bill Ashcroft, Gareth Griffiths and Helen Tiffin discuss the connections between English and non-English words in English texts in a way which seems useful when thinking about Lewis's use of Welsh. They write:

> Untranslated words, the sounds and the textures of the language can be held to have the power and presence of the culture they signify... It is commonly held that in this way words somehow embody the culture from which they derive... The idea that language somehow "embodies" culture in this way is a seductive one for the post-colonial reader. Superficially, it seems to be demonstrable from the texts, where words ...embedded in the English text seem to "carry" the oppressed culture, just as the english which surrounds them may seem to be "tainted" by its colonial origins. Such an essentialist view of language has an appeal... But it is a false and dangerous argument. Because it confuses usage

with property in its view of meaning, and it is ultimately contradictory, since, if it is asserted that words do have some essential cultural essence not subject to changing usage, then post-colonial literatures in English, predicated upon this very changing usage, could not have come into being. Language would be imprisoned in origins and not, as is the demonstrable case, be readily available for appropriation and liberation by a whole range of new and distinctive enterprises.

However, such uses of language as untranslated words do have an important function in describing difference.[27]

In the case of Welsh, these words may not only describe difference, but also inscribe, even memorialise, the loss of linguistic difference. Unlike the movements between English and Scots (which I discuss next in the work of Kathleen Jamie), the movements between English and Welsh are figured repeatedly for Lewis in terms of loss rather than exchange and proliferation. Given the historical demise of the Welsh language, this is perhaps unsurprising.

In section V of her sequence 'Welsh Espionage' (*MWP*, pp.353-54), which was first published in her third book, her first English-language collection, *Parables & Faxes* (1995), Lewis interrogates the relationship between gender and nation explicitly through language. In the poem a father surreptitiously teaches his Welsh-speaking daughter English by pointing to parts of her body, and the poem ends with the father telling the little girl on his knee that they should keep their 'game' secret. The last line asks in a way which is both challenging and suffused with melancholy: 'Was it such a bad thing to be Daddy's girl?'

Importantly, 'Welsh Espionage V', as Lewis has herself pointed out, recalls Act 3 scene 4 in Shakespeare's *Henry V*. It was, of course, Henry V (1387-1422), the English king who was born in Monmouth, who led the English forces to suppress the Welsh uprising led by the Welsh hero and rebel Owain Glyndwr during the reign of Henry IV. Shakespeare's scene, however, takes place, in French, between two women, as Katherine, the French princess, attempts to learn English through the naming and misnaming of body parts. Whereas Shakespeare's scene is comic, there is no room for laughter in Lewis's poem. To read the poem simply as a metaphor for sexual abuse, however, is to reduce the complexity by which the poem positions relations between language, text and the female body. In its dramatisation of the price the female body might metaphorically pay for such a transgression of boundaries the poem becomes the faultline on which colonial history is worked out. The poem highlights the position of the bilingual writer, whose position is too often seen solely in terms of privilege rather than in terms of one that arises directly from a damaging colonial history.

Despite the fact that this poem is ostensibly transparent in terms of its meaning to the non-Welsh speaker, with its untranslated use of Welsh words it must always be read as three different poems dependent upon whether its reader is a Welsh speaker, an English speaker, or a bilingual reader. Non-Welsh-speaking readers must work out for themselves their own translation of the Welsh phrases as the "meanings" of the Welsh phrases and body parts are both revealed and sheltered by their translation. If we unpick the resonances of the first line 'Welsh was the mother tongue, English was his' there is a clear distinction arising in the grammar of the sentence as well as in terms of gender, which points to a rift between the "natural" state of language of the mother tongue and the ownership of language illustrated by the father's possession of it. The mother exists in the sentence only as language, while the father exists outside of language; language is something he can own, language is something the mother *is*. It's important to note, too, that the father is teaching the daughter the body itself, not how to name the body, and such an omission is telling.

That Welsh is spoken first in the poem is in part a necessity of upholding the realism of the anecdote, but Lewis's use of Welsh works importantly to position the English-speaking reader who has no Welsh. This reader is presented with words which he or she has to work to *interpret* within the context of the situation and the poem. The English reader, must in effect, in the reading of the poem, attempt to "read" the Welsh, searching the line for the words which do make sense, for English equivalents, which will then allow the act of "translation" to occur. Such a strategy enacts a reverse colonisation in which Welsh assumes primacy, and demands, uncompromisingly that the English reader hear and speak it. Interestingly, in readings given to English or mixed English- and Welsh-speaking audiences, Lewis has often pointed to the parts of the body she names in Welsh, shifting her own body into the arena of the poem's text. Cultural experience – this 'game' of naming is one played across many cultures in Britain – becomes the bridge between languages, whilst languages also mark the difference between the knowing of those experiences. And the English-speaking reader will always in this process attempt to become the Welsh reader in the movement to understand the line, a process which in fact performs the failure to "know" Welshness through language because of the unfamiliarity of the language that perhaps he or she cannot "hear" or pronounce.

In the poem Lewis refers to the game of naming as a 'fetishist quiz'. Although anthropologically, the fetish is a material object imbued with magical powers, the fetishist, according to Freud is, as Hal Foster neatly paraphrases it, 'a subject who recognises the reality of castration or trauma...but who disavows it'.[28] Is the nature of disavowal in this quiz the fact that English is not the language which through colonial power has superseded Welsh in its power to communicate? If so, who is the fetishist? The father, or the mother, or the little girl on whose body the trauma of lost language becomes figured? The answer is perhaps all three. Being Daddy's girl, with its suggestion of oedipal incestuous relations, is juxtaposed by the only other available option, that of murdering of the mother. In choosing the role of 'fetishist' Lewis does so as an act of preservation, denying that a choice is to be made between languages. But even when the choice to write in two languages is made, it is not uncomplicated. In the poem 'Pentecost' (*Chaotic Angels*, p.10), for example, a monologue written in the voice of a charismatic Christian asserts that 'glossolalia / shall be my passport – I shall taste the tang / of travel on the atlas of my tongue'. Such speaking in tongues is to be admired, and works as a metaphor for secular many-tonguedness, but such abilities are simultaneously seen less positively in the context of European war and American capitalism and globalisation, the 'perpetual Pentecost / of golf course and freeway, shopping mall and car'. 'Oxford Booklicker' (*Chaotic Angels*, p.58), from the 'Parables and Faxes' sequence, is Lewis's most optimistic poem in this respect, 'voracious / for the Word' the speaker of the poem 'lick[s] / the fat from all the books':

> ...When I am ripe
>
> I shall know and then you'll see the caravans,
> processions, fleets, parades come from my mouth
> as I spew up cities, colonies of words
> and flocks of sentences with full-stop birds
> and then, when I'm empty I shall open wide
>
> And out will come fountains for the chosen few...
>
> (*Chaotic Angels*, p.58)

If this poem works as a metaphor for intertextuality it does so offering all texts, in many languages – Tolstoy, Kafka, Ovid, Byron, Keats – as divine offering and sustenance.

Lewis has spoken of her writing in English in terms of a collusion with the 'enemy'. And yet denying the wealth of expression afforded by English would also seem like a denial of an important part of her relationship with a literary tradition of writing in English. That one of her mentors at a formative point in her development as a poet was the Russian poet and political exile, Joseph Brodsky, who finally chose to write in both English and his native Russian, sheds some light on Lewis's decision to write in English at all. In her poem that is most optimistic about her relationship to language, 'The Reference Library' (*Chaotic Angels*, p.50), she writes 'new languages are regicides', concluding

> for in your spines and not in those of books,
> lies the way to live well, the best library;
> for the erudition of your open looks
> shall turn old words to new theologies.

Here it is the body again which works as touchstone for truth; but it is the body's instincts not its learning that are held up in terms of a transformative and once again divine way of knowing.

We see Lewis returning to her exploration of bilingualism in her book-length poem *Keeping Mum* which was published in 2003 at a point in recent Welsh history when, after the establishment of the Welsh Assembly in 1997, Welsh interests in relation to Britain have ostensibly not been stronger. The book is partly based on *Y Llofrudd Iaith*, the first part being a direct translation, the second part moving away from the original Welsh, and the final part being completely new work. Using the vehicle of a detective story, Lewis uses the murdered body of an old woman as a metaphor for the Welsh language in order 'to explore how we could free ourselves of the idea of a "mother tongue" with all its accompanying psychological baggage and its infantalising of native speakers' (*Chaotic Angels*, p.143). The first section of the poem is framed through the device of a police file, and is spoken in the voice of a poet who confesses to the murder of the mother tongue. The second section, 'Memoirs of a Psychiatrist', seen through the persona of a psychiatrist, sees him in dialogue with the voice of a woman, Miss D, and the tapes of her analytic sessions. In the preface to *Keeping Mum* Lewis teases that she will not tell the English reader what happens in the Welsh-language version. Instead we are given in the English version a sequence of twelve sonnets which, using the language of Chaos Theory, describe various kinds of angels, and, like the previous two sections, suggest ways of knowing the self.

What is unusual about *Keeping Mum* is the way in which it holds on to its metaphorical interest in the power of language while still managing to dramatise and make real the intricacies of its characters' thought processes, never falling prey to the straightforwardly or reductively allegorical. The title *Keeping Mum*, with its punning ambivalence about the mother tongue, that also points to the language as a secret, or a silence which cannot be shared, is addressed directly in the sequence's first poem, 'A Poet's Confession' (part 1) (*Chaotic Angels*, p.146) when Lewis writes:

> All I wanted was a bit of fun
> with another body
> but now that she's gone –
> it's a terrible silence.

If the mother tongue here is seen, in the terms of Ashcroft et al, as a dangerous embodiment of culture, Lewis seems to be arguing for a simultaneous acknowledgement of that language's importance at the same time as advocating a relationship between language and nation which is freed of essentialist notions of intrinsic Welshness which are solely dependent *on* the language. Acknowledgment of the reality of bilingualism is not, of course, without its pain. As Lewis explains in the preface to the poem, 'The prospect of losing a whole culture is an existential nightmare for a Welsh speaker, fraught with questions of one's own responsibility in preserving collective values without becoming a parrot for the past.' (*Chaotic Angels*, p.143)

Such tensions are repeatedly returned to in the first section of the poem. In 'What's in a Name' (part 1) Lewis juxtaposes English and Welsh acts of naming, refusing, unlike in the Welsh espionage poem, for them to register in language as exact equivalents within the body. The poem begins with the wagtail which, oblivious of the ways in which it is named, 'kept on rooting in river moss' and continues in its lament for the names which have overwritten the Welsh names for bird. The other ways of naming that are not English represent not the same thing but 'another point of view, // another bird'. This 'culling' represents a blunting of the senses until, the poem seems to suggest, all we have is the silence of the unnamed and simply the thing itself. In 'Mother Tongue' (*Chaotic Angels*, p.148) the anxieties of reading literature in English rather than Welsh (in the context of other European literatures) and the secret desire for other languages are figured in terms of addiction, and again Lewis returns to the idea of language fetishism whereby we see her setting up language as a denial of what appears to be a metaphorical castration. It is in 'Her End' (*Chaotic Angels*, p.154; *MWP*, p.357) that we see the murdering of the Welsh language metaphorically staged in the murdering of a woman.

Perhaps surprisingly, there is much in this poem to remind us of Sitwell's own recourse to the image of the murdered mother and the Kleinian model of a relationship between mother and child as a model for creativity. Like Sitwell, too, Lewis turns to the abject

body as a way of configuring the relationship between language and
the body, and dramatising the separation between mother and child,
poet and the mother tongue: language is 'blood...full of filth', 'then
disgusting pus, and long-lost terms / like *gwelltor* and *rhychor*, her
vomit a road'. It is a 'saliva and sweat / of words' which 'poured
out like ants'. This time the Welsh phrases, proverbs, lines of poem,
single words, are glossed in a note at the end of the page, as ver-
bal debris is violently ejected from the body/nation. In *Sunbathing
in the Rain: A Cheerful Book About Depression*, Lewis draws on the
work of Julia Kristeva and object relations theories to discuss her
own depression and her relationship to language:

> Through her language skills, the daughter isn't aware that she has lost
> the mother because she can speak to and about her. Any unconscious
> rage at the breast that disappeared is directed not at the true mother
> but at her symbolic representation in language which is now part of
> the child. This may be why depressed people hate themselves so much.
> It's too dangerous to turn that rage on the mother – that would make
> the depressed person face a grief they fear would overwhelm them –
> so it's easier to hate the mother whose been symbolically absorbed into
> the patient's self through language.
>   For a poet, this theory has another fascinating implication. If lan-
> guage is a child's way of evading coming to terms with depression,
> how much more true must this be of a poet who has schooled herself
> in fluency and technique for years...Might not being bilingual in this
> instance become a way of evading the experience of despair to an even
> greater degree, as the poet would have so much more linguistic delight
> to distract her before crashing against depression's blank wall.[29]

In 'Aphasia' (*Chaotic Angels*, p.155) Lewis invokes theories of lan-
guage loss to draw wider points about the disconnection the
speaker has from the world of things, with apparent reference to
the linguist Roman Jakobson's famous essay, 'Two Aspects of
Language and Two Types of Aphasic Disturbances'[30] in which he
describes the 'the aphasic defect in the "capacity of naming"' as
being 'properly a loss of metalanguage' (*Language and Literature*,
p.104). Metalanguage is the language we use to describe language,
and in his study Jakobson points out its importance, particularly in
children who are learning the language. 'Loss of bilingualism,' he
writes, 'and confinement to a single dialectical variety of a single
language is a symbolic manifestation' of the kind of aphasia that
'can switch neither from a word to its synonyms or circumlocu-
tions not to its heteronyms (equivalent expressions in other lan-
guages)' (*Language in Literature*, p.104). If the links are being made
here implicitly between colonialism and psychic damage, this damage
is addressed head-on in section 2 of Lewis's poem.

Here the inability to put words to things in Lewis's work is explored in the context of the therapeutic process where a psychiatrist describes how his job in working with his patients is 'to translate / pain into tales they can tolerate / in another language' (*Chaotic Angels*, p.160). This ability to speak and not to speak is central to the book's truth. Lewis writes:

> Therapy's based on the premise that an accurate description of a situation releases the patient from being neurotically bound to it. Psychoanalysts have even more faith in language than do poets. In the face of experience our explanations always break down. Far from being a failure, however, this wordlessness is usually a clue that something more truthful than our own account of the world is being approached: the 'keeping mum' of this book's title. (*Chaotic Angels*, p.144)

In the final section of the poem Lewis turns to the angel as an image of transformation and spiritual communication. The angel for Lewis here is both muse and divine transcendence which sees her escaping from the body. She writes:

> I started to understand what a modern angel might be when I learned that the technical term for an unidentified object on a radar screen is 'an angel', that is a message which we can register, but not fully understand. Perhaps angels are a particularly sympathetic concept in the age of the mass media, when we understand a lot about the process of communication. Annunciations, however, are always mysterious and the message perhaps only partly understood at the time. The angel brings in more than we can understand, with our lives as they are. If the angel's received, then the life has to change to accommodate the message. Angels aren't creatures with wings wearing soft robes, to me, but are any act of communication when the weight of one world is brought down on another more superficial. These are always moments of difficulty and struggle.
> My understanding of religious truths isn't literal at all. I think of Christ as anything or anyone who shows up the nature of God, like dust in a stream of sunlight. Angels are abstract concepts which have taken on convenient figurative forms. For they are just a way of talking – but a dialogue between different worlds (hence the feet *and* wings).[31]

In *Keeping Mum* angels are messages which come from beyond language: the violence inflicted on the Welsh language by English, which blurs with the psychic difficulties of Miss D, are resolved by the divine message and 'Christ bringing cool dock leaves of mercy' (*Chaotic Angels*, p.191.) Such a resolution is especially interesting when read in the light of the relatively recent interest by the French feminist philosophers, in particular Luce Irigaray, who have suggesting that female 'becoming' is dependent on the creation of the divine.[32]

And while I have no space to include a full discussion here, it is worth noting that, after a movement towards the historical and political in Mebbh McGuckian's books *Captain Lavender* (1994), which carries an epigraph from Picasso, 'I have not painted war but I have no doubt that the war is in these paintings I have done', and *Shelmalier* (1997), which concerns the failed rebellion of the United Irishmen in 1798, her most recent volume, *The Book of the Angel* (2004), looks also to the angel as a figure of religious and poetic transformation.

KATHLEEN JAMIE

> We emigrants of no farewell
> who keep our bit language
>
> in jokes and quotes...[33]

Robert Crawford, in his *Identifying Poets: Self and Territory in Twentieth-Century Poetry*, draws on the work of the Russian theorist Mikhail Bakhtin to read modern poetry in terms of the 'identifying poet', one who 'construct[s] poetic selves that may be identified with particular territories' at the same time acknowledging that these territories are 'bound up with the shifting and constructed selves which lie at the heart of the Enlightenment itself and at the heart of post-enlightenment Romantic poetry'.[34] Crawford finds particular use in Bakhtin's idea of heteroglossia or 'other tonguedness' which he discusses in terms of the relationship between Scots and Englishness whereby when standard English words are used 'in the context of a Scots poem they appear to be "quoted" or recontextualised in the zone of Scots and are turned back on their more familiar identity. They become double-voiced, acting out a dialogue between Scots and English.' (*Identifying Poets*, p.7) Whereas in Lewis's work there is no potential for dialogue between languages – they must be kept apart in the oedipal triangle which threatens either murder or incest – in contrast the Scottish poet Kathleen Jamie (born 1962) moves with apparent ease between both English and Scots, and English poems which include Scots phrases or expressions. Jamie published her first collection of poems when she was just 19. Born in Fife, she has travelled extensively, writing about her travels in Pakistan, Baltistan, Amdo and Tibet in both poetry and prose.[35] Jamie juxtaposes these with a desire to write about home, and in *The Queen of Sheba* (1994) her explorations of Scotland and Scottishness are frequently figured in terms of transit and a juxtaposition of Scotland and Scottishness with that of other nations. Home, therefore, becomes imagined through otherness, not as one might perhaps have expected, through familiarity. Crawford argues that Scots is

> a deliberate variation on English, which frequently quotes, re-accents, and realigns elements of English vocabulary, mixing them with a rich impurity with alien elements (in the same way that some "Black English" works). Such Scots is a form of "dialogised heteroglossia", which is why the use of it affects not only Scottish but English identity... (*Identifying Poets*, p.7)

Despite my uneasiness with some of the assumptions Crawford makes here – the 'rich impurity of alien elements' that in spite of itself somehow slips, however ironically spoken, into the very discourse of colonialism it seeks to undermine, his discussion is nevertheless useful. In his use of Bakhtin, Crawford opens an otherwise useful way into thinking about Scottish poetry, and if we take his instances further, to other engagements through national languages with a dominant English:

> In Scotland we live between and across languages. Anyone who stays here and is interested in the spoken or written word is constantly aware of being on the edge of another tongue – of being a speaker of English who understands a bit of Scots, but knows no Gaelic; of being a Gaelic speaker who knows English but no Scots; even in a small number of cases of knowing all three tongues. Few Scottish people are totally monolingual, and the variety of languages between and across which we live is increasing, not simply as a result of education but also as a result of population movements that have given us Scottish people who are trilingual in English, Gaelic and Urdu or Glaswegians one of whose languages is Cantonese. (*Identifying Poets*, p.161)

Such across and betweenness is of course not exclusively a Scottish phenomenon but sees Jamie in a poem like 'The Republic of Fife' (*MMSD*, pp.147-48) juxtaposing different ways of knowing through different ways of speaking, whether in English or in Scots. The poem seems to accord well with Bakhtin's suggestion (paraphrased here by Crawford) that 'the creation of a vital cultural identity, like that of individual and personal literary identity, depends less on a looking in than on a looking out' (*Identifying Poets*, p.12):

> Citizens:
>
>   our spires and doocoots
>   institutes and tinkies' benders,
>   old Scots kings and dancing fairies
>   give strength to my house

> on whose roof we can balance,
> carefully stand and see
> clear to the far off mountains,
> cities, rigs and gardens,
>
> Europe, Africa, the Forth and Tay bridges,
> even dare let go, lift our hands
> and wave to the waving citizens
> of all those other countries.

'The Queen of Sheba' (*MMSD*, pp.111-13), the opening poem of Jamie's 1994 volume of the same title, is also written in both English and Scots. The poem dramatises a feminist response to the often repeated question asked of the woman who is seen to be above herself, 'who do you think you are?' The Queen of Sheba is invoked as a symbol of both sensuality and knowledge, of aspiration and the power of desire: '*All that she desires, whatever she asks* / She will make the bottled dreams / of your wee lasses / look like sweeties':

> Spangles scarcely cover
> her gorgeous breasts, hanging gardens
> jewels, frankincense; more voluptuous
> even than Vi-next-door, whose
> high-heeled slippers
> keeked from dressing gowns
> like little hooves, wee tails
> of pink fur stuffed in the cleavage of her toes...

Here the otherness of the black body does not become a stereotype of eastern exoticism; rather it figures as a model of female power which escapes the boundaries of "race", nation, and, even the text:

> The cool black skin
> of the Bible couldn't hold her,
> nor the atlas green
> on the kitchen table,
> you stuck with thumbs
> and split to fruity hemispheres –
> Yellow Yemen, Red Sea, *Ethiopia*...

In 'The Sea-House' (*MMSD*, p.154), national identity and femininity become figured as equally unfixable, with the establishment of a women's place seen as shifting, and 'neither-nor', transitory in both time and space:

> The sea-house is purdah:
> cormorants' hooked-out wings
> screen every chamber. Inside
> the shifting place, the
> neither-nor

> I knock back and forth
> like the tongue of a bell...

In 'Another Day in Paradise' (*MMSD*, pp.151-53), Jamie seems to be locating the imagination elsewhere, from which she can negotiate the state, making of the debris washed up on her desert island a 'shoppers-survey-cum-government-demand, / with a slightly genetic spelling error' a 'a small boat / that flutters in your cupped hands / and wants to sail' . This she returns to the 'brand shining new / state museum' while placing on board an '*island totem*; an electric blue feather, / a shell, the stretched and cured // pelt of a wild-fruit, / which you wrap around a pebble / in the manner of shepherds / with an orphaned lamb' (*MMSD*, p.151).

Whereas in 'Mrs and Mrs Scotland Are Dead' (*MMSD*, p.134; *MWP*, p.372) the cultural ephemera and detritus which come to represent Scottishness in the previous generation are viewed on the municipal landfill site, in her post-Scottish devolution *The Tree House* (2004),[36] Jamie shifts towards an identification as much with Scottishness and femininity as with nature. Her explorations of a national 'home' are figured in terms of a negotiation with the natural world. *The Tree House* is in part influenced by the ecocritic Jonathan Bate's book *The Song of the Earth* (2000).[37] Jamie writes:

Jonathan Bate writes that there is an essential role for poetry...that since the Romantics, the poet's job has been to mediate between self and world, to explore 'the relationship between external environment and ecology of mind'. Poetry is the place where we consider or calibrate our relationships – with ourselves, our culture, history. However, with the natural world, many of our approaches have been infantalised, or cauterised. 'We have forgotten the language needed for such communication' writes Thomas Berry, who calls our situation 'autistic'.

So, I wanted to think about encounters with the non-human world, and try to bring myself into right, non-autistic, relationship, which is more wranglesome than it sounds. Not least because of language. As humans, our singing, dreaming and being is conducted in language. I used to think that our Fall was the fall into language, that language only served to obfuscate our relationship with the world, but this doesn't stand up to examination. Another book which helped is *Forests*, by Robert Poque Harrison who says 'We dwell not in nature but in relation to nature' and 'Language is the ultimate "place" of human habitation.' Best among language is a poem, which is a "hained" space, an enclosure. A poem sets itself apart from ordinary discourse, but, through image and shared meaning and metaphor, is ever in relationship. I think now that language, especially poetry, can open and clarify our relationships; can sustain communication, and save us from "autism".[38]

The Tree House is a collection suffused with flora and fauna: there are encounters with pipistrelles, kites, whales, daisies, rhododendrons, dolphins, sharks, 'jellyfish: mauve-fringed, luminous bowls / like lost internal organs, / pulsing and slow' (*Tree House*, p.21). Yet rather than providing either a straightforwardly political or a psychic landscape, for Jamie the natural and the human begin, in every sense, to take surreally coalesce. The first poem in the collection, 'The Wishing Tree', draws together these ways of knowing home as the human body merges with a tree (*Tree House*, pp.3-4):

> My limbs lift, scabbed
> with greenish coins
>
> I draw into my slow wood
> fleur-de-lys, the enthroned Britannia.
>
> Behind me, the land
> reaches towards the Atlantic.

The poem concludes with an image of hope for both humanity and the nature of which it is a part: 'look: I am still alive –' she writes, 'in fact, in bud'. The tree house of the title-poem (pp.41-43) is figured as an elsewhere as its narrator sleeps beside 'neither man / nor child, but a lichened branch' the 'hundred other lives, / like taxis strangers hail and hire' that she might have lived. The childish house made of wood that lodges in the tree is a place from where she surveys the landscape, 'gardens of dockens / and lady's mantle, kids' bikes / stranded on the grass'. It is an intermediary place, between nature and "culture":

> a dwelling of sorts; a gall
> we've asked the tree to carry
> of its own dead, and every spring
> to drape in leaf and blossom, like a pall.

Elsewhere we see Jamie playing with the divide between the social and the natural world, and its – to use a phrase from Bate's *The Song of the Earth* which has clearly been important to her – 'complex and delicate web'. In 'Stane-Raw' (*Tree House*, p.35) the marks of the natural world are compared to the marks we make on ourselves and each other as human beings, as the inscriptions on the human body work as a symbol of its interconnectedness with nature, implicitly in parallel perhaps with the marks made by the poem on the page:

> *Our* kisses are fleet, invisible;
> should we wish to
> keep or carry one, we must
> transmute it to a bruise-
> coloured tattoo, hidden
> beneath our clothing, like this
> indelible dog rose

inked on my shoulder,
the finch on my inner thigh.

In 'The Buddleia' (*Tree House*, p.27) Jamie chooses to 'retire the masculine / God of my youth / by evoking instead the divine / in the lupins, or foxgloves, or self- / seeded buddleia'. The clever line break between self and seeded, which makes the human self divine as well as the buddleia, is followed by the interruption into lyricism of 'bumbling, well-meaning bees / which remind me again, / of my father...whom, Christ, / I've forgotten to call'. Here Jamie upbraids herself for getting lost not only in nature but in the lyric moment. In her distraction from a daughter's responsibility – and again relying on a clever ambiguity – she reminds us, not without irony and exasperation, that familial relationships are also holy.

The holiness of nature is a central theme for Hölderlin whose lines 'But it is beautiful to unfold our souls / And our short lives' are an epigraph to the volume. In asking also 'how should we live' in 'The Puddle', Jamie echoes the preoccupations of Heidegger in his 1951 essay on Hölderlin '...Poetically man dwells...', discussed at some length by Bate. Jamie also includes several Scots versions of Hölderlin which are concerned with establishing 'hame' through an exploration of the lush wonders of the natural world. In an analysis of the Hölderlin, Bate writes:

> 'Dwells' (German *wohnet*) suggests a sense of belonging. But what is meant by 'yet poetically' (*doch dichterisch*)? A superficial answer might be 'yet linguistically': well deserving (because of his evolutionary superiority), yet as a language animal, man dwells on this earth. 'Dwelling' and well deserving may be regarded as conditions apprehensible only in language. We understand the terms by means of an instant mental comparison with their linguistic opposites ('homelessness' and 'ill deserving'). Yet they may also be conditions which we convince ourselves we can feel pre-linguistically – instinctively, in the guts. This contradictory apprehension brings us directly to the central paradox of poetry. Poetry is merely language. Yet poetry is not merely language, because when we allow it to act upon us it seems able to conjure up conditions such as dwelling and alienation *in their very essence*, not just in their linguistic particulars. (*Song of the Earth*, p.260)

Heidegger's interest in Hölderlin is as a national poet who can speak in an age when the gods no longer walk among us. In 'Hame' (*Tree House*, p.28), a version of Hölderlin's 'Heimat', Jamie writes of home as an earthly paradise 'whaur ah wunner' (where I wonder)

> – here whaur jags o roses
> and gean-trees
> pit oot thur sweet air,
> aside the birks, at noon

As an English-speaking reader it is only by going to a Scots diction-
ary that I can find out that 'gean-trees' are cherry trees, that 'birks'
are birches, and that the 'yird', to whom the poem is addressed, is
the earth. As in Lewis's poem about the naming of the natural
world, the use of Scots asks that the non-Scots-speaking reader
knows that world differently, even anew. But where Lewis's bilin-
gualism has loss inscribed within it, Jamie's is much more celebra-
tory of the differences of knowing, differences doubly highlighted by
the fact that she draws on a poem itself in another language. The
poems in Scots in her *oeuvre* are addressed to a precise Scots-
speaking readership, and, without glosses, as when reading Lewis's
Welsh, we must feel the Scots in our mouth, speak it and hear it
if we are at least to partially understand it. In marking its cultural
difference in an English-language volume, published by a com-
mercial London publisher, Jamie is offering a version of home
inscribed in Scots, which sits alongside her poems in English. She
negotiates difficult ground here, not, I think, in a way which offers
Scots as the ultimate way of knowing home, but as a way of writing
into the collection its importance as one way of knowing, which
works, as indeed Crawford has suggested, in dialogue with her
English-language poems, changing the way we read the English
poems, and the relationship between body and nation, in the process.

JACKIE KAY

> the blood does not bind confusion,
> yet I confess to my contradiction
> I want to know my blood.[39]

If the black body of 'The Queen of Sheba' comes to represent a
resistant female Scottishness, in *The Adoption Papers* (1991) we see
how Jackie Kay (born 1961) throws into question ways of marking
difference whether by colour or nationality, or gender, asking what it
means to mother, to be a mother, to be Scottish, to be female, to
be black as she tells the story of the adoption of a black baby by a
white Scottish couple in the 1960s. *The Adoption Papers* is written in
three different female voices, that of the adoptive mother, the birth
mother and the birth daughter, and in its format surely recalls that
other poem for three female voices (written in 1962, a year after
Kay's birth), Sylvia Plath's 'Three Women'. The experiences of
Kay's three women, whose voices appear interweaved, distinguished
by differing typefaces, are explored as each begins to come to terms

with her identity as mother and daughter, and each deals with a different sort of loss. The poem unfolds the story of a black child searching for her white birth mother (the poem is divided into ten chapters and spans the years 1961-90) detailing the child's formative experiences as she tries to locate herself culturally and define herself as a black Scottish woman. We see the child looking for black role models whom she finds in the American activist and communist Angela Davis, the only black woman apart from a nurse on TV she had ever seen, and dealing with racism as she questions stereotypes of supposedly genetically determined "black" qualities. Black is something as puzzling to the child as it might be to her white Scottish contemporaries:

> [M]y teacher shouts from the bottom
> of the class Come on, show
>
> us what you can do I thought
> you people had it in your blood.
> My skin is hot as burning coal
> like that time she said Darkies are like coal
> in front of the whole class – my blood
> what does she mean? I thought
>
> she'd stopped all that after the last time
> my dad talked to her on parents' night
> the other kids are all right till she starts;
> my feet step out of time, my heart starts
> to miss beats like when I can't sleep at night –
> *What Is In My Blood?* The bell rings, it is time.
>
> (*Adoption Papers*, p.25)

As well as questioning the essential nature of blackness, Kay also questions the essential nature of maternity as set up against each other, in relation to both "motherhood" and "race". The adoptive mother explains

> Now when people say 'ah but
> it's not like having your own child though is it,'
> I say of course it is, what else is it?
> she's my child, I have told her stories
> wept at her losses, laughed at her pleasures
> she is mine.
>
> I was always the first to hear her in the night
> all this umbilical knot business is nonsense
> – the men can afford deeper sleeps that's all.
> I listened to hear her talk,
> and when she did I heard my voice under hers
> and now some of her mannerisms crack me up...
>
> (*Adoption Papers*, p.23)

As a whole, *The Adoption Papers* offers a wider metaphor for the
self, suggesting that the relationships between gender and the body
are unstable in their ownership. In the rest of the poems that make
up the book Kay shifts the emphasis from a specifically female
black experience to explore gender and sexuality through a series
of dramatic monologues in the voices of both women and men.

As we have seen, the dramatic monologue works as a device
which simultaneously presents and masks in its embodiment. Kay
frequently uses the monologue to deconstruct "difference" as it
becomes constructed through the body. In 'Dressing Up' (*Adoption
Papers*, p.57), for example, a male, working-class Scottish trans-
vestite spends Christmas with his mother who has been battered
by a drunken father:

> ...See at Christmas I had
> on black stockings Santa would kill
> for and even Quentin Crisp would
> look drab beside my beautiful
> feather boa – bright fucking red.
>
> Ma ma didn't touch her turkey
> Finally she said What did I do
> I know what they call you, transvite.
> You look a bloody mess you do.
> She had a black eye, a navy dress.

The mother of the poem wears the violence inflicted on her by her
husband in contrast to the monologist's wearing of his highly-sex-
ualised version of femininity, his 'beautiful / feather boa – bright
fucking red'. The failure of the mother to properly name her son
is a failure to see that his identity, just as hers, is constructed cul-
turally. It is his vestments that she equates with his masculinity;
and yet the irony of the poem is that her own bodily "adornment"
is not chosen, it cannot be taken on and off at will. It is inflicted
on the body in the violence of her relationship.

Kay's second collection, *Other Lovers* (1993),[40] includes more
apparently autobiographical poems as well as a sequence based on
the life of the Blues singer Bessie Smith (1894-1937). Whereas in *The
Adoption Papers* Kay was dramatising an intensely personal exper-
ience of blackness, with the sequence of Bessie poems she seeks to
link herself to a continuum of black women's experience that oper-
ates outside national boundaries, and a tradition which asserts
women's strength and independence. Kay also suggests that unless
we remember the cruelty and violence of women's oppression,
such cruelties might be dangerously repeated. In 'Even the trees'
(*Other Lovers*, p.9) she writes:

down and down, a blue song in the beat of her heart,
in an old car that crossed

a railroad track; the scream of a warning –
is that why we remember certain things and not others;

the sound of the bass, the sound of the whip, the strange
strangled wind, bruises floating through light air

like leaves and landing, landing, here; this place
Everything that's happened once could happen again.

In interview Kay has spoken of the difficulty she finds in calling herself British, and indeed of the labelling which goes on in an attempt to construct an identity for her. In 'Sign' (*Other Lovers*, pp.20-21), a deaf woman has her arms bound behind her back. The suppression of the woman's sign language, where language becomes the body, becomes a metaphor for an attack on specifically female self-expression and creativity, as well as the patriarchal/colonial attempt to stamp out a language which it cannot control or understand:

Imagine

seeing language in shapes
before your eyes – dynamic
and metrical – forcing
you to focus;
your conversation a spatial relation-
ship between mouth eyes and hands.
The space between the planets.
And somebody telling you, *that's miming
that's pantomime.* Somebody who
cannot separate a word
from a thought.
All this

distance

between one language and another; one
culture and another; one religion
and another. The *little languages*
squashed, stamped upon, cleared out
to make way
for the big one, better tongue.
These things happen
between

time

The day they forced her to speak
their tongue, she lost
the black-eyed-susan.
She went back in
time

> They say her voice is very strange.
> They tie her hands behind her back.
> They say repeat after me until
> she has *no language at all.*

Kay's explorations of identity's multifacedness are continued in her most recent collection, *Life Mask* (2005). Rather than a photograph of the author on the back of the book, we are given a photograph of a wax cast with the mould of her face by the sculptor Michael Snowden, a photograph which draws attention to the fact that poems too are made things, inventions and personae which bear a relationship to the poet, but which are not her. Many of the poems in the collection tell of the breakdown of a relationship which becomes figured through the metaphor of the process of sculpture, the imaging and casting of the body, what she describes in one poem as '[t]he staging of my body.' In 'Old Tongue' (*Life Mask*, p.50) language and the body are directly connected as she writes, 'My own vowels started to stretch like my bones / And I turned back on Scotland'. As in Jamie's work, it is language that connects her with Scottishness, but a Scottishness again figured here in resistance to Englishness:

> Out in the English soil, my old words
> buried themselves. It made my mother's blood boil.
> I cried one day with the wrong sound in my mouh.
> I wanted them back; I wanted my old accent back,
> my old tongue. My dour Scottish tongue.
> *Sing-songy.* I wanted to *gie it laldie.*

MONIZA ALVI

Pakistan was a fantasy, nourished by vivid family stories, extraordinary gifts, letters, news items and anecdotes...Perhaps it's because Pakistan and my connection with that country strikes me as so surreal and fantastical in itself that I haven't quite got over it. Perhaps the country of my birth has become a symbol of other losses.[42]

Moniza Alvi, who was born in Pakistan in 1954, moved to England when she was only a few months old. Alvi is non-Urdu speaking, with English as her first language, and she has spoken of only having the confidence to return to Pakistan after she had begun to write about it. Her first collection, *The Country at My Shoulder* (1993),[42] in its evocation of a country, is 'not necessarily...a geographical location, but...a reference to the hidden worlds that can be entered through poetry' (*CWP*, p.36). Throughout the volume the connections between the body and nation are returned to. In the surreal 'The Sari' (*Carrying My Wife*, p.137), for example, the sari becomes a protection and marker of identity, whilst also carrying with it intimations of the corpse's winding cloth:

> All the people unravelled a sari.
> It stretched form Lahore to Hyderabad,
> wavered across the Arabian Sea,
> shot through with stars,
> fluttering with sparrows and quails.
> They threaded it with roads,
> undulations of land.
>
> Eventually
> they wrapped and wrapped me in it
> whispering Your body is your country

These final lines perhaps make reference to Virginia Woolf's famous assertion in *Three Guineas* that 'As a woman I have no country'. In making the body her country, like McGuckian, Alvi draws together the private and the domestic into the public and national realm. In 'Presents from My Aunts in Pakistan' Alvi refers to her country of origin as 'a fractured land / throbbing through newsprint' (*Carrying My Wife*, pp.131-32). With the use of the word fracture the nation state is again metaphorically identified with the body and in her first volume's title poem Alvi writes how '[t]he country has become my body – / I can't break bits off' (*Carrying My Wife*, pp.135-36; *MWP*, pp.321-22).

'Throwing Out My Father's Dictionary' (*Carrying My Wife*, p.128; *MWP*, p.320) is a complex meditation on how we learn language, both on the literal level of the father who has to learn English, and how the poet, the daughter of the language learner who has no Urdu and only English through which to express her dual identities, relates to the places in language where both old and new, generations, sexes and cultures, intersect. The poem, while rejecting the tenets of Empire under which her father's generation were oppressed, seems to suggest that the decay of the old regime also heralds a mulching of cultures, one which within the poem becomes distinctly feminised. The dictionary in the poem which has been thrown away is disposed of with items with powerful symbolic resonances. The metaphorical composting of language takes place alongside imagery associated with birth, femininity, and fecundity as 'Words grow shoots in the bin / with the eggshells and rotting fruit'. The rotting of language, its decomposition, seems to suggest a regeneration or a move towards some kind of cohesion, something emphasised by the toffee-glue revealed when

the dictionary's back fell off. And yet the toffee-glue which is ex-
posed on the dictionary's binding is an ambiguous image because
it is present only because of disintegration. Its sweetness associates
it with the mouth, where of course language takes form.

To write his name in the dictionary, the speaker's father has
asserted authority over the language of imperialism. In this context
it's hard not to register the possible implications of a word like
'rifle', a word which carries connotations of violence in its literal
etymology from the Old French, 'to search with intent to steal',
and with its militaristic associations with the noun 'rifle'. The father
of the poem is identified with tarragon, an aromatic, and bitter herb
associated with the cooking of his country. The new words which
the speaker has, and which are an integrated part of her identity,
work like a hybrid in that they represent the assimilation of non-
English words into an English vocabulary, the *chador* or headscarf
worn by Muslim women as well as new words which derive from
new experiences of the modern world. The clash within the dic-
tionary of tradition and modernity, the wearing of the *chador* which
preserves the female's modesty and 'Sick building syndrome', a
concept which at its core, both literally and metaphorically surely
suggests a basic rottenness at the core of modernity, and ultimately
of capitalism, are both alien to her. The speaker of the poem is
placed between cultures and traditions and she cannot authorita-
tively place her name within this new ordering. Alvi seems to be
suggesting that it is in the place between that she can find a place
for herself. This place between is not the language of the new dic-
tionary either but is the poem itself, product of the rejection of one
culture and the resistance to what one might be if one simply brings
together but does not reconcile or transform the two. It is only by
the hybridity of cultures which coalesce, outside the ordering of
symbolic language, but in a place of decay and regeneration, that
such reconciliation can take place.

The surreal poem 'I Was Raised in a Glove Compartment' (*Carry-
ing My Wife*, p.112) in which an unborn child exists in dark con-
tainment never seeing her mother's face figures the self in terms
that move away from the body: 'sometimes / her gloved hand would
reach for me. // I existed in the quiet – I listened / for the sound
of the engine.' The equally surreal 'I Would Like to be a Dot in a
Painting by Miró' (*Carrying My Wife*, p.118; *MWP*, p.319) also
suggests a desire for the absence of the body, and the desire to
replace the figurative with Miró's biomorphic abstraction.

In *A Bowl of Warm Air* (1996) Alvi's anxiety about the exchange
between languages is directly addressed, as Dowson and Entwistle

have pointed out, in her poem 'Hindi Urdu Bol Chaal' 'stages [a dialogue] between the two major languages of the Indian subcontinent':[43]

> I shall be borrowed from England.
> Pakistan, assalaam alaikum –
> Peace be with you – Helloji.

This idea of finding a place for herself between England and Pakistan is spelled out in the later autobiographical poem 'Go Back to England'.[44] It is perhaps a less successful poem in its explicit approach to the subject, but shows Alvi's need to return to these issues in a way which allows us to usefully reflect on the earlier poem when she writes of becoming English as something which happens to the body through language:

> My mother hoped to be
> a different mother.
>
> The ocean knew
> I would be translated
>
> into an English girl.

In her later work, *Souls* (2002) and *How the Stone Found Its Voice* (2005),[45] Alvi continues to play with ideas of the body and disembodiedness, taking on the persona of the voice of a husband who writes sequences of poems about 'my wife'. These poems are less monologues than canny poems of self-address which see Alvi writing about the self in a manner which serves to distance and reflect, rather than refract. Anxieties about language and the body are returned to again as the image of stickiness we saw in the toffee-glue in 'Throwing Out My Father's Dictionary' recurs in 'England, I am Gazing at Your Body' (*How the Stone Found Its Voice*, p.28), this time resulting in a metaphor of sexual intercourse between the speaker of the poem and the English landscape with which she has union:

> all I can do is sniff you, your industrial belts,
> your hedgerows, your crags and reservoirs,
> rest an elbow on a grass roundabout.

The poem concludes with the lines 'I pull myself off you. / Hard to prise the stickiness from yours' suggesting, if we follow the metaphor, that the relationship to nation involves a potentially fertile, if not especially romantic, exchange.

JO SHAPCOTT

People expect poets to write about themselves and their history. Even when it's not about you, they'll read your poem as if it is. Novelists are allowed to make things up and take things anywhere they want. I love that freedom. In my writing there's lots about boundaries and different skins and different worlds. It may be that I feel the self is enclosing, and I like the idea that you can pass out of it, and get into other places, other imaginations, other skins.[46]

Perhaps surprisingly, and with the exception of Stevie Smith, the exploration of Englishness has been little addressed by women poets. Englishnessness itself is of course not a monolithic identity, and national identities can be complex in their interactions with both regional and cultural as well as class differences. The title-poem of Jo Shapcott's second collection, *Phrase Book* (1992),[47] deals with love and death, language and technology, the role of the personal in the political, and the modern response to advanced warfare in the context of the relationship between language and Englishness. The poem is written in the voice of an English woman who performs her disorientation in the crisis of war through the fractured and fragmented language which is all she has to record her experiences. 'Phrase Book' (*Her Book*, pp.65-66; *MWP*, pp.309-10) is a poem about difficulty and about conflict, and as such seems held together by a kind of centrifugal force as, throughout the poem, phrases and themes pull against each other: meaning becomes doubled and ambiguous. Like Walter Benjamin's angel of history, the speaker of the poem is caught between the past and the future, she is a cultural refugee, her suitcase in hand. Setting her poem in 1991 during the first Gulf War, Shapcott is juxtaposing neatly the failure of both private and public worlds. Communication between the sexes has broken down at a time not only of war, but of a war which was transmitted by satellite to the rest of world. 'This is my own front room,' says the voice of the poem, 'where I'm lost in the action, live from a war, / on screen'. Here the idea of engrossment, being lost in the act of watching the small screen, doubles with the idea of death in war. The syntactic ambiguity and careful line break here, prompting again a sense of doubleness whereby 'live' may also be read as '*live*', giving a sense of the viewer as parasite, feeding off, living on, the images of war. The art critic Hal Foster's autobiographical account of his experiences as a civilian watching the war via CNN describes the effect of the coverage:

Repelled by the politics, I was riveted by the images, by a psycho-techno-thrill that locked me in, as smart bomb and spectator are locked in as one. A thrill of techno-mastery (my mere human perception became a super machine vision, able to see what it destroys and to destroy what it sees), but also a thrill of an imaginary dispersal of my own body, of my own subjecthood. Of course, when the screen of the smart bombs went dark, my body did not explode. On the contrary, it was bolstered: in a classic fascistic trope, my body, my subjecthood, was affirmed in the destruction of other bodies. In this techno-sublime, then, there is a partial return of a fascistic subjecthood, which occurs at the level of the mass too, for such events are massively mediated, and they produce a psychic collectivity – a psychic nation, as it were, that is also defined against cultural otherness both within an without.[49]

Foster refers to the process of watching the war on screen as a

spatio-temporal splitting, the paradox of the immediacy produced through mediation; a moral splitting, the paradox of disgust undercut by fascination, or of sympathy undercut by sadism... If a postmodern subject can be pointed to at all, it is made and unmade in such splittings. (*The Return of the Real*, p.222)

Foster's response is indeed close to the response of the poem. Torn between *eros* and *thanatos* the (whole) notion of selfhood becomes contained within the Human Remains Pouch: a container for the self which will only do for the moment. The skin is simply a body bag for the remnants of a mutilated or disassembled self; but also with its strange intimation of an embryonic or structure, it doubles as the marsupial pouch within which life might be nurtured, and out of which something positive may emerge. Yet Shapcott's poem goes further than Foster's eloquent reading of his emotions. For not only is it interrogating the role of the poet during such a conflict, but it is looking towards the past by way of a response to the present and the future. The camera angles of the first stanza 'Look down there (up here). / Quickly. Slowly' serve to locate the reader as the reader attempts to put together the fragments that are the articulation of this fragmented self. 'What does it mean/ What must I do? Where / can I find? What have I done?' This is a self whose questions echo the painter Gauguin's 'Where do we come from / Who are we? Where are we going?' (*The Return of the Real*, p.208) – questions which became representative of modernity's concern with identity, and postmodernism's insistence on a refusal of such questions' answerability.

Vicki Bertram usefully points out that in Shapcott's monologues the

[r]eaders' constant awareness of the poet herself behind the persona enhances the impression of a self-conscious performance. But there is an interesting twist to this: where conventional representations make

woman the objectified spectacle, in Shapcott's poems she provides a
running commentary on her own physicality, thus insisting on her
existence as a subject. Furthermore, the focus on visuals is replaced with
an emphasis on touch and motion, because it is the speaker's version
of events that dominates, and she is preoccupied with the feel, not the
look of things.[50]

In 'Phrase Book' the idea of self is located in several ways throughout
the poem: the voice which takes on the parodic voice of the phrase
book; the voice which is more knowing, which talks of the war in
the technical language of the war; and finally the voice which gathers
phrases from other works of literature. As a way of establishing a
correspondence between the present and the past, Shapcott' makes
extensive intertextual reference to Book X of Wordsworth's *The
Prelude*, subtitled 'Residence in France and the French Revolution'
– the lines in the third stanza, 'Bliss is how it was in this very room'
echoing Wordsworth's 'Bliss was it in that dawn to be alive, / But
to be young was very heaven.' Like Shapcott's speaker, Wordsworth
too is unable to express himself (both because he has little French)
and because he has no words for his horror at the carnage which
he has seen:

> I crossed (a blank and empty area then)
> The Square of the Carousel, few weeks back
> Heaped up with dead and dying, upon these
> And other sights looking as doth a man
> Upon a volume whose contents he knows
> Are memorable, but from him locked up.
> Being written in a tongue he cannot read,
> So that he questions the mute leaves with pain
> And half upbraids their silence.
>   (Book X, lines 46-54)[50]

Shapcott offers a subtle parody of Wordsworth's poem, based as
much on her sense of connection with his preoccupation with ideas
of memory and language, as his shifting response to the Revoluton
which turns from sympathy ('I was as far as angels are from guilt':
Book X, line 127) to terror and horror. But whereas for Words-
worth it is nature which saves the individual from 'destruction by
material and social pressures' (113) Shapcott's speaker has no sense
of a 'true self'. As Linda Hutcheon has pointed out

> postmodernist ironic rethinking of history is definitely not nostalgic. It
> critically contrasts the past with the present, and vice versa... The crit-
> ique of its irony is double edged; the past and the present are judged
> in each other's light.[51]

Shapcott's choice of Wordsworth, the poet who writes 'in a selection
of language really used by men' in which the 'passions of men are

incorporated with the beautiful and permanent forms of nature' (Wordsworth, p.597) is also doubly ironic. Within 'Phrase Book' language as we know it becomes a kind of debris – at some points decontextualised, at some points sanitised, ostensibly unproblematised – it takes on a purely functional status. The phrase book phrases offer a way of seeing the world without fully understanding the implications. As Wittgenstein asks in *Zettel*:

> 'Say "abcd" and mean: the weather is fine.' – Should I say, then, that the utterance of a sentence in a familial language is a quite different experience from the utterance of sounds which are not familiar to us as a sentence? So if I learnt a language in which 'abcd' meant that – should I come bit by bit to have the familial experience when I pronounced the letters? Yes and no. – A major difference between the two cases is that in the first one I *can't move.* It's as if one of my joints were in splints, and I not yet familiar with the possible movements, so that I as it were keep on stumbling.[52]

Yet this is all that the Englishwoman has left of her language now: so alienated is she from the language of technology and war.

The *Sunday Times* of 3 February 1991 issued what it called an A-Z of war speak. 'The War in the Gulf,' the article begins, 'has produced its own vocabulary, a language of battle that is becoming daily more familiar through the continuous media coverage of the hostilities.' It continues:

> The modern soldier, sailor or airman has his own slang, acronyms and abbreviations, all adapted to the desert battle zone. Much of it is pejorative and used of the enemy; it is an exclusive jargon, a private language that binds together the men who are enduring adversity and risking their lives. Some of it is the jargon of weaponry, affectionate descriptions of the tools of the trade...put together it and must be understood.

The most central of these pieces of war jargon is the acronym that is quoted in the third stanza. The acronym BLISS which the pilots use to fly is ironically juxtaposed with the ecstasy with which the woman meets her lover's body, her body raised to his mouth. At this point of contact the woman is in flight, arms outspread, sacrificial, balanced in the composite figure of bird, aeroplane, angel. Her Molly Bloomish assertions of pleasure and the memory of pleasure are caught by 'The Side-Looking Airborne Radar, and through the J-Stars'. And throughout the poem the terms of war also take on a double meaning. Metaphors for the pursuit and seduction and destruction of the love object: the J-Stars (perhaps even a pun on the poet's own name) are the 'joint surveillance and targeting acquisition radar system'; sexual bliss becomes a strategy for evasion and escape, an acronym that the pilots learn – Blend, Low silhouette, Irregular shape, Small, Secluded. The Killbox, the rectangle on a radar screen in which a target is blown up becomes part of a strategy for finding and destroying the love object – perhaps even a jokey vagina dentata – as sex and destruction become entwined as the Englishwoman asks: "What's love in all this debris? / Just one person pounding another into dust, / into dust.'

Although the poem's narrative voice is fragmented and unstable, it still asserts twice within the poem that it is 'an Englishwoman'. And again we see a double image. For the voice that declares itself an Englishwoman – the upholder of Empire, of femininity, of stiff upper lip in the face of adversity – is simultaneously an English-woman who can't understand, can't collude with the war though the kind of language – born of war, patriarchy, capitalism – which refuses to take responsibility for its own acts of killing. 'HARM', the acronym for 'high speed anti-radiation missile' fitted to the wild weasels to pick off fixed radars, becomes associated with the potentially unfaithful penis. Her assertion at the end of the poem – 'I have done / nothing. Let me pass please.' – is simultaneously an abnegation of responsibility as much as it is a plea to remove itself from the new language of technology which refuses to take responsibility for its actions. The Englishwoman has no reason to be guilty – she hasn't done anything wrong; yet nor has she, in answer to her earlier question, perhaps done enough.

In placing the figure of the woman who speaks in the language of the 1950s language learner's phrase book, Shapcott perhaps offers us a revised image of post-imperial Britannia who has to learn her own broken sense of Englishness. Disorientation from the power of her national identity and alienation from her body – the human remains pouch – culminates in the final lines of the poem, 'Let me pass please, I am an Englishwoman.' The ambiguities of passing – getting past, passing the test of Englishness, and the acute ironisa-tion of that statement of subjectivity – throw into question not only essential Englishness but essential femininity too. In 'Motherland', a 'version' of a Marina Tsvetaeva poem, Shapcott turns instead to a female poetic model – albeit a non-English one – in an attempt to describe her sense of exile from an Englishness what in another poem she refers to as that 'complicated shame'. If in Lewis's work we saw a complicated relationship evolving between the infantali-sation of the speaker, in Alvi an interrogation of the dictionary for a presence of her colonial past, in Shapcott's poem the dictionary resists her attempt to understand the words 'England', 'Motherland', 'Home'.

Shapcott has described how her 'quest has been to discover how to be a different kind of writer, for whom place and language are less certain, and for whom shifting territories are the norm'.[54] Shapcott's model in rethinking a relationship with nation is Elizabeth Bishop (1911-79), whose poem 'The Map', she writes, 'read to me like formal permission to put travel, rootlessness, even lost identity, at the centre' (*Elizabeth Bishop: Poet of the Periphery*, p.116). It is to the importance of Bishop's influence on Shapcott and her contemporaries that I turn in my final chapter.

CHAPTER SEVEN

Objecting to the Subject: Science, Nature, Femininity and Poetic Process

> From neuroscience and cognitive science we now understand that our thinking is "embodied", that the concept of body/mind duality no longer provides a satisfactory account of the way we perceive. I love this idea and its implications for language: that the images we invent are intrinsic to the way we see the world – according to thinkers like Lakoff, metaphors actually structure the way we think. All this puts poetry right at the centre of our (bodily) experience.[1] – JO SHAPCOTT

Anxieties around the establishment of a poetic voice that is able to reach beyond the perceived limitations of femininity in the lyric are, as we have seen, sustained in women's poetic writing throughout the 20th century. Attempts to re-forge the relationship between the gendered body of the poet and the poem are explored variously through a return to the dramatic monologue, the structures of myth and fairytale, and an over-determination of the self in confessional poetry, as well through the use of surrealist techniques.

In the first part of this final chapter I turn to look at the use made of science – as both metaphor and approach – in the work of two very different poets, Jo Shapcott (born 1953) and Lavinia Greenlaw (born 1962). As David Kennedy has pointed out, the burgeoning interest in 'the use of science is inextricable from British poetry's anxiety in the 1980s and early 1990s about its authority, function and role...The use of science is not only a badge of rational "fitness" but a way of bolstering poetry's traditional claims to be the discourse of the ultimate truth.'[2] Such a diagnosis is made with Kennedy's usual clarity, but I want to suggest here that for women these anxieties about poetic authority and 'rational "fitness"' are doubly complicated and compounded because of the traditional associations of femininity with self-effacement and irrationality.

The common influence for Shapcott and Greenlaw – indeed one of the most influential for both male and female poets in contemporary writing – is the American poet Elizabeth Bishop. Bishop has proven an important poet not least because of the contrast – even antidote – she offers to the perceived self-exposure and performance of the women confessionals. Bishop's *Selected Poems* was published in Britain in 1967, and a *Complete Poems* in 1970, 1983 and (in paperback) in 1991,[3] and the slow assimilation of her work into a wider public consciousness occurred almost in parallel with the slow release of Sylvia Plath's books in the 1970s, which culminated in the publication of her *Collected Poems* in 1981. Bishop is not a poet who writes "about" science, but her scrupulously detailed, observant poetic offers an important model for both Shapcott and Greenlaw.

Shapcott and Greenlaw look to science as a way of rethinking fixed structures and empirical givens, using it simultaneously as a discourse of authority associated with masculinity as well as a way of questioning that authority. In the second part of the chapter and, by way of contrast, I think about the poetry of Alice Oswald (born 1966). Oswald, a classicist who later trained as a gardener, is predominantly a nature poet, and I look here in particular at her long poem *Dart*, which finds her making use of a dramatised narrative, as well briefly at the experimental lyrics of her most recent volume *Woods etc.* (2005).

If science has offered itself as a discourse imbued with an often masculinised authority, nature in many ways has functioned as its feminised opposite. Women's relationship to nature has historically been a difficult one because of the Romantic positioning of nature as a feminised "other", and although the potential for rethinking and recoding that relationship are potentially fruitful, they are also traditionally fraught with difficulty. As Margaret Homans writes

> Mother Nature is hardly powerless, but, enormous as her powers are, they are not the ones that daughters want if they are to become poets. A human mother's giving birth may be an extraordinarily active event, but as a model for the daughter's vocational ambitions it is simply not applicable, because it stems from what she is, not from what she does... Mother Nature is also traditionally associated with death as much as with life. Even Wordsworth, who attributes to nature an active and beneficent love, retains the tradition of her amorality in his portrayal of her mixed ministries of fear and love. She has no consciousness, only materiality and an elusive presence, no center only diffuseness.[4]

Oswald's work is ostensibly very different from Shapcott's and Greenlaw's, but the three poets offer three strategically connected ways of negotiating the relationship between body and poetic voice in their work. Oswald's resistance to the personal voice of the lyric can be seen in *Dart* which takes up many voices, not as dramatic monologue but in the interweavings of a long dramatic poem. Although Oswald is much more directly and obviously influenced by Ted Hughes, her use of nature compares particularly interestingly with the way in which Bishop places geography in opposition to history – the spatial versus the temporal – as a way of knowing.

*   *   *

In her essay, 'The Geographical Mirror',[5] Anne Stevenson discusses the way in which Bishop, in her working notebooks, described '[t]he "clear dark glass" of icy river that runs though Great Village into the Bay of Fundy', elaborating that 'It's my idea of knowledge, this cold stream, half drawn, half flowing from a great rocky breast.' Stevenson elucidates:

> It is not unusual to find passages of abstract musing in Bishop's note-books, but only rarely in her poetry did she allow such ideas thinking-room. Though she insisted that the last lines of 'At the Fishhouses' came to her in a dream, there they are, plainly articulated in her notes. 'At the Fishhouses' therefore seems to be a particularly revealing example, not only of how Bishop seized upon the idea of nature's offering of a geographical (as opposed to metaphorical or psychological) mirror, but also of how Bishop thought her way through the composition of a poem, putting it together image by image, memory by memory, testing all the time for what at college she had identified as a 'mind thinking within the poem' (*Poet of the Periphery*, p.39)

For Bishop, in 'The Map' (*CP*, p.3) – the poem which begins her first collection *North and South* (1946) – the topographer's project, which shows geographical features as opposed to historical and political boundaries, is a more subtle and pleasing art and one which Bishop perhaps allied with her own poetic vision. 'Topography displays no favourites; North's as near as West,' she writes, going on to conclude, 'More delicate than the historian's are the map-maker's colors.' Bishop's always subtle often ironic stance in relation to geography is thus established, and culminates in her final volume *Geography III* (1976), which takes as its epigraph chapter headings from a geography textbook which ask 'What is Geography', 'What is a map?'

The connection between landscape, the body and the poem are intimately connected in Bishop's work. Nature is not seen as other. Furthermore, as Margaret Dickie has pointed out, Bishop's

> [i]nterest in geography as a picture of surfaces was not limited to the outside world; it extended (or retracted) its focus to the surface of the body and, still closer in, to the systemic arrangement of the body of the poem or picture...her fascination with bodies –– the world's, her own body, and the poem's – infiltrated everything she wrote... [...] 'The Map' introduces the general topic in a surrealistic treatment of mapping, 'The Weed' interjects the image of the land or nature into the body, and 'Over 2,000 Illustrations and a Complete Concordance' explores the way books and by extension poems arrange and disarrange any understanding of the world derived from direct experience or travels.[6]

If the topography of the land offers Bishop a way of mirroring and exploring the self, and sees her creating what in general Bonnie

Costello has described as a 'drama within the beholding',[7] her poem 'The Monument' (*CP*, pp.23-25), also included in *North and South* (1946), suggests that the relationship between poet and poem artefact is equally unstable and ambiguous in its positioning of relations between subject and object.

Bishop draws for the poem from T.S. Eliot's 1919 essay 'Tradition and the Individual Talent' in which he famously describes his theory of a poetics of impersonality.[8] 'The progress of an artist is a continual self-sacrifice, a continual extinction of personality':

> It is in this depersonalisation that art may be said to approach the condition of science...consider, as a suggestive analogy, the action which takes place when a bit of finely filiated platinum is introduced into a chamber containing oxygen and sulphurdioxide. (*Selected Prose*, p.40)

Continuing, Eliot defines the relationship between the poet and the poem through the scientific analogy of the 'catalyst':

> When the two gases previously mentioned are mixed in the presence of a filament of platinum, they form sulphurous acid. This combination takes place only if the platinum is present; nevertheless the newly formed acid contains no trace of platinum, and the platinum itself is apparently unaffected: has remained inert, neutral, and unchanged. The mind of the poet is the shred of platinum. It may partly or exclusively operate upon the experience of the man himself; but, the more perfect the artist, the more completely separate in him will be the man who suffers and the mind which creates; the more perfectly will the mind digest and transmute the passions which are its material. (*Selected Prose*, p.40)

Eliot uses the metaphor of science not only as an objective method of distancing the reader from more Romantic conceptions of the artist, but to validate poetry by allying it with an authoritative, universal and powerful modern discourse. Although Bishop is obviously drawing on the essay, her relationship to the objective voice is an ambiguous one. While Eliot's essay reads in some ways like an hysterical attempt to cut off emotion and then re-member it in the body of a poem, Bishop's intersection with the essay shows how she will interrogate the relationship between poem and poet, subject and object, personal and literary history, rather than severing it. As Lisa Steinman has shown, developments in science and technology had an important influence on Modernist poetics in America in the 1920s and 1930s, and in particular on the work of William Carlos Williams, Wallace Stevens and Marianne Moore.[9] Yet the fêting of the scientific as a new aesthetic also became part of an elision which equated science with a hard, dry objective voice, which in its turn became equated with masculinity. Such codings, which are infamously and repeatedly to be found in the work of Ezra Pound, and which are, as Marilyn L. Brownstein points out, gleefully deconstructed by Moore, present themselves as a hallmark of canonical modernism.[10] Like myth and fairytale, science offers women poets a narrative of knowing, but one which removes the personal.

'The Monument' ends with an instruction that it 'is the beginning of a painting, or poem, or monument' and that we must '[w]atch it closely'. In a frequently cited letter to Anne Stevenson, Bishop writes:

> reading Darwin one admired the beautiful solid case being built up out of his endless, heroic, observations, almost unconscious or automatic – and then comes a sudden relaxation, a forgetful phrase, and one feels that strangeness of his undertaking, sees the lonely young man, his eyes fixed on facts and minute details, sinking or sliding giddily off into the unknown. What one seems to want in art, in experiencing it, is the same thing that is necessary for its creation, a self-forgetful, perfectly useless concentration.[11]

Here the poet's concentration on the object becomes an examination of the perceiver as well as the object perceived. Not only does the subject construct the object under its scrutiny, but the construction of the object in its turn contributes to the construction of the subject describing it, and this dialogue between self and other, poem and poet, establishes a dynamic relationship which breaks down hierarchical positions between the subject and the object. Thus the objective voice becomes a medium not for the fixing of experience, but for interrogating and renegotiating its multi-facetedness.

At the same time as relating intertextually with Eliot's essay, 'The Monument' is also based on Max Ernst's series of 34 *frottages*, *Histoire Naturelle* (1925).[12] Bishop's interest in surrealism, and her early use of surrealistic imagery, accord well with the aesthetic principles which evolve in 'The Monument' in that one of surrealism's main aims is to break down the relationship between subject and object.[13] As a poetic model for 'The Monument', *Histoire Naturelle* demands an interrogation of perception. As Werner Spies elaborates, *frottage* is:

> bound up with a new objectivity. It creates this objectivity in that the structure that Ernst rubs through is subordinate to a pictorial element that has nothing to do with that structure. Two planes of reality coincide. A structure that refers *a priori* to something unrelated to the pictorial object, that at first glance does not seem adequate, encounters the pictorial object that has hitherto never been expressed in extrapictorial structural elements... This apparent illogic creates the curious state of suspension in which Ernst's figure live... Ernst's *Histoire Naturelle*... calls into question the rational and the explicable, which is the aim of

natural history; through a slight stroke of the hand he again renders inexplicable and indescribable the world as explained and described... To the artist *frottage* is not only a technique in which two object-planes overlap and penetrate each other; it is also a means by which he frees himself from his inhibitions.[14]

'Natural History' does of course also offer an alternative to political or human history. The monument Bishop sets up is a monument to time as much as it is one set up against it. Disorientation of the self in relation to the objects it perceives offers Bishop an emancipatory model which presents her with an opportunity, through an interrogation of the concept of 'the natural', to reconstruct herself in relation to subject and object, history and literary tradition.

JO SHAPCOTT

Jo Shapcott's first collection, *Electroplating the Baby* (1988),[15] is strongly influenced by Bishop in both its adoption of an 'objective' narratorial voice and her use of surrealistic imagery. 'Electroplating the Baby' (*Her Book*, pp.20-24) makes reference to Victorian popular science magazines and describes in intricate detail the process of mummification as figured in the experiments of a French scientist in the 19th century. Obviously indebted to Bishop's 'The Monument', as well as T.S. Eliot's chemical analogy of the poet as a piece of platinum, Shapcott writes with precise, realist descriptions:

> He metallises our entire cadaver.
> He encloses it in an envelope
>
> of bronze, copper, nickel, silver or gold
> according to the wealth or caprice
>
> of those who survive.
> Does this waken your curiosity?
>
> Do you wish to know
> how Dr Variot proceeds?
>
> In a double frame with four uprights
> connected top and bottom by four square plates
>
> is the body of a child which has been
> perforated with a metal rod.

It is the bizarre and surreal elements of scientific exploration which are at the root of Shapcott's interests here, and, as an exercise in a literally morbid fascination, 'Electroplating the Baby' is a self-reflexive critique of objectivity. It also depicts an obsession with technology which denies or marginalises any sense of the human scale. The ethos of the poem is double-edged because it does, despite our better instincts, awaken both Shapcott's and the reader's interest. Objectively detailing, examining, interrogating becomes a grotesque act. 'What is the future in store / for this process of mummification?' the narrator asks, replying that:

> It would be impossible to say.
> It is infinitely probable
>
> that metallised cadavers
> will never figure
>
> except in small numbers
> for a long, long time to come.

Because of its echoes of Mary Shelley's *Frankenstein*, it is difficult to read the poem as a positive proposal for an aesthetic, yet in its intersection with Bishop and Eliot, Shapcott is perhaps making a point about women's relationship to the ethics of scientific experimentation. Although the levels of irony evident in Shapcott's narratorial voice are difficult to discern, the poem seems to work as an overdetermined critique of her own poetic process. Stylistically it remains as a kind of curate's egg, standing apart from much of the rest of her work, but in asking us to re-examine both the method and motivation of our relationship to the world, it is wholly representative of her approach.

By her second collection *Phrase Book* (1992), Shapcott's interest in science does in fact become as much a part of her dialogue with authority as it does with the literary tradition. In 'On Tour: The Alps' (*Her Book*, pp.60-64), the speaker of the poem meets Byron, Goethe and Wordsworth, poets who work as a focus for her exploration of not just the male tradition, but of ways of observing and writing the world. In the first section the speaker imagines herself in a carriage with Byron, in lines which again recall Bishop's interrogations in 'The Monument' when she writes: 'Does a cabinet of drinks / swing out of the mahogany panel? Do the seats // collapse at the touch of a button to throw you / wriggling on your back?' If Byron represents the image of the Romantic poet rattling through the night in his plush-lined carriage, the speaker of Shapcott's poem, who travels in a Volvo with her grumpy lover, is altogether more prosaic. We are told that Wordsworth made the same journey by foot, as the speaker of the poem emphasises her practicality, her rootedness in the world.

> I could have done that too,
> could have matched him step for step

> even in the snow. Everywhere a new pathway
> and I'm there with him, to help turn walking
> into statement, more than just somewhere to go. We talk
> politics as much as topography and I help him
>
> by thinking legs, not imagination

In the penultimate section of the poem the receptionist whispers to the speaker about Goethe who she hears 'stayed here for his geology // to make a study of the mountain stones', exclaiming 'Look at me / supervising sacks of rocks, naming and weighing / just like him, testing and cataloguing too.' If Wordsworth figures as the poet who pronounces that 'we murder to dissect', then Goethe, famously both poet and scientist, figures as his opposite. In both her romanticism and desire, in her imagining, as well as in her scientific approach the speaker of the poem, and implicitly also Shapcott herself, must negotiate her way carefully as a woman. Shapcott explains

> Each encounter is different, but they all represent some aspect of the tradition, and the male tradition, at that. It's a theme with variations, if you like, and a record of the speaker's effort to locate herself both in relation to this tradition and at the same time necessarily outside it.[16]

In the final section the speaker's lover becomes a cipher for all the literary male texts, 'names of stars, of women, of things // in the world outside our wooden box' as the male tradition attempts to drown out her capacity for listening to the cow bells, which work as a symbol for the non-linguistic and non-rational feminine

> it's hard to tune my ear to it
> against so many men's voices shouting
> all the names they know, at the dark.

By contrast, 'In the Bath' (*Her Book*, pp.67-68; *MWP*, p.311) offers an image of the body as a teeming mutable complexity subject to many fluctuations and transformations, rather than a fixed and coherent entity. The body is examined in terms of 'prehistory' as the speaker of the poem imagines 'her body cells spreading like a film to cover the earth, / coating every frond in the tropical rainforest, / every blade of grass on the pampas'. Thus the way of knowing the body becomes located in geography as she concludes:

> ...all she wanted
> was to be a good atlas, a bright school map
> to shine up the world for everyone to see

If the poem perhaps reminds us fleetingly of Frida Kahlo's surreally inflected painting of herself in the bath, 'What I Saw in the Water' or 'What the Water Gave Me' (1938), its emphasis is actually at a far remove from Kahlo's autobiographical and self-narrativising impulse. Seeing the body in terms of its component cells and the molecules of water that cover it offers a kind of transcendence from the reductiveness of 'writing just about what you see'.[17]

Shapcott has spoken in interview of the kind of transcendent experience that she finds in both Bishop and Rilke. Shapcott's extensive engagement with Rilke, what she has frequently referred to when talking about her versions of Rilke's French poems as her 'extended love letter', sees her consciously in dialogue with both masculinity and the tradition when, in *Les Roses*, for example, she gives back to the roses, which she sees as female genitals, their own voice. But it is perhaps Rilke's image of the angel in the *Duino Elegies*, which is an important, if unexplicated part, of Shapcott's thinking about the relationship between inner and outer worlds, body and poem. Rilke's thinking in this respect was important also to Heidegger, and Jonathan Bate's gloss on the Rilkean angel is useful here:

> The enigmatic 'angel' of Rilke's elegies is not a Christian spirit, a har-binger from heaven. The angel is the creature in whom the transfor-mation of the visible into the invisible, of earth into consciousness, is already complete. Potentially, the poet – or perhaps the poem itself – is the angel. The mode of being to which Rilke aspired in poetry was that which he called the 'open' (one of the terms borrowed by Heidegger). The open is akin to Schiller's 'naive', where there is no division between nature and consciousness...as in Romantic meditation on mortality such as Keats's 'Ode to Autumn', the purpose is not to elevate 'naive' modes of being over thoughtful ones, but rather to seek to reconcile the two. Like the Romantic, Rilke is in search of a way of thinking and living which reconciles instrumental rationality with openness to 'the open'. This involves him in the acceptance of finitude and of mortality, but also in a letting-go... [in which he] seemed to become nature itself, to share his being with tree and singing bird as inner and outer were gathered together into a single 'uninterrupted space'. (*Song of the Earth*, p.263)

By becoming a 'self that is permeable, see through', Shapcott cre-ates a body gendered as much like Rilke's as that of the theorist Luce Irigaray (equally, I think, in this respect influenced by Rilke) when she writes of the angel as 'That which unceasingly passes through the envelope(s) or container(s), goes from one side to the other.'[18] For Irigaray the angel is 'a representation of a sexuality that has never been incarnated'. Like Heidegger's desire for an 'alliance between the divine and the mortal' (*Sexual Difference*, p.17):

These swift angelic messengers, who transgress all enclosures in their speed, tell of the passage between the envelope of God and that of the world as micro- or macrocosm. They proclaim that such a journey can be made by the body of a man, and above all the body of a woman. (*Sexual Difference*, p.16)

Margaret Whitford has suggested that the angel is 'an alternative to the phallus. In psychoanalytic terms, the phallus has sometimes been thought of as that which "goes between", creates a bridge'.[19] In *Tender Taxes* (2001),[20] which includes all her versions of Rilke's French poems, Shapcott creates such an angelic bridge between Rilke's writing and her own, thus bringing together male and female poetic traditions until, as her postscript from Borges suggests, 'I do not know which of us has written this page.' Just as Rilke speaks 'through a French mouth', so Shapcott in her versions replies with a female voice to a male one, wresting back the poetic 'I' in a manner which involves dialogue and exchange, not just intertextual assimilation or opposition. In her introduction to *Tender Taxes* Shapcott writes

I began to see that in the sequence Rilke's roses were women. And more than that – petal – space – petal – these poems were versions of female genitalia [...] My roses are given their own voice. They speak. And if you put my poems alongside Rilke's, more often than not you'll find my roses addressing his, saying, in effect: 'It's not like that, it's like this.' And, for me, this parachuted the whole notion of gender relations into the business of translation. Who's doing what to whom? And, more importantly, how does a woman poet relate to the poets who have gone before? (*Tender Taxes*, p.xi)

Shapcott transforms the unnamed roses/women into roses with scientific classifications. Though there is a risk in this strategy – in that removing these women from a state of anonymity she then positions them in a way which rigidly classifies them – Shapcott finds her names through thematic association: they arise, as it were, organically. 'Rosa gallica' (*Tender Taxes*, p.59), the first of Rilke's poems, for example, then makes mention of her French mouth (incidentally, not in the French at all). 'Rosa foetida' (*Tender Taxes*, p.61), a poem which refutes Rilke's positioning of 'her' as '*ô chose par excellence complète*' instead offers a self 'imperfect' and 'brown at the edges / like the air you breathe'.

To conclude I want to look at one of the poems in some detail, to show a little of the way Shapcott's engagement with Rilke works.[21] Rilke's fifth poem reads as follows (here with A. Poulin Jr's English translation):

Abandon entouré d'abandon,	Abandon surrounds abandon.,
tendresse touchant aux tendresses...	tenderness touches tenderness...
C'est ton intérieur qui sans cesse	You'd think your center would caress
se caresse, dirait-on...	itself on and on and on...
se caresse en soi-même,	caress itself in itself and seem
par son propre reflet éclairé.	to glow with its own image
Ainsi tu inventes le thème	Thus you invent the theme
du Narcisse exaucé.	of the fulfilled Narcissus.

Shapcott's version, 'Rosa nitida' (*Tender Taxes*, p.63) reads:

> Space folds against space,
> petal touches petal;
> you look at me
> as though you want to fall in,
>
> make the flower
> glow with your own image,
> change my meaning
> from rose to Narcissus.

Rosa nitida is a pink, wild rose, its name well suited to this, the most obviously genital of the poems. The male voyeur is looked at while he looks, so that rather than this being a poem about the woman's narcissism it becomes a poem about both the male lover (and the poet's) scopophilia. The genitals as well as the poem (Rilke returns several times throughout the sequence to think about the roses as text or book) have become Narcissus' pool in which he might fall as Shapcott swiftly (and deftly) turns the tables on the stereotype of female vanity.

If Shapcott's desire to make for herself a permeable skin is angelic, then this act of translation surely also accords with Irigaray's urge to mimesis as a reappropriation of the feminine when she writes:

> To play with mimesis is thus, for a woman, to try to recover the place of her exploitation by discourse, without allowing herself to be simply reduced to it. It means to resubmit herself – inasmuch as she is on the side of the "perceptible", of "matter" – to "ideas", in particular to ideas about herself that are elaborated in/by a masculine logic, but so as to make "visible", by an effect of playful repetition, what was supposed to remain invisible: the cover-up of a possible operation of the feminine in language.[22]

Irigaray does of course also place at the centre of her strategy of speaking as a woman the matter and metaphor of the female genitals which, with their double nature and permanent self-caress, become a model for such playful mimesis. Such a strategy returns us in particular to the writing of Medbh McGuckian whose work, as we saw in 'Slips', also makes use of an intertextual bridge in her reordered repetition of Freud at the same time as parodying and assuming the "feminine" into a textual style.

In a recent uncollected poem, 'Deft', Shapcott responds to the work of the artist Helen Chadwick. Chadwick's use of fluids in her art, in the 'Bad Blooms' photographs, for example, in which flowers are held in suspensions made of household liquids, see her challenging a fixed feminine identity as the flowers – roses, daisies, iris, narcissi – echo the textures and merge the boundaries with their containing fluid, whether this is hair gel, bubble bath or *Germolene*. The impulse to destabilise the body's boundaries sees the speaker of Shapcott's poem becoming water and soap film as his/her skin is figured as 'this and that, the moving point between, the unsettled / limit, stretching and contracting under the breath / that comes and goes'. It is here that Shapcott reaches a position of what seems to be a postmodern rethinking of a Whitmanesque multitudinous self as the poem concludes: 'I am this one, I am that one, / I breathe in and become everything I see.' In an article in which she discusses the work of Chadwick, Shapcott writes:

> She took up the cause of deftness in response to the problem of the gendered 'I', and she challenged the notion of 'the bipolar tension of either/or', in favour of 'the alchemical principle of both/and'. It's a concept completely removed from the narrow 'I' of so much current autobiographical art, produced in this prurient age of ours: the 'I' as Roman numeral, the upright half of the binary system, hard, phallic. In contrast Chadwick's is a vision of the self that is permeable, see through, empathetic, encompassing, transformed and transformative: 'Use the mirror,' she said, 'to return back through the eye into Paradise...'[23]

Shapcott's interest in Chadwick seems very much a continuation of her Rilkean transformations. Her desire to create a permeable 'I' places her at the forefront of women poets in her attempt to destabilise the relationship between self and other in the lyric and to radically rethink the relationship of the woman poet to both body and text.

LAVINIA GREENLAW

It is Bishop's voice as a model of poetic perception on which Lavinia Greenlaw, like Shapcott, draws in her first full-length collection. In an essay on the relationship between poetry and science she cites 'The Monument' as an example of Bishop's 'exactness and continual and patient acknowledgement of this process', returning, as Stevenson did, to Bishop's discussion of a style when she writes:

The mechanics of perception have always been a major poetic theme. In an early letter, Elizabeth Bishop quotes the physicist W. Croll on the baroque prose style which conveys 'not a thought but a mind thinking ...an idea separated from the act of experiencing it is not the ideas that was experienced. The ardour of its conception in the mind is a necessary part of its truth.'[24]

Throughout her work, Greenlaw makes use of scientific discourse to address multiple anxieties about the way in which to construct a poetic voice and articulate her femininity. *Night Photograph* (1993),[25] her first collection, examines the ethics of science in a socio-historic context as well as the ethics of replacing an unquestioning faith in technology and science. In many poems science is used as a metaphor for human relationships. Admiring Bishop for 'her use of distance, geographical poetic and emotional which she somehow manages to employ without any lack of commitment or involvement from herself ',[26] Greenlaw adopts her doctrine of objectivity, while questioning science as a discourse of authority. In exploiting scientific discourse as both subject-matter and poetic idiom, Greenlaw also offers a critique of pat-riarchy through an examination of scientific methods and the history of science, while also using science as a strategy which gives her, as a woman poet, a special and uncompromised sense of authority and detachment not usually associated – even in the 1990s – with a female poetic voice.

As a precursor to Greenlaw, Bishop's notorious sense of privacy and her refusal to gender herself as a poet – her insistence on never appearing in any women-only anthologies – are of obvious importance. In interview, Greenlaw has spoken of her use of science in her poems in a way that suggests her use of the 'detached' voice evolved directly from anxieties about the way she would be constructed as a woman poet. She explains:

In the past, quite naturally I have used what has been described as the controlled, detached "scientific" voice and I think partly I was concerned about allowing myself too much emotional space within my work. (*Talking Verse*, p.79)

Yet writing against a stereotype of the feminine voice (what Vernon Shatley describes as writing 'from the heart, from nature...to pour forth from the heart in the manner of the sentimental women poets popular in Bishop's youth: Millay, Wylie, Teasdale, Ella Wheeler Wilcox...a writing emotive and overflowing')[27] doesn't lead either Bishop or Greenlaw into a position by which they embrace masculinist models of objectivity that compromise the instabilities of self. Instead, both evolve a position which freely acknowledges indeterminacy and flux, and which is simultaneously desirous of an exploration of the world in terms of series of interrogations which may yield a response of no more than a corresponding set of momentary truths.

In 'Electricity' (*NP*, p.27; *MWP*, p.378) Greenlaw uses circuitry as a metaphor for both power and sexual attraction in a relationship. In the poem, self and other merge and become indistinguishable:

> I was thinking about electricity –
> how at no point on a circuit
> can power diminish or accumulate,
> how you also need lack of balance
> for energy to be released. *Trust it.*
> Once, being held like that,
> no edge, no end and no beginning
> I could not tell our actions apart:
> if it was you who lifted my head to the light,
> if it was I who said how much I wanted
> to look at your face. *Your beautiful face.*

Trust in science, however, must also for Greenlaw be regarded with a degree of scepticism, as she writes to 'a Russian mongrel bitch' in 'For the First Dog in Space' (*NP*, p.52):

> Laika, do not let yourself be fooled
> by the absolute stillness
> that comes only with not knowing
> how fast you are going. As you fall
> in orbit around the earth, remember
> your language. Listen to star dust.
> Trust your fear.

Persistently Greenlaw asks us to relate science to the human scale, with poems about plastic surgery ('The Man Whose Smile Made Medical History', *NP*, pp.24–25), artificial insemination ('The Gift of Life', *NP*, p.21), Marie Curie ('A Letter From Marie Curie', *NP*, p.45) and radium poisoning ('The Innocence of Radium', *NP*, pp.46–47), which look at scientific developments from a personal and historical perspective. Her long poem, 'Galileo's Wife' (*NP*, pp.29–31; *MWP*, pp.378–80) – an attempt at "revisionary myth-making" – is the only poem in the collection to engage directly with a recognisable feminist politics. Here Greenlaw engages with a key point in the history of science to explore perceptions and constructions of reality and anticipates Duffy's *Wife* poems by some six years. In doing this she reconstructs a female subject by engaging with, and questioning, the authority of experience, poetry, and science as ways of formulating knowledge and "truth".

Although the issue is not addressed directly in the poem, in her use of Galileo, Greenlaw is also entering into a debate which dramatises

the struggle between science and religion. Galileo's imprisonment by
the Inquisition for his anti-Catholic endorsement of the Copernican
theory that the earth rotates on its axis and revolves around the
sun once a year raises a series of crucial philosophical questions.
As the historian Maurice Finocchiaro has commented, the 'Galileo
affair':

> involved scientific issues about physical facts, natural phenomena, and
> astronomical and cosmological matters; and it is also involved method-
> ological and epistemological questions about what truth is and the proper
> way to search for it.[28]

Galileo was made Professor of Mathematics at the University of Pisa
at the age of 25, and included in his achievements are the develop-
ment of the modern telescope and the thermometer, the discovery
of four satellites of Jupiter, the ring of Saturn and the spots on
the sun, as well as his foreshadowing of Newton's law of motion.
In her poem, Greenlaw deconstructs the myth of the isolated male
genius, and offers to tell us the "whole" story about the so-called
Father of Modern Science. The unnamed wife of the poem, who
is shown to be deeply involved in and perhaps even responsible
for the generation of ideas that have contributed to her husband's
status in the modern world, is publicly (and privately) unacknow-
ledged. In the first three stanzas which make up the first section of
the poem, we are given a portrait of Galileo which subtly under-
mines the importance of detailed scientific enquiry when it is un-
accompanied by sensitivity to human surroundings and conditions.
The stars are 'brought down' and the riddles of the universe are
demystified as Galileo's wife is left with the stars trapped between
the pages of Galileo's cosmological studies – his *The Starry Messenger*
(1610) and *The Sunspot Letters* (1613). As such, the stars have lost
their dimension: their power and their mystery are only paper in
the hands of Galileo's wife.

Femininity is a riddle which Galileo, despite his appetite for
knowledge, is not even remotely interested in solving. Galileo's wife
holds up femininity as a category which, if subjected to any kind
of experimental testing, would fail to reveal a conclusive result, the
kind of result which Galileo might be capable of understanding:
'If only he could / measure me and find my secrets,' she says, and
'[t]he average speed of descent // was three pulsebeats with a half-
beat variable, / allowing for the different angle and force / with which
each pebble hit the water'. The female body here is not used as a
guarantor of a gendered authority, but it is perceived as a method of
discovery, demonstrating the way Galileo's wife is able to humanise

objective ways of perceiving. Greenlaw offers a critique of the rational which denies feeling or any kind of moral responsibility, as Galileo orders that his dead children are cruelly and surreally subjected to his experiments.

The contrast between Galileo and his wife – and their approach to the value of scientific evaluation – is made metaphorical in a joke about their respective footwear. Galileo wears a pair of velvet slippers, while his wife wears boots: it is a sturdy moral framework which allows her to keep her perspective, to keep her feet on the ground. In section four of the poem Galileo's wife is sent off to find the edges of the world. This magic realist fabularisation of a journey from west to east, in which Galileo's wife is carried and supported by the natural world, dramatises an evolution of the self which, with its fish and tidal imagery, portrays her in Christ-like imagery. She sees the world in terms dependent on immediate sensory responses to the world, and as such seems to counterbalance the Copernican world view, which was typically opposed in its time because of the way it is so obviously deceived immediate sensory perception. Galileo's wife's perceptions act poetically in their reliance on metaphor to communicate emotion and knowledge: a cloud over Dalmatia is the colour of her wedding dress, the 'desert is a sea of orchids', a 'powder' 'turns the sky to thunder and gold'. It is showing – rather than testing or explaining – that is Galileo's wife's prime concern; and yet paradoxically, in the process of her experimentation to find out the shape of the world she offers empirical proof about its physical construction, disproving Galileo's theory – as it is fictionalised in the poem – that the world is flat.

In presenting a search for the truth, 'Galileo's Wife' offers a dialogue between subjective and objective ways of knowing while dramatising a series of binary divisions: between male and female, public and private, rational and emotional, showing and explaining, speech and writing. Similarly, a tension between subjective and objective ways of understanding is seen in Greenlaw's use of free verse. Acting not only in rhythmic terms, free verse is, of course, a highly artificial way of pluralising meaning through a self-conscious juxtaposition of semantic and syntactic structures. Greenlaw is deliberately undermining such aesthetics of uncertainty in her recurrent use of the end-stopped line that results in a pattern of assertion and objectivity, juxtaposed by a simultaneous conveyance of constraint and restriction. We see this particularly in the fourth section of the poem when it is the movements of Galileo's wife in the natural world which are mirrored by enjambement: 'I fall / and the frozen air catches me'; 'a tidal wave / carries me up into the

mountains'. In such a way the end-stopped lines of the poem act
to conjure up the edges of the world; likewise in carrying the line
forward the use of enjambement attempts to emphasise and repre-
sent the circularity of that world. Having been asked to find the
edge of the world, Galileo's wife returns, making her answer by
drawing a circle. Edge and limit, themselves equated symbolically
with masculinity, are countered by an equally symbolic feminised
curve. Galileo is portrayed as incapable of representing knowledge in
a way which can be shared with future generations – his students
sleep – as history is left in the hands of Galileo's wife who must
'leave the truth' amongst her husband's papers while thanking 'the
bears of Natolia' that she 'never taught him how to write'.

   In seeking to assume an ungendered identity as poets it might be
easy to accuse Bishop and Greenlaw of denying the many difficulties
which present themselves for the woman poet – not least in the
appropriation of a subjectivity traditionally denied them. But both
Bishop and Greenlaw, in their suspicion of certainty and fixity, do
not seem to be seeking to write off gender and constructions of a
female voice as a category into which they refuse to fit, but rather
to interrogate and destabilise such categories.

   A World Where News Travelled Slowly (1997)[29] marks a move away
from a direct discussion of science in Greenlaw's work. In 'Iron
Lung', however, she draws parallels between the body and the
machine, using the machine which allows a person to breathe as a
metaphor for the charge of desire which leaves the speaker of the
poem breathless 'your hand on the small of my back, / a whispered
imperative, I rise and fall' (*AWWNTS*, p.35). 'Millefiori' (p.24),
dedicated to the poet Don Paterson, is a poem about a man with a
glass eye. Millefiori is a technique of fusing glass into an intensely
decorated pattern, a patterning which occurs at the end of the poem
when the man's eye is surreally transformed listening to an aria as
'the molecules of his eye / oscillated into a thousand flowers'. Pater-
son's own bright blue eyes and his poetics of looking are undoubtedly
being taken to task here, and Dowson and Entwistle read the poem
as a 'deconstruction of (male) sight' to 'slyly gender the means by
which the apparently opposing domains of science and art, reality
and imagination, rationality and emotion, are meshed and elided' and
which 'turns the objectifying male gaze (a parallel for the scientific
"way of looking") back on itself' (*A History of Twentieth-Century
British Women's Poetry*, p.231). In *Minsk* (2003),[30] Greenlaw's work,
although less playful, moves closer to Shapcott's in her interest in
the body in the story of her parent's courtship in 'The Dissection
Room' (*Minsk*, p.5) in which her father's 'sight was fixed on the

cool blood / struggling to circulate in her hand / as she rolled on a glove to dip a finger // in a dead man's chest'. The scientific way of seeing is not only one ascribed to the male, and here it is the mother's eyes which are 'behind glass / preternaturally unblinking, flexed' as they peer from behind 'hieroglyphic contact lenses' and 'swivelled like a pair / of monumental but well-oiled radar'.

ALICE OSWALD

Oswald's second collection, *Dart* (2002), is a book-length poem in which, at first glance, the ghosts of Eliot's *Waste Land* meet Dylan Thomas's *Under Milk Wood*, where the modernist chorus of emergent subjectivity of Woolf's *The Waves* intermingles with voices garnered from a project not a mile away from the mass observation exercises of the 1930s.

In her preface to *Dart* Oswald explains how she spent two years recording the stories of people who live and work on the River Dart in Devon, describing the poem as 'a series of characters – linking their voices into a sound-map of the river, a songline from source to sea'. The sound-map Oswald describes seems in some ways analogous to the way topography works for Bishop, the 'delicate art' which steps outside history and which offers a way of knowing through the ambiguities of the landscape where border and differentiation are called into question. The use of the word songline draws on Australian aboriginal creation myths in which poetry and the landscape become one as the landscape is literally sung into being. Oswald's references to the process of creating a different kind of history is implicitly linked with the Dream Time when she writes:

> And then I saw the river's dream-self walk
> down to the ringmesh netting by the bridge
> to feel the edge of shingle brush the edge
> of sleep and float a world up like a cork
> out of its body's liquid dark.
> Like in a waterfall one small twig caught
> catches a stick, a straw, a sack, a mesh
> of leaves, a fragile wickerwork of floodbrash
> I saw all things catch and reticulate
> into this dreaming of the Dart
> that sinks like a feather falls, not quite
> in full possession of its weight.
>   (p.28)

Like the Derwent, the river with which Wordsworth begins his earliest version of *The Prelude*, the Dart's name – as one of Oswald's

inset glosses informs us – derives from an ancient word for an oak
tree. In his readings of Drayton and Wordsworth in his *Song of
the Earth*, Bate has referred to a strategy of writing 'history-
through-topography'. Drawing on the work of the 'new geogra-
pher', Wyman Hernedeen, he asks not only what is a river, but
when is a river: 'How does one locate it in time, as one must,
since it is in constant movement, and since it has a history, just as
any other object involving human beings has' (*Song of the Earth*,
p.223). Where Wordsworth used the Derwent as a reflection of his
burgeoning mind, Oswald seems to be offering the lives of those
who live and work alongside the River Dart as a collective version
of a historical moment in which biography and autobiography,
which become our histories, are scrutinised in relation to nature
and thus redefine it as they coalesce into a dramatised autobiogra-
phy of place.

Unlike Bishop's establishment of the 'geographical mirror' as a
reflection and extension of the bodily self, it is for Oswald not the
act of looking which creates the self, but the act of telling through
otherness, a process in which the poet as unifying voice, poet as
river who takes up the voices, attempts to find a voice as she asks
at the beginning of the poem: 'The Dart, lying low in darkness
calls out Who is it? / trying to summon itself by speaking…' (p.1)

Thus we see references to a walker the spirit of Jan Coo who
haunts the river, a chambermaid, a naturalist, an eel watcher, fisher-
man and bailiff, dead tinners, a forester, water nymph, the King
of the Oakwoods, Zeus, a canoeist, town boys, a tin extractor, a
worker at the woollen mills, John Edmunds, a corpse, a swimmer,
a water abstractor, a dairy worker, sewage extractor, a stone waller,
boat voices, a boatbuilder, salmon poacher, oyster gatherers, a ferry-
man, naval cadet, Humphrey Gilbert, former river pilots and a seal
watcher. All these characters find their voice in the river and like-
wise the river finds its voice in them, Oswald seems to be suggesting,
creating an image not of the self but of the flux of time, and nature's
capacity to hold all its histories. The indications in the margin,
Oswald writes in her preface, are 'where one voice changes into
another. These do not refer to real people or even fixed fictions.
All voices should be read as the river's mutterings.'

If the river thus offers us a slice of time, a vision of England – as
the oak tree reference might suggest – it is one which shows both
harmony and disunity. Oblique references to war riddle the poem,
focusing specifically on the turbulence at the point 'where East Dart
smashes into West Dart / two wills gnarling and recoiling / and
finally knuckling into balance' – something we might want to read

at some level as a commentary on wider global concerns. But the poem resists such neat interpretations in its constant return to the primacy of the river's being. Later in the poem Oswald appears to offer the river as a place of dissolution of difference, in which ancient myth and modern technology coalesce:

Glico of the Running Streams   named varieties of
and Spio of the Boulders-Encaved-In-The River's-Edges   water

and all other named varieties of Water
such as Loops and Swirls in their specific dialects
clucking and clapping

Cymene and Semaia, sweeping a plectrum along the stones
and the stones' hollows hooting back at them
    (p.17)

It is hard when reading *Dart* not to be aware of the influence of Ted Hughes, whose series of poems *River* (1983) consists of poems inspired by rivers, largely in the British Isles, but partly in America. *Dart* also seems to recall more particularly Hughes' poem 'Wodwo'[31] in which an unidentified creature begins to take form through language, nosing itself into consciousness as it enters the water:

What am I to split
The glassy grain of water looking upward I see the bed
Of the river above me upside-down very clear
What am I doing here in mid-air? Why do I find
this frog so interesting as I inspect its most secret
interior and make it my own?

But if the 'half-man, half-animal spirit of the forests' in 'Wodwo' recalls, in its attempt to become, the relationship to the world of the Irigarayan angelic, it also differs importantly in its attempt to 'make it my own'. Leonard M. Scigaj sees the Wodwo as discovering 'itself *as* it discovers the world':

As 'exact centre' of existence-for-the-self the Wodwo is the generator, the creator of its own universe, moment by moment. This frees him to inspect, rather than accept unthinkingly, the assumptions and beliefs of other cultures – and frees him especially from acquiescing through habit to the aforementioned destructive alienation of mind from nature, the repression of instinct in Reformed Christianity, and the inert scientific rationalism of our contemporary Western culture. With such freedom the Wodwo becomes, like Hughes himself, the peripatetic, eclectic anthropologist.[32]

There is however no one self to discover in *Dart* – the river is its own anthropologist – and Oswald includes in her hypertextual glosses to the poem the people who daily go about their business on and by the river with myths and stories that accumulate also around the river's banks. The relationship of poem to voice is dramatised at the end of the poem in the movement to a 'perilous selving'. Oswald's role as overseer of the poem seems to be an attempt to find a voice – for herself, and for nature – a voice which constantly becomes redefined in its very interaction with the human and the historical. 'This is me,' says the voice at the end of the poem:

> anonymous, water's soliloquy,

> all names, all voices, Slip-Shape, this is Proteus,
> whoever that is, the shepherd of the seals,
> driving my many selves from cave to cave...

> (p.48)

In *Woods etc.* (2005) Oswald returns to the lyrical writing of her first volume, *The Thing in the Gap-Stone Stile* (1996). Here, however, her writing is more self-consciously experimental when, for example, in her idiosyncratic uses of the full stop Oswald suggests a musicality of halt and pause that runs against syntax and the rules of the sentence, nudging the reader's attentiveness from the telling of the event to the processes of the event itself. The publisher's jacket blurb identifies in Oswald's work a 'listening syntax', a phrase which in some ways recalls Heaney's reading of Eliot's term 'the auditory imagination' when he writes of 'the cultural depth-charges latent in certain words and rhythms, that binding secret between words in poetry that delights not just the ear but the whole backward and abysm of mind and body' (*New Relations*, p.56). In a short and fascinating essay, which also throws light on this idea of 'listening syntax', Oswald describes in detail her method of composition:

> Poems are written in the sound house of a whole body, not just with the hands. So before writing, I always spend a certain amount of time preparing my listening. I might take a day or sometimes as much as a month picking up the rhythms I find, either in other poems or in the world around me. I map them into myself by tapping my feet or punching the air and when my whole being feels like a musical score, I see what glimpses, noises, smells, I see if any creature or feeling come to live there.
>   Then, before putting pen to paper, I ask myself, 'Am I listening? Am I really listening with a soft, slow listening that will not obliterate the speaker.[33]

In the title-poem 'Woods etc.' (*Woods etc.*, p.7), Oswald seems to be charting this moment of creativity when she writes

> I remember walking once into increasing
> woods, my hearing like a widening wound.
> first your voice and then the rustling ceasing.
> the last glow of rain dead in the ground

that my feet kept time with the sun's imaginary
changing position, hoping it would rise
suddenly from the scattered parts of my body...

If this recalls, with its image of the 'widening wound', Vicki Feaver's interest in the *duende*, it does so in a way which assumes a much less fixed relationship with the body. Oswald's scattered body assumes a coherence in voice only as the body and nature coalesce, the sun rising through the body as 'in my throat the little mercury line / that regulates my speech began to fall'.

Oswald's engagement with the provisionality of the self in relationship to nature, and the provisionality of self and nature is well exemplified in 'Leaf' (*Woods etc.*, p.8), a poem which is simultaneously about nature, and the experience of being in nature. The poem, which is dedicated to her children, is as well, it seems, a metaphor for pregnancy in which the relationship between self and the natural world and the self and other of the mother and baby is explored:

Leaf
(for J.O. and L.O.)

the leaf that now lies being made
in its shell of scale, the hush of things
unseen inside, the heartbeat of dead wood.
the slow through-flow that feeds
a form curled under, hour by hour
the thick reissuing starlike shapes
of cells and pores and water-rods
which builds up, which becomes a pressure,
a gradual fleshing out of a longing for light,
a small hand unfolding, feeling about.
into that hand the entire
object of the self being coldly placed,
the provisional, the inexplicable I
in mid-air, meeting the wind and dancing

In a recent review of *Woods etc.*, Carol Rumens has commented how 'Oswald clearly knows her botanical science, but scientific accuracy is not the goal... However, it seems that the very impulse to write scientifically fuels the anthropomorphism.'[34] The bifurcation and overlays of image of leaf and image of gestating baby works in the final four lines as both an image of the leaf's unfurling, but also as an image of the 'I' who meets nature, coldly placed against it, but also it. If this image of fertility is mother nature (and mother in nature) it is a version of nature which is generative, self-constructing and in dialogue with human creativity. Oswald's 'science', her attentiveness to nature shares both Bishop's and Shapcott's desire for the transcendent. In 'Leaf' Oswald perhaps most reminds us of Emerson, when he writes in 'Circles' that there 'are no fixtures in nature. The universe is fluid and volatile. Permanence is but a word of degrees'; or in his essay on 'The Poet' when he writes

> We are symbols, and inhabit symbols; workman, work, and tools, words and things, birth and death, all are emblems; but we sympathise with the symbols, and being infatuated with the economical uses of things, we do not know that they are thoughts.
>
> The poet alone knows astronomy, chemistry, vegetation, and anim-ation, for he does not stop at these facts, but employs them as signs. He knows why the plain, or meadow of space, was strewn with these flowers we call suns, and moons, and stars; why the great deep is adorned with animals, with men, and gods; for in every word he speaks he rides on them as the horses of thought.[35]

How radical – or even desired – this provisionality is in relation to a gender politics for Oswald is perhaps more difficult to discern. In the sonnet concluding 'Three Portraits of a Radio Audience', 'Rachel Raynor', (*Woods etc.*, pp.36-37), Oswald writes

> Not her incomparable soul, not its unique
> Fidelity to failure, not the churr
> Of its thin birdthroat, struggling to speak
> On the bare perches of what stands for her.
> Nor any name that anyone might try
> To catch her with. As either she or I.

The suggestion that the soul has a 'unique / fidelity to failure' begs all sorts of questions about the way in which Oswald is construct-ing the relationship between body and soul. What is the nature of the failure and what is the fidelity she is invoking? A fidelity of representation? A Platonic failure of the soul to remember the perfect forms before its inhabitation of the body? Or a moral failure, a kind of postlapsarian original sin? Judith Butler is useful here when, drawing on Michel Foucault, she discusses the relationship between body and soul. Her argument is complex, but is worth quoting at some length:

> The figure of the interior soul understood as "within" the body is signi-fied through its inscription on the body, even though its primary mode of signification is through its very absence, its potent invisibility. The effect of structuring inner space is produced through the signification of a body as a vital and sacred enclosure. The soul is precisely what the body lacks; hence, the body presents itself as a signifying lack. That lack which is the body signifies the soul as that which contests and displaces the inner/outer distinction itself, a figure of interior psychic space inscribed *on* the body as a social signification that perpetually renounces itself as such.[36]

Without getting too lost in the intricacies of Butler's philosophy, what remains important is the way in which this discussion returns us to question Oswald's construction of the poetic subject. The analogy Oswald draws is between the soul as 'birdthroat' (importantly the vehicle by which the bird articulates itself, not the whole bird) and the self as the branches on which the soul might perch, which transforms the Rachel of her poem into a metaphorical Daphne (who was turned into a laurel tree). Such a transformation of woman into tree echoes the beginning lines of the poem 'Who is Rachel. What is she. Not she', which parody Shakespeare's song of love in *Two Gentlemen of Verona*, 'Who is Sylvia, what is she' (3. II). And Sylvia's name recalls, of course, not only 'the sylvan' in which *Two Gentlemen* is set, but also the forest where Proteus attempts to rape Silvia.

As well, then, as questioning the essential nature of feminine, the poem also deconstructs romantic positioning of woman as desired object. Both Sylvia and Daphne are objects of male pursuit, and here, the poem seems to suggest, Rachel suffers in an attempt to speak out of such positionings, like Philomel, the woman who was turned into a nightingale after her tongue was cut out so she couldn't tell who raped her. Rachel in Oswald's poem is not 'the substantial substance of a woman'; knowing her is neither a question of her material presence nor her own speaking 'of what stands for her'. The final lines of the poem work to suggest that we can neither know her as subject or object, body or soul. Such inability to know is also one which must be shared with the speaker of the poem, whose 'I', which in the ambiguities of the poem's final line is both Rachel *and* the voice of the poem, we cannot know either. The poem thus resists a knowing of the self, and does so in resistance to male ways of positioning, knowing and ultimately abusing femininity.

If the subject of Rachel Raynor appears damaged and silenced in such a state of provisionality, in contrast 'Hymn to Iris' (*Woods etc.*, p.39) praises the goddess 'whose being is only an afterglow of a passing-through'. 'Hymn to Iris' is a poem in homage to a rainbow, 'a bridge built out of the linked cells of thin air'. Iris is, like Hermes, and like the angel, a messenger, and the poem ends with the lines 'And may I often wake on the broken bridge of a word, / Like in the wind the trace of a web. Tethered to nothing'. Here the rainbow, which is also, in a homophonic pun, 'a bent-down bough of nothing', again subject to Oswald's sylvan transformations.

The poem is a companion poem to her response to Wordsworth's 'On Westminster Bridge' [37] (many of the poems in the volume do in fact work in this kind of dialogue), which rather than praise the beauty of the city, rejects its commerce and 'teetering structures of administration', where 'the weather trespasses into strip-lit offices / through tiny windows into tiny thought and authorities'. Although the river is praised, the social world of the poem is reduced to 'bored-street walkers' and 'tiny subjugated minds'; and the city is a place from which to wander 'swiftly away'. In contrast to the way in which Oswald creates a relationship in *Dart* between the human and the natural, the city offers no such potential for exchange. Oswald's problem with the city appears to be its confinement of human beings, and the 'million shut-away eyes' of those who 'glance once / restlessly at the river's ruts and glints'. By contrast the rainbow's bridge 'built out of the linked cells of thin air' appears to symbolise union and connection in more spiritual terms. If this recalls Shapcott's angelic poetics of mediation, it does so with more conservatism, for although it offers a critique of urban capitalism with which we might have strong sympathies, it appears to do so also at the blanket expense of the differences and individuality of its inhabitants.

There is much more to be said about Oswald's work, and the potential it holds in opening up a new direction for women's writing, and a new, if precarious, way of exploring the self, and the poetic relationship between text, voice and body. Although she has identified as important poetic influences Dante, Ovid and Gerard Manley Hopkins, Oswald's use of the dramatised long poem also connects her work with women poets of the 19th and 20th centuries who used the form (see, for example, Sheila Wingfield, *MWP*, pp.87-91; Lynette Roberts, *MWP*, pp.96-99). In *Woods etc.* Oswald blends the scrutiny and attentiveness of naming that scientific detail brings, with an altogether more precarious version of the self who looks. The chromatic dispersion of white light as it hits water in the atmosphere, that refracts into the drop separating the light's component colours and then refracts out again, remaining in this process intangible and mysteriously movable seems a good – if also necessarily provisional – metaphor for Oswald's poetics, the broken bridge of a word in which she allows the self to form as it knows the world, and then disappears, before reappearing differently elsewhere.

NOTES

Introduction *(pp.11-29)*

1. First published in 1854, its two volumes revised through until 1862, the poem glorifies female subservience, passivity and dependence. See *A Room of One's Own*.

2. See *Feminist Literary Theory: A Reader*, ed. Mary Eagleton (Oxford: Blackwell, 1988), p.2. In Woolf's writing there is a degree of slippage between the terms writer and poet; the "problem" of the woman poet is clearly central to her preoccupations, although this is not always spelled out. Woolf's *Orlando*, her "pseudo-biography" of the poet Vita Sackville-West, her friend and lover, is a narrative which tells the story over four centuries of a poet modelled on West. Woolf's only other "biography", *Flush*, is an account of Elizabeth Barrett Browning's life, as seen through the eyes of her dog.

3. Judith Butler, *Gender Trouble: Feminism and the Subversion of Identity* (New York and London: Routledge, 1990), p.136. Hereafter *Gender Trouble* in the text.

4. *Literary Theory: A Very Short Introduction* (Oxford: Oxford UP, 1997), p.203.

5. 'Cultural Studies, Critical Theory and Critical Discourse Analysis: Histories, Remembering and Futures' in *Linguistik online* 14, 2/03 [www.linguistik-online.de/14_03/threadgold.html]

6. Cited by Connor, 'British Surrealist Poetry in the 1930s', in *British Poetry, 1900-50* (Basingstoke: Macmillan, 1995), p.176.

7. 'Syllepsis', *Critical Enquiry*, VI (1980), p.625. Cited by Michael Worton and Judith Still, *Intertextuality: Theories and Practices* (Manchester: Manchester UP, 1990), p.25.

8. Linda Hutcheon, *A Theory of Parody: Teachings of Twentieth-Century Art Forms* (London: Routledge, 1985), p.129.

9. Linda Hutcheon, *A Poetics of Postmodernism: History, Theory, Fiction* (London: Routledge, 1988), p.35.

10. Relations between male and female poets at the beginning of the century were of course complex in their personal and gender politics. Both Pound and Eliot, for example, came to dislike the writing and lecturing of Amy Lowell who did much to espouse the cause of modernism. Pound initially published Lowell's work, but later dismissed her imagist writing as 'Amygism'. Pound also championed the work of Marianne Moore, under the illusion at first that she was a black woman. Pound brought H.D. to prominence, creating her public persona as 'imagiste' but was overbearing in a way which later made both H.D. and Edith Sitwell uncomfortable.

11. See, for example, photographs by Maurice Beck in Elizabeth Salter, *Edith Sitwell* (London: Bloomsbury, 1988), p.50.

12. *Selected Letters*, cited by Elizabeth Salter, *Edith Sitwell* (London: Bloomsbury, 1988), p.50.

13. Headwear was something of an issue at this gathering of poets, as Elizabeth Bishop recounts in her memoir of Marianne Moore, 'Efforts of Affection'. Moore was asked to remove her trademark wide-brimmed hat because it took up too much space. She refused. See Elizabeth Bishop, *Collected Prose* (London: Chatto, 1984), pp.150-51.

14. Charles Baudelaire, *The Painter of Modern Life and Other Essays* (London:

Phaidon, 1995), p.27. Hereafter *Painter of Modern Life* in the text.

15. 'Female Female Impersonators' in *No Man's Land: The Place of the Woman Writer in the Twentieth Century* (New Haven and London: Yale UP, 1989), p.60.

16. Laura Severin, *Poetry Off the Page: Twentieth Century British Women Poets in Performance* (Aldershot: Ashgate), pp.45-46. Hereafter *Poetry Off the Page* in the text.

17. *Stevie Smith: A Selection*, edited by Hermione Lee (London: Faber, 1983), p.17.

18. *Men and Women Writers of the 1930s: The Dangerous Flood of History* (London: Routledge, 1996), p.84.

19. Cited by Jacqueline Rose in *The Haunting of Sylvia Plath* (London: Virago, 1991), p.154. See pp.150-54 for a fascinating and valuable discussion of Plath and Hughes's response to Graves. Hereafter all references *The Haunting of Sylvia Plath* in the text.

20. See Rebecca O'Rourke, 'Mediums, Messengers and Noisy Amateurs', *Women: A Cultural Review*, 1 no. 3 (Winter 1990), 275-86.

21. See Anne Stevenson, *Poems 1955-2005* (Tarset: Bloodaxe Books, 2005), pp.384-86.

22. See the biographical note on Greenlaw in *Modern Women Poets*, p.377.

23. *The New Poetry*, revised edition (Harmondsworth: Penguin, 1966), p.27 and p.28.

24. Some of whom were in mental institutions themselves. See *Anne Sexton: A Self-Portrait in Letters*, edited by Linda Gray Sexton and Lois Ames, with a new foreword by Linda Gray Sexton (Boston: Houghton Mifflin, 1991), p.276.

25. *Anne Sexton: The Complete Poems*, with a foreword by Maxine Kumin (Boston: Houghton Mifflin, 1981), p.xix-xx.

26. *Slipshod Sibyls: Recognition, Rejection and the Woman Poet* (London: Viking, 1995), p.390. Hereafter *Slipshod Sibyls* in the text.

27. *Edith Sitwell: The Symbolist Order* (Carbondale and Edwardsville: Southern Illinois UP, 1968), p.iv.

CHAPTER ONE: **Wheels, Peacocks, Ghosts, Hambones and Hearts: Edith Sitwell's Self-Fashioning**
(pp.33-69)

1. From *The Letters of Virginia Woolf*, volume 3, cited by Victoria Glendinning, *Edith Sitwell: A Unicorn Among Lions* (London: Weidenfeld & Nicolson, 1981), p.111. Hereafter all references to Glendinning, *Unicorn Among Lions*, in the text.

2. For an interesting selection of Cunard's poetry, and an invaluable introduction to her life and work, see *The Selected Poems of Nancy Cunard*, edited by John Lucas (Nottingham: Trent Editions, 2005).

3. 'And slowly we perambulate / With spectacles that concentrate, / In one short hour, Eternity, In one small lens, / Infinity.// With children our primeval curse, /We overrun the universe' Edith Sitwell, *Collected Poems* (London: Sinclair-Stevenson, 1993), p.165. Hereafter all references to Sitwell's poems which refer to the *Collected Poems* will appear as CP in the text.

4. *Edith Sitwell: The Symbolist Order* (Carbondale and Edwardsville: Southern Illinois UP, 1968), p.110.

5. *Wheels: An Anthology of Verse,* second edition (New York: Longman, March 1917).

6. The continuing thematic preoccupation with death in the poems stems, in almost all cases, in reaction to the First World War. See for example the soldier Victor Perowne's poem 'The Lady of Shalott' ; Osbert Sitwell's poem 'Black Mass' describes 'the music of the evil things of Night', or his description of the French battlefields: 'Long writhing bodies fall and twist and rise, / And one can hear them playing in the mud. / Upon the ruined walls there gleam and shine / The track of those grey vast monstrosities – / As some gigantic snail had crawled along'. Such trauma is equally resonant in the poems by women: in Iris Tree's 'Zeppelins' the body at war cannot contain its terror: 'Now every muscle weakens, every pulse / Is set at gallop pace, and every nerve / Stretched taut with terror and a mad revolt. / The fear of death, the longing still to live, –/ Lie in a vain world racked with hundred pains / Limp in a dull street housed with crumbling dreams;/ Only to breathe and eat and sleep and love / A little longer...' Helen Rootham's poem 'The Great Adventure', recalls at its end J.M. Barrie's line from *Peter Pan*, that death must be an 'awfully big adventure':

> Then in my hands that trustingly advanced
> To take the gifts that Time new-born might offer,
> I found a sword.
> In my young mind which hardly yet saw clear
> To order rules of life,
> They wrote the rules of death.
> In my young heart which had not yet lived long enough
> To know its mate,
> They placed an enemy, full-grown;
> And where I looked for Life
> Death stands – The Great Adventure.

7. See David Batchelor, Briony Fer and David Wood, *Realism, Rationalism, Surrealism: Art Between the Wars* (Yale UP, in association with the Open University, 1993), pp.36–40.

8. *Radio Corpse: Imagism and the Cryptaesthetic of Ezra Pound* (Cambridge, Mass, and London, England: Harvard UP, 1995), p.73.

9. *Façades: Edith, Osbert and Sacheverell Sitwell* (London: Macmillan, 1978), p.98. Hereafter *Façades* in the text.

10. See for example Sandra Gilbert and Susan Gubar, 'Soldier's Heart: Literary Men, Literary Women, and the Great War', in *No Man's Land: The Place of the Woman Writer in the Twentieth Century,* vol. 2: Sexchanges (New Haven and London, Yale UP, 1989), pp.258–323.

11. See Trudi Tate, *Modernism, History and the First World War* (Manchester: Manchester UP, 1998), p.44.

12. *Selected Poems*, with an essay on her own poetry (London: Duckworth, 1936). Hereafter *Selected Poems* in the text.

13. *Black Sun: Depression and Melancholia* (New York and Oxford: Columbia UP, 1989), p.63.

14. *Psychoanalytic Criticism: Theory in Practice* (London: Routledge, 1989), p.8.

15. Not unsurprisingly, Sitwell's "murderous" impulses were channelled and fuelled by the events of the war. A pacifist, Sitwell published six poems by Wilfred Owen in the fourth cycle of *Wheels* in 1919 – Owen had been killed in action in 1918 – and began a friendship with Siegfried Sassoon when she wrote to support him following his removal to Craiglockhart in 1917. Sitwell later became embroiled with Sassoon in a dispute concerning the posthumous publication of Owen's poems and Sitwell's letter to Owen's mother uncomfortably but tellingly echoes the dynamic set-up in 'The Mother' when she writes: 'I am dumb when I think what not only you, his mother, but we all have lost. I shall keep the 4th November always, as long as I live, as a day of mourning. I know you are broken hearted, but oh, you are just the mother for such a son. Tomorrow, his first poems in book form will be with you – the immortality of his great soul.' See the *Selected Letters of Edith Sitwell*, ed. Richard Greene (London: Virago, 1998), pp.31-32. Hereafter *Selected Letters*. Tellingly, Sitwell's biographer Victoria Glendinning recounts how Alice B. Toklas, Stein's lover and lifelong companion, described Sitwell on first meeting as 'a grenadier... A gendarme' and that in Paris Sitwell was chased by French children who called out to her 'Soldat anglais, soldat anglais' on account of what Toklas described as her 'double-breasted coats with large buttons'. See *Edith Sitwell: A Unicorn Among Lions*, p.115.

16. See Rimbaud, *Collected Poems*, introduced and edited by Oliver Bernard, with plain prose translations of each poem (Harmondsworth: Penguin, 1986), pp.242-43. The French poem reads:

Ô le plus violent Paradis de la grimace enragée! Pas de comparaison avec vos Fakirs et les autres bouffonneries scéniques. Dans les costumes improvisés avec le goût du mauvais rêve ils jouent des complaintes, des tragédies de malandrins et de demi-dieux spirituels comme l'histoire ou les religions ne l'ont jamais été. Chinois, Hottentots, bohémians, niais, hyènes, Molochs, vieilles démences, démons sinistres, ils mêlent les tours populaires, maternels, avec les poses et les tendresses bestiales. Ils interpreteraient des pièces nouvelles et des chansons « bonnes filles ». Maîtres jongleurs, ils transforment le lieu et les personnes et usent de la comedies magnétique. Les yeux flambent, le sang chante, les os s'élargissent, les larmes et des filets rouges ruissellent. Leur raillerie ou leur terreur dure une minute, ou des mois entiers.

J'ai seul la clef de cette parade sauvage.

17. *The Radical Twenties: Writing, Politics and Culture* (New Brunswick, NJ: Rutgers UP, 1999), pp.209-10.

18. *Desire in Language: A Semiotic Approach to Literature and Art*, edited by Leon S. Roudiez and translated by Thomas Gora, Alice Jardine and Leon S. Roudiez (Oxford: Blackwell, 1982), p.78.

19. Cited by David Batchelor in 'This Liberty and This Order: Art in France After the First World War' in *Realism, Rationalism, Surrealism: Art Between the Wars*, p.63.

20. *Modernism: An Anthology of Sources and Documents*, edited by Vassiliki Koloctroni, Jane Goldman and Olga Taxidou (Edinburgh: Edinburgh UP, 1998), p.310. Hereafter *Modernism: An Anthology* in the text.

21. The use of the Sengerphone also resembles the image one of the original set designs for Picasso's character the American Manager, with his megaphone, in *Parade*.

22. He continues: 'No one who has not felt it has understood their secret language...cold wind is the trance in which inspiration has descended. It is in that chill wind upon the wrists and temples that the muse has come down to earth.' *Poltergeists* (London: Faber, 1940), p.37.

23. 'The Machine in the Ghost: Spiritualism, Technology and the "Direct Voice"' in *Ghosts: Deconstruction, Psychoanalysis and History* (Basingstoke: Palgrave, 1999), p.203. Hereafter 'The Machine in the Ghost' in the text.

24. Rimbaud's French reads:

> Au gibet noir, manchot aimable,
> Dansent, dansent les paladins,
> Les maigres paladin du diable,
> Les squelettes de Saladins.

> Messire Belzébuth tire par la cravate
> Ses petits pantins noirs grimaçant sur le ciel,
> Et, leur claquant au front un revers de savante,
> Les fait danser, danser aux sons d'un vieux Noël!

Helen Rootham's translations, prose poems from *Illuminations* (a series of which were in the first edition of *Wheels*), were published by Faber, with an introduction by Sitwell, in 1932.

25. *Rabelais and His World*, translated by Helene Iswolsky (Bloomington: Indiana UP, 1984), p.41.

26. The story of Proserpine or Persephone is a myth which tells of the persistence of a mother's love as Proserpine's mother Demeter roves the earth to find her; the world is plunged into Winter, and only on Proserpine's return, for six months of the year is the earth's fertility returned.

27. *Victorian Poetry: Poetry, Poetics and Politics* (London: Routledge, 1993), p.405.

28. Graves defines texture as 'the relations of a poem's vowels and consonants, other than rhyme, considered as mere sound'. Cited by Glendinning, *A Unicorn Among Lions*, p.37.

29. Cited by Anthea Trodd, *Women's Writing in English: Britain, 1900-1945* (London and New York: Longman, 1998), p.87. Trod suggests that 'the discrepancy between the peacock's decorative plumage and its discordant shriek' is important, bearing in mind Sitwell's high-pitched voice'. Sitwell even owned a rather unoriginally named pet peacock 'Peaky' as a child.

30. *No Man's Land: The Place of the Woman Writer in the Twentieth Century*, vol. 2: Sexchanges (New Haven and London: Yale UP, 1989), p.327.

31. *No Man's Land: The Place of the Woman Writer in the Twentieth Century*, vol. 3: Letters from the Front (New Haven and London: Yale UP, 1994), p.60.

32. *Bodies That Matter: On the Discursive Limits of Sex* (London and New York: Routledge, 1993), pp.234-35.

33. The image of the peacock does in fact recur as a motif throughout Sitwell's prose work. In her only novel, *I Live Under a Black Sun* (John Lehmann: London, 1937) (Holiday Library Edition, 1948), which anachronistically sets the story of Jonathan Swift's relationships with women in the period of the First World War, Sitwell associates the peacock with modernity, sexlessness and fashion. It's hard to know exactly how such a description is to be read in terms of Sitwell's own dress and voice. In a paragraph that is satirical and yet simultaneously admiring, Esther, who is described as 'a plump young woman whose whole appearance and manner,...gave the impression that she was on the point of slipping down a hill', is contrasted with her friends:

> Geometrical ciphers, sexless figures of indestructible, highly varnished Birmingham hardware, but with a metropolitan polish, and turned out according to the latest international taste in hardware. Their faces were

like the definition of Zero... 'Nothing – nought – duck's egg – goose's egg – cypher – none nobody' and from these epitomes would issue the new fashionable voice, deliberately colourless and wooden, or tinny and tiny and as circumscribed and meaningless as if issued from an inferior and worn-out musical box, or rich and artificially hoarse. It might be said that Respectability was the only outcast with whom they were not on speaking terms. ...To these were added a crowd of young men, screaming about 'chic' and 'the latest thing, my dear', in voices high and shrill as those of parrots or peacocks. Their costumes were as striking as the feathers of these birds...(pp.158-59)

Here the fashionable are unsexed, a great zero, in which the self is extinguished, surrendered to the artifice of costume and the fashionable voice and most notably it is the camp young men who are peacocks. In her later book, *English Women* (1942; London: Prion, 1997), a series of brief hagiographies which includes chapters on Catherine Blake, Mary Wollstonecraft, Esther Johnson, Dorothy Wordsworth and Christina Rossetti, Sitwell's great heroine, Elizabeth Tudor, is praised in Blake's words for the 'pride of the peacock which is the glory of god' (p.10). Sitwell also describes there the discrepancy between public and private roles of woman and Queen, a discrepancy she perhaps perceived between her private self and public role as poet.

    34. Cited by Elaine Showalter, *Sexual Anarchy: Gender and Culture at the Fin de Siècle* (London: Bloomsbury, 1991), p.169. Hereafter *Sexual Anarchy* in the text.

    35. Cited by Garber, *Vested Interests: Cross-Dressing and Cultural Anxiety* (New York: Routledge, 1992), p.343. Hereafter *Vested Interests* in the text.

    36. Mallarmé: *Collected Poems*, translated and with a commentary by Henry Weinfield (London and Berkeley: University of California Press, 1994), p.32.

    37. *Mallarmé on Fashion* (New York and London: Berg, 2004), p.98. It is unlikely that Sitwell would have known at this point Mallarmé's writings on fashion, but interesting to remember here his brief career as editor of the Parisian fashion magazine *La Dernière Mode*. Often "disguised" as a woman he would comment on contemporary fashion. In its first issue *La Dernière Mode* initiates a discussion on women, fashion and poetry (1874).

    38. *Modernisms: A Literary Guide* (Berkeley and Los Angeles: University of California Press, 1995), pp.61-62. Hereafter *Modernisms* in the text.

    39. *Troy Park* (London: Duckworth, 1925). Hereafter *TP* in the text.

    40. *Rustic Elegies* (London: Duckworth, 1927).

    41. Cited by Ulrich Lehmann in *Tigersprung: Fashion in Modernity* (Cambridge, Mass. and London, England: MIT Press, 2000), p.271.

    42. *Geography and Plays*, with an introduction by Cyrena N. Pondrom (Madison: University of Wisconsin Press, 1993).

    43. See Cyrena N. Pondrom, 'Influence? Or Intertextuality?: The Complicated Connection of Edith Sitwell with Gertrude Stein', in *Influence and Intertextuality in Literary History*, edited by Jay Clayton and Eric Rothstein (Wisconsin: Wisconsin UP, 1991), p.210. Hereafter *Influence and Intertextuality* in the text.

    44. *English Women* (London: Prion, 1997), pp.76-77.

    45. Cited in P. Adams Sitney, *Modernist Montage: The Obscurity of Vision in Cinema and Literature* (Columbia: Columbia UP, 1990), p.150.

    46. *Gold Coast Customs* (London: Duckworth, 1929).

    47. Such imagery, it's worth pointing out, is very much in contrast with Nancy Cunard's later pamphlet *Black Man and White Ladyship* (1931), which is an attack on her mother's and her mother's circle's racism.

48. *Powers of Horror: An Essay on Abjection* (New York: Columbia UP, 1982), p.10. Hereafter *Powers of Horror* in the text.

49. *The Compulsion to Create: A Psychoanalytic Study of Women Artists* (London: Routledge, 1993), p.286.

50. *Elizabeth Bishop and Marianne Moore: The Psychodynamics of Creativity* (Princeton: Princeton UP, 1993), p.5.

CHAPTER TWO: **'Tirry-Lirry-Lirry All the Same':**
The Poetry and Performance of Stevie Smith
(pp.70-92)

1. 'Of Absent friends' in *In Search of Stevie Smith*, edited with an introduction by Sanford Sterlicht (New York: Syracuse UP, 1991), p.153. Hereafter *In Search of Stevie Smith* in the text.

2. *The Bloodaxe Book of Contemporary Women Poets: Eleven British Writers*, edited by Jeni Couzyn (Newcastle: Bloodaxe Books, 1985), p.35.

3. *Stevie Smith: A Critical Biography* (London: Faber, 1988), p.246.

4. 'Frivolous and Vulnerable' in *In Search of Stevie Smith*, p.77.

5. 'On Writing' in *Stevie Smith: A Selection*, edited by Hermione Lee (London: Faber, 1983), p.185. Hereafter *SS* in the text.

6. In Smith's early poem 'The Hound of Ulster', for example, which was the first poem in *A Good Time Was Had By All*, Smith recalls the popular song 'How much is that doggy in the window' in combination with an evocation of Blake's 'Little Boy Lost' and 'Little Boy Found' and Yeats' 'Stolen Child'. Hermione Lee has pointed to Blake's 'Mad Song' as ur-text to Smith's 'Breughel'.

7. Janet Montefiore, *Men and Women Writers of the 1930s: The Dangerous Flood of History* (London: Routledge, 1996), p.115.

8. *The Collected Poems of Stevie Smith*, edited with a preface by James MacGibbon (Harmondsworth: Penguin, 1985), p.195. Hereafter all references to *CP* in the text.

9. Smith's first name was Florence. She took on the persona Stevie, after, according to Spalding, some boys yelled at her when she was riding, drawing attention to the fact that she looked like the well-known jockey Steve Donaghue.

10. Only two short stories were published post-1950: 'To School in Germany' and 'Getting Rid of Sadie', both in 1955.

11. *Me Again: The Uncollected Writings of Stevie Smith*, edited by Jack Barbera and William McBrien, with a preface by James MacGibbon (London: Virago, 1981), p.115. Hereafter *Me Again* in the text.

12. Smith's drawings of women are rarely bosomy. Most have no breast definition at all. Some exceptions are the nursing mother in infant, 'Peggy to Joey' (*CP*, p.468), 'Venus When choosing Death' (*CP*, p.454), 'The Smile' (*CP*, p.200), 'Death of Mr Mounsel' (*CP*, p.76), 'Appetite' (*CP*, p.66) and 'Angel of Grace' (*CP*, p.64). These women are all figured, perhaps with the exception of the nursing mother, as being subject to excessive love.

13. *Poetry Off the Page: Twentieth Century British Women Poets in Performance* (Aldershot: Ashgate, 2004), p.61.

14. 'The Machine in the Ghost: Spiritualism, Technology and the "Direct Voice" ' in *Ghosts: Deconstruction, Psychoanalysis History*, edited by Peter Buse and Andrew Stott (Basingstoke: Macmillan, 1999), p.209.

15. *Alexander Pope: A Critical edition of the Major Works* (Oxford: Oxford UP, 1993), p.337.

16. *William Wordsworth*, edited by Stephen Gill (Oxford and New York: Oxford UP, 1984), p.246.

17. *Gerard Manley Hopkins*, edited by Catherine Phillips (Oxford and New York: Oxford UP, 1986), pp.157-58.

18. For detailed discussions of the relationship between the poetry and the prose, see Romana Huk, *Stevie Smith: Between the Lines* (Basingstoke: Palgrave Macmillan, 2005).

19. Spalding does not mention a particular poem here but clearly had in mind Sitwell's poem from *Façade*, 'Rain', with its lines, 'For this is the hour when like a swan //The silence floats so still and wan'.

20. Pointed out and cited by Huk in *Stevie Smith: Between the Lines*, p.78. Smith had a brief correspondence with Osbert Sitwell and though given the opportunity was uncertain about whether she wanted to meet Edith herself. Smith took it upon herself to try to find homes for Edith's three cats after her death.

21. See especially Celia's attempted suicide in *The Holiday*, where she is rescued by her cousin/brother.

22. *Stealing the Language: The Emergence of Women's Poetry in America* (London: The Women's Press, 1986), p.213. Hereafter *Stealing the Language* in the text.

CHAPTER THREE: **Liberty Belles and Founding Fathers: Sylvia Plath and the Search for a Gendered Writing Self** *(pp.93-127)*

1. *The Journals of Sylvia Plath, 1950-1962*, edited by Karen V. Kukil (London: Faber, 2000), pp.457-58. Hereafter *Journals* in the text.

2. See *Johnny Panic and the Bible of Dreams and other prose writings* (London: Faber, 1977). Hereafter *JP* in the text. The only other woman represented in the text, Miss Milleravage, seems curiously to embody female power as having masculine and female elements, but such a conflation becomes repellent to Plath's narrator: 'Something about her merely smoking and drinking her coffee in the cafeteria at the ten o'clock break put me off so I never went to sit next to her again.' The narrator's revulsion stems from the seemingly brutish cut of Miss Milleravage's figure, a portrayal which seems to align her with some stereotypical representation of a concentration camp warden. Miss Milleravage functions as part of the repressed psyche of the narrator, which resides in these waters: 'Lake Nightmare, Bog of Madness, it's here the sleeping people lie and toss together among the props of their worst dreams.' (*JP*, p.20) And part of the narrator's act of repressing the figure of this 'female man' results in her inability to remember her name: 'She has a funny name I don't ever quite remember correctly, something really odd, like Miss Milleravage. One of those names that seems more like a pun mixing up Milltown and Ravage than anything in the city telephone directory.' (*JP*, p.23) Like Johnny Panic, the fearful presence who dominates the story, Miss Milleravage is a double-headed figure whose name is composed of oppositional mental states. 'Miltown', the brandname of a tranquilliser, was the wonder-drug of the 1950s, prescribed exuberantly as a panacea for restlessness, anxiety and depression. Miss Milleravage, then, figures as an emblem of anxiety about femininity that seems to merge the masculine with the feminine, energy with destruction, control and suppression. For a more detailed reading see my doctoral thesis, 'Anxiety and Role: Four Postwar Women Poets' (University of London, 1995).

3. In an essay on Rich first published in 1973, the critic Helen Vendler writes of coming across Rich's first book, describing it in powerful terms: 'I read it in almost disbelieving wonder; someone my age was writing down my life...here was a poet who seemed, by a miracle, a twin: I had not known till then how much I had wanted a contemporary and a woman as a speaking voice of life.' See Adrienne Rich, *Collected Early Poems 1950-1970* (London and New York: Norton, 1993), p.83-84. Rich's first two collections compare interestingly with Plath's first. But while Rich's poetry was to take its cue from the burgeoning of the Women's Movement in the US, her third collection *Snapshots of a Daughter-in-Law* (1963) looked to the recovery of women's history and a reconstruction of the self through both personal and political engagement. 'Snapshots of a Daughter-in-Law' (see *MWP*, pp.137-41), a key poem in Rich's development as both poet and feminist, was written between 1958 and 1960. Rich's poems take a discursive, more analytical stance ('mere talent was enough for us – / glitter in fragments and rough drafts // Sigh no more, ladies. / Time is male'). In comparison, Plath, while certainly not apolitical, sought to establish the self through metaphor.

4. Plath writes: 'Am reading Elizabeth Bishop with great admiration. Her fine originality, always surprising, never rigid, flowing, juicier than Marianne Moore who is her godmother.' *Journals*, p.516.

5. 'No reason why I should not surpass at least the facile Isabella Gardner and even the lesbian and fanciful Elizabeth Bishop.' *Journals*, p.322.

6. *Collected Poems*, edited with an introduction by Ted Hughes (London: Faber, 1981), pp.129-30. Hereafter *CP* in the text.

7. Hughes sees Plath and himself in terms of this relationship in *Birthday Letters* (London: Faber, 1998).

8. Sylvia Plath, *Letters Home: Correspondence 1950-1963*, selected and edited with a commentary by Aurelia Schober Plath (London: Faber, 1975), p.244. Hereafter *Letters Home* in the text.

9. See 'Isis' in *Birthday Letters*, p.111: 'The morning we set out to drive around America / She started with us. She was our lightest / Bit of luggage. And you had dealt with Death. You had come to an agreement finally: / He could keep your Daddy and you could have a child.' While I certainly don't want to construct a definitive reading of Plath via Hughes, the poem adds an interesting dimension to my argument.

10. With its reference to fairytales, this stanza reminds us in particular of Plath's short story 'The Wishing Box' (1956).

11. De Chirico, *La Révolution Surréaliste* (1 December 1924). Cited by Hal Foster, *Compulsive Beauty* (Cambridge, Mass. & London, England: MIT Press, 1993), pp.73-75. Foster's footnote continues:

> In *Hebdomeros*, his 1929 novel that recaptured some surrealist favor [sic], this glance returns – in the body of a woman: 'All at once, Hebdomeros saw that this woman had his father's eyes; and he understood... "Oh Hebdomeros," she said, "I am Immortality".'
> *Hebdomeros*, trs Margaret Crosland (New York, 1988), p.132.

12. Translated extract in Herschel B. Chipp, ed., *Theories of Modern Art* (Berkeley, 1968), pp.397-402; pp.446-53. Cited by Foster, *Compulsive Beauty*, p.65.

13. *Feminism and Psychoanalysis: A Critical Dictionary*, edited by Elizabeth Wright (Oxford: Blackwell, 1992), p.114.

14. See Elizabeth Grosz, 'lesbian fetishism?', *differences* 3/2 (1991), pp.39–42.

15. *Envy and Gratitude and Other Works 1946-1963* (London: Virago, 1988), p.289.

16. *The Other Sylvia Plath* (London: Longman, 2001), p.61. Hereafter *The Other Sylvia Plath* in the text.

17. *Monuments and Maidens: The Allegory of the Female Form* (London: Vintage, 1996), p.3. Hereafter *Monuments and Maidens* in the text.

18. Emma Lazarus's poem 'The New Colossus' appears in *Eliza's Babes: Four Centuries of Women's Poetry in English, c. 1500-1900*, edited by Robyn Bolam (Tarset: Bloodaxe Books, 2005), p.329. It is worth comparing Plath's 'The Colossus' also with Adrienne Rich's earlier poem, 'Villa Adriana', from *The Diamond Cutters* (1955), which begins: 'When the colossus of the will's dominion / Wavers and shrinks upon a dying eye, / Enormous shadows sit like birds of prey, / Waiting to fall where blistered marbles lie.' Like the speaker of Plath's poem, the speaker of Rich's poem is 'searching for an answer, / Passionately in need to reconstruct'.

19. *A Hitchcock Reader*, edited by Marshall Deutelbaum and Leland Poague (Ames: Iowa State UP, 1986), p.58. Hereafter *A Hitchcock Reader* in the text.

20. See film stills in Joel W. Finler, *Alfred Hitchcock: The Hitchcock Years* (London: B.T. Batsford Ltd, 1992), p.127.

21. For a discussion, to which I am indebted, of Plath's attitude towards American and England, see Tracy Brain, *The Other Sylvia Plath* (London: Longman, 2001).

22. See *Landscape and Memory* (London: Fontana, 1996), pp.385-99.

23. First published posthumously in *Crossing the Water* (London: Faber, 1971).

24. *Penguin Freud Library*, vol. 10 (Harmondsworth: Penguin, 1993), p.94. Cited by Malcom Bowie, *Feminism and Psychoanalysis: A Critical Dictionary*, p.29.

25. As pointed out by Heather Cam, ' "Daddy": Sylvia Plath's Debt to Anne Sexton', *American Literature*, 59 (3), October 1987, pp.429-32. Cited by Tim Kendall, in *Sylvia Plath: A Critical Study* (London: Faber, 2001), p.122.

26. Unpublished essay by Sylvia Plath, 'Edith Sitwell and the Development of her Poetry', 25 March 1953. Plath mss. II, Box 10, f.7. Courtesy Lilly Library, Indiana University, Bloomington and the Sylvia Plath Estate. Hereafter 'Edith Sitwell' in the text.

27. *The Mass Psychology of Fascism*, trs Vincent R. Carfagno (Harmondsworth: Penguin, 1970), p.87.

28. *Escape from Freedom* (New York: Henry Holt, 1969), p.4. Hereafter *Escape from Freedom* in the text.

29. *The Feminine Mystique* (Harmondsworth: Penguin, 1963), pp.265-66.

30. *The Captive Wife: Conflicts of Housebound Mothers*, new edition with new introduction by Ann Oakley (London: Routledge and Kegan Paul, 1983), p.143.

31. Cited by Wagner-Martin, in *Sylvia Plath: A Literary Life*, pp.115-16.

32. Paraphrased from James R. Lewis and Evelyn Dorothy Oliver, *Angels A-Z*, pp.52-53.

33. Dylan Thomas, *Collected Poems 1934-1952* (London: Dent, 1952), pp.95-97 & 155-58.

34. The lines in Plath's 'Lesbos', 'I should wear tiger pants, I should have an affair' are also possibly echoing (Riding) Jackson's 'The Tiger'. See *MWP*, pp.73-76. Reading Stevie Smith's poem 'Die Lorelei' (*CP*, p.380) it is easy to imagine the emotional charge such a poem would carry for Plath.

35. Cited by Anne Stevenson, *Bitter Fame: A Life of Sylvia Plath* (Harmondsworth: Penguin, 1989), p.268.

36. *Sylvia Plath: A Critical Study* (London: Faber, 2001), pp.153-54.

37. *Sylvia Plath and the Theatre of Mourning* (Oxford: Clarendon Press, 1999), p.130.

38. *The Observer*, 17 February 1963.

39. Cited by C.B. Cox and A.R. Jones in 'After the Tranquillised 50s: Notes on Sylvia Plath and James Baldwin', *Critical Quarterly*, 6 (Supp. 1964), p.107.

CHAPTER FOUR: **Consorting with Angels:**
Anne Sexton and the Art of Confession
(pp.128-144)

1. *Anne Sexton: A Biography* (London: Virago, 1992), p.303. Hereafter *Anne Sexton* in the text.

2. Elisabeth Bronfen: *The Knotted Subject: Hysteria and its Discontents* (Princeton, NJ: Princeton UP, 1998), p.297. Hereafter *The Knotted Subject* in the text.

3. *Complete Poems*, pp.6-7. Hereafter *CP* in the text.

4. Does the Eagle know what is in the pit?
   Or wilt thou go ask the Mole:
   Can wisdom be put in a silver rod?
   Or Love in a golden bowl.

See *Blake's Poetry and Designs*, edited by Mary Lynn Johnson and John E. Grant (New York and London: Norton, 1979). p.61. Hereafter *Blake's Poetry* in the text.

5. See Robert Lowell, *Collected Poems*, edited by Frank Bidart and David Gwanter with the editorial assistance of DeSales Harrison (New York: Farrar, Straus & Giroux, 2003; London: Faber, 2003), p.641.

6. These final lines, as Diane Wood Middlebrook points out in her biography of Sexton, echo the lines of the play Sexton wrote in 1962, in which a woman patient attempts to deal with the guilt she feels for assuaging psychological difficulty through analysis and not a relationship with God.

7. *The Uses of Enchantment: The Meaning and Importance of Fairy Tales* (London: Penguin, 1979), p.234.

8. Kumin describes Sexton's working method in the introduction to her *Complete Poems*: 'the impetus for creation usually came when Anne directly invoked the muse at her desk. Here, she read favorite poems of other poets – most frequently Neruda – and played certain evocative records over and over.' (p.xxvi)

9. I heard an Angel singing
   When the day was springing
   Mercy Pity Peace
   Is the worlds release
      (*Blake's Poetry*, p.187)

10. See Neruda, *Odes to Opposites*, selected and illustrated by Ferris Cook, trans. Ken Krabbenhoft (New York: Little Brown and Co., 1995), pp.76-77. 'Of all / my friends / and / enemies, / you're / the hardest to handle. / Everybody

else / carries you tied up, / a demon in their pockets, / a hurricane locked away / in boxes and decrees. / But not me. I carry you right alongside me, / and I'm telling you this: / It's high time / you showed me / what you can do. / Open up, let down / your tangled / hair, / leap up and singe / the heights of heaven.'

11. Sexton's insecurity about her own validity within a male-domain had resulted in her sly reprimand of Ted Hughes in a much earlier letter (1967) in which she displays an anxiety about her positioning as both woman and poet and confessional:

> It looks as if I will be the only female poet at the festival (not counting Ginsberg!)...is that so? How strange. I look drawn and haggard now, I will be no addition. I will work on a tan. Not, of course, that you asked me because I was another sex. No. That is another lump I dislike[:] 'female poets lump', the 'confessional lump', or the 'Lowell, Sexton, Plath lump'.

See *Anne Sexton: A Self Portrait in Letters*, edited by Linda Gray Sexton and Lois Ames, with a new foreword by Linda Gray Sexton (New York: Houghton Mifflin, 1991), p.308.

CHAPTER FIVE: **Myth, Fairytale and Feminism after the Women's Movement** *(pp.147-173)*

1. *One Foot on the Mountain: British Feminist Poetry 1969-1979* (London: Onlywomen Press, 1979).

2. 'Poetry and the Women's Movement in Postwar Britain', in *Contemporary British Women's Poetry: Essays in Theory and Criticism*, edited by James Acheson and Romana Huk (New York: SUNY Press, 1996), p.91.

3. *Feminism and Poetry: Language, Expereince and Identity in Women's Writing* (London: Pandora, 1987), p.42.

4. *Myth and Fairytale in Contemporary Women's Fiction* (Basingstoke: Palgrave, 2001) pp.7-8.

5. Letter to the author, 1998.

6. Cited by Jules Smith, http://www.contemporarywriters.com/authors/ ?p=auth02D2K462412627167, accessed 31 October 2005.

7. 'The Handless Maiden', in *How Poets Work*, edited by Tony Curtis (Bridgend: Seren, 1996), p.146. Hereafter *How Poets Work* in the text.

8. Interestingly, there are also echoes in the use of the relationship between creativity and the damaging of hands, and mother and daughter relationships, of Jane Campion's film *The Piano* (1993).

9. *Powers of Horror: An Essay on Abjection* (New York: Columbia UP, 1982), p.70. Hereafter *Powers of Horror* in the text.

10. *Judith, Sexual Warrior: Women and Power in Western Culture* (New Haven and London: Yale UP, 1998), p.3.

11. Notes for the attention of Professor Rosario Portale, copied to the author, 1998.

12. Letter to the author, February 1998.

13. *Elizabeth Bishop: Poet of the Periphery*, edited by Linda Anderson and Jo Shapcott (Tarset/Newcastle: Bloodaxe Books/University of Newcastle, 2002), p.100.

14. See for example John Newsinger's essay ' "Do You Walk the Walk":

Aspects of Masculinity in Some Vietnam War Films', in *You Tarzan: Masculinity, Movies and Men* (London: Lawrence and Wishart, 1993), pp.126-36. Newsinger points to Kubrick's film *Full Metal Jacket* 'which opens with young men having their heads shaved, being ritually de-feminised by having their relatively long hair cut' (p.132).

15. *Complete Poems* (London: Chatto, 1983), p.200-01

16. From 'Mrs Beast' in *The World's Wife* (London: Picador, 1999), p.72. Hereafter *TWW* in the text.

17. *Carol Ann Duffy* (Plymbridge: British Council/ Northcote House, 1999), p.18.

18. There remain many issues of inequality for women, in terms of the pay gap, female poverty, the domination by men of political systems, gender discrimination, and equality in the home. See the website of the Fawcett Society, which has campaigned for women's rights in Britain since 1866, at http://www.fawcettsociety.org.uk/index.asp?Pageid=5

19. '"Small Female Skull": Patriarchy and Philosophy in the Poetry of Carol Ann Duffy', in *The Poetry of Carol Ann Duffy: Choosing Tough Words*, edited by Angelica Michelis and Antony Rowland (Manchester: Manchester UP, 2003), p.111; p.117.

20. *Rapture* (London: Picador, 2005). All references hereafter *Rapture* in the text.

21. Interview with the author, Norwich, 30 May 1990.

22. Interview with Lidia Vianu, http://www.contemporarywriters.com/authors/?p=auth191 accessed 31 October, 2005.

23. André Breton, *Manifestoes of Surrealism*, trans. Richard Seaver and Helen R. Lane (London and New York: Ann Arbor, 1972), p.26.

24. Briony Fer, 'Surrealism, Myth and Psychoanalysis' in *Realism, Rationalism, Surrealism: Art Between the Wars* (London: Yale UP in association with the Open University, 1993), p.212.

25. Cited by Sarane Alexandrian, *Surrealist Art*, trans. Graeme Hough (London: Thames & Hudson, 1970), p.28.

26. Cited by Whitney Chadwick, *Women Artists and the Surrealist Movement* (London: Thames & Hudson, 1985), p.16.

27. Hélène Cixous with Catherine Clément, *The Newly Born Woman*, trans. Betsy Wing with an introduction by Sandra M. Gilbert (Manchester: Manchester UP, 1987), p.23. Hereafter *The Newly Born Woman* in the text.

28. *Saying Hello at the Station* – along with three other Hill collections – is published in *Trembling Hearts in the Bodies of Dogs: New & Selected Poems* (Newcastle: Bloodaxe Books, 1994). Hereafter *THIBD* in the text.

29. Interview with the author, Norwich, 30 May 1990.

30. *A Little Book of Meat* (Newcastle: Bloodaxe Books, 1993). Hereafter *LBOM* in the text.

31. *Contemporary Poetry and Postmodernism: Dialogue and Estrangement* (Basingstoke: Macmillan, 1996), p.240.

32. *Violet* (Newcastle: Bloodaxe Books, 1997). Hereafter *Violet* in the text.

33. *The Deregulated Muse: Essays on Contemporary British and Irish Poetry* (Newcastle: Bloodaxe Books, 1998), p.257.

34. See Jules Smith http://www.contemporarywriters.com/authors/?p=auth191, accessed 31 October 2005.

CHAPTER SIX: **Motherland and Mothertongues:**
Writing the Poetry of Nation
(pp.217-240)

1. *New Relations: The Refashioning of British Poetry 1980-1994* (Bridgend: Seren, 1996), p.22.

2. 'A Small Piece of Wood' from *Marconi's Cottage* (Oldcastle: Gallery, 1991), p.31.

3. *Facing the Music: Irish Poetry in the Twentieth Century* (Omaha, Nebraska: Creighton UP, 1999), p.355.

4. *Improprieties: Politics and Sexuality in Northern Irish Poetry* (Oxford: Clarendon Press, 1993), pp.50-51. Hereafter *Improprieties* in the text.

5. Such a comparison often overlooks the fact that Irigaray is Bulgarian, and Cixous, Algerian, and that their theoretical positions might arise from an experience of colonisation.

6. *This Sex Which is Not One*, trans. Catherine Porter with Carolyn Burke (New York: Cornell UP), p.71.

7. M.T.P. McCaughan [Medbh McGuckian], 'Gothic Influence on 19th-century Anglo-Irish Fiction', M.A. thesis, Queen's University Belfast, 1973, pp.143-44.

8. Source unknown. Transcript in the possession of Selima Hill.

9. For example, McGuckian draws on John Clare ('The Flitting'), Swift ('Vanessa's Bower'), Lewis Carroll ('The Rising Out'), Samuel Johnson ('The Seed Picture'), Chekhov ('A Small Piece of Wood'), Henry James' 'Turn of the Screw' ('Tulips'), Gwen John ('Road 32, Roof 13-23, Grass 23'), and as Clair Wills has brilliantly shown, 'The Dream-Language of Fergus' is 'almost entirely constructed out of quotations from Mandelstam's essays, most obviously "Conversation about Dante", "About the Nature of the Word", and 'Notes About Poetry".' See *Improprieties*, p.173.

10. McGuckian's first collection *The Flower Master* (Oxford: Oxford UP, 1982) was revised and expanded when republished as *The Flower Master and Other Poems* (Oldcastle: Gallery, 1993). Hereafter *TFM* in the text.

11. *The Psychopathology of Everyday Life*, Penguin Freud Library, vol. 5 (Harmondsworth: Penguin, 1976), p.83. Hereafter *Psychopathology* in the text.

12. Introduction to *The Psychopathology of Everyday Life*, translated by Anthea Bell (London: Penguin, 2002), p.xxxiv. Hereafter *Psychopathology* in the text.

13. *English Poetry Since 1940* (Harlow: Longman, 1993), p.223.

14. 'Screen Memories', Standard Edition of the *Complete Psychological Works of Sigmund Freud*, vol. 3, translated under the editorship of James Strachey in collaboration with Anna Freud, assisted by Alix Strachey and Alan Tyson (London: Hogarth Press, 24 volumes, 1953-74), p.319. Hereafter *Screen Memories* in the text.

15. *Mythologies*, selected and translated by Annette Lavers (St Albans: Granada, 1972), p.37. Barthes distinguishes between 'advertisements based on psychology and those based on psychoanalysis':

'*Persil* Whiteness' for instance, bases its prestige on the evidence of a result; it calls into play vanity, a social concern with appearances, by offering for comparison two objects, one which is *whiter than* the other. Advertisements for *Omo* also indicate the effect of the product (and in superlative fashion incidentally), but they chiefly reveal its mode of action;

in doing so, they involve the consumer in a kind of direct experience of the substance, make him the accomplice of a liberation rather than a mere beneficiary of a result; matter here is endowed with value bearing states.

16. *Collected Poems* (London: Faber, 1979), p.30. Hereafter, *CP*, in the text.

17. *Poetry in the Wars* (Newcastle: Bloodaxe Books, 1986), p.137. Hereafter *Poetry in the Wars* in the text.

18. There might here be a double joke on McGuckian's part, in that another town with a name like a woman's Christian name is Nancy, a town of great significance to Freud because it was the centre of an alternative to the psycho-analytic thought of Charcot's school at the Salpêtrière in Paris. The differ-ences arose from the Nancy's school's emphasis on hypnotism's therapeutic uses, rather than Charcot's use for display and entertainment.

19. Cited by Shane Murphy, in *Éire-Ireland: An Interdisciplinaray Journal of Irish Studies*, XXXI: 3&4, pp.85-86.

20. Medbh McGuckian, interview with Clair Wills (20 November 1986) in *Improprieties*, pp.62-63.

21. Interview with Rebecca E. Wilson, *Sleeping with Monsters: Conversations with Scottish and Irish Women Poets* (Polygon: Edinburgh, 1990), p.4.

22. 'Christ as Angel as the Will of God' from *Keeping Mum* (Tarset: Blood-axe Books, 2003), reprinted in *Chaotic Angels: Poems in English* (Tarset: Blood-axe Books, 2005), p.191. All references to poems hereafter *Chaotic Angels* in the text.

23. In the 2001 census this total had risen to 21%, with 24% being able to understand Welsh, and 16% being able to speak, read and write Welsh. See the website for the Office of National Statistics, at: http://www.statistics.gov.uk/cci/nugget.asp?id=447 (accessed 11 September 2005).

24. *The Bloodaxe Book of Modern Welsh Poetry: 20th Century Welsh-Language Poetry in Translation*, edited by Menna Elfyn and John Rowlands (Tarset: Bloodaxe Books, 2003). Hereafter *Modern Welsh Poetry* in the text.

25. See Robert Minhinnick's *The Adulterer's Tongue: An Anthology of Welsh Poetry in Translation* (Manchester: Carcanet, 2003).

26. *Y Llofrudd Iaith* (Swansea: Cyhoeddiadau Barddas, 1999).

27. *The Empire Writes Back: Theory and Practice in Post-colonial Literatures* (London and New York: Routledge, 1989), pp.52-53.

28. *The Return of the Real: The Avant-garde at the End of the Century* (Cam-bridge, Mass, and London, England: MIT Press, 1996), p.118. Hereafter *The Return of the Real* in the text.

29. *Sunbathing in the Rain: A Cheerful Book About Depression* (London: Flamingo, 2002), pp.41-42.

30. *Language in Literature* (Cambridge, Mass. & London: Belknap Press, 1987), pp.95-120. Hereafter *Language in Literature* in the text.

31. Letter to the author, 17 March 1996.

32. See for example 'Divine Women' in *Sexes and Genealogies*, trans. Gillian C. Gill (New York: Columbia UP, 1993), pp.57-72.

33. Kathleen Jamie, 'The Graduates', in *Jizzen* (London: Picador, 1999), pp.3-4.

34. *Identifying Poets: Self and Territory in Twentieth Century Poetry* (Edin-burgh: Edinburgh UP, 1993), p.3. Hereafter *Identifying Poets* in the text.

35. For poetry, see *The way we live* (Newcastle: Bloodaxe Books, 1987) and *The Autonomous Region* (Newcastle: Bloodaxe Books, 1993), both collected in *Mr and Mrs Scotland Are Dead: Poems 1980-1994*, selected by Lilias Fraser

(Tarset: Bloodaxe Books, 2002), hereafter *MMSD* in the text; also her prose account *The Golden Peak* (London: Virago, 1992).

36. *The Tree House* (London: Picador, 2004). Hereafter *Tree House* in the text.

37. *The Song of the Earth* (London: Picador, 2000). Hereafter *Song of the Earth* in the text.

38. See http://www.st-andrews.ac.uk/~www_se/jamie/treehouse.html

39. *The Adoption Papers* (Newcastle: Bloodaxe Books, 1991). Hereafter *The Adoption Papers* in the text.

40. *Other Lovers* (Newcastle: Bloodaxe Books, 1993). Hereafter *Other Lovers* in the text.

41. 'The Least International Shop in the World' in *Contemporary Women's Poetry: Reading / Writing / Practice*, edited by Alison Mark and Deryn Rees-Jones (Basingstoke: Palgrave, 2000), p.36. Hereafter *CWP* in the text.

42. *The Country at My Shoulder* (Oxford: Oxford UP, 1993), reprinted in *Carrying My Wife* (Newcastle: Bloodaxe Books, 2000). Hereafter *Carrying My Wife* in the text.

43. *A History of Twentieth Century Women's Poetry* (Cambridge: Cambridge UP, 2005), p.204.

44. *Souls* (Tarset: Bloodaxe Books, 2002), pp.61-62.

45. *How the Stone Found Its Voice* (Tarset: Bloodaxe Books, 2005). Hereafter *How the Stone Found Its Voice* in the text.

46. Interview with Janet Phillips, *Poetry Review*, 91 no.1 (Spring 2001), pp.18-21. See http://www.poetrysociety.org.uk/review/pr91-1/Shapcot1.htm

47. *Phrase Book* (Oxford: Oxford UP, 1992), reprinted in *Her Book* (London: Faber, 2000). Hereafter *Her Book* in the text.

48. Hal Foster: *The Return of the Real: The Avant-garde at the End of the Century* (Cambridge, Mass, and London, England: MIT Press, 1996), p.222. Hereafter *The Return of the Real* in the text.

49. *Gendering Poetry: Contemporary Women and Men Poets* (London: Pandora, 2005), p.103.

50. See *William Wordsworth*, edited by Stephen Gill (Oxford and New York: Oxford UP, 1984), pp.532-558. Hereafter Wordsworth in the text.

51. *A Poetics of Postmodernism: History Theory Fiction* (London: Routledge, 1988), p.39.

52. Wittgenstein, *Zettel*, edited by G.E.M. Anscombe and G.H. von Wright, trans. G.E.M. Anscombe (Oxford: Blackwell, 1975), p.1. Shapcott's poem can be interestingly compared with Veronica Forrest-Thomson's 'Phrase-Book' in *Language Games* (1971), itself strongly influenced by Wittgenstein's *Zettel*. See Veronica Forrest-Thomson, *Collected Poems and Translations*, edited by Anthony Barnett (Lewes, East Sussex: Allardyce, Barnett, 1990).

53. 'Confounding Geography' in *Elizabeth Bishop: Poet of the Periphery*, edited by Linda Anderson and Jo Shapcott (Tarset/Newcastle: Bloodaxe Books/ University of Newcastle, 2002), p.115.

CHAPTER SEVEN: **Objecting to the Subject: Science, Nature, Femininity and the Poetic Process** *(pp.00-00)*

1. E-mail to the author, October 2005.

2. *New Relations: The Refashioning of British Poetry 1980-1994* (Bridgend:

Seren, 1996), pp.169-70. Hereafter all references *New Relations* in the text.

3. Elizabeth Bishop, *Complete Poems* (London: Chatto, 1991). Hereafter *CP* in the text.

4. *Women Writers and Poetic Identity: Dorothy Wordsworth, Emily Brontë and Emily Dickinson* (Guildford and Princeton: Princeton UP, 1980), pp.16-17.

5. *Elizabeth Bishop: Poet of the Periphery*, edited by Linda Anderson and Jo Shapcott (Tarset/Newcastle: Bloodaxe Books/University of Newcastle, 2002). All references hereafter *Poet of the Periphery* in the text.

6. *Stein, Bishop and Rich: Lyrics of Love, War, Place* (Chapel Hill and London: University of North Carolina Press, 1997), p.127.

7. *Elizabeth Bishop: Questions of Mastery* (Cambridge, Mass., and London, England: Harvard UP, 1991), p.215.

8. 'Tradition and the Individual Talent', in *Selected Prose of T.S. Eliot*, edited with an introduction by Frank Kermode (London: Faber, 1975), pp.37-44. Hereafter *Selected Prose* in the text.

9. *Made in America: Science, Technology and American Modernist Poets* (New Haven and London: Yale UP, 1987).

10. *The Gender of Modernism: A Critical Anthology*, edited by Bonnie Kine Scott (Bloomington: Indiana UP, 1990), p.331. Brownstein shows how

Subversion of binarisms...typically takes three forms. First, Moore takes conventionally negative words in contexts that make them positive... second, "masculine" and "feminine" words...lose their gender distinct and biased functions without losing meaning; "strong" women write "erect" poems, "violent" ones... Third, Moore employs paired oppositions, wittily exposing individual meanings based on difference ('controlled ador', 'clean violence') and operating anterior to their oppositional judgement-weighted relations. As a consequence meaning is made more precise - and closer to Moore's goal of "depersonalised" usage.

11. Cited by Anne Stevenson, *Elizabeth Bishop* (New York: Twayne, 1966), p.66.

12. In *Elizabeth Bishop: Questions of Mastery*, Bonnie Costello argues that the poem is based specifically on the frottage 'False Positions', but I would see the poem as more generally inspired by the sequence. The poem does not need a single (or monumental) original: the poem becomes it itself.

13. See 'Surrealist Situation of the Object', *Manifestoes of Surrealism*, trans. Richard Seaver and Helen R. Lane (London and New York, Ann Arbor, 1972), pp.255-78 (p.260). Here André Breton, outlining Surrealism's debt to Hegel, defines surrealism in both poetry and the plastic arts as being a process which '[l]iberated from the need to reproduce forms essentially taken from the outer world' depends on 'inner representation'. Surrealism:

confronts this inner representation with that of the concrete forms of the real world, seeks in turn...to seize the object in its generality, and as soon as it has succeeded in so doing, tries to take that supreme step par excellence: excluding (relatively) the external object as such and considering nature only in its relationship with the inner world of consciousness.

14. See Max Ernst, *Frottages*, translated by Joseph M. Bernstein (London: Thames and Hudson, 1986).

15. *Electroplating the Baby* (Newcastle: Bloodaxe Books, 1988), reprinted in *Her Book* (London: Faber, 2000). Hereafter all references to Shapcott's poems as *Her Book*, unless otherwise indicated.

16. Jo Shapcott: e-mail to the author, October 2005.

17. See interview with Janet Phillips, *Poetry Review*, 91 no.1 (Spring 2001). See http://www.poetrysociety.org.uk/review/pr91-1/shapcot1.htm

18. 'Sexual Difference' in *An Ethics of Sexual Difference*, trans. Carolyn Burke and Gillian C. Gill (London: The Athlone Press 1993), p.16. Hereafter *Sexual Difference* in the text.

19. Cited by Gail Schwab, 'Mother's Body, Father's Tongue', in *Irigaray: Feminist Philosophy and Modern European Thought*, edited by Carolyn Burke, Naomi Schor and Margaret Whitford (New York: Columbia UP, 1994), p.367.

20. *Tender Taxes* (London: Faber, 2001). Hereafter *Tender Taxes* in the text.

21. See *The Complete French Poems of Rainer Maria Rilke*, trans. A. Poulin Jr (St Paul: Graywolf Press, 1986).

22. Luce Irigaray, 'The Power of Discourse and Its Subordination', in *This Sex Which Is Not One*, trans. Catherine Porter with Carolyn Burke (Ithaca, New York: Cornell UP, 1985), p.76.

23. http://www.blinking-eye.co.uk/writer/shapcott.html: accessed 9 September 2005.

24. 'Unstable Regions: Poetry and Science' in *Cultural Babbage: Technology, Time and Invention*, edited by Francis Spufford and Jenny Uglow (London: Faber, 1996), p.220.

25. *Night Photograph* (London: Faber, 1993). Hereafter *NP* in the text.

26. Interview with Raymond Friel, London, 1994, in *Talking Verse: Interviews with Poets* (St Andrews and Williamsburg: Verse, 1995), pp.78-81 (p.79). Hereafter *Talking Verse* in the text.

27. *After the Death of Poetry: Poet and Audience in Contemporary America* (Durham and London: Duke UP, 1993), p.44.

28. *The Galileo Affair: A Documentary* (London: University of California Press, 1989), p.6.

29. *A World Where News Travelled Slowly* (London: Faber, 1997). Hereafter *AWWNTS* in the text.

30. *Minsk* (London: Faber, 2003). Hereafter *Minsk* in the text.

31. See Ted Hughes, *Wodwo* (London: Faber, 1967); *Collected Poems*, edited by Paul Keegan (London: Faber, 2003), p.183.

32. 'Oriental Mythology in *Wodwo*' in *The Achievement of Ted Hughes*, edited by Keith Sagar (Manchester: Manchester UP, 1983), p.146.

33. BBC *Get Writing* website: www.bbc.co.uk/dna/getwriting/module18p

34. 'Mysterious Nature' in *The Guardian*, 24 September 2005.

35. *Nature and Other Writings*, edited by Peter Turner (Boston and London: Shambala, 2003), pp.168-69.

36. *Gender Trouble*, p.135. Hereafter *Gender Trouble* in the text.

37. See '*Earth has not any thing to shew more fair: A Bicentennial Celebration of Wordsworth's Sonnet 'Composed upon Westminster Bridge, 3 Sept. 1802*', edited by Peter Oswald and Alice Oswald and Robert Woof (Shakespeare's Globe & The Wordsworth Trust, 2002).

Modern Women Poets
CHRONOLOGY

This listing covers poetry titles published by all the poets included in *Modern Women Poets*, the companion anthology to *Consorting with Angels*. Titles marked § are first collections. Dates denote year of first publication (often earlier in the US than in Britain in the case of American writers).

1909
Gertrude Stein: *Three Lives* § (London: Owen; New York: Grafton Press)

1910
Frances Cornford: *Poems* § (Hampstead, London: Priory Press; Cambridge: Bowes & Bowes)

1911
Anna Wickham: *Songs of John Oland* § [as John Oland] (London: privately printed)

1912
Elizabeth Daryush: *Charitessi 1911* § (Cambridge: Bowes & Bowes)

1914
Gertrude Stein: *Tender Buttons: Objects, Food, Rooms* (New York: Claire Marie)

1915
Frances Cornford: *Spring Morning* (London: Poetry Bookshop)
Edith Sitwell: *The Mother and Other Poems* § (printed for the author, Oxford: Blackwell)
Anna Wickham: *The Contemplative Quarry* (London: Poetry Bookshop)

1916
Elizabeth Daryush: *Verses* (Oxford: Blackwell)
Hilda Doolittle: *Sea Garden* § (London: Constable)
Charlotte Mew: *The Farmer's Bride* § (London: Poetry Bookshop)
Anna Wickham: *The Man with a Hammer* (London: Grant Richards)
Edith Sitwell: *Twentieth Century Harlequinade*, with Osbert Sitwell (Oxford: Blackwell)

1918
Edith Sitwell: *Clown's Houses* (Oxford: Blackwell)

1920
Ruth Pitter: *First Poems* § (London: Cecil Palmer)
Edith Sitwell: *The Wooden Pegasus* (Oxford: Blackwell)

1921
Elizabeth Daryush: *Sonnets from Hafez and Other Verses* (London: H. Milford)
Hilda Doolittle: *Hymen* (London: Egoist Press; New York: Henry Holt)
Charlotte Mew: *The Farmer's Bride*, reprint with 11 additional poems (London: Poetry Bookshop; New York: Macmillan, Saturday Market)

Marianne Moore: *Poems* § (London: Egoist Press)
Anna Wickham: *The Little Old House* (London: Poetry Bookshop)

1922
Edith Sitwell: *Façade* (Kensington, London: Favil Press)

1923
Frances Cornford: *Autumn Midnight* (London: Poetry Bookshop)
Mina Loy: *Lunar Baedecker* § (Paris: Contact Publishing)
Edith Sitwell: *Bucolic Comedies* (London: Duckworth)

1924
Hilda Doolittle: *Heliodora and Other Poems* (London: Jonathan Cape; Boston: Houghton Mifflin)
Marianne Moore: *Observations* (New York: Dial Press)
Edith Sitwell: *The Sleeping Beauty* (London: Duckworth; New York: Knopf)

1925
Hilda Doolittle: *Collected Poems of H.D.* (New York: Boni & Liveright)
Edith Sitwell: *Troy Park* (London: Duckworth)
Edith Sitwell: *Poor Young People*, with Osbert Sitwell (London: Fleuron)
Sylvia Townsend Warner: *The Espalier* § (London: Chatto & Windus)

1926
Laura (Riding) Gottschalk Jackson: *The Close Chaplet* (London: Leonard & Virginia Woolf at the Hogarth Press; New York: Adelphi)
Naomi Mitchison: *The Laburnum Branch* § (London: Jonathan Cape)

1927
Laura (Riding) Jackson: *Voltaire: A Biographical Fantasy* (London: Leonard & Virginia Woolf at the Hogarth Press)
Ruth Pitter: *First and Second Poems 1912-1925* (London: Sheed & Ward)
Edith Sitwell: *Rustic Elegies* (London: Duckworth; New York: Knopf)

1928
Frances Cornford: *Different Days* (London: Leonard & Virginia Woolf at The Hogarth Press)
Laura (Riding) Jackson: *Love as Love, Death as Death* (London: Seizin Press)
Edith Sitwell: *Popular Song* (London: Faber & Gwyer)
Edith Sitwell: *Five Poems* (London: Duckworth)
Sylvia Townsend Warner: *Time Importuned* (London: Chatto & Windus)

1929
Charlotte Mew: *The Rambling Sailor* (London: Poetry Bookshop)
Edith Sitwell: *Gold Coast Customs* (London: Duckworth)

1930
Elizabeth Daryush: *Verses* (London: Oxford UP)
Laura (Riding) Jackson: *Poems: A Joking Word* (London: Jonathan Cape)
Laura (Riding) Jackson: *Twenty Poems Less* (Paris: Hours Press)
Laura (Riding) Jackson: *Though Gently* (Deyá, Majorca: Seizin Press)
Una Marson: *Tropics Reveries* § (Kingston, Jamaica: Gleaner, the author)
Edith Sitwell: *Collected Poems* (London: Duckworth)

1931

Hilda Doolittle: *Red Roses for Bronze* (London: Chatto & Windus; New York: Random House, 1929)

Laura (Riding) Jackson: *Laura and Francisca* (Deyá, Majorca: Seizin Press)

Una Marson: *Heights and Depths* (Kingston, Jamaica: the author)

Ruth Pitter: *Persephone in Hades* (Auch, Gers, France: Sauriac) [privately printed]

Sylvia Townsend Warner: *Opus 7* (London: Chatto & Windus)

1932

Frances Cornford: *Before and After Socrates* (Cambridge: Cambridge UP)

Elizabeth Daryush: *Verses: Second Book* (London: Oxford UP)

Sylvia Townsend Warner: *Rainbow* (New York: Knopf)

1933

Elizabeth Daryush: Verses: *Third Book* (London: Oxford UP)

Laura (Riding) Jackson: *The Life of the Dead* (London: Arthur Barker)

Laura (Riding) Jackson: *Poet: A Lying Word* (London: Arthur Barker)

Laura (Riding) Jackson: *The First Leaf* (Deyá, Majorca: Seizin Press)

Naomi Mitchison: *The Delicate Fire: Short Stories and Poems* (London: Jonathan Cape)

Edith Sitwell: *Five Variations on a Theme* (London: Duckworth)

Sylvia Townsend Warner: *Whether a Dove or a Seagull*, with Valentine Ackland (New York: Viking; London: Chatto & Windus, 1934)

1934

Frances Cornford: *Mountains and Molehills* (Cambridge: Cambridge UP)

Elizabeth Daryush: *Verses: Fourth Book* (London: Oxford UP)

Laura (Riding) Jackson: *Americans* (Los Angeles: Primavera)

Ruth Pitter: *A Mad Lady's Garland* (London: Cresset Press; New York: Macmillan)

1935

Elizabeth Daryush: *Selected Poems* (London: Macmillan)

Laura (Riding) Jackson: *The Second Leaf* (Deyá, Majorca: Seizin Press)

Marianne Moore: *Selected Poems* (New York: Macmillan; London: Faber & Faber)

1936

Elizabeth Daryush: *The Last Man and Other Verses* (London: Oxford UP)

Marianne Moore: *The Pangolin and Other Verse* (London: Brendin)

Ruth Pitter: *A Trophy of Arms: Poems 1926-1935* (London: Cresset Press; New York: Macmillan)

Edith Sitwell: *Selected Poems* (London: Duckworth)

Anna Wickham: *Anna Wickham* (Richard Shilling Selections) (London: Richards Press)

1937

Elizabeth Daryush: *Verses: Sixth Book* (Oxford: the author)

Laura (Riding) Jackson: *Collected Poems* (New York: Random House; London: Cassell)

Una Marson: *The Moth and the Star* (Kingston, Jamaica: the author)

Stevie Smith: *A Good Time Was Had by All* § (London: Jonathan Cape)

1938
Stevie Smith: *Tender Only to One* (London: Jonathan Cape)
Sheila Wingfield: *Poems* § (London: Cresset Press)

1939
Naomi Mitchison: *The Alban Goes Out* (Harrow: Raven Press)
Ruth Pitter: *The Spirit Watches* (London: Cresset Press; New York: Macmillan)
Anne Ridler: *Poems* § (London: Oxford UP)

1940
Edith Sitwell: *Poems New and Old* (London: Faber & Faber)

1941
Marianne Moore: *What Are Years* (New York: Macmillan)
Ruth Pitter: *The Rude Potato* (London: Cresset Press)
Anne Ridler: *A Dream Observed* (London: Editions Poetry London)

1942
Edith Sitwell: *Street Songs* (London: Macmillan)
Stevie Smith: *Mother, What is Man?* (London: Jonathan Cape)

1943
Frances Cornford: *Poems from the Russian* (London: Faber & Faber)
Kathleen Raine: *Stone and Flower: Poems 1935–43* § (London: Nicholson & Watson)
Anne Ridler: *The Nine Bright Shiners* (London: Faber & Faber)

1944
Marianne Moore: *Nevertheless* (New York: Macmillan)
Lynette Roberts: *Poems* § (London: Faber & Faber)
E.J. Scovell: *Shadows of Chrysanthemums* § (London: Routledge)
Edith Sitwell: *Green Song and Other Poems* (London: Macmillan)

1945
Gwendolyn Brooks: *A Street in Bronzeville* § (New York: Harper)
Una Marson: *Towards the Stars* (Bickley, Kent: University of London Press)
Ruth Pitter: *The Bridge: Poems 1939–1944* (London: Cresset Press; New York: Macmillan)
Kathleen Raine: *Ecce Homo* (London: Enitharmon)
Edith Sitwell: *The Song of the Cold* (London: Macmillan; New York: Vanguard Press)

1946
Frances Bellerby: *Plash Mill and Other Poems* § (London: Peter Davies)
Elizabeth Bishop: *North and South* § (Boston: Houghton Mifflin)
Hilda Doolittle: *Trilogy* (*The Walls Do Not Fall, Tribute to the Angel and The Flowering of the Rod*) (London: Oxford UP)
Denise Levertov: *The Double Image* § (London: Cresset Press)
Kathleen Raine: *Living in Time* (London: Editions Poetry London)
E.J. Scovell: *The Midsummer Meadow* (London: Routledge)
Gertrude Stein: *Selected Writing of Gertrude Stein* (New York: Random House)
Sheila Wingfield: *Beat Drum, Beat Heart* (London: Cresset Press)

1947

Ruth Pitter: *On Cats* (London: Cresset Press)

Edith Sitwell: *The Shadow of Cain* (London: John Lehmann)

1948

Frances Cornford: *Travelling Home and Other Poems* (London: Cresset Press)

Elizabeth Daryush: *Selected Poems* (New York: Swallow Press)

1949

Frances Bellerby: *The Brightening Cloud* (London: Peter Davies)

Gwendolyn Brooks: *Annie Allen* (New York: Harper)

Kathleen Raine: *The Pythoness and Other Poems* (London: Hamish Hamilton; New York: Farrar, Straus, 1952)

Edith Sitwell: *The Canticle of the Rose: Selected Poems 1920-1947* (London: Macmillan)

Sheila Wingfield: *A Cloud Across the Sun* (London: Cresset Press)

1950

Ruth Pitter: *Urania* (London: Cresset Press)

Edith Sitwell: *Façade and Other Poems 1920-1935* (London: Duckworth)

Stevie Smith: *Harold's Leap* (London: Chapman & Hall)

1951

Marianne Moore: *Collected Poems* (New York: Macmillan)

Adrienne Rich: *A Change of World* § (New Haven: Yale UP; London: Oxford UP)

Anne Ridler: *The Golden Bird and Other Poems* (London: Faber & Faber)

Lynette Roberts: *Gods with Stainless Ears: A Heroic Poem* (London: Faber & Faber)

1952

Kathleen Raine: *The Year One and Other Poems* (London: Hamish Hamilton; New York: Farrar, Straus, 1953)

Edith Sitwell: *Selected Poems* (Harmondsworth: Penguin)

Muriel Spark: *The Fanfarlo and Other Verse* § (Aldington, Ashford, Kent: Hand and Flower Press)

1953

Elizabeth Jennings: *Poems* § (Swinford, Eynsham, Oxford: Fantasy Press)

Mairi MacInnes: *Splinters: Twenty-Six Poems* § (Reading: University of Reading Press)

Charlotte Mew: *Collected Poems* (London: Duckworth)

Ruth Pitter: *The Ermine: Poems 1942-1952* (London: Cresset Press)

Edith Sitwell: *Gardens and Astronomers: New Poems* (London: Macmillan)

Gertrude Stein: *Bee Time Vine and Other Pieces 1913-1927* (New Haven, Connecticut: Yale UP; London: Oxford UP)

1954

Frances Cornford: *Collected Poems* (London: Cresset Press)

Edith Sitwell: *Collected Poems* (London: Macmillan; New York: Vanguard Press, 1957)

Sheila Wingfield: *A Kite's Dinner: Poems 1938-1954* (London: Cresset Press)

1955

Elizabeth Bishop: *A Cold Spring* (Boston: Houghton Mifflin)

Elizabeth Jennings: *A Way of Looking* (London: André Deutsch)

Adrienne Rich: *The Diamond Cutters and Other Poems* (New York: Harper)

1956

Elizabeth Bishop: *Poems* (London: Chatto & Windus)

Marianne Moore: *Like a Bulwark* (New York: Viking; London: Faber & Faber)

Kathleen Raine: *Collected Poems* (London: Hamish Hamilton)

E.J. Scovell: *The River Steamer* (London: Cresset Press)

Gertrude Stein: *Stanzas in Meditation and Other Poems 1929-1933* (New Haven: Yale UP)

1957

Frances Bellerby: *The Stone Angel and the Stone Man* (Plymouth: Ted Williams)

Denise Levertov: *Here and Now* (San Francisco: City Lights Pocket Bookshop)

Stevie Smith: *Not Waving but Drowning* (London: André Deutsch)

1958

Elizabeth Jennings: *A Sense of the World* (London: André Deutsch)

Mina Loy: *Lunar Baedeker and Time-tables* (Highlands, NC: Jonathan Williams)

1959

Patricia Beer: *The Loss of the Magyar and Other Poems* § (London: Longmans)

Marianne Moore: *O to be a Dragon* (New York: Viking Press)

Anne Ridler: *A Matter of Life and Death* (London: Faber & Faber)

1960

Gwendolyn Brooks: *The Bean Eaters* (New York: Harper)

Frances Cornford: *On a Calm Shore* (Cambridge: Saint Nicholas Press for Cresset Press)

Jenny Joseph: *The Unlooked-for Season* § (Northwood: Scorpion Press)

Denise Levertov: *With Eyes at the Back of our Heads* (New York: New Directions)

Sylvia Plath: *The Colossus* § (London: Heinemann; New York: Random House, 1962)

Anne Sexton: *To Bedlam and Part Way Back* § (Boston: Houghton Mifflin; Cambridge, Massachusetts: Riverside Press)

Sylvia Townsend Warner: *Boxwood* (London: Chatto & Windus)

1961

Hilda Doolittle: *Helen in Egypt* (New York: Grove Press)

Elizabeth Jennings: *The Sonnets of Michelangelo* [translation] (London: Folio Society)

Elizabeth Jennings: *Song for a Birth or a Death and Other Poems* (London: André Deutsch)

Denise Levertov: *The Jacob's Ladder* (New York: New Directions)

Anne Ridler: *Selected Poems* (New York: Macmillan)

1962

Eavan Boland: *23 Poems* § (Dublin: Gallagher Press)
Anne Sexton: *All My Pretty Ones* (Boston: Houghton Mifflin)
Edith Sitwell: *The Outcasts* (London: Macmillan)
Stevie Smith: *Selected Poems* [including eleven new poems] (London: Longmans)

1963

Patricia Beer: *The Survivors* (London: Longmans)
Gwendolyn Brooks: *Selected Poems* (New York: Harper & Row)
Adrienne Rich: *Snapshots of a Daughter-in-law: Poems 1954-1962* (New York: Harper & Row; revised edition, New York: Norton, 1967; London: Chatto & Windus, 1970)
Anne Ridler: *Who is My Neighbour?; and How Bitter the Bread* (London: Faber & Faber)
Rosemary Tonks: *Notes on Cafés and Bedrooms* § (London: Putnam)

1964

Fleur Adcock: *The Eye of the Hurricane* § (Wellington, NZ: Reed)
Elizabeth Jennings: *Recoveries* (London: André Deutsch)
Marianne Moore: *The Arctic Ox* (London: Faber & Faber)
Denise Levertov: *O Taste and See* (New York: New Directions)
Sheila Wingfield: *The Leaves Darken* (London: Weidenfeld & Nicolson)

1965

Elizabeth Bishop: *Questions of Travel* (New York: Farrar, Straus & Giroux)
Sylvia Plath: *Ariel* (London: Faber & Faber; New York: Harper & Row)
Kathleen Raine: *The Hollow Hill and Other Poems 1960-1964* (London: Hamish Hamilton)
Edith Sitwell: *Selected Poems* (London: Macmillan)
Anne Stevenson: *Living in America* § (Ann Arbor: Generation)

1966

Gwendolyn Brooks: *We Real Cool* (Detroit: Broadside Press)
Ruth Fainlight: *Cages* § (London: Macmillan; New York: St Martin's Press)
Elaine Feinstein: *In a Green Eye* § (London: Goliard Press)
Elizabeth Jennings: *The Mind Has Mountains* (London: Macmillan)
Marianne Moore: *Tell Me, Tell Me: Granite, Steel, and Other Topics* (New York: Viking)
Ruth Pitter: *Still by Choice* (London: Cresset Press)
Adrienne Rich: *Necessities of Life: Poems 1962-1965* (New York: Norton)
Anne Sexton: *Live or Die* (London: Oxford UP; Boston: Houghton Mifflin)
Stevie Smith: *The Frog Prince and Other Poems* (London: Longmans)

1967

Fleur Adcock: *Tigers* (London: Oxford UP)
Patricia Beer: *Just like the Resurrection* (London: Macmillan)
Eavan Boland: *New Territory* (Dublin: Allen Figgis)
Gwendolyn Brooks: *The Wall* (Detroit: Broadside Press)
Veronica Forrest-Thomson: *Identi-Kit* § (London: Outposts)
Frances Horovitz: *Poems* § (Aylesford: St Albert's Press)
Elizabeth Jennings: *Collected Poems* (London: Macmillan)

Denise Levertov: *The Sorrow Dance* (New York: New Directions; London:
   Jonathan Cape, 1968)
Marianne Moore: *The Complete Poems of Marianne Moore* (New York:
   Macmillan/Viking; revised edition 1981)
Adrienne Rich: *Selected Poems* (London: Chatto & Windus / Hogarth Press)
Muriel Spark: *Collected Poems 1* (London: Macmillan)
Rosemary Tonks: *Iliad of Broken Sentences* (London: Bodley Head)

1968
Gwendolyn Brooks: *In the Mecca* (New York: Harper & Row)
Ruth Fainlight: *To See the Matter Clearly and Other Poems* (London:
   Macmillan)
Louise Glück: *Firstborn* § (New York: New American Library; Northwood,
   Middlesex: Anvil Press, 1969)
Audre Lorde: *The First Cities* § (New York: Poets Press)
Ruth Pitter: *Poems 1926-1966* (London: Barrie & Rockcliff)
Kathleen Raine: *Ninfa Revisited* (London: Enitharmon)
Kathleen Raine: *Six Dreams and Other Poems* (London: Enitharmon)
Sylvia Townsend Warner: *King Duffus and Other Poems* (London & Wells:
   Clare)

1969
Elizabeth Bishop: *The Complete Poems* (New York: Farrar, Straus & Giroux;
   London: Chatto & Windus)
Gwendolyn Brooks: *Riot* (Detroit: Broadside Press)
Elizabeth Jennings: *The Animals' Arrival* (London: Macmillan)
Ruth Pitter: *Collected Poems* (London & New York: Macmillan)
Adrienne Rich: *Leaflets: Poems 1965-1968* (New York: Norton; London:
   Chatto & Windus / Hogarth Press, 1972)
Anne Sexton: *Love Poems* (London: Oxford UP; Boston: Houghton Mifflin)
Anne Stevenson: *Reversals* (Middletown, CT: Wesleyan UP)

1970
Frances Bellerby: *The Stuttering Water* (Gillingham, Kent: Arc)
Frances Bellerby: *Selected Poems* (London: Enitharmon)
Gwendolyn Brooks: *Family Pictures* (Detroit: Broadside Press)
Veronica Forrest-Thomson: *Twelve Academic Questions* (Cambridge: the
   author)
Laura (Riding) Jackson: *Selected Poems: In Five Sets* (London: Faber &
   Faber)
Elizabeth Jennings: *Lucidities* (London: Macmillan)
Denise Levertov: *Relearning the Alphabet* (New York: New Directions;
   London: Jonathan Cape)
Audre Lorde: *Cables to Rage* (London: Paul Breman)

1971
Fleur Adcock: *High Tide in the Garden* (London: Oxford UP)
Patricia Beer: *The Estuary* (London: Macmillan)
Gwendolyn Brooks: *Aloneness* (Detroit: Broadside Press)
Gwendolyn Brooks: *Black Steel: Joe Frazier and Muhammed Ali* (Detroit:
   Broadside Press)

Gwendolyn Brooks: *The World of Gwendolyn Brooks* (New York: Harper & Row)

Gillian Clarke: *Snow on the Mountain* § (Llandybie: Christopher Davies)

Elizabeth Daryush: *Verses: Seventh Book* (Oxford: Carcanet)

Elaine Feinstein: *The Magic Apple Tree* (London: Hutchinson)

Veronica Forrest-Thomson: *Language-Games* (Leeds: School of English Press, University of Leeds)

Denise Levertov: *To Stay Alive* (New York: New Directions)

Sylvia Plath: *Winter Trees* (London: Faber & Faber; New York: Harper & Row, 1972)

Sylvia Plath: *Crossing the Water* (London: Faber & Faber; New York: Harper & Row)

Sylvia Plath: *Crystal Gazer and Other Poems* (London: Rainbow Press)

Sylvia Plath: *Fiesta Melons* (Exeter: Rougemont Press)

Sylvia Plath: *Lyonesse: Poems* (London: Rainbow Press)

Kathleen Raine: *The Lost Country* (Dublin: Dolmen Press; London: Hamish Hamilton)

Adrienne Rich: *The Will to Change: Poems 1968-1970* (New York: Norton; London: Chatto & Windus, 1972)

Anne Sexton: *Transformations* (Boston: Houghton Mifflin; London: Oxford UP, 1972)

Stevie Smith: *Two in One* [*Selected Poems* and *The Frog Prince and Other Poems*] (London: Longmans)

Anna Wickham: *Selected Poems* (London: Chatto & Windus)

1972

Gwendolyn Brooks: *Aurora* (Detroit: Broadside Press)

Elizabeth Daryush: *Selected Poems: Verses I-VI* (Oxford: Carcanet)

Hilda Doolittle: *Hermetic Definition* (Oxford: Carcanet; New York: New Directions; West Newbury, Massachusetts: Frontier Press, privately printed, 1971)

Elizabeth Jennings: *Relationships* (London: Macmillan)

Denise Levertov: *Footprints* (New York: New Directions)

Liz Lochhead: *Memo for Spring* § (Edinburgh: Reprographia)

Eiléan Ní Chuilleanáin: Acts and Monuments § (Dublin: Gallery Press)

Anne Ridler: *Some Time After and Other Poems* (London: Faber & Faber)

Anne Sexton: *The Book of Folly* (Boston: Houghton Mifflin; London: Chatto & Windus, 1974)

Stevie Smith: *Scorpion and Other Poems* (London: Longman)

1973

Ruth Fainlight: *Twenty-one Poems* (London: Turret Books)

Ruth Fainlight: *The Region's Violence* (London: Hutchinson)

Elaine Feinstein: *The Celebrants and Other Poems* (London: Hutchinson)

Audre Lorde: *From a Land Where Other People Live* (Detroit: Broadside Press)

Kathleen Raine: *On a Deserted Shore* (Dublin: Dolmen Press; London: Hamish Hamilton)

Adrienne Rich: *Diving into the Wreck: Poems 1971-1972* (New York & London: Norton)

Carol Rumens: *A Strange Girl in Bright Colours* § (London: Quartet Books)

1974

Fleur Adcock: *The Scenic Route* (London: Oxford UP)

Veronica Forrest-Thomson: *Cordelia or 'A Poem Should Not Mean, But Be'* (Loughborough: the author)

Jenny Joseph: *Rose in the Afternoon and Other Poems* (London: Dent)

Audre Lorde: *New York Head Shop and Museum* (Detroit: Broadside Press)

Adrienne Rich: *Poems: Selected and New, 1950-1974* (New York & London: Norton)

Anne Sexton: *The Death Notebooks* (Boston: Houghton Mifflin; London: Chatto & Windus, 1975)

Anne Stevenson: *Correspondences: A Family History in Letters* (Middletown, CT: Wesleyan UP; London: Oxford UP)

Anne Stevenson: *Travelling Behind Glass: Selected Poems 1963-1973* (London & New York: Oxford UP)

1975

Patricia Beer: *Driving West* (London: Gollancz)

Frances Bellerby: *The First Known and Other Poems* (London: Enitharmon)

Eavan Boland: *The War Horse* (London: Gollancz; Dublin: Arlen House, 1980)

Gwendolyn Brooks: *Beckonings* (Detroit: Broadside Press)

Louise Glück: *The House on Marshland* (New York: Ecco Press; London: Anvil Press, 1976)

Elizabeth Jennings: *Growing Points* (Cheadle: Carcanet)

Denise Levertov: *The Freeing of the Dust* (New York: New Directions)

Eiléan Ní Chuilleanáin: *Site of Ambush* (Dublin: Gallery Press)

Ruth Pitter: *End of Drought* (London: Barrie & Jenkins)

Anne Sexton: *The Awful Rowing Toward God* (Boston: Houghton Mifflin; London: Chatto & Windus)

Stevie Smith: *Collected Poems* (London: Allen Lane)

1976

Elizabeth Bishop: *Geography III* (New York: Farrar, Straus & Giroux; London: Chatto & Windus, 1977)

Frances Cornford: *Fifteen Poems from the French* (Edinburgh: Tragara Press)

Elizabeth Daryush: *Collected Poems* (Manchester: Carcanet New Press)

Menna Elfyn: *Mwyara: Cerddi* § (Llandysul: Gomer Press)

Ruth Fainlight: *Another Full Moon* (London: Hutchinson)

Veronica Forrest-Thomson: *On the Periphery* (Cambridge: Street Editions)

Louise Glück: *The Garden* (New York: Antaeus)

Audre Lorde: *Coal* (New York: Norton)

Audre Lorde: *Between Our Selves* (Point Reyes, CA: Eidolon Editions)

Elma Mitchell: *The Poor Man in the Flesh* (Stockport: Peterloo Poets)

Anne Sexton: *45 Mercy Street* (Boston: Houghton Mifflin; London: Secker & Warburg)

Stevie Smith: *Selected Poems* (Harmondsworth: Penguin)

1977

Freda Downie: *A Stranger Here* § (London: Secker & Warburg)

Elaine Feinstein: *Some Unease and Angels* (London: Hutchinson; Michigan: Green River Press)

Elizabeth Jennings: *Consequently I Rejoice* (Manchester: Carcanet)
Eiléan Ní Chuilleanáin: *Cork* (Dublin: Gallery Press)
Eiléan Ní Chuilleanáin: *The Second Voyage* (Dublin: Gallery Press; Winston-Salem, NC: Wake Forest UP; revised edition 1986: Dublin: Gallery Press; Newcastle: Bloodaxe Books)
Kathleen Raine: *The Oval Portrait* (London: Enitharmon / Hamish Hamilton)
Adrienne Rich: *Twenty-One Love Poems* (Emeryville, CA: Effie's Press)
Denise Riley: *Marxism for Infants* § (Cambridge: Street Editions)
Denise Riley: *No Fee*, with Wendy Mulford (Cambridge: Street Editions)
Anne Stevenson: *Enough of Green* (Oxford: Oxford UP)
Sheila Wingfield: *Admissions: Poems 1974-1977* (Dublin: Dolmen Press; London: John Calder)
Sheila Wingfield: *Her Storms: Selected Poems 1938-1977* (Dublin: Dolmen Press; London: John Calder)

1978
Gillian Clarke: *The Sundial* (Llandysul: Gomer Press)
Menna Elfyn: *'Stafelloedd Aros* (Llandysul: Gomer Press)
U.A. Fanthorpe: *Side Effects* § (Liskeard: Peterloo Poets)
Jenny Joseph: *The Thinking Heart* (London: Secker & Warburg)
Denise Levertov: *Life in the Forest* (New York: New Directions)
Audre Lorde: *The Black Unicorn* (New York & London: Norton)
Naomi Mitchison: *The Cleansing of the Knife and Other Poems* (Edinburgh: Canongate)
Kathleen Raine: *Fifteen Short Poems* (London: privately printed at the Tragara Press for Enitharmon Press [for the author])
Adrienne Rich: *The Dream of a Common Language: Poems 1974-1977* (New York & London: Norton)
Carol Rumens: *A Necklace of Mirrors* (Belfast: Ulsterman Publications)
Anne Sexton: *Words for Dr Y* (Boston: Houghton Mifflin)
Stevie Smith: *Selected Poems* (Harmondsworth: Penguin)

1979
Fleur Adcock: *Below Loughrigg* (Newcastle: Bloodaxe Books)
Fleur Adcock: *The Inner Harbour* (Oxford: Oxford UP)
Patricia Beer: *Selected Poems* (London: Hutchinson)
Elizabeth Jennings: *Selected Poems* (Manchester: Carcanet)
Denise Levertov: *Collected Earlier Poems 1940-1960* (New York: New Directions)
Elma Mitchell: *The Human Cage* (Liskeard: Peterloo Poets)

1980
Eavan Boland: *In Her Own Image* (Dublin: Arlen House)
Ruth Fainlight: *Sibyls and Others* (London: Hutchinson)
Elaine Feinstein: *The Feast of Eurydice* (London: Next Editions/Faber & Faber)
Louise Glück: *Descending Figure* (New York: Ecco Press)
Jorie Graham: *Hybrids of Plants and of Ghosts* § (Princeton: Princeton UP)
Frances Horovitz: *Water Over Stone* (London: Enitharmon)
Laura (Riding) Jackson: *The Poems of Laura Riding*, a new edition of the 1938 *Collected Poems* (Manchester: Carcanet)

Elizabeth Jennings: *Moments of Grace* (Manchester: Carcanet New Press)

Sharon Olds: *Satan Says* § (Pittsburgh: University of Pittsburgh Press; London: Feffer & Simons)

Kathleen Raine: *The Oracle in the Heart and Other Poems 1975-78* (London: Allen & Unwin; Dublin: Dolmen Press)

Anne Ridler: *Dies Natalis: Poems of Birth and Infancy* (Oxford: Perpetua)

Penelope Shuttle: *The Orchard Upstairs* § (Oxford: Oxford UP)

Gertrude Stein: *The Yale Gertrude Stein: Selections* (New Haven & London: Yale UP)

Sylvia Townsend Warner: *Twelve Poems* (London: Chatto & Windus)

1981

Gillian Allnutt: *Spitting the Pips Out* (London: Sheba)

Eavan Boland: *Introducing Eavan Boland* (Princeton, NJ: Ontario Review Press)

Gwendolyn Brooks: *Black Love* (Chicago: Brooks Press)

Gwendolyn Brooks: *To Disembark* (Chicago: Third World Press)

Freda Downie: *Plainsong* (London: Secker & Warburg)

Vicki Feaver: *Close Relatives* § (London: Secker & Warburg)

Liz Lochhead: *The Grimm Sisters* (London: Next Editions/Faber & Faber)

Charlotte Mew: *Collected Poems and Prose* (Manchester: Carcanet in association with Virago)

Eiléan Ní Chuilleanáin: *The Rose-Geranium* (Dublin: Gallery Press)

Nuala Ní Dhomhnaill: *An Dealg Droighin* (Dublin: Cló Mercier)

Sylvia Plath: *Collected Poems* (London: Faber & Faber; New York: Harper & Row)

Kathleen Raine: *Collected Poems 1935-1980* (London: Allen & Unwin)

Adrienne Rich: *A Wild Patience Has Taken Me This Far: Poems 1978-1981* (New York & London: Norton)

Carol Rumens: *Unplayed Music* (London: Secker & Warburg)

Anne Sexton: *The Complete Poems* (Boston: Houghton Mifflin)

Stevie Smith: *Me Again: The Uncollected Writings of Stevie Smith* (London: Virago)

1982

Eavan Boland: *Night Feed* (Dublin: Arlen House; London: Marion Boyars; revised edition, Manchester: Carcanet, 1994)

Gillian Clarke: *Letter from a Far Country* (Manchester: Carcanet)

Menna Elfyn: *Tro'r Hual Arno* (Llandysul: Gomer Press)

U.A. Fanthorpe: *Standing To* (Liskeard: Peterloo Poets)

Kathleen Jamie: *Black Spiders* § (Edinburgh: Salamander Press)

Elizabeth Jennings: *Celebrations and Elegies* (Manchester: Carcanet)

Denise Levertov: *Candles in Babylon* (New York: New Directions)

Audre Lorde: *Chosen Poems, Old and New* (New York & London: Norton)

Medbh McGuckian: *The Flower Master* § (Oxford: Oxford UP); revised and enlarged edition, *The Flower Master and Other Poems* (Oldcastle, Co. Meath: Gallery Press, 1993)

Carol Rumens: *Scenes from the Gingerbread House* (Newcastle: Bloodaxe Books)

E.J. Scovell: *The Space Between* (London: Secker & Warburg)

Muriel Spark: *Going up to Sotheby's and Other Poems* (London: Granada)

Anne Stevenson: *Minute by Glass Minute* (Oxford: Oxford UP)
Sylvia Townsend Warner: *Collected Poems* (Manchester: Carcanet)

1983

Fleur Adcock: *Selected Poems* (Oxford: Oxford UP)
Fleur Adcock: *The Virgin & the Nightingale: medieval latin lyrics* (Newcastle: Bloodaxe Books)
Elizabeth Bartlett: *Strange Territory* (Liskeard: Peterloo Poets)
Patricia Beer: *The Lie of the Land* (London: Hutchinson)
Elizabeth Bishop: *The Complete Poems 1927-1979* (New York: Farrar, Straus & Giroux; London: Chatto & Windus, paperback edition 1991)
Amy Clampitt: *The Kingfisher* § (New York: Knopf; London: Faber & Faber, 1984)
Hilda Doolittle: *H.D.: Collected Poems 1912-1944* (New York: New Directions; Manchester: Carcanet, 1984)
Helen Dunmore: *The Apple Fall* § (Newcastle: Bloodaxe Books)
Ruth Fainlight: *Climates* (Newcastle: Bloodaxe Books)
Ruth Fainlight: *Fifteen to Infinity* (London: Hutchinson; Pittsburgh: Carnegie-Mellon UP, 1986)
Jorie Graham: *Erosion* (Princeton: Princeton UP)
Frances Horovitz: *Snow Light, Water Light* (Newcastle: Bloodaxe Books)
Jenny Joseph: *Beyond Descartes* (London: Secker & Warburg)
Denise Levertov: *Poems 1960-67* (New York: New Directions)
Elma Mitchell: *Furnished Rooms* (Liskeard: Peterloo Poets)
Grace Nichols: *i is a long memoried woman* § (London: Karnak House)
Adrienne Rich: *Sources* (Woodside, CA: Heyeck Press)
Carol Rumens: *Star Whisper* (London: Secker & Warburg)
Penelope Shuttle: *The Child-Stealer* (Oxford: Oxford UP)
Stevie Smith: *Stevie Smith: A Selection* (London: Faber & Faber)
Sheila Wingfield: *Collected Poems 1938-1983* (London: Enitharmon; New York: Hill & Wang)

1984

U.A. Fanthorpe: *Voices Off* (Liskeard: Peterloo Poets)
Selima Hill: *Saying Hello at the Station* § (London: Chatto & Windus)
Denise Levertov: *Oblique Prayers* (New York: New Directions; Newcastle: Bloodaxe Books, 1986)
Liz Lochhead: *Dreaming Frankenstein and Collected Poems* (Edinburgh: Polygon)
Medbh McGuckian: *Venus and the Rain* (Oxford: Oxford UP); revised edition, Oldcastle, Co. Meath: Gallery Press, 1994)
Paula Meehan: *Return and No Blame* § (Dublin: Beaver Row Press)
Grace Nichols: *The Fat Black Woman's Poems* (London: Virago)
Nuala Ní Dhomhnaill: *Féar Suaithinseach* (Maynooth, Co. Kildare: An Sagart)
Sharon Olds: *The Dead and the Living* (New York: Knopf)
Adrienne Rich: *The Fact of a Doorframe: Poems Selected and New 1950-1984* (New York & London: Norton)
Anna Wickham: *The Writings of Anna Wickham: Freewoman and Poet* (London: Virago)

1985

Amy Clampitt: *What the Light was Like* (New York: Knopf; London: Faber & Faber)

Gillian Clarke: *Selected Poems* (Manchester: Carcanet)

Carol Ann Duffy: *Standing Female Nude* § (London: Anvil Press)

Menna Elfyn: *Mynd Lawr I'r Nefoedd* (Llandysul: Gomer Press)

Louise Glück: *The Triumph of Achilles* (New York: Ecco Press)

Frances Horovitz: *Collected Poems* (Newcastle: Bloodaxe Books; London: Enitharmon)

Elizabeth Jennings: *Extending the Territory* (Manchester: Carcanet)

Liz Lochhead: *True Confessions and New Clichés* (Edinburgh: Polygon)

Mina Loy: *The Last Lunar Baedeker* (Highlands, North Carolina: Jargon Society; Manchester: Carcanet)

Sylvia Plath: *Selected Poems* (London: Faber & Faber)

Denise Riley: *Dry Air* (London: Virago)

Carol Rumens: *Direct Dialling* (London: Chatto & Windus)

Anne Stevenson: *The Fiction-Makers* (Oxford: Oxford UP)

Sylvia Townsend Warner: *Selected Poems* (Manchester: Carcanet)

1986

Fleur Adcock: *The Incident Book* (Oxford: Oxford UP)

Elizabeth Bartlett: *The Czar is Dead* (London: Rivelin Grapheme Press)

Frances Bellerby: *Selected Poems* (London: Enitharmon)

Eavan Boland: *The Journey and Other Poems* (Dublin: Arlen House; Manchester: Carcanet, 1987)

Gwendolyn Brooks: *The Near-Johannesburg Boy and Other Poems* (Chicago: David)

Wendy Cope: *Making Cocoa for Kingsley Amis* § (London: Faber & Faber)

Maura Dooley: *Ivy Leaves & Arrows* § (Newcastle: Bloodaxe Books)

Helen Dunmore: *The Sea Skater* (Newcastle: Bloodaxe Books)

U.A. Fanthorpe: *Selected Poems* (Liskeard: Peterloo Poets; Harmondsworth: Penguin)

Elaine Feinstein: *Badlands* (London: Hutchinson)

Rita Ann Higgins: *Goddess on the Mervue Bus* § (Galway: Salmon)

Laura (Riding) Jackson: *The Poems of Laura Riding*, new edition (Manchester: Carcanet)

Kathleen Jamie: *A Flame in Your Heart*, with Andrew Greig (Newcastle: Bloodaxe Books)

Elizabeth Jennings: *Collected Poems 1953-1985* (Manchester: Carcanet)

Jenny Joseph: *Persephone* (Newcastle: Bloodaxe Books)

Denise Levertov: *Selected Poems* (Newcastle: Bloodaxe Books, 1986)

Audre Lorde: *Our Dead Behind Us* (New York: Norton; London: Sheba)

Paula Meehan: *Reading the Sky* (Dublin: Beaver Row Press)

Eiléan Ní Chuilleanáin: *The Second Voyage*, revised edition (Dublin: Gallery Press; Newcastle: Bloodaxe Books)

Nuala Ní Dhomhnaill: *Selected Poems / Rogha dánta* (Dublin: Raven Arts Press)

Adrienne Rich: *Your Native Land, Your Life* (New York & London: Norton)

E.J. Scovell: *Listening to Collared Doves* (Hitchin: Mandeville Press)

Penelope Shuttle: *The Lion from Rio* (Oxford: Oxford UP)
Anne Stevenson: *Wintertime* (Ashington, Northumberland: MidNAG)

1987

Gillian Allnutt: *Beginning the Avocado* (London: Virago)
Gwendolyn Brooks: *Blacks* (Chicago: David)
Amy Clampitt: *Archaic Figure* (New York: Knopf; London: Faber & Faber, 1988)
Carol Ann Duffy: *Selling Manhattan* (London: Anvil Press)
Ruth Fainlight: *Selected Poems* (London: Hutchinson)
U.A. Fanthorpe: *A Watching Brief* (Calstock: Peterloo Poets)
Jorie Graham: *The End of Beauty* (New York: Ecco Press)
Kathleen Jamie: *The way we live* (Newcastle: Bloodaxe Books)
Denise Levertov: *Breathing the Water* (New York: New Directions; Newcastle: Bloodaxe Books, 1988)
Elma Mitchell: *People Etcetera: Poems New and Selected* (Calstock: Peterloo Poets)
Sharon Olds: *The Gold Cell* (New York: Knopf)
Sharon Olds: *The Matter of this World: New & Selected Poems* (Nottingham: Slow Dancer)
Ruth Pitter: *A Heaven to Find* (London: Enitharmon)
Kathleen Raine: *The Presence: Poems 1984-87* (Ipswich: Golgonooza Press; Rochester, Vermont: Inner Traditions)
Carol Rumens: *Selected Poems* (London: Chatto & Windus)
Carole Satyamurti: *Broken Moon* § (Oxford: Oxford UP)
Anne Stevenson: *Selected Poems 1956-1986* (Oxford: Oxford UP)

1988

Fleur Adcock: *Meeting the Comet* (Newcastle: Bloodaxe Books)
Patricia Beer: *Collected Poems* (Manchester: Carcanet)
Sujata Bhatt: *Brunizem* § (Manchester: Carcanet)
Jean 'Binta' Breeze: *Riddym Ravings and Other Poems* § (London: Race Today Publications)
Gwendolyn Brooks: *Winnie* (Chicago: David)
Imtiaz Dharker: *Purdah and other poems* § (Delhi, Oxford: Oxford UP; with *Postcards from god*, Newcastle: Bloodaxe Books, 1997)
Maura Dooley: *Turbulence* (Clapham via Lancaster: Giant Steps)
Helen Dunmore: *The Raw Garden* (Newcastle: Bloodaxe Books)
Rita Ann Higgins: *Witch in the Bushes* (Galway: Salmon)
Selima Hill: *My Darling Camel* (London: Chatto & Windus)
Medbh McGuckian: *On Ballycastle Beach* (Oxford: Oxford UP); revised edition, Oldcastle, Co. Meath: Gallery Press, 1995)
Mairi MacInnes: *The House on the Ridge Road* (Boston: Rowan Tree Press)
Kathleen Raine: *To the Sun* (Child Okeford, Dorset: Words Press)
Kathleen Raine: *Selected Poems* (Ipswich: Golgonooza Press)
Anne Ridler: *New and Selected Poems* (London: Faber & Faber)
Carol Rumens: *The Greening of the Snow Beach* (Newcastle: Bloodaxe Books)
E.J. Scovell: *Collected Poems* (Manchester: Carcanet)
Jo Shapcott: *Electroplating the Baby* § (Newcastle: Bloodaxe Books)
Penelope Shuttle: *Adventures with My Horse* (Oxford: Oxford UP)

1989

Eavan Boland: *Selected Poems* (Manchester: Carcanet)

Gillian Clarke: *Letting in the Rumour* (Manchester: Carcanet)

Selima Hill: *The Accumulation of Small Acts of Kindness* (London: Chatto & Windus)

Elizabeth Jennings: *Tributes* (Manchester: Carcanet)

Jenny Joseph: *The Inland Sea: A Selection from the Poems of Jenny Joseph* (Watsonville, CA: Papier-Mache Press)

Denise Levertov: *A Door in the Hive* (New York: New Directions; with *Evening Train*, Newcastle: Bloodaxe Books, 1992)

Eiléan Ní Chuilleanáin: *The Magdalene Sermon* (Oldcastle, Co. Meath: Gallery Press)

Grace Nichols: *Lazy Thoughts of a Lazy Woman* (London: Virago)

Adrienne Rich: *Time's Power: Poems 1985-1988* (New York & London: Norton)

Carol Rumens: *From Berlin to Heaven* (London: Chatto & Windus)

Pauline Stainer: *The Honeycomb* § (Newcastle: Bloodaxe Books)

1990

Meg Bateman: *Orain Ghaoil* (Dublin: Coiscéim)

Eavan Boland: *Outside History* (Manchester: Carcanet; New York: Norton)

Amy Clampitt: *Westward* (New York: Knopf; London: Faber & Faber, 1991)

Menna Elfyn: *Aderyn Bach Mewn Llaw: Cerddi 1976-90* (Llandysul: Gomer Press)

Ruth Fainlight: *The Knot* (London: Hutchinson)

Elaine Feinstein: *City Music* (London: Hutchinson)

Veronica Forrest-Thomson: *Collected Poems and Translations* (London: Allardyce, Barnett)

Louise Glück: *Ararat* (Hopewell, NJ: Ecco Press)

Gwyneth Lewis: *Cyhoeddodd Sonedau Redsa* § (Llandysul: Gomer Press)

Nuala Ní Dhomhnaill: *Pharaoh's Daughter* (Oldcastle, Co. Meath: Gallery Press)

Ruth Padel: *Summer Snow* § (London: Hutchinson)

Ruth Pitter: *Collected Poems* (Petersfield: Enitharmon)

Carole Satyamurti: *Changing the Subject* (Oxford: Oxford UP)

Anne Stevenson: *The Other House* (Oxford: Oxford UP)

Carol Ann Duffy: *The Other Country* (London: Anvil Press)

1991

Fleur Adcock: *Time-Zones* (Oxford: Oxford UP)

Elizabeth Bartlett: *Look No Face* (Bradford: Redbeck Press)

Sujata Bhatt: *Monkey Shadows* (Manchester: Carcanet)

Gwendolyn Brooks: *Children Coming Home* (Chicago: David)

Maura Dooley: *Explaining Magnetism* (Newcastle: Bloodaxe Books)

Helen Dunmore: *Short Days, Long Nights: New & Selected Poems* (Newcastle: Bloodaxe Books)

Elizabeth Garrett: *The Rule of Three* § (Newcastle: Bloodaxe Books)

Jorie Graham: *Region of Unlikeness* (Hopewell, NJ: Ecco Press)

Jackie Kay: *The Adoption Papers* § (Newcastle: Bloodaxe Books)

Mimi Khalvati: *In White Ink* § (Manchester: Carcanet)

Jenny Joseph: *Beached Boats* (London: Enitharmon)
Liz Lochhead: *Bagpipe Muzak* (London: Penguin)
Medbh McGuckian: *Marconi's Cottage* (Oldcastle, Co. Meath: Gallery Press; Newcastle: Bloodaxe Books, 1992)
Sarah Maguire: *Spilt Milk* § (London: Secker & Warburg)
Paula Meehan: *The Man Who was Marked by Winter* (Oldcastle, Co. Meath: Gallery Press)
Eiléan Ní Chuilleanáin: *The Magdalene Sermon and Earlier Poems* (Winston-Salem, NC: Wake Forest UP)
Nuala Ní Dhomhnaill: *Feis* (Maynooth. Co. Kildare: An Sagart)
Sharon Olds: *The Sign of Saturn: Poems 1980-1987* (New York: Knopf; London: Secker & Warburg)
Kathleen Raine: *Living with Mystery* (Ipswich: Golgonooza Press)
Adrienne Rich: *An Atlas of the Difficult World: Poems 1988-1991* (New York & London: Norton)
E.J. Scovell: *Selected Poems* (Manchester: Carcanet)
1992
Jean 'Binta' Breeze: *Spring Cleaning* (London: Virago)
Anne Carson: *Short Talks* § (London, Ontario: Brick)
Wendy Cope: *Serious Concerns* (London: Faber & Faber)
U.A. Fanthorpe: *Neck-Verse* (Calstock: Peterloo Poets)
Louise Glück: *The Wild Iris* (Hopewell, NJ: Ecco Press; Manchester: Carcanet)
Rita Ann Higgins: *Philomena's Revenge* (Galway: Salmon)
Laura (Riding) Jackson: *First Awakenings: The Early Poems* (Manchester: Carcanet)
Elizabeth Jennings: *Times and Seasons* (Manchester: Carcanet)
Denise Levertov: *Evening Train* (New York: New Directions; with *A Door in the Hive*, Newcastle: Bloodaxe Books, 1993)
Jenny Joseph: *Selected Poems* (Newcastle: Bloodaxe Books)
Audre Lorde: *Undersongs: Chosen Poems Old and New* (New York: Norton)
Nuala Ní Dhomhnaill: *The Astrakhan Cloak* (Oldcastle, Co. Meath: Gallery Press)
Sharon Olds: *The Father* (New York: Knopf; London: Secker & Warburg, 1993)
Denise Riley: *Stair Spirit* (Cambridge: Equipage)
Jo Shapcott: *Phrase Book* (Oxford: Oxford UP)
Penelope Shuttle: *Taxing the Rain* (Oxford: Oxford UP)
Pauline Stainer: *Sighting the Slave Ship* (Newcastle: Bloodaxe Books)
Susan Wicks: *Singing Underwater* § (London: Faber & Faber)
Eva Salzman: *The English Earthquake* § (Newcastle: Bloodaxe Books)
1993
Moniza Alvi: *The Country at My Shoulder* § (Oxford: Oxford UP)
Patricia Beer: *Friend of Heraclitus* (Manchester: Carcanet)
Gillian Clarke: *The King of Britain's Daughter* (Manchester: Carcanet)
Carol Ann Duffy: *Mean Time* (London: Anvil Press)
Menna Elfyn: *Dal Cler* (Cardiff: Hughes a'i Fab)
Menna Elfyn: *Madfall ar y Mur* (Llandysul: Gomer Press)

Jorie Graham: Materialism: *Poems* (Hopewell, NJ: Ecco Press)
Lavinia Greenlaw: *Night Photograph* § (London: Faber & Faber)
Selima Hill: *A Little Book of Meat* (Newcastle: Bloodaxe Books)
Kathleen Jamie: *The Autonomous Region: poems & photographs from Tibet*,
    with Sean Mayne Smith (Newcastle: Bloodaxe Books)
Jackie Kay: *Other Lovers* (Newcastle: Bloodaxe Books)
Denise Levertov: *A Door in the Hive* with *Evening Train* (Newcastle:
    Bloodaxe Books)
Audre Lorde: *The Marvelous Arithmetics of Distance: Poems 1987-1992* (New
    York: Norton)
Mairi MacInnes: *Elsewhere & Back: New & Selected Poems* (Newcastle:
    Bloodaxe Books)
Ruth Padel: *Angel* (Newcastle: Bloodaxe Books)
Adrienne Rich: *Collected Early Poems: 1950-1970* (New York & London:
    Norton)
Denise Riley: *Mop Mop Georgette: New and Selected Poems 1986-1993*
    (Cambridge & London: Reality Street Editions)
Carol Rumens: *Thinking of Skins: New & Selected Poems* (Newcastle:
    Bloodaxe Books)
Edith Sitwell: *Collected Poems* (London: Sinclair-Stevenson)
Gertrude Stein: *A Stein Reader* (Illinois: Northwestern UP)
Anne Stevenson: *Four and a Half Dancing Men* (Oxford: Oxford UP)
1994
Gillian Allnutt: *Blackthorn* (Newcastle: Bloodaxe Books)
Eavan Boland: *In a Time of Violence* (Manchester: Carcanet; New York:
    Norton)
Amy Clampitt: *A Silence Opens* (New York: Knopf)
Imtiaz Dharker: *Postcards from god* (New Delhi: Viking/Penguin Books India;
    with *Purdah*, Newcastle: Bloodaxe Books, 1997)
Carol Ann Duffy: *Selected Poems* (London: Penguin in association with Anvil
    Press)
Helen Dunmore: *Recovering a Body* (Newcastle: Bloodaxe Books)
Ruth Fainlight: *This Time of Year* (London: Sinclair-Stevenson)
Vicki Feaver: *The Handless Maiden* (London: Jonathan Cape)
Elaine Feinstein: *Selected Poems* (Manchester: Carcanet)
Vona Groarke: *Shale* § (Oldcastle, Co. Meath: Gallery Press)
Selima Hill: *Trembling Hearts in the Bodies of Dogs: New & Selected Poems*
    (Newcastle: Bloodaxe Books)
Laura (Riding) Jackson: *A Selection of the Poems of Laura Riding*
    (Manchester: Carcanet)
Kathleen Jamie: *The Queen of Sheba* (Newcastle: Bloodaxe Books)
Elizabeth Jennings: *Familiar Spirits* (Manchester: Carcanet)
Jenny Joseph: *Extended Similes* (Newcastle: Bloodaxe Books)
Medbh McGuckian: *Captain Lavender* (Oldcastle, Co. Meath: Gallery Press)
Paula Meehan: *Pillow Talk* (Oldcastle, Co. Meath: Gallery Press)
Eiléan Ní Chuilleanáin: *The Brazen Serpent* (Oldcastle, Co. Meath: Gallery
    Press; Winston-Salem, NC: Wake Forest UP, 1995)
Anne Ridler: *Collected Poems* (Manchester: Carcanet)

Carole Satyamurti: *Striking Distance* (Oxford: Oxford UP)
Penelope Shuttle: *Taxing the Rain* (Oxford: Oxford UP)
Pauline Stainer: *The Ice-Pilot Speaks* (Newcastle: Bloodaxe Books)
Susan Wicks: *Open Diagnosis* (London: Faber & Faber)

1995

Elizabeth Bartlett: *Two Women Dancing: New & Selected Poems* (Newcastle: Bloodaxe Books)
Sujata Bhatt: *The Stinking Rose* (Manchester: Carcanet)
Eavan Boland: *Collected Poems* (Manchester: Carcanet)
Anne Carson: *Glass, Irony and God* (New York: New Directions)
Anne Carson: *Plainwater: Essays and Poetry* (New York: Knopf)
Kate Clanchy: *Slattern* § (London: Chatto & Windus; London: Picador, 2001)
Julia Copus: *The Shuttered Eye* (Newcastle: Bloodaxe Books)
Freda Downie: *Collected Poems* (Newcastle: Bloodaxe Books)
Jane Duran: *Breathe Now, Breathe* § (London: Enitharmon)
Menna Elfyn: *Eucalyptus: Detholiad o Eerddi 1978-1994* (Llandysul: Gomer Press)
Ruth Fainlight: Selected Poems (London: Sinclair-Stevenson)
U.A. Fanthorpe: *Safe as Houses* (Calstock: Peterloo Poets)
Louise Glück: *The First Four Books of Poems* (Hopewell, New Jersey: Ecco Press)
Jenny Joseph: *Ghosts and other company* (Newcastle: Bloodaxe Books)
Mimi Khalvati: *Mirrorwork* (Manchester: Carcanet)
Gwyneth Lewis: *Parables & Faxes* (Newcastle: Bloodaxe Books)
Sharon Olds: *The Wellspring* (New York: Knopf; London: Jonathan Cape, 1996)
Katherine Pierpont: *Truffle Beds* § (London: Faber & Faber)
Adrienne Rich: *Dark Fields of the Republic: Poems 1991-1995* (New York & London: Norton)
Carol Rumens: *Best China Sky* (Newcastle: Bloodaxe Books)

1996

Moniza Alvi: *A Bowl of Warm Air* (Oxford: Oxford UP)
Eavan Boland: *An Origin Like Water: Collected Poems 1967-1987* (New York: Norton)
Gillian Clarke: *Selected Poems*, new edition (Manchester: Carcanet)
Frances Cornford: *Selected Poems* (London: Enitharmon)
Maura Dooley: *Kissing a Bone* (Newcastle: Bloodaxe Books)
Jane Draycott: *No Theatre* § (Huddersfield: Smith/Doorstop Books)
Menna Elfyn: *Cell Angel* (Newcastle: Bloodaxe Books)
Louise Glück: *Meadowlands* (Hopewell, NJ: Ecco Press; Manchester: Carcanet, 1998)
Jorie Graham: *The Dream of the Unified Field: Selected Poems, 1974-1994* (New York: Knopf; Manchester: Carcanet)
Kerry Hardie: *A Furious Place* § (Oldcastle, Co. Meath: Gallery Press)
Rita Ann Higgins: *Higher Purchase* (Cliffs of Moher, Co. Clare: Salmon)
Rita Ann Higgins: *Sunny Side Plucked: New & Selected Poems* (Newcastle: Bloodaxe Books)

Elizabeth Jennings: *In the Meantime* (Manchester: Carcanet)
Denise Levertov: *Sands of the Well* (New York: New Directions; Newcastle: Bloodaxe Books, 1998)
Gwyneth Lewis: *Cyfrif Un ac Un yn Dri* (Felindre, Abertawe: Barddas)
Mina Loy: *The Lost Lunar Baedeker* (New York: Farrar, Straus & Giroux; Manchester: Carcanet, 1997)
Paula Meehan: *Mysteries of the Home* [selection from *The Man who was Marked by Winter* and *Pillowtalk*] (Newcastle: Bloodaxe Books)
Sinéad Morrissey: *There was a Fire in Vancouver* (Manchester: Carcanet)
Grace Nichols: *Sunris* (London: Virago)
Alice Oswald: *The Thing in the Gap-Stone Stile* (Oxford: Oxford UP)
Ruth Padel: *Fusewire* (London: Chatto & Windus)
Ruth Pitter: *Collected Poems*, revised edition (London: Enitharmon)
Penelope Shuttle: *Building a City for Jamie* (Oxford: Oxford UP)
Pauline Stainer: *The Wound-dresser's Dream* (Newcastle: Bloodaxe Books)
Anne Stevenson: *The Collected Poems 1955-1995* (Oxford: Oxford UP; Newcastle: Bloodaxe Books, 2000)
Susan Wicks: *The Clever Daughter* (London: Faber & Faber)

1997
Fleur Adcock: *Looking Back* (Oxford: Oxford UP)
Gillian Allnutt: *Nantucket and the Angel* (Newcastle: Bloodaxe Books)
Meg Bateman: *Aotromachd agus dain eile / Lightness and Other Poems* (Edinburgh: Polygon)
Patricia Beer: *Autumn* (Manchester: Carcanet)
Sujata Bhatt: *Point No Point: Selected Poems* (Manchester: Carcanet)
Jean 'Binta' Breeze: *On the Edge of an Island* (Newcastle: Bloodaxe Books)
Amy Clampitt: *The Collected Poems of Amy Clampitt* (New York: Knopf; London: Faber & Faber, 1998)
Gillian Clarke: *Collected Poems* (Manchester: Carcanet)
Imtiaz Dharker: *Postcards from god* [with *Purdah*] (Newcastle: Bloodaxe Books)
Helen Dunmore: *Bestiary* (Newcastle: Bloodaxe Books)
Ruth Fainlight: *Sugar-Paper Blue* (Newcastle: Bloodaxe Books)
Elaine Feinstein: *Daylight* (Manchester: Carcanet)
Loiuse Glück: *The First Five Books of Poems* (Manchester: Carcanet)
Jorie Graham: *The Errancy* (Hopewell, NJ: Ecco Press; Manchester: Carcanet, 1998)
Lavinia Greenlaw: *A World Where News Travelled Slowly* (London: Faber & Faber)
Selima Hill: *Violet* (Newcastle: Bloodaxe Books)
Mimi Khalvati: *Entries on Light* (Manchester: Carcanet)
Medbh McGuckian: *Selected Poems 1978-1994* (Oldcastle, Co. Meath: Gallery Press)
Sarah Maguire: *The Invisible Mender* (London: Jonathan Cape)
Charlotte Mew: *Collected Poems and Selected Prose* (Manchester: Carcanet)
Carol Rumens: *The Miracle Diet*, with Viv Quillin (Newcastle: Bloodaxe Books)
Eva Salzman: *Bargain with the Watchman* (Oxford: Oxford UP)

Penelope Shuttle: *Selected Poems 1980-1996* (Oxford: Oxford UP)

Jean Sprackland: *Tattoos for Mother's Day* § (Liverpool: Spike)

1998

Eavan Boland: *The Lost Land* (Manchester: Carcanet; New York: Norton)

Anne Carson: *Glass and God* (London: Jonathan Cape)

Anne Carson: *Autobiography of Red: A Novel in Verse* (New York: Vintage; London: Jonathan Cape, 1999)

Gillian Clarke: *Five Fields* (Manchester: Carcanet)

Elizabeth Garrett: *A Two-Part Invention* (Newcastle: Bloodaxe Books)

Elizabeth Jennings: *Praises* (Manchester: Carcanet)

Jackie Kay: *Off Colour* (Newcastle: Bloodaxe Books)

Gwyneth Lewis: *Zero Gravity* (Newcastle: Bloodaxe Books)

Medbh McGuckian: *Shelmalier* (Oldcastle, Co. Meath: Gallery Press)

Nuala Ní Dhomhnaill: *Cead Aighnis* (Dingle/An Daingean: An Sagart)

Ruth Padel: *Rembrandt Would Have Loved You* (London: Chatto & Windus)

Pascale Petit: *The Heart of the Deer* § (London: Enitharmon)

Carol Rumens: *Holding Pattern* (Belfast: Blackstaff Press)

Carole Satyamurti: *Selected Poems* (Oxford: Oxford UP; Newcastle: Bloodaxe Books, 2000)

Jo Shapcott: *My Life Asleep* (Oxford: Oxford UP)

1999

Kate Clanchy: *Samarkand* (London: Picador)

Gillian Clarke: *The Animal Wall* (Llandysul: Pont Books)

Jane Draycott: *Prince Rupert's Drop* (Oxford: Oxford UP)

Carol Ann Duffy: *The World's Wife* (London: Picador)

Veronica Forrest-Thomson: *Selected Poems: Language Games, On the Periphery and Other Writings* (London: Invisible Books)

Vona Groarke: *Other People's Houses* (Oldcastle, Co. Meath: Gallery Press)

Kathleen Jamie: *Jizzen* (London: Picador)

Denise Levertov: *This Great Unknowing: Last Poems* (New York: New Directions; Tarset: Bloodaxe Books, 2001)

Gwyneth Lewis: *Y Llofrudd Iaith: Ffeil Heddlu* (Llandybie: Barddas)

Mairi MacInnes: *The Ghostwriter* (Newcastle: Bloodaxe Books)

Charlotte Mew: *Selected Poems* (London: Bloomsbury)

Nuala Ní Dhomhnaill: *The Water Horse* (Oldcastle, Co. Meath: Gallery Press)

Sharon Olds: *Blood, Tin, Straw* (New York: Knopf; London: Jonathan Cape, 2000)

Adrienne Rich: *Midnight Salvage: Poems 1995-1998* (New York & London: Norton)

Penelope Shuttle: *A Leaf Out of His Book* (Manchester: Oxford Poets / Carcanet)

Pauline Stainer: *Parable Island* (Newcastle: Bloodaxe Books)

2000

Fleur Adcock: *Poems 1960-2000* (Newcastle: Bloodaxe Books)

Moniza Alvi: *Carrying My Wife* (Newcastle: Bloodaxe Books)

Sujata Bhatt: *Augatora* (Manchester: Carcanet)

Jean 'Binta' Breeze: *The Arrival of Brighteye and other poems* (Newcastle: Bloodaxe Books)

Colette Bryce: *The Heel of Bernadette* § (London: Picador)
Anne Carson: *Men in the Off Hours* (New York: Knopf; London: Jonathan Cape)
Gillian Clarke: *Nine Green Gardens* (Llandysul: Gomer Press)
Gillian Clarke: *Owain Glyn Dwr 1400-2000* (Aberystwyth: Llyfrgell
    Genedlaethol Cymru)
Carol Ann Duffy: *The Salmon Carol Ann Duffy: Poems Selected and New,
    1985-1999* (Cliffs of Moher, Co. Clare: Salmon)
U.A. Fanthorpe: *Consequences* (Calstock: Peterloo Poets)
Elaine Feinstein: *Gold* (Manchester: Carcanet)
Louise Glück *The Seven Ages* (New York: Ecco; Manchester: Carcanet, 2001)
Louise Glück: *Vita Nova* (New York: Ecco; Manchester: Carcanet)
Jorie Graham: *Swarm* (New York: Ecco Press; Manchester: Carcanet)
Kerry Hardie: *Cry for the Hot Belly* (Oldcastle, Co. Meath: Gallery Press)
Mimi Khalvati: *Selected Poems* (Manchester: Carcanet)
Mairi MacInnes: *The Pebble: Old and New Poems* (Baltimore: University of
    Illinois Press)
Paula Meehan: *Dharmakaya* (Manchester: Carcanet)
Kathleen Raine: *The Collected Poems of Kathleen Raine* (Ipswich: Golgonooza
    Press; Washington, D.C.: Counterpoint, 2001)
Denise Riley: *Selected Poems* (London: Reality Street Editions)
Carole Satyamurti: *Love and Variations* (Newcastle: Bloodaxe Books)
Jo Shapcott: *Her Book: Poems 1988-1998* (London: Faber & Faber)
Anne Stevenson: *Granny Scarecrow* (Newcastle: Bloodaxe Books)

2001

Gillian Allnutt: *Lintel* (Tarset: Bloodaxe Books)
Elizabeth Bartlett: *Appetites of Love* (Tarset: Bloodaxe Books)
Eavan Boland: *Against Love Poems* (New York: Norton)
Eavan Boland: *Code* (Manchester: Carcanet)
Anne Carson: *The Beauty of the Husband: A Fictional Essay in 29 Tangos*
    (London: Jonathan Cape; New York: Knopf; New York: Vintage, 2002)
Wendy Cope: *If I Don't Know* (London: Faber & Faber)
Imtiaz Dharker: *I Speak for the Devil* (Tarset: Bloodaxe Books; New Delhi:
    Penguin Books India, 2003)
Helen Dunmore: *Out of the Blue: Poems 1975-2001* (Tarset: Bloodaxe Books)
Menna Elfyn: *Cusan Dyn Dall / Blind Man's Kiss* (Tarset: Bloodaxe Books)
Rita Ann Higgins: *An Awful Racket* (Tarset: Bloodaxe Books)
Selima Hill: *Bunny* (Tarset: Bloodaxe Books)
Elizabeth Jennings: *Timely Issues* (Manchester: Carcanet)
Sarah Maguire: *The Florists at Midnight* (London: Jonathan Cape)
Eiléan Ní Chuilleanáin: *The Girl Who Married the Reindeer* (Oldcastle, Co.
    Meath: Gallery Press; Winston-Salem, NC: Wake Forest UP, 2002)
Medbh McGuckian: *Drawing Ballerinas* (Oldcastle, Co. Meath: Gallery Press)
Caitríona O'Reilly: *The Nowhere Birds* § (Tarset: Bloodaxe Books)
Pascale Petit: *The Zoo Father* (Bridgend, Wales: Seren)
Adrienne Rich: *Fox: Poems 1998-2000* (New York & London: Norton)
Jo Shapcott: *Tender Taxes: Versions of Rilke's French Poems* (London: Faber
    & Faber)
Greta Stoddart: *At Home in the Dark* § (London: Anvil Press)

2002

Moniza Alvi: *Souls* (Tarset: Bloodaxe Books)
Sujata Bhatt: *A Colour for Solitude* (Manchester: Carcanet)
Jean 'Binta' Breeze: *The Arrival of Brighteye* (Tarset: Bloodaxe Books)
Anne Carson: *If Not, Winter: Fragments of Sappho* (New York: Knopf;
    London: Virago, 1993)
Maura Dooley: *Sound Barrier: Poems 1982-2002* (Tarset: Bloodaxe Books)
Carol Ann Duffy: *Feminine Gospels* (London: Picador)
Jane Duran: *Silences from the Spanish Civil War* (London: Enitharmon)
Ruth Fainlight: *Burning Wire* (Tarset: Bloodaxe Books)
U.A. Fanthorpe: *Christmas Poems* (London: Enitharmon)
Elaine Feinstein: *Collected Poems and Translations* (Manchester: Carcanet)
Jorie Graham: *Never* (New York: Ecco; Manchester: Carcanet)
Vona Groarke: *Flight* (Oldcastle, Co. Meath: Gallery Press)
Selima Hill: *Portrait of My Lover as a Horse* (Tarset: Bloodaxe Books)
Elizabeth Jennings: *New Collected Poems* (Manchester: Carcanet)
Mimi Khalvati: *The Chine* (Manchester: Carcanet)
Denise Levertov: *Selected Poems* (New York: New Directions; as *New
    Selected Poems*, Tarset: Bloodaxe Books, 2003)
Medbh McGuckian: *The Face of the Earth* (Oldcastle, Co. Meath: Gallery Press)
Sinéad Morrissey: *Between Here and There* (Manchester: Carcanet)
Sharon Olds: *The Unswept Room* (New York: Knopf, 2002; London:
    Jonathan Cape, 2003)
Alice Oswald: *Dart* (London: Faber & Faber)
Ruth Padel: *Voodoo Shop* (London: Chatto & Windus)
Carol Rumens: *Hex* (Tarset: Bloodaxe Books)
Eva Salzman: *One Two* (Manchester: Jones Press)

2003

Julia Copus: *In Defence of Adultery* (Tarset: Bloodaxe Books)
U.A. Fanthorpe: *Queuing for the Sun* (Calstock: Peterloo Poets)
Lavinia Greenlaw: *Minsk* (London: Faber & Faber)
Kerry Hardie: *The Sky Didn't Fall* (Oldcastle, Co. Meath: Gallery Press)
Gwyneth Lewis: *Keeping Mum* (Tarset: Bloodaxe Books)
Liz Lochhead: *The Colour of Black and White: Poems 1984-2003* (Edinburgh:
    Polygon)
Medbh McGuckian: *Had I a Thousand Lives* (Oldcastle, Co. Meath: Gallery
    Press)
Sarah Maguire: *Haleeb Muraq (Selected Poems)* (Syria: Al-Mada House)
Marianne Moore: *The Poems of Marianne Moore* (New York: Viking; London:
    Faber & Faber)
Caitríona O'Reilly: *Three-Legged Dog*, with David Wheatley (Bray, Co.
    Wicklow: Wild Honey Press)
Eva Salzman: *One Two II* (Hull: Wrecking Ball Press)
Jean Sprackland: *Hard Water* (London: Jonathan Cape)
Pauline Stainer: *The Lady & the Hare: New & Selected Poems* (Tarset:
    Bloodaxe Books)
Anne Stevenson: *A Report from the Border: New & Rescued Poems* (Tarset:
    Bloodaxe Books)

2004

Gillian Allnutt: *Sojourner* (Tarset: Bloodaxe Books)

Elizabeth Bartlett: *Mrs Perkins and Oedipus* (Tarset: Bloodaxe Books)

Kate Clanchy: *Newborn* (London: Picador)

Gillian Clarke: *Making Beds for the Dead* (Manchester: Carcanet)

Jane Draycott: *The Night Tree* (Manchester: Oxford Poets / Carcanet)

Carol Ann Duffy: *New Selected Poems* (London: Picador)

Louise Glück: *October* (Louisville, KY: Sarabande Books)

Selima Hill: *Lou-Lou* (Tarset: Bloodaxe Books)

Kathleen Jamie: *A Tree House* (London: Picador)

Mebdh McGuckian: *The Book of the Angel* (Oldcastle, Co. Meath: Gallery Press)

Sharon Olds: *Strike Sparks: Selected Poems 1980-2002* (New York: Knopf; as *Selected Poems*, London: Jonathan Cape, 2005)

Ruth Padel: *The Soho Leopard* (London: Chatto & Windus)

Adrienne Rich: *The School Among the Ruins: Poems 2000-2004* (New York & London: Norton)

Carol Rumens: *Poems 1968-2004* (Tarset: Bloodaxe Books)

Eva Salzman: *Double Crossing: New & Selected Poems* (Tarset: Bloodaxe Books)

Muriel Spark: *All the Poems of Muriel Spark* (Manchester: Carcanet; New York: New Directions)

2005

Moniza Alvi: *How the Stone Found Its Voice* (Tarset: Bloodaxe Books)

Colette Bryce: *The Full Indian Rope Trick* (London: Picador)

Anne Carson: *Decreation: Poetry, Essays, Opera* (New York: Knopf)

Carol Ann Duffy: *Rapture* (London: Picador)

Jane Duran: *Coastal* (London: Enitharmon)

Menna Elfyn: *Perffaith Nam* (Llandysul: Gomer Press)

U.A. Fanthorpe: *Collected Poems 1978-2003* (Calstock: Peterloo Poets)

Jorie Graham: *Overlord* (New York: Ecco; Manchester: Carcanet)

Rita Ann Higgins: *Throw in the Vowels: New & Selected Poems* (Tarset: Bloodaxe Books)

Jackie Kay: *Life Mask* (Tarset: Bloodaxe Books)

Gwyneth Lewis: *Chaotic Angels: Poems in English* (Tarset: Bloodaxe Books)

Gwyneth Lewis: *Tair Mewn Un* (Llandybie: Barddas)

Sinéad Morrissey: *The State of the Prisons* (Manchester: Carcanet)

Alice Oswald: *Woods etc.* (London: Faber & Faber)

Pascale Petit: *The Huntress* (Bridgend: Seren)

Pascale Petit: *The Wounded Deer: Fourteen Poems after Frida Kahlo* (Huddersfield: Smith/Doorstop)

Carole Satyamurti: *Stitching the Dark: New & Selected Poems* (Tarset: Bloodaxe Books)

Edith Sitwell: *Collected Poems* (London: Duckworth)

Anne Stevenson: *Poems 1955-2005* (Tarset: Bloodaxe Books)

2006

Elizabeth Bishop: *Edgar Allan Poe & The Juke-Box: Uncollected Poems, Drafts, and Fragments* (New York: Farrar, Straus & Giroux)

Sujata Bhatt: *Pure Lizard* (Manchester: Carcanet)

Jean 'Binta' Breeze: *The Fifth Figure: a poet's tale* (Tarset: Bloodaxe Books)

Imtiaz Dharker: *The Terrorist at My Table* (Tarset: Bloodaxe Books)
Ruth Fainlight: *Moon Wheels* (Tarset: Bloodaxe Books)
Vicki Feaver: *The Book of Blood* (London: Jonathan Cape)
Louise Glück: *Averno* (New York: Farrar, Straus & Giroux; Manchester: Carcanet, 2007)
Vona Groarke: *Juniper Street* (Oldcastle, Co. Meath: Gallery Press)
Selima Hill: *Red Roses* (Tarset: Bloodaxe Books)
Jenny Joseph: *Extreme of things* (Tarset: Bloodaxe Books)
Caitríona O'Reilly: *The Sea Cabinet* (Tarset: Bloodaxe Books)
Penelope Shuttle: *Redgrove's Wife* (Tarset: Bloodaxe Books)

INDEX

This index covers *Consorting with Angels* (excluding Chronology) and *Modern Women Poets* (*MWP*), edited by Deryn Rees-Jones (Bloodaxe Books, 2005), the companion anthology to this study. Bold face figures indicate chapter or section on the person concerned. Italicised *n* indicates further comment in a note.

Classical Women Poets

edited by JOSEPHINE BALMER

'Their songs delight the gods...and mortals too for all time'

Fragmented and forgotten, the women poets of ancient Greece and Rome have long been overlooked by translators and scholars. Yet to Antipater of Thessalonica, writing in the first century AD, these were the 'earthly Muses' whose poetic skills rivalled those of their heavenly namesakes.

Today only a fraction of their work survives – lyrical, witty, often innovative, and always moving – offering surprising insights into the closed world of women in antiquity, from childhood friendships through love affairs and marriage to motherhood and bereavement.

Josephine Balmer's translations breathe new life into long-lost works by over a dozen poets from early Greece to the late Roman empire, including Sappho, Corinna, Erinna and Sulpicia, as well as inscriptions, folk-songs and even graffiti. Each poet is introduced by a brief bibliographical note, and where necessary her poems are annotated to guide readers through unfamiliar mythological or historical references.

In an illuminating introduction, Josephine Balmer examines the nature of women's poetry in antiquity, as well as the problems (and pleasures) of translating such fragmentary works. *Classical Women Poets* is a complete collection for anyone interested in women's literature, the ancient world, and – above all – poetry. It is a companion volume to Josephine Balmer's edition *Sappho: Poems and Fragments*, also published by Bloodaxe.

SAPPHO
Poems & Fragments
translated by **JOSEPHINE BALMER**

The Greek poet Sappho was one of the greatest poets in classical literature. Her lyric poetry is among the finest ever written, and although little of her work has survived and little is known about her, she is regarded not just as one of the greatest women poets but often as the greatest woman poet in world literature.

She lived on the island of Lesbos around 600 BC, and even in her lifetime her work was widely known and admired in the Greek world. Plato called her 'the tenth muse', and she was a major influence on other poets, from Horace and Catullus to more recent lyric poets. Yet in later centuries, speculation about her sexuality has tended to diminish her poetic reputation. One medieval pope considered her so subversive that her poems were burned.

Some of her poems were written for the women she loved, but her circle of women friends and admirers was not unlike Socrates' circle of followers. She may have been a lesbian in the modern sense, or she may not, but to call her a lesbian poet is an oversimplification. What remains is her poetry, or the fragments which have survived of it, and her intense, sensuous, highly accomplished love poems are among the finest in any language.

Josephine Balmer's edition brings together all the extant poems and fragments of Sappho. In a comprehensive introduction, she discusses Sappho's poetry, its historical background and critical reputation, as well as aspects of contemporary Greek society, sexuality and women.

'Balmer's translations are the best I have read to date. She gives me the trace of a spirited, deed-minded, direct, guileless soul, and she modestly fulfils Boris Pasternak's demand that "ideally translation too will be a work of art; sharing a common text, it will stand alongside the original, unrepeatable in its own right" ' – CHRISTOPHER LOGUE, *Literary Review*

'If Josephine Balmer's new translations can bring Sappho's sensuous clarity, her genius, back into prominence, they will perform an invaluable service not only to us, but to poetry' – HARRIETT GILBERT, *Sunday Times*

ANNE STEVENSON
Five Looks at Elizabeth Bishop

Elizabeth Bishop is one of the greatest and most influential American poets of the 20th century. First published in hardback in 1998, *Five Looks at Elizabeth Bishop* is a highly illuminating reader's guide written by another leading poet which makes full use of the letters Elizabeth Bishop wrote to Anne Stevenson from Brazil in the 1960s.

Anne Stevenson is a major American and British poet who has published many books of poetry, including her *Poems 1955-2005* in 2005. Her other books include *Bitter Fame: A Life of Sylvia Plath* (1989), the first critical study of Elizabeth Bishop (1966), and a book of essays, *Between the Iceberg and the Ship* (1998).

Each of her five chapters looks at a different aspect of Bishop's art. *In the Waiting Room* links her life-long search for self-placement to her unsettled childhood. *Time's Andromeda* shows how a youthful fascination with 17th-century baroque art ripened, in the 1930s, into a unique brand of metaphysical surrealism. *Living with the Animals* considers ways in which Bishop, like Walt Whitman, deserted the literary mode of the fable to give autonomy and authority to natural creatures. Two final chapters focus on the poet's Darwinian acceptance of evolutionary change and her steady look at the 'geographical mirror' that in her later work replaced the figure of the looking-glass as an emblem of imagination.

Five Looks at Elizabeth Bishop represents a view of her work Bishop herself would have recognised and approved. A chronology and a set of maps serve as practical guides to the poet's life and travels.

'A compelling book; patiently and intelligently, Stevenson elucidates and illuminates her subject, relating work and life with exemplary tact. I read it with mounting excitement and, ultimately, gratitude. In a healthy culture, it would be a bestseller' – LACHLAN MACKINNON, *Thumbscrew*

'Biography and close reading of Bishop's poems and prose…complement each other in [this study] which must surely be the best available introduction to that marvellous poet' – JOHN MOLE, *TLS*

Elizabeth Bishop:
Poet of the Periphery

edited by **LINDA ANDERSON & JO SHAPCOTT**

Elizabeth Bishop is one of the greatest poets of the 20th century. When she died in 1979, she had only published four collections, yet had won virtually every major American literary award, including the Pulitzer Prize. She maintained close friendships with poets such as Marianne Moore and Robert Lowell, and her work has always been highly regarded by other writers. In surveys of British poets carried out in 1984 and 1994 she emerged as a surprising major choice or influence for many, from Andrew Motion and Craig Raine to Kathleen Jamie and Lavinia Greenlaw.

A virtual orphan from an early age, Elizabeth Bishop was brought up by relatives in New England and Nova Scotia. The tragic circumstances of her life – from alcoholism to repeated experiences of loss in her relationships with women – nourished an outsider's poetry notable both for its reticence and tentativeness. She once described a feeling that 'everything is interstitial' and reminds us in her poetry – in a way that is both radical and subdued – that understanding is at best provisional and that most vision is peripheral.

Since her death, a definitive edition of Elizabeth Bishop's *Complete Poems* (1983) has been published, along with *The Collected Prose* (1984), her letters in *One Art* (1994), her paintings in *Exchanging Hats* (1996) and Brett C. Millier's important biography (1993). In America, there have been numerous critical studies and books of academic essays, but in Britain only studies by Victoria Harrison (1995) and Anne Stevenson (1998/2006) have done anything to raise Bishop's critical profile.

Elizabeth Bishop: Poet of the Periphery is the first collection of essays on Bishop to be published in Britain, and draws on work presented at the first UK Elizabeth Bishop conference, held at Newcastle University. It brings together papers by both academic critics and leading poets, including Michael Donaghy, Vicki Feaver, Jamie McKendrick, Deryn Rees-Jones and Anne Stevenson. Academic contributors include Professor Barbara Page of Vassar College, home of the Elizabeth Bishop Papers.